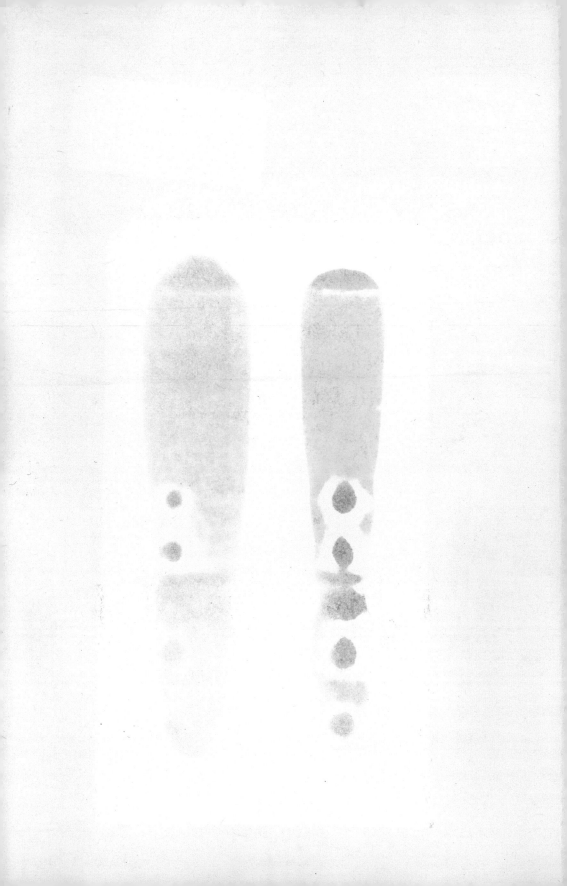

EDUCATION AND SOCIETY IN MEDIEVAL
AND RENAISSANCE ENGLAND

Ewelme (Oxfordshire) possesses one of the few surviving medieval school buildings, still used by the local primary school. A seigneurial foundation, it was built and endowed by William de la Pole, duke of Suffolk (d. 1450), outside the gates of his palace.

EDUCATION AND SOCIETY
IN MEDIEVAL AND
RENAISSANCE ENGLAND

NICHOLAS ORME

THE HAMBLEDON PRESS
LONDON AND RONCEVERTE

Published by The Hambledon Press, 1989

102 Gloucester Avenue, London NW1 8HX (U.K.)

309 Greenbrier Avenue, Ronceverte, WV 24970 (U.S.A.)

ISBN 1 85285 003 5

British Library Cataloguing in Publication Data

Orme, Nicholas
  Education and society in medieval and
  renaissance England.
  1. England. Education, 1066-1616. Social aspects.
  I. Title
  370.19'0942

Library of Congress Cataloging-in-Publication Data

Orme, Nicholas.
  Education and society in medieval and
  Renaissance England.

  Includes index.
  1. Education, Medieval – England.
  2. Education – England – History – 16th century.
  3. England – Social conditions – Medieval period, 1066-1485.
  4. England – Social conditions – 16th century.
  I. Title.
  LA631.3.0737   1989   370'.942   88-11009

Printed and bound by WBC Ltd., Bristol and Maesteg

29438

CONTENTS

PERMISSIONS

The British Library (4); The dean and chapter of
Exeter Cathedral (5); Lt.-Col. W. Luttrell, MC (3);
The Public Record Office (1); The Royal Commission
on the Historical Monuments of England (Frontispiece)

LIST OF ILLUSTRATIONS AND MAPS

MAGISTRIS MEIS

PREFACE

This book is a complement to my earlier studies, *English Schools in the
Middle Ages* (1973) and *From Childhood to Chivalry* (1984). Like them it
deals with education in England in schools, great households and
religious houses during the middle ages and the early Renaissance, but
not (save marginally) with the universities. It has two aims: to give the
new reader an outline of the history of non-university education from the
twelfth to the sixteenth centuries, and to examine specific topics in a
more detailed way than was possible in the earlier books. The first and
final chapters are original; chapters 3-5, 12 and 15 are revised versions of
previously published papers, and the remaining nine chapters are exact
reprints of earlier articles.

The chapters have been arranged and rewritten to form a co-ordinated
series of studies. They fall into four quartets. The first group deals with
schools and schoolmasters, at both a national and local level. The second
examines the teaching in grammar schools, through the surviving note-
books written by masters and pupils, and the third explores the wider
education of the lay aristocracy and the clergy. The last group considers
the treatment of education by four English writers – Langland, Chaucer,
Barclay and Shakespeare, who demonstrate how education was viewed
by intelligent onlookers. A common theme of the whole book is the
extent of continuity and change in English education between the twelfth
century and the Renaissance and Reformation.

I have many obligations to acknowledge. Five of the chapters include
editions of original texts, which are reproduced by kind permission of
the Beinecke Library, University of Yale (Chapter Five), the Rector and
Fellows of Lincoln College, Oxford (Chapter Six), Lt.-Col. W. Luttrell
(Chapter Seven), the British Library (Chapters Eight and Ten) and the
Public Record Office (Chapter Ten). I am grateful to many people, since
the publication of my first book, who have shared with me their
knowledge about early education, especially Dr R. Bowers, Mr L.S.
Colchester, Professor N. Davis, Professor C. Garton, Dr M.A. Hicks,
the Revd. Dom S.F. Hockey, the late Dr N.R. Ker, Miss Imogen
Luxton, Dr Joann H. Moran, Mrs Peter Opie, Dr I. Rowlands, Mrs Joan

Simon, Sir Richard Southern, the Revd. Dr D. Thomson, Professor
Linda E. Voigts and Dr E. Wilson. It is also proper, in a book about
education, to thank my own teachers: Mr J.B. Dalziel, Mr Edward
Martin and the late Arthur Sabin, who taught me at school; the late K.B.
McFarlane, Professor K.J. Leyser and Dr J. Stoye, my tutors at Oxford;
and Professor Frank Barlow, my head of department for many years at
Exeter. To these, my masters, I dedicate this book.

Nicholas Orme
Exeter
October 1987

ACKNOWLEDGEMENTS

The author and publishers gratefully acknowledge the permission of the following editors and publishers to revise and reprint material which has already appeared elsewhere:

Chapter Two, originally published in *History of Education*, xvi (1987), pp 81-9 (Messrs. Taylor and Francis);

Chapter Three, originally published in *Worcestershire Archaeological Society Transactions*, 3rd series, vi (1978), pp 43-51 (the Society);

Chapter Four, originally published in *Profession, Vocation and Culture in Later Medieval England*, ed. C.H. Clough (Liverpool, 1982), pp 218-41 (Liverpool University Press);

Chapter Five, originally published in *The Yale Library Gazette*, lx (1985), pp 47-57 (the Editor, Mr S. Parks);

Chapter Six, originally published in *Traditio*, xxxviii (1982), pp 301-26 (Fordham University Press);

Chapter Seven, originally published in *Somerset Archaeology and Natural History*, cxxviii (1984), pp 55-63 (the Editor, Dr R.W. Dunning);

Chapter Eight, originally published in *Renaissance Quarterly*, xxxiv (1981), pp 11-39 (the Editor, Dr Bridget Gellert Lyons);

Chapter Nine, originally published in *English Court Culture in the Later Middle Ages*, ed. V.J. Scattergood and J.W. Sherborne (London, 1983), pp 63-85 (Messrs. Duckworth);

Chapter Ten, originally published in *The Bulletin of the Institute of Historical Research*, lvii (1984), pp 119-30 (the Editor, Professor F.M.L. Thompson);

Chapter Eleven, originally published in *The Journal of Ecclesiastical History*, xxxii (1981), pp 265-83 (Cambridge University Press);

Chapter Twelve, originally published in *Bristol and Gloucestershire Archaeological Society Transactions*, xcvi (1978), pp 33-52 (the Society);

Chapter Thirteen, originally published in *The Chaucer Review*, xvi (1981), pp 38-59 (The Pennsylvania State University Press);

Chapter Fourteen, originally published in *History of Education*, xi (1980), pp 251-66 (Messrs. Taylor and Francis); and

Chapter Fifteen, originally published in *Devon and Cornwall Notes and Queries*, xxxv (1984), pp 84-9 (the Editor, Mrs M.M. Rowe).

ACKNOWLEDGEMENTS

The author and publishers gratefully acknowledge the permission of the following authors and publishers to reprint the material which has already appeared elsewhere.

LIST OF ABBREVIATIONS

BL	British Library, London
EETS	London, Early English Text Society
Emden, *BRUO*, i–iii	A.B. Emden, *A Biographical Register of the University of Oxford to AD 1500*, 3 vols (Oxford, 1957-9)
Emden, *BRUO*, iv	A.B. Emden, *A Biographical Register of the University of Oxford, 1501-1540* (Oxford, 1974)
Orme, *English Schools*	N.I. Orme, *English Schools in the Middle Ages* (London and New York, 1973)
Orme, *From Childhood to Chivalry*	N.I. Orme, *From Childhood to Chivalry* (London and New York, 1984)
Orme, *West of England*	N.I. Orme, *Education in the West of England, 1066-1548* (Exeter, 1976)
PRO	Public Record Office, London
VCH	*Victoria History of the Counties of England*

ENGLISH SCHOOLS 1100 – 1300

Norham

Carlisle Hexham
Cockermouth Durham
Yarm Guisborough
Helmsley Malton
Lancaster York Beverley
Clitheroe Pontefract Hedon
Wakefield Louth
Chesterfield Lincoln
Newark
Derby Nottingham Rudham
Kinoulton
Shrewsbury Lichfield Leicester Stamford Taverham Norwich
Ludlow Beccles
Warwick Huntingdon Mildenhall Dunwich
Worcester Northampton Cambridge Bury St Edmunds
Hereford Stratford Bedford
Brecon Dunstable Colchester
Gloucester Oxford St Albans
Awre Cirencester Berkhamsted
Wotton Abingdon London
Malmesbury
Bristol Reading Canterbury
Bath Marlborough Guildford Dover
Wells Winchester
Bridgwater Wilton
Taunton Salisbury Arundel Lewes Battle
Shaftesbury Chichester Hastings
Bridport Christchurch
Exeter Newport
Plympton

Known sites of schools
● In the twelfth century
○ In the thirteenth century
◐ Both

0   75 ml
0   150 km

1

SCHOOLS AND SOCIETY FROM THE TWELFTH CENTURY
TO THE REFORMATION

Education, like charity, begins at home. What is true today, of course, has also been true in the past. In the earliest days of English history, in the fifth and sixth centuries AD, children got their education in the homes of their parents or other people. Even in later times when other centres of instruction appeared – first monasteries, then schools, such centres were confined to a minority of the population and to older children at that. The home retained its importance as the place of first education for all, and all education for most. Home education is primarily social and domestic. It ranges from learning to eat, walk, speak and dress oneself, to coping with one's surroundings and dealing with other people. It also involves absorbing the customs and beliefs of one's elders. Langland and Chaucer in the fourteenth century refer to the habits and experience which parents teach their children: proverbs, religious observances, even love-making.[1] And medieval homes were also places of training for work. Boys and girls shared in their parents' tasks and acquired their parents' skills – the only instruction many children got for their adult careers.

Nor was the home in medieval or even later times a place of only rudimentary education. On the contrary, it showed a remarkable ability to accommodate the teaching of specialised techniques as these developed in society. When literacy spread to the laity, beginning in Anglo-Saxon times, literate homes became places where parents taught the knowledge of letters. Asser pays tribute to King Alfred's mother for encouraging her son to read, and by about 1300 it was possible to make the general statement that 'woman teacheth child on book'.[2] The home could also be a place of technical training. Children, especially boys, were often sent away from their own homes to be servants in the homes of other people, where they learnt particular crafts and trades in a parallel domestic environment. An early example of this was St William of

---

[1] Below, pp 223–4, 246–7.
[2] *Asser's Life of King Alfred*, ed. W.H. Stevenson (Oxford, 1959), p 20; W.W. Skeat, 'Nominale sive Verbale', *Transactions of the Philological Society (1903-6)*, p 7*.

Norwich, one of the boys alleged to have been killed by the Jews, who left his home at Haveringford in Norfolk at the age of seven, in about 1140, to be trained in the house of a master skinner at Norwich.[3] When formal apprenticeship developed (the word is first encountered in the thirteenth century), the placing of boys in the households of merchants, craftsmen and shopkeepers came to be accompanied by written contracts specifying duties, discipline, maintenance and instruction, and sometimes even schooling or language-teaching.[4] Yet such apprentices still lived and worked as part of their masters' families. The largest household involved in teaching boys was that of the king.[5] The royal household 'below stairs' took in children to help in the kitchens, storehouses and stables, and trained them to succeed their seniors. The household 'above stairs' likewise accepted noble boys as wards and pages, and educated them to be courtiers, warriors and landlords able to give the king good service in adulthood. Such practices endured with little change for hundreds of years. The hero of *Beowulf*, written in the mid eighth century, who was brought up in the royal court of the king of the Geats, had his successors in Shakespeare's time.[6] *The Two Gentlemen of Verona* and *All's Well That Ends Well* both feature adolescent noblemen going off to finish their education at the court of the local monarch.[7]

In 597 Christianity was introduced to England, with great effect on education. Monasteries and nunneries were established, which soon admitted English boys and girls to be trained for the religious life. In this training memory and literacy were both important. Much of the daily work of the clergy – saying the liturgy – was committed to memory, but it was also desirable that they should be able to read the Bible and other religious works. The western Church used Latin for speaking and writing, which meant instructing the Church's recruits in that language. The earliest mention of a school for the purpose in England is of one set up in East Anglia in about 631,[8] but references to separate schools are uncommon before the twelfth century. Most education in Anglo-Saxon England probably went on in monasteries, or at any rate in the earlier centuries. Writers like Bede and Alcuin make clear that scholars and students were to be found in the larger abbeys, and mention them being taught in schools within the houses. The teachers were monks, doing the

[3] Thomas of Monmouth, *The Life and Miracles of St William of Norwich*, ed. A. Jessopp and M.R. James (Cambridge, 1896), pp 14–16.

[4] On apprenticeship, see Sylvia L. Thrupp, *The Merchant Class of Medieval London* (Chicago, 1948) and E. Lipson, *The Economic History of England*, 11th ed., vol i (London, 1956), pp 308–28.

[5] On this subject, see Nicholas Orme, *From Childhood to Chivalry; the education of the English kings and aristocracy, 1066-1530* (London & New York, 1984), pp 48–55, and below, chapter 9.

[6] *Beowulf*, lines 2428–31.

[7] Below, chapter 16.

[8] Bede, *Ecclesiastical History*, book iii, chapter 18.

duty as part of their general work, and the pupils were usually monks too, ranging from children under monastic vows to young adults. As pupils came and went, so the teaching might resume or cease, without much continuity or institutional development. It may be unwise to imagine early monastic schools as permanent organisations of a modern kind.

Still, if early monastic education was simple in organisation, it was sophisticated in content. It ranged from elementary reading through Latin grammar to the liberal arts and theology. Two notable contributions to the history of education were made in Anglo-Saxon England. Latin was a difficult language for the English to learn, compared with western Europeans who spoke dialects based on Latin. Its teaching consequently needed comprehensive textbooks, dealing with all the problems of grammar and construction. Grammars already existed on the continent, notably those of Donatus and Priscian which dated from the Roman Empire, but they assumed a knowledge of Latin, and merely sought to improve it, like English grammars for the English today. Anglo-Saxon teachers (and also the Irish) had to extend and improve Donatus for their pupils, and they ended by writing a number of new Latin grammars, the first to be written in Europe for non-Latin speakers.[9] Moreover, since even these aids did not altogether overcome the problems of learning Latin, the Anglo-Saxons began to use the Latin alphabet for writing in their own language. Religious works, secular poems, laws and charters conferring land all came to be written in English, and a vernacular literature was created. The consequence of this (though it is not specifically recorded) was that a system of elementary education evolved, in which many children learnt only the Latin alphabet and then went on to read and write English. This too was new in European terms, since on the continent the vernacular languages were not yet used for writing.

The teaching of letters, Latin and English, cannot have been entirely based in religious houses, however, by late Saxon times. There was a widespread knowledge and use of letters by the eleventh century, particularly in English, which makes it likely that literary education, of an informal kind at least, was available outside the monasteries. Possible places for such teaching include noble households, parish churches and towns. Two writers of about 1000 AD recommend priests (i.e. of parishes) to teach the young and enable them to help in church.[10] But it is not until after the Norman Conquest, in the late eleventh and twelfth centuries, that schools begin to be mentioned as separate institutions in

[9] On this subject, see Vivien Law, *The Insular Latin Grammarians* (Woodbridge, 1982).
[10] *Councils and Synods, I: 871-1204*, ed. D. Whitelock, M. Brett, & C.N.L. Brooke, 2 vols (Oxford, 1981), i, 331.

particular places in significant numbers. Much of the evidence for this in
the period 1066–1200 comes from charters issued by the king, bishops
and other important people, granting or confirming control of local
schools to nearby monasteries.[11] Other sources mention schools
controlled by bishops, cathedrals, archdeacons, secular lords and the
parish clergy. These newly recorded schools were generally located in
towns. The controlling power or 'patron' appointed the teacher and gave
him a local monopoly, so that he could collect enough fee-paying pupils
to give him a living. The teacher was a priest, clerk or layman, not a
monk, instructing a class numbering anything from twenty to 120
pupils, sometimes assisted by a 'submaster' or 'usher'. The pupils were
males, ranging from boys to young adults, who intended to become
priests, monks, administrative clerks, or literate laymen. Sometimes
there was a separate 'song' or elementary school for the younger ones,
and a 'grammar' or Latin school for the older. Girls were not catered for,
to any great extent. Their literary education remained informal and
inferior, confined to the home or at best to an elementary school. Most of
them who learnt to read did so in a vernacular language, English or later
French, and only rarely in Latin.

The question arises whether these town schools of the post-Conquest
period were new, or were older institutions appearing in records for the
first time. This is difficult to answer. England in the late Anglo–Saxon
period undoubtedly possessed many of the cultural institutions necessary
for the existence of schools. There were royal and noble administrators,
secular clergy, towns, the reading and writing of books, the use of
documents. The twelfth-century evidence refers to schools in existence
rather than being founded, and this is particularly true of the charters
granting schools to monasteries. It can be argued that Norman and
Angevin England inherited a network of schools from the late Anglo–
Saxon period, which simply came to be recorded in the greater surviving
volume of twelfth-century literature. Against this, it is possible that the
Conquest itself set in motion educational changes. The Normans like
other western Europeans were used to literature and documents in Latin,
not in the local vernacular. Gradually, after the Conquest, this habit was
introduced to England too, increasing the amount of Latin that was read
and written, and decreasing that of English. Learning letters now
involved a greater study of Latin. Moreover, many who learnt were
French, and many (if not most) twelfth-century schoolmasters must
have taught Latin in French, their English pupils having to know French
as a pre-requisite for learning Latin. This, as we shall see, was still the
case in the early fourteenth century. Schooling, in short, became more
complicated, and the appearance of more formal 'schools' may be a

---

[11] For examples, see A.F. Leach, *Educational Charters and Documents, 598 to 1909*
(Cambridge, 1911), pp 58-117 passim (the dates need revising).

consequence of this and a development from an earlier less formal system of teaching in which English played more part. Whatever the truth, the post-Conquest period undoubtedly marks a new era of educational history in terms of evidence. Schools appear in records for the first time as a distinctive group, and they can be studied continuously from that point down to the present day.

At least 36 places in England are known to have possessed a school at one time or another between 1066 and 1200, and at least 70 during the thirteenth century. They include London (where there were three authorised schools), virtually all the cathedral cities, and many county towns, ports and market towns. The evidence is presented on the map opposite page 1.[12] It is incomplete, and the examples are only representative ones, because nobody kept systematic records of medieval schools. Mentions occur by chance in a wide variety of documents; others remain to be found, and some schools may have left no trace.[13] Moreover, though schools were fairly common from the twelfth century onwards, the number open from year to year must have fluctuated as masters came and went, especially in the smaller towns. Gradually, from the twelfth to the nineteenth centuries, schools built up resources which helped them to survive: patrons, buildings, books, scholarships, and eventually endowments to give the masters salaries. But notwithstanding these, the life of schools was often interrupted. Most medieval schoolmasters relied on taking fees. Plagues, disturbances, public apathy, rival teachers, or simply a better job could cause them to stop work and close their schools, sometimes temporarily, sometimes permanently. Even the schools of the cathedral cities, which had a good deal of oversight, support and prestige, could be suspended in this way. At Salisbury the master was accused of failing to teach in 1350 and dismissed two years later; in 1418, 1440 and 1454 the mastership is mentioned as vacant, and in 1468 another unsatisfactory occupant was sacked.[14] Locally, therefore, the supply of teaching varied and sometimes collapsed. There seems to have been less local variation, on the other hand, in how schools were organised. True, we can find some regional peculiarities. In the counties of Huntingdon,

[12] For a list, see Nicholas Orme, *English Schools in the Middle Ages* (London & New York, 1973), pp 293–325. To this should be added Abingdon, 1100x1117 (*Chronicon Monasterii de Abingdon*, ed. J. Stevenson, vol ii (London, Rolls Series, 1858), p 123); Bath, c. 1113 (Orme, *Education in the West of England, 1066-1548* (Exeter, 1976), pp 93–4); Brecon, 1155x66 (R.W. Banks, 'Cartularium Prioratus de Brecon', *Archaeologia Cambrensis*, 4th series, xiv (1883), pp 154–5); Bristol, probably 1166x83 (Orme, *West of England*, p 36); Dunwich, 1109x31 (*Liber Eliensis*, ed. E.O. Blake, Royal Historical Society, Camden 3rd series, xcii (1962), pp 270–4); Newport, Isle of Wight, 1269 (London, Public Record Office, SC6/984/2); and Wilton, 1238 (Orme, *West of England*, p 108).

[13] For new discoveries of schools in York diocese after 1340, see Joann H. Moran, *The Growth of English Schooling, 1340-1548* (Princeton, 1985).

[14] Orme, *West of England*, p 73.

Lincoln, Nottingham and York there was more centralised control of education by local religious dignitaries. Norfolk appears to have had a system of schools based on rural deaneries.[15] But generally, organisation, teaching and development were similar everywhere. England was a united country, compared with its continental neighbours, and this affected the development of schools.[16]

The town schools are a notable group, and they have common characteristics with modern schools in being self-contained, open to the public, and taught by specialist teachers. Occasionally, there is even a direct link through sites and endowments between the schools of then and now. But the town schools did not monopolise teaching, no matter how much they tried to do so. Private and informal tuition was also important. By the later middle ages the larger towns, besides their principal, authorised or 'high' school, often had one or two other masters unobtrusively instructing groups of pupils in private houses.[17] Teaching continued in monasteries, indeed it expanded after 1200 to include groups of almonry boys and choristers, sometimes with special masters to teach them. The large abbey of Glastonbury had 39 non-monastic 'clerks' in its school in 1377, the size of a town school,[18] and significant numbers of such clerks and lay boys went on being educated in monasteries down to the Reformation. Noble households were also centres of education, and by the fifteenth century were employing professional schoolmasters to teach the lord's children, wards and pages.[19] Less fortunate groups like women, people in remote areas and the poor, who had no access to the male, town-centred fee-paying schools, could learn some letters from a local priest or clerk or lay person. Clergy sometimes trained up boys, partly as servants, partly as trainee priests, as they had been bidden to do in Anglo-Saxon times. Priests with pupils appear in such places as Braughing (Hertfordshire) in the 1450s, Bridgwater (Somerset) at about the same time, and Burrough (Leicestershire) in 1508.[20] Parish clerks are mentioned teaching boys at two Bristol churches in the fifteenth century, and elsewhere thereafter.[21]

[15] Orme, *English Schools*, pp 144 n 5, 145–7.

[16] For the teaching of standard texts and methods at the remote school of Barlinch Priory, Somerset, see below, chapter 7.

[17] E.g. at Coventry, 1318 (Orme, *English Schools*, p 219), York, 1375–1528 (Joann H. Moran, *Education and Learning in the City of York, 1300–1560* (York, Borthwick Institute of Historical Research, Borthwick Papers, lv (1979), pp 9–13), and London, 1404–65 (Orme, *English Schools*, pp 210–12).

[18] Orme, *West of England*, p 206.

[19] On this process in households, see Orme, *From Childhood to Chivalry*, pp 22–4.

[20] Orme, *English Schools*, pp 66–7, 220–1; *West of England*, pp 7–8.

[21] Ibid., p 38; cf. pp 11–12, 117, 150.

Nor was all informal teaching necessarily received in childhood. William Smith the early Leicester Lollard of the 1380s learnt to read and write as an adult, yet subsequently even wrote books on religious topics.[22]

Education, like its pupils, is touched by the passing of time. Ever since the twelfth century schools have undergone changes, some generated within, some due to outside forces operating now to the schools' advantage, now to their detriment. At every point in time since their appearance they have experienced development in some respects and decline in others. It is therefore hazardous to call any single period a time of 'educational revolution' in a special sense, as has sometimes been said of the Tudor era, for example, or the reign of Victoria. Even at the outset of their recorded history in the twelfth century, schools had certain special features not repeated since.[23] This was a time before the evolution of universities. Learning was not yet clearly stratified into school studies and higher studies, and the latter were not yet concentrated at Oxford and Cambridge. As a result there was a greater range of teaching in the major English towns than at any time until the development of provincial universities in the nineteenth century. Cathedral cities like Canterbury, Exeter, Hereford, Lincoln and York, and the two important towns of Northampton and Oxford, harboured masters teaching not only Latin grammar but the liberal arts, canon and Roman law, or theology. There were only one or two masters in each place, and the reputation and even the existence of their schools depended on them personally. But for a rare brief period higher studies flourished in the English provinces. It was also a relatively good time to be a schoolmaster in terms of one's career prospects. Teaching seems to have conferred more status in the twelfth century than it did in the later middle ages. References to teachers are common in letters and chronicles, and several schoolmasters and private tutors were promoted to high offices in the Church.[24] This was not to happen again on a large scale until the sixteenth century.

Another characteristic of masters and schools in this period was their internationalism. The Norman Conquest had joined England to the continent politically and socially, and the continental connection was further enlarged with the Angevin Empire of Henry II. Scholars moved freely across the English Channel, and studied and taught in France and England indiscriminately. The Roman lawyer Vacarius, an Italian, is known to have lectured at Canterbury, while William de Montibus, born in Lincolnshire, went to the schools of Paris before returning to

---

[22] *Chronicon Henrici Knighton*, ed. J.R. Lumby, vol ii (London, Rolls Series, 1895), pp 180-1.

[23] For a good survey of early twelfth-century English schools, see F. Barlow, *The English Church, 1066-1154* (London & New York, 1979), pp 217-67.

[24] Ibid., pp 229-32; see also below, chapter 4.

lecture at Lincoln. Well-travelled men like these were no doubt commonest among the best scholars, lecturing on higher studies in the cathedral cities, but one or two worked even in the grammar schools of smaller towns. The school in Dunstable (Hertfordshire) was taught first by a Frenchman, Geoffrey de Gorroy, invited to England by the abbot of St Albans, and later by Alexander Neckham, the foster-brother of Richard Coeur-de-Lion, who had studied and taught at Paris.[25] The contacts with Europe enabled the works of continental grammarians to spread into English schools. Several of the standard Latin textbooks used by English masters and their pupils down to the early sixteenth century were the products of twelfth- and early thirteenth-century authors working on the continent. Alexander of Ville-Dieu's comprehensive grammar, the *Doctrinale*, Evrard of Béthune's combination of grammar and dictionary, the *Grecismus*, Hugutio of Pisa's etymological dictionary, the *Derivationes*, and the simpler works on homonyms and synonyms ascribed to John of Garland, were all enabled to take root in England because of its close links with mainland Europe.[26]

These links continued in the thirteenth century. Indeed, they were reinforced by the creation of the friars in the 1210s. The four orders of friars combined an international organisation with an enthusiasm for education. Friars established themselves in all the major English towns, and set up a network of friary schools for members of their orders. But the friars were not confined to particular houses; they moved from one region and country to another, and this included their teachers and students as well. The famous John Duns, 'Duns Scotus', was born on the Anglo-Scottish border, entered the friary in Dumfries (Scotland), studied and taught at Oxford and Paris, alternating between the two, and ended his life at Cologne.[27] Foreign friars came to study in English friaries until the fifteenth century, notably the Greek Peter Philarges who resided at Norwich and Oxford before embarking on a career in Europe which ended with his election as Pope Alexander V in 1409.[28] In another important respect, however, education changed in the thirteenth century with the emergence of universities at Oxford and Cambridge. This led to a geographical separation between universities and schools, and between their respective studies. Teachers and students of higher studies – the liberal arts, medicine, civil and canon law, and theology – gathered in the universities. The other towns were left only with schoolmasters teaching elementary learning and grammar, with but a few lecturers in theology and canon law at some of the cathedral cities. The distinction was not absolute; the word 'school' went on being used of schools and

[25] *Gesta Abbatum Monasterii Sancti Albani*, ed. H.T. Riley, vol i (London, Rolls Series, 1867), pp 72-3, 196.

[26] On these works, see Orme, *English Schools*, pp 89-91, 93.

[27] Emden, *BRUO*, i, 607-10.

[28] Ibid., pp 345-6.

universities, and there was some overlap of studies. Some schools remained involved with logic, a university subject, while the university towns continued to have grammar schools and to teach grammar in the arts course. Lectures in theology and canon law continued to be given in some cathedrals, friaries and monasteries. But a divergence began which had significant results.

In one respect the rise of the universities benefited school education. University study was dominated by Aristotle, one of whose works, the *Politics*, distinguishes children from adults and proposes a model curriculum for educating boys.[29] Out of this the university friars developed an interest in childhood: a more sustained and systematic interest than before. Some previous scholars, of course, had been aware of children. In England Aelfric's tenth-century *Colloquy* and William FitzStephen's twelfth-century description of London both contain accounts of children's lives and activities.[30] But most educational works before the thirteenth century did not distinguish children from adults, or divide their material into what was suitable for each group. This changed in the thirteenth century, as three great friar authors, centred in France, made childhood a separate topic of educational writing. Bartholomew Glanville, Vincent of Beauvais and Giles of Rome wrote encyclopaedias and treatises in which they described the physical and mental characteristics of children, the methods of bringing them up, and the matters they needed to learn.[31] True, the friars directed their remarks chiefly to royal and noble children and to boys rather than girls, but they perceived and mapped the territory of childhood more fully than before. No comprehensive book about education in future could afford to ignore children as a distinct group. The interest in childhood gradually spread beyond the friars. One of their English associates, Robert Grosseteste, bishop of Lincoln (d. 1253) was moved to write the Latin poem on good behaviour, *Stans Puer ad Mensam*, which is one of the earliest pieces of literature in England directed specifically at children. And Walter of Bibbesworth, an English knight, produced a poem in French about everyday life, to assist in teaching French, which also centred on children, how they behave and what they should learn – one of the first such texts in a vernacular language.[32]

In other ways the rise of the universities was less to the schools' advantage. It relegated schoolmasters to a lower division, concerned with younger pupils and more elementary subjects. Whereas the higher studies, their teachers and students profited from being concentrated together in two cities, the schoolmasters were left isolated, one or two

[29] Aristotle, *Politics*, i.13, vii.13–17, viii.1–7.
[30] Aelfric, *Colloquy*, ed. G.N. Garmonsway, 2nd ed. (Exeter, 1978); *Materials for the History of Thomas Becket*, ed. J.C. Robertson, vol iii (London, Rolls Series, 1877), pp 4–5, 8–10.
[31] Orme, *From Childhood to Chivalry*, pp 90–4.
[32] Ibid., pp 15, 137.

per town, in what were now 'the provinces' in intellectual terms. The movement of scholars internationally, while still common in the thirteenth-century universities, grew rare between the schools which now became staffed purely by Englishmen. New continental textbooks ceased to reach the English schools, one of the last to do so being John of Genoa's standard Latin dictionary, the *Catholicon*, finished in 1286.[33] Nor did the friars' interest in royal and noble children in households do much at first to help the more plebeian schools. Instead, schools after 1200 seem to have had a lower public profile. In literature for example, from *Tristan* in the twelfth century onwards, there are mentions of noble children and their tutors, but virtually nothing about schools or schoolchildren or schoolmasters.[34] Chaucer and Langland, though often aware of education, rarely made schools a major topic of their work.[35] A decline of autobiography and biography after 1200 means that we hear less about masters, their relationship with their pupils, and the regard in which they were held. Economically, too, schools attracted fewer benefactions and endowments than the universities. In 1193 Abbot Samson of Bury St Edmunds founded what was almost a free school in the town, with a pension of £2 a year for the master to teach forty scholars for nothing.[36] During the thirteenth and fourteenth centuries certain schools were given other amenities in the form of buildings and alms or scholarships for the pupils.[37] But the universities benefited far more than this, through the foundation of endowed colleges like Merton (Oxford, 1264) and Peterhouse (Cambridge, 1284). Not until the late fourteenth century did the school sector receive even one large similar foundation in Winchester College.

The schools of the thirteenth century were therefore rather neglected by contemporary observers, and this was to continue in the fourteenth. Yet meanwhile changes took place within their walls in both the method and content of education. According to the historian Ranulph Higden, in his well-known observation of the 1320s, Latin was taught in grammar schools through the oral medium of French.[38] This was presumably a legacy of the twelfth century, when schools primarily catered for the French-speaking élite, and meant that English speakers needed to learn French to partake of grammar-school education. During the thirteenth century this situation gradually altered. Although the use of French increased for literary purposes (the writing of romances, devotional works and documents), the spoken language became less common and

---

[33] Orme, *English Schools*, p 93; but cf. p 96.
[34] Orme, *From Childhood to Chivalry*, pp 82–6.
[35] Below, chapters 13–14.
[36] Orme, *English Schools*, p 184.
[37] Ibid., pp 178–84.
[38] Ranulph Higden, *Polychronicon*, ed. C. Babington, vol ii (London, Rolls Series, 1869), pp 158–61.

had to be formally learnt rather than picked up informally. French grammars and vocabularies began to be written to assist with this process,[39] and it is possible that some schoolmasters formally taught French as an alternative to, or preparation for, learning Latin. By the middle of the fourteenth century even this arrangement was no longer feasible, and schoolmasters abandoned French for English as the medium of teaching Latin. John Trevisa's famous remarks of 1387 ascribe the change, rightly or wrongly, to the Oxford schoolmaster, John Cornwall, at about the time of the Black Death (1348-9).[40] Along with this linguistic change, but unconnected, was another in the content of the Latin curriculum. Previously boys who had learnt their grammar went on to read Latin poems, including works of the late classical period dealing with mythology, fable and love. Now, these works ceased to be read and were replaced by more recent poems of the twelfth and thirteenth centuries on topics of Christian wisdom, morality and behaviour. The reading matter in schools became more overtly religious and didactic.[41]

The decline of French at the expense of English, first in speech, later in writing, led in due course to the production of educational books wholly or partly in English. In the theoretical sphere, the works of Bartholomew Glanville and Giles of Rome were translated into English at the turn of the fourteenth and fifteenth centuries. Other translations and one or two original works came out in the course of the fifteenth.[42] In the sphere of school text-books, John Cornwall's *Speculum Grammaticale* (1346) was the first grammatical treatise which, though chiefly in Latin, included a number of English glosses and translations.[43] Soon after 1400 authors like the Oxford schoolmaster John Leland were producing short grammatical tracts entirely in English, save for the Latin examples, and versions of these tracts eventually became universal in schools.[44] A Latin-to-English dictionary, the *Medulla Grammatice*, was compiled by 1438, and an English-to-Latin one, the *Promptorium Parvulorum*, was completed in 1440 primarily for children.[45] The increasing use of English in the grammar schools not only affected the schools but English too. By explaining Latin grammar in English, with the use of English parallels,

[39] W. Rothwell, 'The Role of French in Thirteenth-Century England', *Bulletin of the John Rylands Library*, lviii (1975-6), pp 458-62.

[40] Higden, *Polychronicon*, ii, 158-61. The reason for questioning Trevisa's accuracy is that one would expect the change to have happened first in provincial schools, rather than in Oxford whose schools were important and also took pupils from various English dialect areas.

[41] Orme, *English Schools*, pp 102-6.

[42] Orme, *From Childhood to Chivalry*, pp 98-106.

[43] Below, chapter 5.

[44] David Thomson, *A Descriptive Catalogue of Middle English Grammatical Texts* (New York & London, 1979), pp 6-12.

[45] Orme, *English Schools*, pp 97-8.

masters caused their pupils to think of English in Latin grammatical terms. By making them write sentences in English for translation into Latin, and vice versa, masters also imposed methods of spelling English and writing it stylistically.[46] Several school exercise-books kept by fifteenth-century masters and pupils survive, and tell us a good deal about the work of schools in this period and the mentality of their inmates.[47]

The fourteenth and fifteenth centuries in England were notable for demographic and social changes. Severe mortality in the famine of 1316–17, the Black Death of 1348–9, and later epidemics caused the population to fall drastically. Popular discontent manifested itself, coming to a head in the Peasants' Revolt of 1381, but subsequently in the fifteenth century a smaller population enjoyed a better standard of living. Villeinage, a chief complaint in 1381, gradually faded away, though it was not extinct until the late sixteenth century. These changes and events affected schools. The impact of the plague of 1348–9 is not very clear, but there is no doubt about that of epidemics in general. Masters died or left, and were sometimes hard to replace. At York in 1350 the cathedral school had to be given to a local rector as temporary *custos*, and in 1368 the patron of the school, the cathedral chancellor, spoke of the difficulty of finding a suitable master since the last plague. Pupils were also victims of diseases.[48] At Winchester College 23 scholars died in one particularly bad period between 1401 and 1410: five in 1401 and eight in the following year. Eleven of the 44 scholars admitted in 1401 failed to survive their schooldays.[49] A schoolbook written at Magdalen College School, Oxford, in the early sixteenth century shows epidemics to have been a constant preoccupation. The least case of illness caused scholars to withdraw for fear of a general outbreak, and when such outbreaks came the whole school moved, together with the college community, to a rural manor which was felt to be safer. One boy is represented as saying that he has missed schooling for much of the year because of epidemics, and that if another should come, he will go elsewhere.[50]

The social tensions of the late fourteenth century also impinged on schools. The aristocracy and some writers accused ignoble people of bettering themselves through education, and hostility to schools was attributed to some of the peasants in 1381.[51] It is rather odd, therefore, that most modern writers on education in this period state that parliament, a body dominated by the aristocracy, struck a blow for

[46] Below, pp 67–9.
[47] Below, chapters 5–8.
[48] A.F. Leach, *Early Yorkshire Schools*, vol i (Yorkshire Archaeological Society, xxvii, 1899), p 23; Moran, *Education and Learning in York*, p 39.
[49] T.F. Kirby, *Winchester Scholars* (London & Winchester, 1888), pp 25–38.
[50] Below, pp 132–3.
[51] Orme, *English Schools*, pp 192–3.

education in 1406 by taking away the rights of lords of manors to control the education of their villeins.[52] Previously, villeins needed their lords' consent to go to school, lest they become priests and thereby incapable of villein service; fees were usually levied for the permission. A statute of 1406 indeed contains a clause that 'any man or woman, of whatever estate or condition, be free to put his son or daughter to learn letters at any school in the kingdom', but the statement is misleading. The statute was about restricting apprenticeship, and the clause (a subordinate one) seems intended to say that the restrictions shall not apply to schooling. It would be amazing if parliament had so casually abandoned lords' control over their villeins' education, and there is no sign that any change took place. Lords continued levying fines on villeins who went to school without permission, and treatises on how to hold manorial courts went on enquiring 'if there be any bondman of blood that putteth his son unto the school to make him a priest or a prentice' until as late as 1552, when villeinage itself was all but dead.[53] Attractive though it seems, there was no educational 'emancipation of the serfs'.

In 1439 or thereabouts William Bingham, rector of a London city church, addressed a petition to the young King Henry VI, drawing attention to the decline of grammar teaching in England. Seventy schools, he claimed, had disappeared from the eastern half of England alone within the last fifty years, for lack of men to teach in them, and to remedy this he proposed to create a college at Cambridge to train schoolmasters.[54] Bingham was virtually unique in commenting on the state of school education in later medieval England, but as an activist on behalf of schools he was one of a number of people who attempted to improve their situation in the 1430s and 40s, particularly by the endowment of free grammar schools. The origins of the endowed-school movement go back to the thirteenth century.[55] Walter de Merton, the founder of Merton College in 1264 had provided for the maintenance there of some boy-scholars and a grammar master to teach them. During the fourteenth and fifteenth centuries other colleges of secular clergy were founded in the universities and elsewhere, some (but by no means all) of which included masters to instruct the choristers of the college or the boys of the surrounding area. The most important such scheme was at Winchester College, established by William of Wykeham in 1382 for

[52] A.F. Leach, *The Schools of Medieval England*, 2nd ed. (London, 1916), p 236; Joan Simon, *Education and Society in Tudor England* (Cambridge, 1967), p 24; J. Lawson & H. Silver, *A Social History of Education in England* (London, 1973), p 83.

[53] Orme, *English Schools*, p 52. See also editions of the treatise *Modus Tenendi Cur. Baron* listed in A.W. Pollard & G.R. Redgrave, *A Short Title Catalogue of Books Printed in England, 1475-1640*, 2nd ed., 2 vols (London, 1976-86), i, 350, particularly *The Maner of Keping a Courte Baron* (London, 1552) (STC 7721), f Aiii.

[54] A.H. Lloyd, *The Early History of Christ's College, Cambridge* (Cambridge, 1934), pp 356-7; Leach, *Educational Charters and Documents*, pp 402-3.

[55] On what follows, see Orme, *English Schools*, pp 184-90, 194-7.

various clergy, two schoolmasters, and seventy scholars learning grammar.[56] Meanwhile, two years later, Lady Katherine Berkeley created the first endowed grammar school pure and simple at Wotton-under-Edge (Gloucestershire), for a single schoolmaster teaching all who came to him for nothing. A few more small endowed grammar schools later made their appearance at Durham in 1414, Oswestry (Shropshire) in about 1423, and Sevenoaks (Kent) in 1432. Up to about 1440, however, it is difficult to see a pattern in these school endowments. They were widely separated in time, place and form, and their founders seem to have been individualists rather than sharers in a common cause.

This changed in the late 1430s and 40s when Henry VI emerged from his childhood to become an active monarch. Henry was unusual among English kings in the extent of his interest in grammar schools. The interest may have been instilled by elder statesmen at his court, like Archbishop Chichele and Walter Lord Hungerford, but Henry soon developed it enthusiastically.[57] In his late teens he started to plan an ambitious new endowed free school at Eton (Buckinghamshire), which ended by equalling Winchester College in size and wealth. School foundations became fashionable at court. They were made by Lords Cromwell, Hungerford and Suffolk, all leading lay courtiers, and by John Ferriby, controller of the king's household. A few schoolmasters were promoted to important offices, a rare event since the twelfth century. The king's own master, John Somerset, became chancellor of the exchequer, John Chedworth (a Hungerford family tutor) bishop of Lincoln, and William Wainfleet (headmaster of Winchester College) bishop of Winchester.[58] Chedworth and Wainfleet went on to found grammar schools themselves, as did some others of Henry's bishops. It became known that the king was favourable to schools, and at least three petitions were directed to him on the subject. One, by William Bingham in 1439, has already been mentioned. Another, by the schoolmasters of Oxford in 1442, complained about the dues imposed upon them by the university and led to Henry's intervention on their behalf.[59] A third, by prominent London clergy via the House of Commons in 1447, petitioned for more schools to be established in the capital, and also got a sympathetic answer.[60] For a short period in the 1440s we can therefore talk of an educational movement, based on the king and the court, in favour of grammar schools. There is evidence too of a court interest in

---

[56] The latest work on Wykeham and Winchester is in *Winchester College: sixth centenary essays*, ed. R. Custance (Oxford, 1982).

[57] I have discussed the question in *West of England*, p 143.

[58] On this topic, see also below, p 59.

[59] *Epistolae Academicae Oxon*, ed. H. Anstey, vol i (Oxford Historical Society, 1898), pp 210-11.

[60] Orme, *English Schools*, pp 212-13.

higher education. It can hardly be a coincidence that this period sees the first recorded eldest sons of peers being sent to study at Oxford and Cambridge, in what seems to be an attempt by some of the lay aristocracy to give their heirs a more formal education in a university setting.[61]

The movement, unfortunately, ran into trouble in the 1450s, like the court itself. Suffolk was murdered in 1450, and Henry experienced his first outbreak of madness in 1453. The court became disrupted by politics, then by civil war, and in 1461 by a change of dynasty; school education lost its brief celebrity. The endowment of schools did not entirely cease during the Wars of the Roses, for some of Henry's circle like Chedworth and Wainfleet went on with educational schemes, but the rate slowed down. Whereas more than a dozen schools had been founded or projected during the late 1430s and 40s, the next three decades (1450–80) produced only three or four each. Gradually, in the 1480s, interest revived, and the last two decades of the century each saw about ten new endowments. This further increased in the sixteenth century, so that from about the 1480s we can talk once more of a movement, but now a national one not centred on a single group of men. By this time there were enough endowed schools in existence for their value to be apparent, and plenty of models for would-be founders to copy. Indeed, the popularity of educational foundations grew so much that other religious institutions began to be partly or wholly converted to educational uses.[62] Resources were set aside for endowed schools in some collegiate churches, hospitals and guilds which had not hitherto possessed them, and even the patrons of some chantries in the early sixteenth century started to appoint priests to teach school as well as to say prayers. The idea of transferring ecclesiastical revenues to education became well established on the eve of the Reformation.

The fifteenth century was notable, therefore, in the growth of interest in schools by people in authority, and in the giving of endowments so that masters could teach wholly or partially free. Such school foundations, however, were only part of an increasing awareness of education in general.[63] As we began by observing, much that went on in homes and at work involved learning and teaching, but it took a long time for people to notice this and to try to affect it in a conscious way. Grosseteste, as we saw, wrote a poem on table manners for boys, and during the fourteenth and fifteenth centuries a genre of similar poems grew up in Latin, French and English, so that by the fifteenth pages and schoolboys learnt good manners from books as well as in practice. In 1391 Chaucer wrote his treatise on *The Astrolabe* primarily for his young son Lewis, the first example in England of a work to teach science to

---

[61] Orme, *From Childhood to Chivalry*, pp 71–2.
[62] Below, pp 211–12.
[63] On what follows, see Orme, *From Childhood to Chivalry*, pp 216–17.

children. In the sphere of sport, John Hardyng identified hunting as educational for children in 1457, and a treatise on hunting called *Tristram* was written, supposedly by a mother for her son; this too could be formally learnt. In the late 1460s Sir John Fortescue in his *De Laudibus Legum Anglie* (intended to teach the young Lancastrian prince of Wales) identified wardship as an educational process, and wrote the first description of legal education at the inns of court. His contemporary, the anonymous author of 'The Black Book of the Royal Household' was one of the first to point to boy-servants and pages in households as learners, even of menial tasks. In 1484 Caxton published his translation of *The Book of the Knight of the Tower* which made widely available a treatise about the education of women. By 1500 therefore, more activities than ever before were perceived as educational. There were more descriptions of them and treatises about them by which they could be studied formally, and many others were to be written during the sixteenth century.

The coming of humanism to England added to this ferment of educational schemes and ideas.[64] The first English schoolmaster to follow humanist approaches appears to have been John Anwykyll, master of Magdalen College School, Oxford, *c.* 1481–88. From here humanism gradually spread through all the English schools, achieving complete diffusion by about the 1520s. Humanism brought changes of its own. The teaching of grammar and its textbooks were revised away from medieval usages to accord more closely with classical Latin practices. The list of authors read in schools was changed to include the great classical writers, in place of most of the Christian poetry read in the last two centuries. There was also an influx of new grammars and schoolbooks from the continent, for the first time since the thirteenth century, including the grammars of the Italian scholars Perotto, Sulpizio and Valla, the Latin poems of another Italian, Battista Mantovano and the *Colloquies* of Erasmus. Finally, humanism succeeded in attracting the interest of the royal family and the lay aristocracy. Since the late twelfth century royal and noble boys had not learnt Latin to a high level unless there was a chance that they would become clerics or lawyers. Late-medieval kings and lay noblemen tended to know only a little Latin, and to do most of their reading and writing in French or English. Now there was a revival of Latin among them, first recorded in the family of Henry VII whose eldest son, Arthur, is said to have read twenty-four Latin authors and grammarians by the time that he died, aged fifteen, in 1502. During the sixteenth century, the schooling of all noblemen and gentlemen came to place a greater emphasis on Latin, and continued to do so for the next four hundred years.

The triumph of humanism was long-lived, and its supporters have

---

[64] On what follows, see Orme, *English Schools*, pp 106–15, and *From Childhood to Chivalry*, pp 142–56.

rated its achievements highly ever since. Some caution is advisable in this respect. There was nothing new about English schools being influenced by continental grammarians, as we have seen. Even during the period of greatest isolation in the fourteenth and fifteenth centuries, older continental authors went on being studied. Moreover the English schoolmasters who began teaching humanism did so within the strong native tradition of how to teach, enshrined in grammatical treatises like the English *Accidence* and *Parvula* which had developed during the fifteenth century. They incorporated humanism into this tradition. The *Accidence* and *Parvula* were revised to make the grammar, prosody and syntax harmonise better with classical forms. But the methods of teaching, as opposed to the content, remained similar. 'Apposing' or examining boys, the use of treatises in question–and–answer form, the ways of analysing and presenting Latin grammar developed during the middle ages, mnemonic verses to memorise rules and vocabulary, and the writing of model passages in Latin and English (*latinitates* and *vulgaria*) continued during the sixteenth century as they had done before. Even elementary Latin reading went on being dominated by *Cato*, who had been read throughout the middle ages, and by parallel poems to Grosseteste's *Stans Puer ad Mensam*. A schoolmaster, transported from 1450 to 1600, would still have recognised much that went on in schools.

The introduction of humanism coincided with the arrival of printing. Caxton opened his Westminster press in 1476, and in the following year he issued *Cato* in Latin and English, the first schoolbook to be printed in England. Other printers gradually did the same, notably at Oxford, where the English treatise on composition called the *Long Parvula* and John Anwykyll's *Compendium totius Grammatice* came out in the early 1480s. The impact of printing on schools, like that of humanism, was a gradual one. Although schools offered a potential market for multiple copies of books, Caxton himself printed few school texts, preferring to concentrate on literary works. The Oxford press was short-lived, and not until the 1490s did the London printers Richard Pynson and Wynkyn de Worde begin to issue schoolbooks in large numbers. It took time for all the texts in use to become available in printed versions. As late as 1505–10 an enterprising French bookbinder in Exeter, Martin Coeffin, arranged for the printing in France of schoolbooks which were not yet available from London.[65] The turning point in the relationship of printing and the schools seems to have come in about 1510. John Stanbridge who died in that year, was master first of Magdalen College School and later of Banbury, and the man chiefly responsible for revising the standard Latin schoolbooks in the direction of humanism. His revisions now began to be published frequently, both in England and on the continent for the English market, and printed schoolbooks soon

[65] Orme, 'Martin Coeffin: The First Exeter Publisher', *The Library: Transactions of the Bibliographical Society* (1988), forthcoming.

became common, if not dominant in schools. In some respects, however, printing affected school education in degree rather than principle. Even before printing, the standard works of grammar had been widely available to masters. New works had spread from school to school (as Leland's did in the fifteenth century), and some boys had possessed their own copies of the shorter works or parts of the longer ones.[66] Printing simply accelerated the speed, efficiency and cheapness with which copies could be made. At the same time, it helped to bring about one early qualitative change. The imposition of uniform schoolbooks, which we shall shortly encounter in the 1540s, was a policy born of printing and made feasible by it.

From the 1520s onwards education became increasingly involved with religious changes, due to the Reformation. In part, the Reformation was the outcome of educational developments. The higher education of the monarch and the nobility, and wider education among other lay people, made necessary and helped bring about a reassessment of their roles within the Church. The conversion of ecclesiastical endowments from liturgical to educational purposes, already mentioned, offered precedents for the transfer of other religious property. Schools provided the Reformers, consciously or unconsciously, with a model on which to base the reform of worship. What had previously been a sacred drama in colourful surroundings now became a sedentary lesson, as in a plain schoolroom, with a teacher, a class, oral responses and written texts on the walls. In turn, the Reformation affected education, particularly schools. The leaders of the Church became more confident than their predecessors that they possessed the truth, and more anxious to enforce it. Control of the schools came to be seen as a proper (and politic) means of establishing orthodoxy, and suppressing the heterodoxy of opponents. It helped you to win the next generations for your Church, and if you did not control the schools your enemies might do so. Up to the 1520s most religious leaders had taken it for granted that the schools were on their side. Now it was more and more necessary to scrutinise the teachers and their lessons, and to bring education into line with the policies of Church and State. The easiest way to control the schools, as to control religion, was through imposing common practices. So Church and education experienced two new policies at the same time: royal control and uniformity.

Considering how important education eventually became to lay and clerical authorities throughout Europe, it is notable how slowly this was realised in England. The slowness is an example of the strong religious and cultural conservatism of the English. Henry VIII, the first Reformation monarch, was probably the best-educated king in a literary

---

[66] On boys' own copies before printing, see Orme, *English Schools*, pp 126-7, and below, chapter 7.

sense since Henry II.[67] He had been schooled in humanist Latin to a high degree by graduate schoolmasters. In 1521 he posed as the author of the Latin treatise *Assertio Septem Sacramentorum*, an unprecedented royal claim to scholarship. Yet for the first thirty years of his thirty-eight year reign, he and his ministers showed little inclination to develop an educational policy, or to meddle with schools or universities.[68] When Wolsey fell in 1530, Henry took no steps to save the cardinal's great school at Ipswich, a foundation equal in size to Eton and Winchester. At Oxford he converted Wolsey's academic college, Cardinal College, into a less academic collegiate church. In 1534-5, as a consequence of the breach with Rome, the king ordered schoolmasters to declare his headship of the Church to their pupils, and in 1535 royal visitors made some changes to the studies at the universities. But these were isolated actions. When the monasteries began to be dissolved in 1536 there was at first little official realisation of the implications for education. None of the internal schools was preserved which the monasteries had kept for others than monks, i.e. almonry boys and choristers, and there was no general arrangement for dealing with the public town schools which some monasteries still governed and supported. Such schools survived as much through initiatives by local people as through any general royal policy.[69]

It was not until about 1539-40 that such policies developed, through the imposition of a uniform grammar and the foundation of new cathedral schools. The first of these, however, was not an idea of the king or his current ministers; it had originated as far back as 1525, perhaps from Wolsey's brain, and had been approved by a Church convocation in London in 1530. Henry's contribution was to make the policy effective by imposing a uniform advanced Latin grammar on all schools in 1540. An elementary Latin grammar was added in 1542, and a 'primer' or collection of prayers for schools in 1545.[70] The foundation of new cathedral schools, projected in 1539 and carried out in 1540-44, was Henry's main original contribution to educational history, and the chief attempt to replace monasticism and its schools by education wholly available to the laity.[71] But quite apart from the paucity of monastic property transferred for the purpose, the new Henrician foundations (thirteen cathedral schools and three or four others) formed a haphazard

---

[67] Orme, *From Childhood to Chivalry*, pp 23-4.

[68] G.R. Elton has argued in favour of Thomas Cromwell's interest in education (*Reform and Renewal: Thomas Cromwell and the Common Weal* (Cambridge, 1973), pp 28-34). He shows Cromwell in contact with scholars, but kings and statesmen had been so since the twelfth century. What was new in the sixteenth was sustained policy and intervention in education, and here there is little sign of Cromwell's interest.

[69] Orme, *English Schools*, pp 258-61.

[70] Ibid., pp 255-8.

[71] On what follows, see ibid., pp 262-8.

scheme. The initial plans were scaled down in their execution, and the cathedrals were not treated equally, some receiving smaller schools than others. Two of them, Norwich and Winchester, were excluded from the plans throughout, and a third, Oxford, lost its school after a few years. Still, by about 1540, the crown at least conceived of saving endangered schools, and when soon afterwards it started to suppress the collegiate churches, there was more care to preserve the public schools associated with them. By 1547 when Henry was dead and the new government of Edward VI extended the Reformation to the chantries and religious guilds, the need was recognised for a general policy towards the schools associated with these bodies. This was written into the parliamentary statute for the dissolution of chantries, passed in December 1547.[72] The preamble of the statute declared the intention of transferring chantry endowments from superstitious uses to educational purposes, and the enactments undertook to maintain all grammar schools connected with chantries. Even so, the elementary reading schools kept by certain chantries were allowed to perish without any intervention.

Edward VI's regime, therefore, can be said to have advanced on Henry VIII's in having from the beginning a policy towards schools. The execution of the policy, however, was once again rather erratic. Although most chantry grammar schools were saved, only about nine new schools were endowed out of chantry property, showing small desire by the government to enlarge the national facilities for education. And the regime showed curiously little interest in the majority of schools, which were not associated with chantries. In view of the fact that it set up a distinctively Protestant Church, one might expect it to have used the schools as a means of establishing Protestantism locally. The ineffectiveness of such a policy can be illustrated by reference to the cathedral school of Wells, the leading school in Somerset. Here the headmasters between 1547 and 1553 included the poet Alexander Barclay, an ex-friar and notorious conservative, and an ex-Cistercian monk, Richard Edon, who returned to the monastic life under Mary Tudor.[73] It was not until her reign, between 1553 and 1558, that a government appeared which possessed both a policy towards schools and the determination to carry it out. The Marian regime, so often accused of conservatism and sterility, was bold and innovative in the educational field.[74] In 1554 the queen instructed the bishops to examine all schoolmasters and replace those of suspect opinions by Catholic men. In 1556 the regular licensing of all schoolmasters by the bishops was introduced, a measure so in tune with the Reformation that it survived

[72] Ibid., pp 272-7.
[73] Orme, West of England, pp 87-8.
[74] On what follows, see Orme, English Schools, pp 285-7. The latest study of Mary's reign, D.M. Loades, The Reign of Mary Tudor (London, 1979), scarcely even mentions its educational features (see e.g. pp 346-52, and index sub 'education').

Mary's death and continued under her Protestant successors. Deliberate appointments of active Catholic teachers were made in some of the major schools. At Wells a new headmaster and usher were imported from Corpus Christi College, Oxford, a stronghold of traditional religion; the former became a Jesuit in later life.[75] They left the school after Mary died, as did their colleagues at the cathedral schools of Durham, St Paul's and Salisbury, and at Winchester College. More was done in Mary's short reign than ever before to create a relationship between government and the schools. Education was at last a branch of royal policy, and the schools had come under a measure of state control.

'Medieval' is a term of abuse in the modern world, including the world of education, for what is alleged to be primitive. Medieval and also Renaissance schools were indeed modest in their size and resources, by modern standards, but they were the product of different societies with lower standards of living. Ignoring the economic differences between then and now, the English schools of 1100–1550 appear perfectly rational and realistic in the way that they operated. Like schools today they were the object of political and social forces outside their control, to which they responded as best they could. Like modern schools they depended on finance from outside (in their case from fee-payers and benefactors) for their existence. But with the support they got they were capable of effective work and development. No one who studies medieval schoolbooks can fail to be impressed by the complexity of school work, and the ingeniousness of masters' methods. The modern school, autonomous with professional staff, and the modern educationist aware of the needs and potentialities of children, are the respective heirs of the town schools of the twelfth century and the friars who rediscovered childhood in the thirteenth, to which they are linked by continuous tradition. As Newman remarked of the Church, those who talk boldly against it owe to it that they can talk at all.

[75] Orme, *West of England*, p 88.

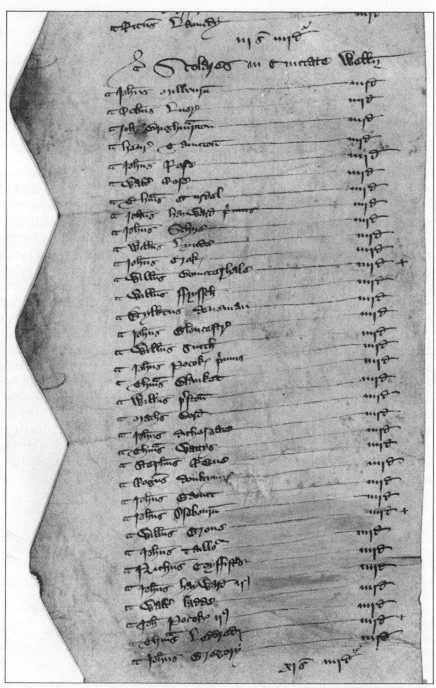

1 A rare list of the pupils in a medieval school. Compiled for the poll-tax of 1377, it names
the 34 boys of Wells cathedral school (Somerset) aged over fourteen and liable to tax. Two
pairs of boys with the same surname are distinguished as 'primus' and 'secundus', a custom
which survived till modern times.

2

THE 'LAICISATION' OF ENGLISH SCHOOL EDUCATION

A. F. Leach's book *The Schools of Medieval England* (1915) was a pioneer of topic rather than method. Notable as the first general survey of the subject, it earns poor marks for presentation: unintegrated lists of facts about schools intermingled with 'the rashest judgment about the most disputable matters', as Maitland once remarked of Leach's work. And yet, sorting through the jumbled heap, one finds from time to time perceptive comments. When Leach came to describe the fifteenth century, he rightly pointed out that it was not a time of decadence in learning, as many people then thought, but of activity in the endowment of schools and colleges. This activity had two contrasting features: 'the sacerdotal and the anti-sacerdotal'. On the one hand, the clerical interest in education was strengthened by the foundation of chantry grammar schools taught by priests. On the other hand many of these schools were founded by laymen or entrusted to the governance of laymen, and in schools other than the chantry schools examples of married lay schoolmasters could often be found. The fifteenth century, therefore, also saw a 'growth of the interest of the laity in the schools'.[1]

Recent writers on late-medieval education, whatever their other disagreements with Leach, concur with him in this. They too see, after 1400, a perceptible lay involvement with school education. Kenneth Charlton viewed it in 1965 as a shift away from a previous domination by the clergy. Assuming a situation in the thirteenth and fourteenth centuries in which the Church authorities took the lead in licensing and visiting schools, he saw this give way to 'the growth of purely lay-sponsored education which...had begun to gather momentum in the fifteenth century'.[2] Joan Simon, writing a year later, was more cautious in assessing clerical control of education before 1400, pointing out that 'schools sponsored by the Church were adjuncts of semi-autonomous religious corporations rather than units in a system under diocesan control'. But she too saw a growing lay involvement in education after about 1400. Laymen improved their right to attend school; clerical monopolies of schools were challenged; lay benefactors, guilds and municipal bodies took part in founding and governing schools; and 'in these various ways laymen established an increasing stake in education'.[3] In 1973 John Lawson was more cautious still, pointing out cases of lay involvement with schools long before 1400, but he agreed that 'the Church's influence, even in the traditionally ecclesiastical field of [the grammar schools], was lessening'. Lay literacy was increasing, and more boys were going to school without the intention of becoming priests.[4] Finally, I wrote myself, in 1973, that the activity of laymen in the specific areas of the endowment and government of schools 'constitutes a major development in the history of English education, so much more is it apparent after 1400

---

1 A. F. Leach, *The Schools of Medieval England* (London, 1915), 235, 243–6, 269.
2 K. Charlton, *Education in Renaissance England* (London, 1965), 15, 91–2.
3 J. Simon, *Education and Society in Tudor England* (Cambridge, 1967), 19–32 *passim.*
4 J. Lawson and H. Silver, *A Social History of Education in England* (London, 1973), 43–85 *passim.*

than in the centuries before'. But I added a caveat, that 'it would be foolish to underestimate the share of the clergy' or to see the lay involvement as anti-sacerdotal or carried out at the expense of the ancient clerical interest in education. 'Rather the clergy shared in what was a general growth of interest.'[5]

In 1985 Jo-Ann Hoeppner Moran published a new book on late-medieval education, *The Growth of English Schooling, 1340–1548*. Despite its general title, this is particularly concerned with a single region, the diocese of York, but the judgement about the laity is the same, indeed it is stressed more. Whereas previous writers mentioned lay involvement in passing rather than as a central issue, Moran develops the idea into a major thesis which provides the title of one chapter ('Literacy and the Laicization of Education') and the subtitle of the whole book ('Learning, Literacy and Laicization'). Her arguments are partly traditional, partly new. Lay people are mentioned endowing and governing schools, and new material from Yorkshire wills shows laymen arranging for their children to go to school, often as a prelude to a specific lay career. An increase in lay literacy is postulated, which Moran believes to be both motive and result of the lay involvement in education. She is careful not to underestimate the clergy. Clerics founded schools, school curricula even in institutions under lay control were often clerical and liturgical, and schools still turned out 'impressively high numbers of priests'. 'It is difficult to find any educational institutions, even those that were lay-founded or endowed, that did not retain some ecclesiastical characteristics'. But the main premise of the book appears to be the lay activity, and this is reiterated in the concluding chapter:

> It is the expanding lay interest in schooling that is crucial to an understanding of the growing momentum in education which northern England experienced in the fifteenth and early sixteenth centuries. Laity of all classes – nobles, gentry, townspeople, and villagers – were turning their attention to the schools in a new and dramatic way.[6]

It seems, therefore, to be agreed that laicization of education took place in the fifteenth century, while not wholly replacing clerical interests. The historians differ slightly in their emphasis and evidence, but they generally accord with the idea. So much agreement may appear to leave no room for anything else to be said; on the contrary, I think the time has come to examine laicization more fully than we have yet done. While the lay status of founders and governors were merely observed in passing, such an examination did not seem necessary, but if laicization is to be enlarged into a major thesis, it requires more consideration than (I respectfully suggest) it receives in Moran's book. Wide-ranging though her discussion is, it does not thoroughly explore the five chief areas of school education in which lay and clerical forces can be traced. These are the government of schools by the authorities; the funding of schools by fees, bequests and benefactions; schoolmasters; the school curriculum; and the pupils in schools. I propose to examine the nature and extent of laicization in each of these areas, and as the dates of Moran's survey (1340–1548) seem a little too narrow to show the history of the process to its best advantage, I shall start in the thirteenth century and occasionally go beyond 1548 into the following decade.

'The teaching of boys is a spiritual matter.' So said Chief Justice Thirning in the famous legal judgment of 1410 in which the Justices of the Common Pleas refused to

5 N. Orme, *English Schools in the Middle Ages* (London, 1973), 205–7.
6 J. A. H. Moran, *The Growth of English Schooling, 1340–1548: Learning, Literacy and Laicization in Pre-Reformation York Diocese* (Princeton, 1985), 150–84, 223.

exercise jurisdiction in a suit between rival schoolmasters in Gloucester.[7] Yet, as Joan Simon pointed out in 1966, there was little general oversight of schools by the medieval Church authorities; indeed, one can go further and say there was virtually none. Popes, councils, bishops, and *pace* Kenneth Charlton chancellors and archdeacons, seldom concerned themselves with schools as a group. The few exceptions are mainly confined to Lincolnshire, Nottinghamshire and parts of Yorkshire where the cathedral chancellors exercised a rare authority in this respect.[8] Elsewhere there were no general arrangement for licensing schoolmasters or visiting schools, only a system of local patronage similar to that over parish churches but far less well developed. Bishops, chancellors and archdeacons claimed the right to appoint schoolmasters in the cathedral cities, and the lords of some other towns and rural manors made similar claims in those places.[9] Even so, there were many settlements, including a town as large as Bristol,[10] where claimants to the appointment of schoolmasters were weak or non-existent and where masters could usually teach unchecked and uncontrolled. Where there were effective patrons, we know of vastly more cases up to 1400 in which they were clerics (about 67) than where they were laymen (only 5), for as with parish churches some lay lords had given their patronage of schools to monasteries in the twelfth century. If we took account of the fourteenth-century schools where no patronage is known (at least 30, probably many more), this might reduce the clerical predominance, but many more schools not under clerical patronage would have to be found to establish a non-clerical or lay dominance. At the moment, it looks as though the clergy appointed to a large percentage of schools, particularly grammar schools, and perhaps to the majority.

During the fifteenth century, as the writers already mentioned have noted, this clerical dominance began to be eroded. Between about 1380 and 1450 the fashion developed for founding endowed free grammar schools, requiring governors to administer the endowments and appoint and pay the schoolmasters.[11] Some founders put their schools under clerical governors, particularly monasteries and university colleges, but others entrusted the duty to laymen, thereby increasing the lay patronage of schools. These laymen included noble and gentle families, groups of lay feoffees, London city companies, and religious guilds made up of urban merchants or rural yeomen. One or two schools such as Richmond (Yorkshire), noted by Moran (by 1486),[12] and the famous example of St Paul's, London (1508–12),[13] even changed through endowment from ecclesiastical to lay patronage.

No one denies that this process caused more of the aristocracy, merchants and rural yeomen to become involved in managing school endowments and appointments; there was, indeed, a partial laicization in this respect. What can be doubted is whether it had much impact on schools. Did lay patrons and governors act differently from clerical ones? There is little evidence that they did. Some school statutes required the master to be a priest, but the schools concerned were under both clerical and lay patronage. Where the schoolmaster did not need to be a priest, as in a fee-paying town school, we

7 N. Orme, *Education in the West of England, 1066–1548* (Exeter, 1976), 62–3.
8 Orme, *English Schools*, 145.
9 For a map of the patronage of schools up to 1400, see *ibid.*, 147.
10 Orme, *Education in the West of England*, 35–42.
11 Orme, *English Schools*, 187–90, 194–207.
12 Moran, *The Growth of English Schooling*, 169.
13 M. F. J. McDonnell, *The History of St Paul's School* (London, 1909), 13–20.

find clerical patrons willing to appoint layman as masters, at least by the late fourteenth century. John Cornwall, a married man, was tolerated at Oxford by the (clerical) university in the 1340s, and John Burdon, another married man, was appointed schoolmaster of Carlisle by the bishop, in 1362.[14] Further research may show a greater tendency by clerical patrons to appoint clerical schoolmasters, but it is very unlikely to reveal an absolute policy to that end. Nor does the status of school patrons seem to have affected school curricula. A good deal of curricular material survives from the fifteenth century in the form of masters' and pupils' personal notebooks. But, as we shall see presently, there is nothing in these books to indicate a difference between 'lay' and 'clerical' schools; they share a common approach to common material. The process of laicization at patron and governor level looks less significant given its apparent failure, up to the Reformation, to affect what went on in the schools.

This changed at the Reformation, but not in a straightforward way. At first, under Henry VIII and Edward VI, the laicization of school governors continued and accelerated. The dissolution of the monasteries and chantries removed a great many schools from clerical control. Comparatively few remained under ecclesiastical government after 1550, except for the cathedral schools and such endowed schools as were under the supervision of university colleges. Even the cathedral schools were sometimes now confronted by a town school under lay control, as happened at Bristol, Gloucester, Salisbury and Worcester. This enabled such schools to reflect the rivalries of town and gown, clericalism and anti-clericalism. But in 1554–6 the laicization process was turned on its head by Mary I and Cardinal Pole when they introduced a new general system of examining and licensing schoolmasters. This grew from a typical sixteenth-century conviction, which had been rather slow to develop under Henry VIII and Edward VI, that schools were crucial to the political and religious settlement, and ought to be more closely controlled from outside. Since it was under Mary that this view became a policy, the oversight was given to the bishops not to lay supervisors, and when Elizabeth I succeeded in 1558 she continued both the policy and the bishops as its agents.[15] From the 1550s onwards, therefore, lay government of schools was subjected to a higher ecclesiastical scrutiny. Paradoxically, the conscious control of schools by the clergy, which had not been strong in the Middle Ages, increased during the Reformation, which is rightly regarded in some other respects as a movement of laicization.

Closely allied to the control of schools is their funding. Most medieval schools were fee-paying until the 1440s, and probably as late as the 1540s, and for institutions which depend on fees the fee-payers are as potent a force as the governors. The history of the funding of schools is better recorded the later we go. The increasing survival of wills and private accounts from the late fourteenth century onwards reveals bequests and payments by wealthy people, laity and clergy, for the schooling of their children, relatives and other protégés. The endowment of free schools by other wealthy clergy and laity, particularly after the 1440s, brought in new methods of funding which benefited not only individuals but all who cared to attend these schools. It is important for us not to confuse new records for the funding of education, and new methods by which it was done, with the principle of lay funding, which can be traced back to the

14 For Cornwall, see A. B. Emden, *A Biographical Register of the University of Oxford to AD 1500* (3 vols., Oxford, 1957–9), vol. 1, 490; and for Burdon, Carlisle Record Office, Reg. Gilbert Welton, f 103, and *Testamenta Karleolensia*, ed. R. S. Ferguson, Cumberland and Westmorland Antiquarian and Architectural Society, 9 (1893), 101.
15 Orme, *English Schools*, 286–7.

earliest days of English history. The oldest form of subsidy was the taking of a boy into a royal household, as Beowulf is said to have been at the court of Hrethel, king of the Geats.[16] When Christianity was introduced, kings and noblemen began to found monasteries which included the educational function of bringing up children. They duly sent their children to these places, and also other boys, sometimes to be trained as monks, sometimes as lay aristocracy. Eventually they paid money for the service. When town schools started to proliferate in the twelfth century, wealthy laymen patronized them too, alongside the monasteries. Gerald of Wales was set to study letters by his baronial father in the 1150s and 1160s, first at Gloucester Abbey and then at the Paris schools.[17] Henry II sent his bastard son Geoffrey to the schools of Tours a decade later, and Henry III paid for a boy to attend Bury St Edmunds school in 1255.[18] It can be objected that we do not have many records of early lay funding, that ecclesiastics bore much of the responsibility, and that most of the boys involved were going on to become clerics not laymen. But none of these objections disproves the proposition that large numbers of lay parents and patrons subsidized the education of their children and other boys in households, monasteries and schools before there were free schools in the fifteenth century.

What happened in that century was therefore not a change in the principle of lay funding, but perhaps in the extent to which it was done, and more certainly in the method. The question of extent is a difficult one. Perhaps more parents, particularly from groups below the aristocracy, paid to send their children to school, and more often so that they should follow lay careers. The impression is distorted by greater documentation in the fifteenth century, leading to more records of scholars, schools and personal literacy, but the increase seems likely. That wealthy laymen were contributing *more* money to education, and clergy *less*, than before, as Moran suggests from the evidence of Yorkshire wills, seems to me rather doubtful.[19] Wills were usually drawn up late in life, in a variable mixture of personal sentiments and conventional actions, and are unreliable guides to their makers' behaviour for most of their lives, before their wills were made. Such records are good illustrative sources, but dangerous statistical ones.[20] There was certainly a partial change in the method of funding education, through the invention of the endowed free school. But why this change occurred, chiefly after the 1440s, is rather mysterious. One might suppose that the declining English population (which seems to have reached a bottom in the first half of the fifteenth century) made it less easy for masters to live off fees, prompting interventions to endow them with salaries. But the only contemporary commentator, William Bingham in about 1439, suggests the opposite: a shortage of masters, not of potential pupils. Seventy grammar schools, he claimed, were vacant in the eastern half of England for lack of teachers, and his remedy was to subsidize their training at

16 *Beowulf*, lines 2428–31.
17 *The Autobiography of Giraldus Cambrensis*, ed. and trans. H. E. Butler (London, 1937), 35–7, 79.
18 N. Orme, *From Childhood to Chivalry: the Education of the English Kings and Aristocracy, 1066–1530* (London, 1984), 67; *English Schools*, 119.
19 Moran, *The Growth of English Schooling*, 170. Moran provides figures for the numbers of laity and clergy leaving educational bequests in wills from 1400 to 1530 to show a clerical decline. But surely we also need to know the percentages of such lay benefactors against all lay testators, and likewise those of the clergy, since Moran admits that the numbers of lay and clerical wills fluctuate.
20 The works of the late W. K. Jordan exemplify the failure of the attempt to estimate total charity from statistical work on selected surviving wills.

university.[21] Perhaps by the 1430s there were easier and better-paid jobs than teaching and the endowed schools were prompted by the need to attract men into school work (especially in lesser towns) through higher and more reliable salaries.

The endowment of schools had some effect on the status of schoolmasters. Before about 1350, masters are a shadowy group whose members' biographies are difficult to reconstruct, including their lay or clerical affiliations.[22] The nine secular cathedral schools probably tended to attract clerics, at least in minor orders. Sometimes the masters of these schools had to attend the choral services as well as teach, and committed clerics stood to gain more than laymen, through combining the school with a chantry or vicar-choralship, or being promoted to a parish church in the cathedral's gift. In the schools of the other towns, including the monastic cathedral cities, these factors did not apply and masters may have included priests, clerks in minor orders and laymen from an early date. A cleric could supplement his teaching with other clerical work, but a layman could marry and thereby acquire a housekeeper to look after his boarders. Certainly by the second half of the fourteenth century we encounter married masters of the kind we have mentioned at Carlisle and Oxford. When the endowed schools began to be founded, those attached to colleges (like Magdalen College School, Oxford, and Rotherham, Yorkshire) often continued the tradition of employing clergy *or* laity, but the smaller ones, or chantry schools, which formed the majority, required the master to be a chantry priest and hence a committed cleric. The rise of the chantry schools therefore caused a slight *clericization* of the teaching vocation between about 1440 and 1548, and as some of these schools replaced earlier town schools, there was an exact reverse of the process by which school governors were becoming laicized. The clericization was only slight, however, because there were plenty of non-endowed fee-paying schools even at the height of the chantry school movement, and the opportunities for laymen to teach were never seriously restricted. Moreover, with the coming of the Reformation, the connection between schools and ecclesiastical bodies such as colleges and chantries was reduced or abolished, and by 1550 few schools existed where the master had to be a cleric.

We have doubted whether the status of patrons and governors affected schools; but did that of schoolmasters? A clerical master had to say the liturgy every day (a task of several hours if properly done) and a chantry schoolmaster also had to say mass. School duties had to be fitted in beside these tasks, and we know that schoolboys in chantry schools were sometimes used as servers or assistants at chantry masses. But there is nothing to show that this depressed the standard of the education given (else why did bishops and noblemen found chantry schools?), or greatly changed its character. The teaching of both reading and grammar in schools was a blend of the sacred and secular. The alphabet was presented in a Christian framework, starting with the cross and ending with 'amen', and reading practice centred on Church service books (the psalter and antiphonal) and on the basic prayers (paternoster, Ave Maria, creed and so on).[23] Writers of Latin grammars and masters setting exercises for Latin

21 For versions of Bingham's petition to Henry VI about the state of the English schools, see A. H. Lloyd, *The Early History of Christ's College, Cambridge* (Cambridge, 1934), 356–7, and A. F. Leach, *Educational Charters and Documents, 598 to 1909* (Cambridge, 1911), 402–3.
22 On medieval schoolmasters, see Orme, *English Schools*, 150–63, supplemented and revised in 'Schoolmasters, 1307–1509', in *Profession, Vocation and Culture in Later Medieval England*, ed. C. H. Clough (Liverpool, 1982), 218–41, and 'English schoolmasters, 1100–1500', in *Medieval Lives and the Historian: Studies in Medieval Prosopography*, ed. N. Bulst and J. P. Genet (Kalamazoo, Mich., 1986), 303–12; now below pp 49–71.
23 Orme, *English Schools*, 60–3.

composition or translation freely mingled sacred and secular themes and examples. Translation sentences from a Bristol grammar school in the 1420s varied references to fasting on Candlemas eve, confession in Lent and pilgrimage to Compostella, with observations about food, marriage, tradesmen, birds and animals, and scraps of popular songs.[24] The student who wrote a grammar notebook at Barlinch Priory, Somerset, between about 1480 and 1520 is impossible to classify as an intending monk, secular priest or layman, given the similarly wide range of material he was copying, from moral and religious precepts to secular references and jokes.[25] Nor is this mixture unexpected. Schoolmasters had to teach for a variety of careers and eventualities, and their teaching was accordingly diverse and flexible, as the market demanded.

Lay or clerical bias in the curriculum is most evident in the study of Latin literature. During the thirteenth century a set of six Latin poets, the *Sex Auctores*, frequently appears in manuscripts and was probably widely read in schools.[26] The authors were late- and post-classical Latinists, and their works included the collection of wise precepts known as the *Distichs of Cato*, the *Eclogue of Theodulus* which compares classical mythology unfavourably with biblical history, Avianus's fables, Maximian's love poems, Claudian's *Rape of Proserpine* and Statius's account of the youth of Achilles. Thirteenth-century pupils were therefore exposed to poetry mostly by Christian authors, but including pagan and amatory subjects. By the fourteenth century tastes were changing, and the *Sex Auctores* seemed too difficult linguistically or too unsuitable culturally. The first two, the most Christian, were retained but the others dropped out and were replaced by twelfth- and thirteenth-century moral and religious poems on penitence (*Peniteas cito*), the vanity of the world (*Cartula*) and good behaviour (*Facetus*), together with the wise proverbs of Alain de Lille. This group of texts was dominant in schools until about 1490–1520 when (except for Cato) it was discarded in its turn for the classical pagan authors introduced by the humanists: Cicero, Horace, Livy, Ovid and Virgil.[27] If the yardstick of laicization is applied, school literature became less lay in about the fourteenth century and more lay in the early sixteenth. But the reintroduction of pagan authors after the 1490s was not necessarily seen by its supporters as a piece of laicization. On the contrary, the authors were taught in a framework of Christianity, as in earlier times. Early Tudor schools often had corporate prayers at the beginning and end of the day, and this practice continued after the Reformation. Indeed, in 1545, Henry VIII issued the first official primer of prayers to be used in schools.[28] Moran suggests that Archbishop Holgate's three schools founded in Yorkshire in 1546 were new in that they 'no longer delineate a specific religious function' and that 'it is clear that the purpose behind Holgate's foundation was primarily educational rather than religious'.[29] They were not indeed chantry schools, but were they less religious than traditional town schools, since they were ordered to have daily prayers? It is most unlikely that Holgate, a leader of the Reformation, would have distinguished education from religion at a time when people (as we have seen with licensing) thought of the two as so intimately connected.

24 N. Orme, 'A grammatical miscellany of 1427–65 from Bristol and Wiltshire',| now below pp 87-112.
25 N. Orme, 'A school note-book from Barlinch Priory', *Somerset Archaeology and Natural History*, 128 (1984), 55–63; now below pp 113-21.
26 On what follows, see Orme, *English Schools*, 102–6.
27 Presumably even in the north of England, since printed editions ceased in the 1510s (*ibid.*, 113). East Retford School, described by Moran as the first to 'institute a markedly humanistic curriculum' (*The Growth of English Schooling*, 183) is probably only original in having the matter stated in its foundation documents.
28 Orme, *English Schools*, 130, 258.
29 Moran, *The Growth of English Schooling*, 183.

Laicization, then, is a difficult theme to pursue in the curriculum. Is it easier to discern in the history of those who studied in schools, the pupils? All of them started their lives as laymen, of course, but in the thirteenth and fourteenth centuries there was a tendency to regard them, while at school, as clerics. We hear of the 'clerks of the school' at Exeter and Glastonbury, just as in Chaucer the schoolboy is a 'clergeoun' or little clerk and the Oxford scholar 'the clerk of Oxenford'. Schoolboys were often tonsured; they sometimes fell for jurisdictional purposes under ecclesiastical rather than secular authority, and the older ones might pay clerical rather than lay taxation.[30] Such clerical status, however, was provisional or partial rather than fixed and complete. The tonsure and the degree of acolyte which came above it in the ordination ladder did not force a schoolboy to be a cleric for ever. He could go on to marry and follow a lay career, claiming his 'clergy' only to escape the lay courts if he was accused of a crime. A permanent commitment to clerical life could only be made in his late teens when he took religious vows or was ordained as a subdeacon and deacon. But you could not become a priest until you were 24, and many preferred to delay becoming subdeacons and deacons until they reached that age. 'Be not too hasty of taking of [holy] orders', as Margaret Paston warned her 17-year old son Walter on his departure for Oxford University in 1473.[31] This situation made it possible for schoolboys to be clerks while intending to take up lay careers on finishing their education, and for some who meant to be priests to fall by the wayside through lack of aptitude, inadequate finance, or the inheritance of property through the deaths of elder brothers.[32] Even those who did survive to become priests were not necessarily clerical in their behaviour; they might wear secular dress, fall in love and fight with weapons. The vast number of medieval complaints about the ignorance and worldliness of the adult clergy hardly suggest that schooling was an effective clerical training.

We shall be wise, therefore, not to overestimate the clerical status of early schoolboys, or its decline in the fifteenth and early sixteenth centuries. For there was some decline; the term 'clerk' dropped out and was replaced by 'scholar' and 'schoolboy', and the tonsure (the original mark of clericality) fell into disuse in schools. By early Tudor times ordination records cease to include long lists of tonsured clerks, and woodcuts of schools at work do not appear to show the boys with shaven heads.[33] This change is another sign of the carelessness of the Church authorities in keeping their hold over schools. Perhaps, too, it accompanied an increase in the proportion of schoolboys who intended to go on to secular careers as household servants, secretarial clerks, lawyers, merchants or gentlemen. One assumes that the number of such boys was gradually increasing in the later Middle Ages, though the increase is impossible to measure at present from the small number of available schoolboy biographies. And, as Moran very properly reminds us, the laicization of careers was not a straightforward process. There was a rise in the number of clergy being ordained in the diocese of York during the fifteenth century that was greater than the rise in the population. Ordinations of priests rose from about 100 a year in the first half of the century to a peak of 239 in 1509.[34] Since it has long been known that the number of monks and

---

30 Orme, *English Schools*, 120–2, 135; *Education in the West of England*, 206.
31 *Paston Letters and Papers of the Fifteenth Century*, ed. N. Davis (Oxford, 1971), vol. 1, 370.
32 For some examples of changes of plans by university scholars, see Orme, *From Childhood to Chivalry*, 70.
33 The woodcuts are listed in E. Hodnett, *English Woodcuts, 1480–1535* London, Bibliographical Society Monographs, 22 (1935).
34 Moran, *The Growth of English Schooling*, 126–30.

regular canons also increased in the fifteenth century,[35] more boys in total may have left school to become clergy at the end of the century than did so at the beginning. Later, after 1509, the level both of York ordinations and monastic vocations declined, and the quota of future clerics in schools must have done so too. And with the removal of so many clerical posts in religious houses and chantries at the Reformation, the number of school-leavers who became clergy grew very small indeed.

The history of laicization in schools, therefore, turns out to be a complicated process. In the thirteenth century, when we might expect schools to have been at their most ecclesiastical, they appear neglected by the Church in general and managed by local patrons whose policies were rarely consciously religious. The funding of education was provided by the laity on a significant scale, as well as by the clergy. Schoolmasters probably came from both groups, and the grammar course was a mixture of Christianity and pagan literature. Schoolboys, though classed as clerks, were not irrevocably destined to be clergy, and many who did become so were imperfectly clericized by their education. In the fourteenth and fifteenth centuries some of these elements were laicized but others became more clerical. There was some laicization of the management of schools, a waning of the clerical status of pupils and probably a growing number of boys who passed into lay careers. On the other hand the grammar curriculum became more Christian in content, the chantry school movement introduced a new body of clerical schoolmasters, and the late fifteenth century saw a rising number of clerical vocations. In the early sixteenth century the curriculum became more secular, and the Reformation introduced more changes in a secular direction. Most schools under ecclesiastical management were closed or had the management transferred to secular hands; most schoolmasterships became open to laymen; and an absolute decline in the number of clergy led to less clerical funding of schools and fewer clerical careers. Yet even at the Reformation, the opposite process went on, with the imposition first of an official primer of prayers for schools and later of general ecclesiastical control on schoolmasters and teaching. For the Reformation was not a movement to destroy religion but to increase its effectiveness among the laity. While it ended clerical independence and reduced clerical numbers, it maintained and even strengthened the bishops and parish clergy as agents of religious policy.

What was clerical and what was lay is a problem which affects the history not only of education but of politics, religion and society. Medieval and Tudor people had well-developed theories of who were clergy and laity, but in practice these were inadequate. Clergy could be lay in their activities (from ecclesiastical barons to hunting parsons) just as laymen could be clerical (from pious members of guilds to criminals pleading benefit of clergy). When clergy and laity are such complex terms, it is not surprising that laicization is so hard to establish. The word is a useful label for historians to use for distinguishing particular changes in the history of education. But it fails to summarize what happened to English school education in general between 1250 and 1560.

35 D. Knowles and R. N. Hadcock, *Medieval Religious Houses: England and Wales* (2nd edn, London, 1971), 494.

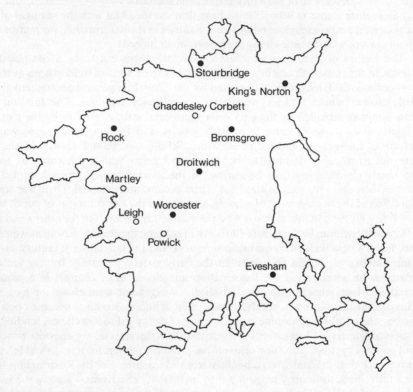

WORCESTERSHIRE SCHOOLS 1500-1550

Stourbridge

King's Norton

Chaddesley Corbett

Rock

Bromsgrove

Droitwich

Martley

Leigh

Worcester

Powick

Evesham

● Recorded grammar schools
○ Recorded elementary, or unspecified, schools
〰 Ancient county boundary

0   15ml

0   25km

3

EDUCATION IN AN ENGLISH COUNTY: WORCESTERSHIRE

The history of English school education before the Reformation is largely a matter of local history. International and national sources hardly exist. Popes and church councils, kings and parliaments, rarely concerned themselves with schools as such, and consequently generated few records about them. Schoolmasters were not an organised profession, nationally or locally, but worked as individuals. True, schools, schoolmasters and scholars are mentioned in the archives of the crown, but on the same terms as other people and for legal or financial reasons unconnected with education. Even in the field of Latin teaching, where similar grammars and reading texts circulated all over western Europe, it is still necessary to verify their use and trace the variations among them in manuscripts produced at local schools. In short, the general history of schools must be built up by collecting local examples. This is true of their numbers and distribution, their constitutional history (patrons, buildings, fees and endowments), their studies and the names and careers of their masters and pupils. The student of medieval school education is perforce a local historian.

The following chapter demonstrates the difficulties and rewards of research in a single area: the old county of Worcestershire.[1] Schools, as we have seen, first become manifest as separate organisations in the twelfth century, particularly in the English cathedral cities and county towns. Unfortunately, since medieval schools are mainly recorded by chance, there are several important towns where no school has yet been discovered in the twelfth or even the early thirteenth centuries. Worcester falls into this category, the earliest extant mentions of its school belonging to the second half of the thirteenth. In 1266 (new style) Bishop Cantilupe of Worcester set up a chantry of four priests to serve the Carnary chapel near the cathedral, and ordered them to attend school every day.[2] In 1291 his successor Bishop Giffard arbitrated in a dispute between the schoolmaster (*rector scolarum*) of Worcester and the rector of the city church of St Nicholas. The master and scholars, it appears, were accustomed to celebrate the feast of the saint (the patron of scholars) in

---

[1] On Worcestershire schools in general, see A.F. Leach, *Documents Illustrating Early Education in Worcester, 685-1700*, Worcestershire Historical Society, xxi (1913), and his article on 'Schools' in *VCH Worcestershire*, vol iv (1924), pp 473-540.

[2] Leach, *Education in Worcester*, pp 19-22.

the church each year. The rector claimed the candles they used as his perquisite, but the bishop upheld the right of the master and scholars to do what they wished with the candles.[3]. At about the same time, in 1294, the 'Priory Register' of Worcester Cathedral (which was a Benedictine monastery) reveals that the monastery maintained a number of boys in its almonry, and sent them to the schoolmaster of Worcester for their teaching.[4] From this time onwards there are further occasional references to the school, which make it likely that the organisation continued in existence (apart from short gaps) down to the Reformation.

If the general history of schools is based on local data, the converse is also true: local data are best interpreted by reference to general history. It is unlikely that Worcester school originated in the thirteenth century, and more probable that it dated back to the twelfth when we know that schools existed in similar neighbouring towns like Gloucester, Hereford and Warwick. The thirteenth-century evidence, confirmed by later records, also shows that the school had closer links with the city than with the cathedral. It was hardly a 'cathedral school'. The master was not appointed by the monks of the cathedral, but by the archdeacon of Worcester, or failing him the bishop. The site of the school, though not at present clear, is also likely to have been outside the monastic precinct. Also tellingly, the school community went for its major annual festival on St Nicholas Day to a church in the city. The cathedral connection seems to have been limited to the master's duty of teaching the almonry scholars and his right in return to send one of his other scholars every day in term (and three scholars in Lent) to receive a meal in the almonry.[5] Apart from this modest patronage, the school appears to have been self-supporting. The master charged his scholars fees and lived off the proceeds, his livelihood being guaranteed by a prohibition against anyone else teaching in the city.[6] The school curriculum is first mentioned in 1312 when the institution is referred to as a 'grammar school',[7] but from its earliest days the master is likely to have taught the whole range of school subjects: reading, plainsong and Latin grammar.

The appearance of schools in lesser market towns can also be traced as early as the twelfth century, and was quite common by the thirteenth. None has yet been found in Worcestershire at such a date, but once again the lack of evidence is no sure guide that none existed. On the contrary, the presence of schools in nearby towns like Cirencester, Ludlow and Stratford-on-Avon during the thirteenth century suggests that one or two at least were to be found within the borders of Worcestershire.[8] As it

[3] Ibid., pp 23–6.
[4] Ibid., pp 22–3.
[5] Ibid.
[6] Ibid., pp 98–9.
[7] Ibid., p 34.
[8] Orme, *English Schools*, pp 300, 310, 317.

is, we have to wait until the fourteenth century before the necessary evidence appears. It relates to two places: Droitwich and Evesham. The borough records of Droitwich reveal that a school existed there, apparently during the reign of Edward III, when certain of the inhabitants were accused of carrying away doors and windows from its building.[9] In 1379 a clerk in minor orders named Henry Scholmayster contributed to a clerical subsidy in the parish of St Andrew, Droitwich, and it is possible that his surname referred to his work.[10] The clergy of Evesham also included a man named William the schoolmaster in 1379, the name being there spelt out in its Latin form: *magister scolarum*.[11] It is not clear, however, whether he taught a school in the abbey, a public school, or both. The continuity of education in smaller English towns should never be relied upon but, as we shall see, both Droitwich and Evesham possessed schools in the 1520s and 30s, and it is not impossible that the latter descended from those of the earlier period.

During the fourteenth and early fifteenth centuries a major development took place in English education with the evolution of endowed schools to provide teaching free of charge. An important early example was the school at Wotton-under-Edge in Gloucestershire, founded in 1384. Endowed schools are easier to investigate than their unendowed predecessors, because they possessed income, buildings and often statutes which have better survived in records. We can be more confident of knowing how many such schools there were, and how they were organised. Usually the master of an endowed school received a salary of £10 a year from the endowment, and had the use of a dwelling and a schoolroom for his teaching. He was expected to give lessons in grammar, and often too in reading and plainsong, to all comers, free of charge. In most cases he had also to be a priest and to celebrate a daily mass for the repose of the founder's soul. Hence the terms 'free school' and 'chantry school' by which such institutions are often known. Schools of this kind began to be founded in appreciable numbers during the 1440s and 50s, when Henry VI gave royal patronage to the movement with his foundation of Eton College. The impetus declined for a time with the rise of political unrest and civil war, and only a few foundations were made under Edward IV, but a revival of interest took place during the 1480s and 90s. A steady stream of endowed schools came into existence under the early Tudors, and the movement continued without much abatement throughout the sixteenth century.[12]

Worcestershire acquired two educational endowments during the first period of activity, under Henry VI. Both were the work of the bishop of Worcester, John Carpenter, and both for this reason are connected with

[9] *VCH Worcs.*, iii, 76.
[10] PRO, E 179/58/11.
[11] Ibid.
[12] On this subject, see Orme, *English Schools*, pp 188–90, 194–207.

the interest in education at Henry's court, with which Carpenter himself was associated.[13] Neither endowment, however, led to the creation of a public grammar school in the usual sense. The first, carried out in 1462, allowed the monks of Evesham Abbey to appropriate the revenues of the church of Eyford in Gloucestershire on condition that they paid a salaried schoolmaster to teach the novices of the abbey and the boys of its almonry.[14] It is possible that Evesham's later endowed public school evolved from this arrangement, but public education was not a stated part of the original scheme. The second endowment, completed in 1464, was a reformation of Bishop Cantilupe's Carnary chapel in Worcester, whose original staff had become reduced to a single priest. Carpenter determined to make the Carnary chapel a centre for the study of theology, one of two such centres in the diocese, for he erected another in Bristol, which will be described in a later chapter.[15] His aim appears to have been to improve the learning of the parish clergy to strengthen their pastoral work and their struggle against Lollard heresy. The secular English cathedrals each possessed a dignitary (usually the chancellor) charged with lecturing in theology or canon law to the local clergy. Recently in London, another John Carpenter (perhaps a relative of the bishop) had helped set up the Guildhall Library, a collection of religious books for a similar purpose.[16] Worcester, with its monastic cathedral, does not appear to have enjoyed such facilities, and Carpenter had to provide them himself. Between 1458 and 1464 he rebuilt the Carnary chapel to include a library and a set of chambers for the chaplain to live in.[17] Finally, on 5 May 1464, he issued a set of statutes for the conduct of the institution.[18]

The statutes increased the qualifications demanded of the Carnary chaplain and gave him new duties. Henceforth he was to be a university graduate, familiar with both the Old and New Testaments, and preferably a bachelor of theology. He was appointed as before by the cathedral sacrist (a monk), but in future under the bishop's supervision. He had to act as keeper of the library and open it each weekday for two hours before noon and two afterwards, to all who wished to enter in order to learn.[19] During these hours he was to be at hand to explain

---

[13] On Carpenter's career, see R.M. Haines, 'Aspects of the Episcopate of John Carpenter', *Journal of Ecclesiastical History*, xix (1968), pp 11–40.

[14] Hereford and Worcester Record Office (hereafter HWRO), Reg. J. Carpenter, vol i, f 186ᵛ; Worcester Cathedral, Dean and Chapter Muniments, A.6(1) f 34.

[15] Below, chapter 12.

[16] On the Guildhall Library, see Orme, *English Schools*, pp 83–4.

[17] HWRO, Reg. Carpenter, vol i, ff 167ᵛ, 175-ᵛ; Reg. S. de Gigli, ff 132-133ᵛ.

[18] HWRO, Reg. S. de Gigli, ff 132-133ᵛ.

[19] *per duas horas ante nonam et duas post nonam* (ibid.). *Nonam* is sometimes translated as 9.00 am, but 'noon' or 'none' (the late morning service) is preferable. The clergy for whom the library was mainly intended would have been saying their offices and masses between 7.00 am and 11.00 am.

doubtful and obscure points of theology. He had also to deliver a lecture on one of the Testaments once or twice a week, to preach a solemn sermon once a year, and to celebrate mass in the Carnary chapel each day. In return, he received £10 a year and cloth for a gown and hood. The library appears to have functioned on these lines until the Reformation. Five of the chaplains' names are known: William Scrivener (instituted 1462),[20] Richard Wolsey (instituted 1475),[21] Peter Webb (occurs 1487),[22] Henry Lewis (occurs 1513, resigned 1528),[23] and Roger Neckham (instituted 1528).[24] All were university men, Scrivener and Lewis being masters of arts, Wolsey a bachelor of theology and the other two doctors. Little is known of the library's history, but it was evidently flourishing in 1503 when Robert Inkberrow, rector of St Swithin's, Worcester, bequeathed two of his books to be chained inside. One was William Lyndwood's *Provinciale*, the important fifteenth-century treatise on English canon law, and the other, identified simply as 'Vienna' may have been one of the biblical commentaries ascribed to Hugh of St Cher, alias Hugh of Vienne, who died in 1263.[25] The nature of these books, together with what is known of the parallel foundations in Bristol and London, suggest that the library's holdings centred on scholarly works of theology written in Latin. It is therefore unlikely that they attracted the lay public, whose reading mainly consisted of works in the vernacular. A weekly lecture was still being given in January 1540 when the Carnary and its library were dissolved along with the cathedral monastery. Two years later the last chaplain, Roger Neckham, was given a pension by the crown in compensation.[26]

Meanwhile, in the early sixteenth century, the foundation of chantry grammar schools in Worcestershire began in earnest. Six institutions came into being during this period at Bromsgrove, Evesham, King's Norton, Rock, Stourbridge and Worcester itself. The only one to which a definite date of origin can be assigned is Rock, which was founded in 1513 by Sir Humphrey Coningsby, one of the justices of the king's bench and a wealthy landowner in the county and elsewhere.[27] The dates of the others, for various reasons, remain obscure. At Worcester, to anticipate what will be argued presently, the city school changed from a fee-paying establishment to a partially endowed one at the beginning of the reign of Henry VIII. At Evesham a free grammar school was endowed by the

---

[20] HWRO, Reg. Carpenter, vol i, f 167ᵛ. For his career, see Emden, *BRUO*, iii, 1658.
[21] HWRO, Reg. Carpenter, vol ii, f 59ᵛ. For his career, see Emden, *BRUO*, iii, 2077.
[22] HWRO, Reg. R. Morton, f 12ᵛ.
[23] HWRO, Reg. S. de Gigli, ff 9, 132; Reg. J. Ghinucci, f 34.
[24] Ibid. For his career, see Emden, *BRUO*, iv, 413.
[25] PRO, Prob 11/14 (PCC 6 Holgrave). I am indebted for this reference, and for note 32 below, to the kindness of Miss Imogen Luxton.
[26] PRO, E 315/101 f 147.-ᵛ.
[27] *Letters and Papers, Foreign and Domestic, Henry VIII*, vol i part ii, no 2055(53).

abbey during the reign of Abbot Lichfield, between 1513 and 1538.[28] The other three schools appear for the first time in 1548. They all originated as chantries pure and simple, founded in the fifteenth or the early sixteenth centuries to provide priests to say mass and to do the duties of a curate. At some point before 1548 the parishioners of Bromsgrove, King's Norton and Stourbridge, who administered the chantry endowments and appointed the priests, laid the further duty upon them of teaching a grammar school. The exact times of these changes are not known, but probably lie in the 1530s and 40s when interest in chantries was declining and fears arose about their future. The three parishes are not very far apart, and it is likely that the decision of one was copied by the others.[29]

Besides these six foundations, all of which taught grammar and probably also reading and song, there are indications of other schools in the county during the 1530s and 40s. The existence of one at Droitwich in 1530 is revealed by a letter from Robert Joseph, monk of Evesham, to its schoolmaster named Sir John, asking the latter for comments on his Latin prose style.[30] The title 'Sir' explains that the master was one of the secular clergy in the town, and we may reasonably assume from the contents of the letter that he was a Latinist involved in teaching grammar. A school of unknown character seems to have flourished for a time at Chaddesley Corbett, probably during the 1530s. When the king's commissioners surveyed the chantries of Worcestershire in 1548, the parishioners told them that an endowment in their parish had formerly been used to pay a priest-schoolmaster, 'but they named no priest, nor did they show no foundation'. The arrangement, whatever it was, had evidently lapsed.[31] Other teaching of a modest nature can be traced in the rural parishes of Martley, Powick and Leigh. At Martley in 1547 the rector, William Noxton, bequeathed 40s. and some books to his young nephew, John Spowling, 'to find him to school with Sir Roger, if it please him to teach him'.[32] Sir Roger was the parish curate. At Powick reading, writing and song were taught in the late 1540s by the parish clerk, Harry Kent, in return for a contribution of 4d. a year from each of the parishioners.[33] Finally at Leigh, four miles west of Worcester, it was

[28] Below, p 40.

[29] A.F. Leach, *English Schools at the Reformation* (London, 1896), part ii, pp 268–71.

[30] *The Letter Book of Robert Joseph*, ed. H. Aveling and W.A. Pantin, Oxford Historical Society, new series, xix (1967), pp 79–81.

[31] Leach, *Schools at the Reformation*, part ii, p 271; PRO, C 3/194/43.

[32] HWRO, Registers of Wills, vol v, p 176.

[33] PRO, E 315/121 nos 27–8; E 321/37/28. Allegations were made in these documents that Powick possessed an endowed chantry school before 1548, but they were evidently designed to excuse the concealment of chantry lands from the chantry commissioners, and carry no conviction.

claimed in 1548 that the chantry priest, John Kayse, whose salary was only £2.2s.8d., had 'used to keep a free school'.[34] It has been assumed that the school was one of grammar, but there is no evidence for the assumption and something against it. The location is an unlikely one for a grammar school, and the foundation was not preserved by the king's chantry commissioners as were all the undoubted chantry-grammar schools in the county. It is more likely that the teaching at Leigh, like that at Powick, was elementary in scope.

The two schools of which most is known in the early sixteenth century are those at Evesham and Worcester. The previous history of education in Evesham is obscure, save for the mention of a schoolmaster in 1379, the endowment of teaching in the monastery in 1464, and a reference to William Fellows, grammar master of Evesham, who died in 1483.[35] We do not know whether the teaching was just for the novices and boys of the abbey, or open to the public. Then, in the 1520s, the educational arrangements at Evesham suddenly emerge into light, largely through the survival of Robert Joseph's remarkable letter-book.[36] Joseph was a monk of the abbey who went up to Oxford to study theology in about 1523. Six years later he was summoned back before his studies were over to carry out duties in the abbey, first as chaplain to the abbot and then as schoolmaster of the novices. Deprived of the congenial life and company of Oxford, he found solace through corresponding in Latin with his university acquaintances and others whom he knew in the monasteries and parish churches of the Severn Valley. His elegant letters, modelled on humanist, classical lines and full of wit and erudition, show himself and his friends to have been more lively, modern and cultured than is sometimes supposed of the clergy on the eve of the Reformation. Incidentally they contain some valuable references to local education. There were evidently two schools in Evesham by Joseph's time. In the abbey itself the novices, who were all aged over eighteen, received instruction in Latin grammar of an advanced nature from an experienced monk, Joseph himself discharging the duty between 1530 and 1532. Two of the addresses that he gave the novices survive in his letter-book. The first, on the *Eunuchus* of Terence, was his inaugural lecture on taking up the office of schoolmaster in 1530.[37] The second, on a poem by Battista

---

[34] Leach, *Schools at the Reformation*, part ii, p 277.
[35] Emden, *BRUO*, ii, 675.
[36] Above, note 30.
[37] *The Letter Book of Robert Joseph*, pp 56-9.

Mantovano in praise of St Katherine, was given later in the same year.[38] All this accorded with the papal law of 1336 that monasteries should maintain a teacher, preferably a monk, to instruct their novices in advanced grammar, logic and philosophy.

The other school in Evesham was open to the public. It owed its foundation, or its refoundation if we suppose a medieval origin, to Clement Wich alias Lichfield, who reigned as abbot from 1513 to 1538.[39] According to a Latin chronicle of the abbey written apparently in the early months of 1536,[40] 'he made the free school for the teaching of boys, assigning rents for the support of a schoolmaster'.[41] The date is not clear within the limits of 1513 and 1536, but probably preceded 1524 when the first of the known schoolmasters of the Tudor period took up his office. It is interesting to note in this connection that a similar project was carried out in 1521 at the nearby town of Winchcombe (Gloucs.) by its local Benedictine abbot, Richard Kidderminster. This also involved the creation of a free public grammar school in close association with an abbey, and one of the enterprises may have stimulated the other.[42] Besides endowing Evesham school Abbot Lichfield erected a building for it, the porch of which is still to be seen on Merstow Green, outside and opposite what was the main gate of the abbey. According to the local antiquary, George May, writing in 1845, it bore the abbey coat of arms, the initials 'C.L.', and the inscription 'Orate pro anima Clementis abbatis'. There was also a date, interpreted by May as 1546 which cannot be correct.[43] The building, as we shall see, is mentioned in 1538. The school was a grammar school, its master was appointed by the abbey, and three of the incumbents before the Reformation are known by name. The earliest is Robert Lyster. He was admitted a fellow of Magdalen College, Oxford, in 1520 and left after taking his MA degree in 1524 because he was about to begin teaching boys at Evesham. He did not teach for long, since in 1526 he was instituted as rector of Willersey (Gloucs.), five miles east of the abbey and one of its livings. Some later references to him in Joseph's letter-book suggest that Lister kept in touch with the monks. He held Willersey until 1554, when he was deprived by

[38] Ibid., pp 124-7.

[39] For Lichfield's career, see Emden, *BRUO*, ii, 1183.

[40] Brussels, Bibliothèque Royale, MS 7965, ff 131-4. An English translation of another text of this chronicle is in T. Habington, *A Survey of Worcestershire*, ed. J. Amphlett, vol ii, Worcestershire Historical Society (1899), pp 84-91. The chronicle is dated in the 23rd year of Abbot Lichfield (Dec. 1535-Dec. 1536) and in the 27th of Henry VIII (Apr. 1535-Apr. 1536), hence the suggested date of early 1536. I am grateful to Dr D.C. Cox for this and note 43.

[41] Brussels, Bibl. Roy., MS 7965, f 134.

[42] Orme, *West of England*, pp 186-90.

[43] G. May, *A Descriptive History of the Town of Evesham* (Evesham, 1845), p 196; *VCH Worcestershire*, iv, 498.

the Marian regime (as were so many others) for having married under Edward VI. He recovered it in 1559 after Elizabeth's accession and kept it for the rest of his life, dying in 1570.[44]

The next master of whom we know was Edmund Field, who held office between 1530 and 1534. Field was a local man, who was born at Haselor near Alcester (Warws.) about 1500, one of a large family of which four other sons and two daughters reached maturity. He was ordained deacon and priest in 1527 to a title provided by the nearby priory of Studley and, on coming to Evesham, became a special friend of Joseph who frequently mentions him in his letters. There is no sign that Field was a university graduate, but he evidently had studious tastes, possessing books and joining in the literary correspondence that went on within Joseph's circle. Two of Joseph's letters are addressed to him, and a third informs us that Field corresponded on his own account with William Dalam, one of the Studley canons. Field was probably a good specimen of an early-Tudor schoolmaster, but his ambition, like Lyster's, was set on a cure of souls and by 1535 he had become vicar of St Lawrence's, Evesham. It is likely that he resigned the school at about the same time. He remained on good terms with his successor, William Scollowe, to whom he bequeathed half of his books, the others going to John Higgins, vicar of Hampton near Evesham. Both men were present at Field's bedside when, sick in body, he made his will on 4 September 1545. He asked to be buried in his own churchyard, and left small sums of money to the church itself, to the light maintained there by the guild of the young men, and to the poor of the parish. The residue of his goods, consisting chiefly of clothes and bedding, was distributed among his mother, brothers and sisters. He died in the autumn of that or the following year.[45]

William Scollowe, the last of these masters, was also a native of the district with a family of relatives at Alvechurch (Worcs.). He took his BA degree at Oxford in 1534, receiving like Lyster a dispensation from some of the requirements because 'through force of necessity' he was teaching scholars 'in the country'.[46] This was not necessarily at Evesham. A William Scollowe is mentioned as schoolmaster of St Albans at an unknown date between 1531 and 1538,[47] and it is unlikely that Scollowe

---

[44] Emden, *BRUO*, iv, 370.

[45] Field was ordained deacon on 7 Apr. and priest on 15 June 1527 (HWRO, Reg. R. Morton, appended folios). He was schoolmaster at Evesham by 1530 (*The Letter Book of Robert Joseph*, p 48) and in 1534 (HWRO, ref. 802, p 89), chaplain of the charnel-chapel by 1532 (ibid., p 46), and vicar of St Lawrence, Evesham, by 1535 (*Valor Ecclesiasticus*, ed. J. Caley, 6 vols (London, Record Commission, 1810-24), iii, 255). His will was dated 4 Sept. 1545 and proved 12 Oct. 1546 (unless that is a mistake for 1545) (HWRO, Registers of Wills, vol v, f 125, no 324).

[46] *The Letter Book of Robert Joseph*, p xxvi.

[47] *VCH Herts.*, ii, 56.

came to Evesham before the spring of 1537 when he was ordained.[48] He was not formally appointed as schoolmaster until 10 December 1538, by an indenture drawn up between the abbey and himself. This document is of great value for the information it contains about the school in the last years of the monastery. Scollowe's appointment bound him to carry out two kinds of duties, educational and liturgical. He had to celebrate mass whenever possible in the charnel chapel by the abbey gate, and teach all comers freely in the public grammar school of Evesham. He was expected to give free instruction to the brethren of the abbey, if required, and also, it seems, to the boys of the monastic almonry. He could not be absent from the school or suspend his teaching for more than two days without getting the abbot's permission or appointing an usher to teach in his place. He was bound to give six months' notice of his intention to resign, on pain of losing 40s. The monks for their part promised that he should receive £10 a year with the dwelling house and garden next to the school, as his predecessors had done. He was further entitled to choose a scholar to help him teach, and send the boy to receive meat and drink in the almonry.[49] Scollowe remained in office until Michaelmas 1546, when he resigned to become vicar of Salford Priors (Warws.).[50] He stayed there unmarried until his death in the summer of 1559. His will of 2 May 1557 included bequests to various relatives and ordered bushels of rye to be distributed among 34 of his poor parishioners. His books, worth £3, went to a kinsman, also named William Scollowe, together with money for his education.[51] The boy entered Winchester College, proceeded to Oxford, and himself became a schoolmaster in later years.[52]

The history of Worcester school presents problems of its own. Broadly speaking, it shared in the changes which took place in the county as a whole. The medieval school, relying on fees to survive, became a partially endowed institution in close association with a religious body, the Trinity Guild. The date of this change is elusive. Some writers would assign it to the fifteenth century, on the basis of a payment of 3s. 4d. by John Pynnyngton, schoolmaster of Worcester, to the clerical subsidy of 1487.[53] It has been suggested that Pynnyngton made this payment because he was in receipt of a stipend which was paid by the Trinity

[48] Scollowe was still only an acolyte on 20 Feb. 1537 when he sought permission to proceed to all holy orders (*Faculty Office Registers, 1534-49*, ed. D.S. Chambers (Oxford, 1966), p.87). This suggests that he was not yet schoolmaster, since his appointment in the following year involved priestly duties.

[49] PRO, E 315/101 ff 36ᵛ-37.

[50] Emden, *BRUO*, iv, 507.

[51] HWRO, Wills, 1558 no 864.

[52] T.F. Kirby, *Winchester Scholars* (London, 1888), p 134; *Register of the University of Oxford*, ed. C.W. Boase, vol i, Oxford Historical Society, i (1885), p 268; *VCH Worcs.*, iv, 529.

[53] Leach, *Education in Worcester*, pp xxvi, 90.

Guild. Colour is given to the suggestion by the assertion of the citizens of Worcester in 1548 that the guild had supported the school, 'time out of mind'.[54] Unfortunately, the theory does not bear close examination. There is no evidence that Pynnyngton was being paid by the Trinity Guild in 1487, merely that he had a taxable income. As for the assertion of 1548, it is both vague and tendentious, reflecting the citizens' anxiety to establish the educational functions of the guild so that its property might escape confiscation as a chantry. It is more probable that the guild took over the school in the early sixteenth century, since as late as 1504 the schoolmaster of Worcester was still holding office on the same terms as his medieval predecessors. Hugh Cratford, who became schoolmaster in that year, was appointed by the bishop (on behalf of the archdeacon), he was not required to be a priest, he took fees from his pupils and he held a monopoly of teaching in the city.[55] All these were characteristics of the medieval school. We shall see, on the other hand, that the school was certainly associated with the Trinity Guild in 1532. This gives us outline dates for the change. It remains to note the evidence of an inquisition held on the origin and character of the school in 1559. Witnesses were asked how long they could remember the guild's association with the school. Their evidence was also of a tendentious nature, but several of them believed that the guild had supported the school in the 1520s, and one or two asserted that the connection went back as early as 1509.[56] On the whole, it is likely that the guild took over the school in the early years of Henry VIII's reign, during the 1510s or 20s, but certainly after 1504.

The Trinity Guild was a religious and charitable brotherhood of the citizens of Worcester, with a guildhall and a chapel in the parish of St Nicholas, about 100 yards from the church. The chapel, also dedicated to the Trinity, contained two chantries. The first of them, the Trinity Chantry proper, was founded in 1371 by Richard Norton and other citizens of Worcester for a priest to intercede for their souls.[57] Incumbents were presented in due succession by the bailiffs of Worcester, but had no educational duties. The second chantry, usually called the Trinity Guild, was apparently founded during the reign of Henry IV for three priests, though in later times there was only one or two.[58] These were the chantry priests of the guild itself, and were probably appointed by its governing body. It was they, and not the incumbent of the older chantry, who came to be concerned with education. In 1532 the list of Worcester clergy paying the clerical subsidy includes, under the heading 'Trinity Guild', Richard Stone (actually the chaplain of the Trinity Chantry) and two schoolmasters, presumably the

---

[54] Ibid., pp 176–7.
[55] Ibid., pp 98–9.
[56] Ibid., pp 195–201.
[57] *Calendar of Patent Rolls, 1370–4*, pp 48–9; Leach, *Education in Worcester*, p 173.
[58] Ibid., p 174.

priests of the guild itself. One, Master George Batkyn, 'formerly schoolmaster', had recently died, so that his executors had to be charged with his contribution. The other, described as Master Standish, was still in office.[59] Evidently the guild was supporting two priests at this time, both of whom were schoolmasters, but we do not know if they taught for nothing. By the date of the next clerical subsidy in 1534 there had been a change of personnel. Under the heading 'Chapel of the Holy Trinity' we find Richard Stone as before, John Byrkyn as chaplain and John Preston as schoolmaster. The latter was not assessed for payment, probably because he was the same man as the rector of St Swithin's and had already been charged in that capacity.[60] The guild, it appears, was still maintaining two priests, but only one of them was now a schoolmaster and he was holding the appointment in plurality.

If we discount the name of Richard Stone from these lists, we see that the Trinity Guild supported two chaplains in the early 1530s, one or both of whom might serve as schoolmasters. Its financial resources, however, were not very strong and by 1538 the school had become a heavy burden. This emerges from a letter of that year written by the bishop of Worcester, Hugh Latimer, to the king's minister Thomas Cromwell. Latimer was anxious to put the schools in the leading towns of his diocese upon a sound footing. He had already solicited Cromwell's help with the endowment of Bristol Grammar School and the Crypt School, Gloucester, and he now commended the case of Worcester to Cromwell's attention. This city, he wrote in a badly spelt letter,

> is greatly charged with three things: their school, their bridge and their wall. As for their school, it hath been maintained heretofore by a brotherhood called a guild, I trow not without some guile, popishly pardoning, and therefore now worthily decayed, so that I am fain myself, as poor as I am, to retain the schoolmaster there with his livery, meat and drink upon the holiday and some part of his living besides, because he is honest and bringeth up the youth after the best form.[61]

We learn from this that the schoolmaster was of good quality, but that the guild was giving him little or no support. He was probably having to charge his pupils fees, and the bishop was helping to maintain him during the holidays.

Latimer's remedy was to ask for Cromwell's assistance in granting the two Worcester friaries to the city to help maintain the school. The friaries had been dissolved on 4 August 1538, and the city council had made an

[59] HWRO, ref. 802, p 33.

[60] Ibid., p 77. John Preston occurs as rector of St Swithin's in 1534 and died in 1536 (HWRO, Reg. J. Ghinucci, f 70; Reg. H. Latimer, vol i, f 3). For his will dated 4 November 1536 see HWRO, Wills, 1536 no 194.

[61] PRO, SP 1/137, pp 111–12; *Letters and Papers, Foreign and Domestic*, xiii part ii, no 543.

immediate bid to secure the sites and the dependent property in order to use the building stones for repairing the city walls and Severn bridge.[62] Further pleas were made in the spring of 1539, and in the following December the two friaries, with certain other property, were finally sold to the city by the crown for just over £541.[63] There are no grounds, however, for judging the sale as a benefaction for education, as has sometimes been done.[64] Latimer evidently hoped that the school would benefit, but the citizens did not mention the school in their petitions and did nothing to help it after the grant was made. On the contrary, the school of the Trinity Guild was allowed to die. This is said to have occurred in about 1543 or 1544, but may have been earlier and was due no doubt to the foundation of a new grammar school at the cathedral in 1541, the present King's School. During the mid 1540s the guild was apparently maintaining only a single priest, William Halberton, and when the chantry commissioners came round for the first time in 1546, no educational activities were reported to them.[65] Then, in 1547, the attitude of the guild to the school underwent a sudden change. The new Chantry Act passed in December of that year provided for the dissolution of all chantries and religious guilds, but the preservation of any grammar schools associated with them. The guild hastened to revive the school, and when the chantry commissioners arrived again in the spring of 1548 they were told that the guild was once more paying a schoolmaster, John Oliver, BA, with a salary of £6.13s.4d., and that he was teaching over a hundred scholars. The guild could not deny that the school had lapsed 'four or five years or more ago', but they claimed that this was due to the costs of maintaining the bridge and the city walls, and that apart from this the guild had kept the school in its guild hall for as long as anyone could remember.[66]

Before concluding the history of Worcester school, we must retrace our steps to consider what had already happened to education in the county through the suppression of the monasteries in 1536-40. The educational role of the monasteries was less than that of the public schools, but it was not without significance. Each house received novices from time to time, which it was supposed to teach in advanced grammar, logic and philosophy. The greater foundations, and some of the lesser ones, also maintained and educated a small number of almonry boys and choristers. Worcester, where such boys are first mentioned in 1294, maintained fourteen or so on the eve of the Reformation.[67] Evesham had

[62] Ibid., no 32.

[63] Ibid., no 540; xiv part i, nos 102, 543; xiv part ii, no 780(9).

[64] E.g. by F.V. Follett, *A History of the Royal Grammar School, Worcester* (Worcester, 1951), pp 11-12, and by Mrs Joan Simon, 'The Reformation and English Education', *Past and Present*, xi (1957), p 56.

[65] Leach, *Education in Worcester*, pp 172-4.

[66] Ibid., pp 175-8.

[67] Ibid., pp 22-3, 114-15.

an unstated number, and other places like Halesowen and Pershore probably had such boys as well. Throughout the county there may have been fifty or sixty boys, the size of a large public school. Finally, Evesham was one of the very few English monasteries to maintain a public school as well. The dissolution of the monasteries put an end to all the maintenance and schooling of novices, almonry boys and choristers, but it was compensated for in Worcestershire by the foundation of a new grammar school, the King's School, Worcester, endowed by Henry VIII from monastic property and providing free board, lodging and education for forty scholars as well as education alone for anyone else who so desired.[68] At Evesham no formal arrangement was made for the public school to continue, but it did so in practice. The master, William Scollowe, was allowed to remain in his house with his salary,[69] and on his resignation in 1546 a new master, Humphrey Atwood alias Taylor, a secular priest and Oxford BA, was appointed instead. Atwood's tenure was uncertain, his salary was suspended after March 1547 and he was forced to give up teaching from the following summer till the spring of 1548, but he was then restored to office and his status confirmed by the crown.[70] Except for this temporary disruption, education in Worcestershire survived the Dissolution rather well. The balance between gains and losses appears to have been roughly equal.

The effects of the Chantry Act of 1547 were also satisfactory from the educational point of view. The act, as we have seen, expressly provided for the continuance of chantry grammar schools, and this provision was duly observed in Worcestershire. On 20 July 1548 the chantry commissioners ordered that the foundations at Bromsgrove, King's Norton, Rock and Stourbridge should be preserved, and made similar arrangements for the former monastic school at Evesham.[71] The only immediate casualties were the chantry school at Leigh, which was probably of an elementary kind, and the school of the Trinity Guild in Worcester. It is hardly surprising, in view of the neglect into which this school had fallen, that the commissioners regarded its revival with suspicion. They seem to have been undecided as to whether or not to preserve it. A note appended to the chantry certificates suggests that it should cease, 'for there is one other in the town of the king's foundation, and this is no school of any purpose, as it is credibly said'. In July 1548 the chantry commissioners in London ordered the school to continue, but this was soon countermanded. The endowment was confiscated, and the master received no more than a pension.[72] The four schools which *were*

---

[68] *Letters and Papers, Foreign and Domestic*, xvi, no 1421; *VCH Worcs.*, iv, 481–3.

[69] PRO, SC 6/Hen. VIII/4054 m 7; SC 6/Hen. VIII/4055 m 7; E 315/292 ff 30, 43, 53ᵛ; E 315/101 ff 36ᵛ-7.

[70] Leach, *Schools at the Reformation*, pp 278–9. For Atwood's career, see Emden, *BRUO*, iv, p 559.

[71] Leach, *Schools at the Reformation*, pp 279–80; *Education in Worcester*, pp 178–80.

[72] Ibid., pp 178–81.

continued also had their endowments confiscated by the crown in 1548, but these were replaced by annuities at the same rate that the endowments had produced in that year. The same was done for Evesham. The annuities were paid regularly under Edward VI, and in 1552 Stourbridge school was refounded by the crown with a landed endowment producing an improved income of £17.10s.8d. a year.[73] The remaining schools received their annuities during the first two years of Mary's reign, but in 1555 these were suspended, as was generally the case elsewhere in England, probably due to the transfer of responsibility for ecclesiastical pensions from the crown to the Church. The suspension, however, did not last for long. In 1556 the crown re-endowed Bromsgrove school with land to the value of its earlier income of £7,[74] and the other three schools petitioned the Court of the Exchequer in London for the restoration of their rights, with success. Rock regained its annuity by a decree of 17 May 1557, Evesham by one of 28 May and King's Norton by one of 27 June 1558.[75] At length in 1559 even the citizens of Worcester managed to reverse the previous decision against the school of the Trinity Guild. The Court of the Exchequer awarded the school an annuity of £6.13s.4d. in lieu of its confiscated endowments, and even added arrears of £80 for the twelve years since 1548.[76] Finally in 1561 the school was refounded by Elizabeth and given an endowment of land.[77]

The main Worcestershire schools seem to have been respectable institutions in the Reformation period. The nearest we can come to estimating their quality is through examining the careers and qualifications of the men who operated them. Thirteen names have been preserved of those who taught in the seven known grammar schools between 1532 and 1548, that is to say in the six endowed foundations and Droitwich.[78] All save one (John Oliver of Worcester in 1548) were priests, a fact which reflects the preponderance of chantry schools involved. The teaching profession in England as a whole included large numbers of laymen at this time. Six of the masters held degrees, four being BAs and two MAs, and two others, entitled 'Master', may have done. The remaining five were probably non-graduates: a proportion

[73] *Calendar of Patent Rolls, 1550-3*, pp 303-4.

[74] *Calendar of Patent Rolls, 1555-7*, pp 260-1.

[75] PRO, LR 6/123/1-3, LR 6/115/1.

[76] Ibid.

[77] *Calendar of Patent Rolls, 1560-3*, p 215; Leach, *Education in Worcester*, pp 203-13.

[78] The masters were Humphrey Atwood alias Taylor, BA (Evesham, appointed 1547); 'Master' George Batkyn (Worcester, died 1532); Edmund Field (Evesham, occurs 1530-4); William Fownes (Bromsgrove, occurs 1548); 'Sir John' (Droitwich, occurs 1530); Robert Lyster, MA (Evesham, appointed 1524); John Oliver, BA (Worcester, appointed 1547); John Preston (Worcester, occurs 1534); John Ree, BA (Rock, occurs 1535-48); Nicholas Rock (Stourbridge, occurs 1548); Henry Saunders, MA (King's Norton, occurs 1548); William Scollowe, BA (Evesham, appointed 1538); and 'Master Standish' (Worcester, occurs 1532).

nearer the national average, in which non–graduates seem to have predominated. Two of the thirteen corresponded in Latin with Robert Joseph in the 1530s, one being Sir John of Droitwich and the other Edmund Field of Evesham. Neither appears to have been a graduate, which reminds us that Latinity was not dependent on possessing a degree. The chantry certificates of 1548 also include some brief comments on the schoolmasters who feature in them. Those in Bromsgrove, Rock and Stourbridge were described as 'learned' and those of King's Norton and Worcester as 'well learned'; none was unsatisfactory.[79] In short these Worcestershire schoolmasters, graduates or not, seem to have been men of adequate attainments by the standards of their day.

As elsewhere in England, however, their status and rewards were modest, at least in economic terms. The best paid were those of Evesham and King's Norton who received £10 a year. This was still the usual rate for the job in the 1540s, but it was not very generous and some contemporary writers on education considered it inadequate.[80] At Bromsgrove moreover the master's salary was only £7, at Stourbridge £6.4s., and at Rock £5.14s., though the incumbents of the two latter schools are only mentioned teaching the children of the poor for nothing and may have taken fees from the wealthy. Masters with £10 a year were better off than hired curates or simple chantry priests whose annual wages were often only £5 or £6, but they were inferior to many beneficed rectors and vicars whose incomes often exceeded the £10 mark. It was therefore the aim of most clerical schoolmasters to escape when the chance arose into the relative comfort of a rectory or vicarage. At least seven of our twelve achieved this ambition, but the achievement remained a limited one even so. The benefices they got, mostly in the Worcestershire area, were worth about the same or slightly more than the schools they left behind them.[81] None of them rose to positions of wealth or power in the Church, and in that respect they were typical of most of their profession. For all the interest in education in Tudor England, the ordinary schoolmaster continued to occupy a relatively modest place in the commonwealth.

[79] Leach, *Schools at the Reformation*, part ii, pp 267–72.

[80] Orme, *English Schools*, p 159.

[81] Atwood probably became a rector in Berks. or Bucks. (Emden, *BRUO*, iv, 559); Field became vicar of St Lawrence, Evesham (above, note 45); and Fownes became rector of Welland in 1556 and of Hill Croome in 1558-9 (HWRO, Reg. R. Pates, f 22; Davenport's MS Calendar). For his will, see HWRO, Wills, 1586, no 59c. Lyster became rector of Willersey, Gloucs. in 1526 (above, note 44); Preston was also rector of St Swithin's, Worcester (above, note 60); and Saunders died as rector of Oldberrow in 1570 (HWRO, Wills, 1570 no 39). Scollowe became vicar of 'Salford Priors in 1546 (above, note 50).

4

SCHOOLMASTERS

One of the most enduring achievements of twelfth-century England was the formation of a distinct body of schoolteachers. There had been teachers of a literary kind before that time, first monks in monasteries and later probably also priests and even lay people, but in the Anglo-Saxon period those who taught did so as part of other duties. Their role as teachers was subsumed in their status as monks or priests, and contemporaries did not usually regard them or refer to them as teachers pure and simple. This changed in the twelfth century with the emergence, or at any rate the greater prominence, of autonomous schools distinct in their own right.[1] The masters of these schools were primarily teachers, or at least teachers as much as they were priests or other functionaries. There went on being other kinds of teachers: monks and later friars in religious houses, and parish clergy, parish clerks and lay people giving instruction for part of their time. But from at least 1100, the teaching of letters had a recognisable core of specialised instructors: schoolmasters, as it has done ever since. It is with these masters, the lineal ancestors of modern schoolteachers, that we shall be concerned.

Specialised groups of people take or receive names to describe themselves. Schoolmasters, perhaps because they were masters of words, invented several names. In Latin we find the term *magister scolarum* (meaning, despite the plural, the master of one school), *rector scolarum*, *informator*, *monitor*, *pedagogus*, *didascalus* and its compounds *archididascalus* and *hypodidascalus*. The master's assistant, if he had one (most medieval schools were run by only one or two staff) was called the *submagister*, *submonitor* or *(h)ostiarius*. There were fashions in the use of these words. *Rector scolarum* occurs from the twelfth to the fourteenth centuries, but fades out afterwards. *Informator* was popular from the fifteenth century onwards, and *archididascalus* (meaning a headmaster where there were at least two teachers) emerged at the Reformation. *Didascalus*, *monitor* and *pedagogus* are rather rare in any period. The commonest term, with the greatest staying power from the twelfth century to the sixteenth, was *magister scolarum*, no doubt because it was the closest to 'schoolmaster' which was the standard word in English from at least the early thirteenth. Assistant masters were called

[1] Above, pp 3–5.

submagistri in Latin, 'submasters' or 'undermasters' in English, up to about 1400, and subsequently (*h*)*ostiarii* or its English equivalent 'ushers', with *hypodidascalus* also coming into use in the sixteenth century. Because most teachers were men, women seem at first to have been called the same, for the *Ancrene Rule* of about 1225 advises women anchoresses against acting as school*masters*.[2] Schoolmistresses so named are first encountered in the early fifteenth century, when we find Matilda Maresflete as *magistra scolarum* in Boston in 1406, and E. Scolemaysteresse and Elizabeth Scolemaystres in London in 1408 and 1441 respectively.[3] But specialised women teachers were uncommon, and there are not enough to be included in our discussion.

It is a requirement when considering a group of people to know its size. This, unfortunately, is hard to establish in the case of medieval schoolmasters. We are not sure how many schools there were, and the total must have undergone changes during the period between 1100 and 1530. Medieval schools and schoolmasters are recorded by chance, and the later we go the more records survive and the more schools are mentioned. If the number was related to the size of the population, however, we would expect a peak to have been reached in the early fourteenth century, with a decline thereafter due to the Black Death of 1348-9 and other factors. William Bingham's assertion in 1439 that over seventy schools had closed in the last fifty years in eastern England south of Ripon would mean, if true, a national decline of 150-200 in the early fifteenth century.[4] As a working hypothesis, let us assume that the average medieval English county contained between five and ten schools with professional masters. Multiplied nationally, this produces a figure of 200-400 schools and masters. We need to add to this, in the later middle ages, another 100-200 masters working in monasteries and private households, giving us a total of 300-600, probably nearer the larger figure. Such a rough estimate is intended not as a statistic but an indication of how few of the population were schoolmasters, even among literate and clerical people. Taken together they were vastly inferior to the 4,500 monks and regular canons, the 2,200 friars, the 1,500 nuns and the several thousands of parish clergy who made up the clerical estate, even at its lowest ebb in the late fourteenth century. Locally, masters were also thin on the ground. The average English town had only one, with perhaps an assistant; in a few larger places like Bristol and York the total may have reached half a dozen, and in London and Oxford as many as a dozen. But these were exceptions; normally the master was a lonely figure in his community.

The dawn of the profession of schoolmaster in England seemed to

---

[2] *The Oxford English Dictionary*, sub 'schoolmaster' 1(d). 'Schoolmaster' also became a surname, borne by wives and children of schoolmasters.

[3] Orme, *English Schools*, pp 54-5.

[4] Above, p 13.

augur well for its development as a well-esteemed and well-rewarded occupation. At least four English cathedrals in the twelfth century – St Paul's, Salisbury, Wells and York – possessed a *magister scolarum* as a member of the cathedral chapter. He is mentioned in statutes; he kept the chapter's seal and wrote its letters as well as teaching; he also shared with the rest of the chapter in the cathedral's income, and was therefore salaried.[5] In the royal family, Matthew the tutor who taught the future Henry II to read Latin at Bristol in the 1140s was important enough to witness some of Henry's charters with the title *doctor ducis*, and may have become the chancellor of Queen Eleanor of Aquitaine.[6] Several other schoolmasters are known to have gone on to hold important posts in the Church. Among bishops with English connections, Guy of Etampes, bishop of Le Mans, John of Salisbury, bishop of Chartres, Robert of Béthune, bishop of Hereford, and William of Corbeil, archbishop of Canterbury, had all been teachers privately or in a public school. In the monasteries, Geoffrey de Gorroy schoolmaster of Dunstable became abbot of St Albans, Guy an Italian schoolmaster prior in turn of Merton, Taunton and Bodmin, and Alexander Neckham who taught at both Dunstable and St Albans, abbot of Cirencester.[7] The success of such men came no doubt from the width of their knowledge, which in that pre-university period meant that they often taught not simply elementary Latin but the liberal arts and other advanced studies. A twelfth-century schoolmaster could be as learned as anyone, and consequently well qualified for appointment to high office.

By the end of the century, however, the auspicious dawn was turning into a chill grey morning. At the cathedrals the *magistri scolarum* were growing more concerned with their secretarial functions. They took the new and more exalted title of 'chancellor', and while retaining their membership of the cathedral chapter, became mere supervisors of the local schools. The title of *magister scolarum* and the duty of teaching passed to a deputy schoolmaster, lower in status, paid (if at all) with a small stipend, and dependent for his living on charging fees.[8] In the royal family, an office of schoolmaster failed to develop. Literature in French competed for interest with Latin literature, and although the king's sons went on learning some Latin, the subject seems to have been regarded as only moderately important and suitable to entrust to chaplains and clerks who were not professional teachers. Not until the 1420s do we hear of

[5] Kathleen Edwards, *The English Secular Cathedrals in the Middle Ages*, 2nd ed. (Manchester & New York, 1967), pp 176-84, 205-6.

[6] H.G. Richardson, 'The Letters and Charters of Eleanor of Aquitaine', *English Historical Review*, lxxiv (1959), pp 193-4.

[7] Most of these masters are mentioned in F. Barlow, *The English Church, 1066-1154* (London & New York, 1979), pp 217-67 passim. On William of Corbeil, see H.G. Richardson, 'Gervase of Tilbury', *History*, xlvi (1961), p 103.

[8] Edwards, *English Secular Cathedrals*, p 178.

schoolmasters teaching the royal family.[9] The rise of the universities in the thirteenth century further depressed the status of schoolmasters. They ceased to be concerned with the teaching of higher subjects, and became chiefly confined to the lowlier subjects of reading, plainsong and Latin grammar. For the next three hundred years, knowledge of university studies – arts, canon and civil law and theology – or of the common law of the king's courts was the qualification for high office in both the king's service and the Church. Schools became humble institutions, schoolmasters lowly and peripheral figures, and their best students university men with university loyalties. A period ensued of lower status and prominence for masters, and it is this period, up to the early sixteenth century, that we shall now explore.

How did you become a schoolmaster after 1200? As with most occupations there were two requirements to be met: you had to possess certain basic qualifications and to secure appointment to an actual school in a particular place. The qualifications were relatively simple. Walter Bradewylle, clerk, who became schoolmaster of Ottery St Mary in about 1380, was chosen for his 'ability and knowledge in teaching young men in grammar' and for 'the merit of his other virtues'.[10] John Bredel, chaplain, appointed to Worcester school in 1429, had 'knowledge of letters, honesty of morals, and a [satisfactory] manner of life'.[11] A third master, William Breter, who started to teach at Gloucester in the following year and was not described as any kind of cleric, survives as 'a fit and honest man, competently learned in the art of grammar'.[12] These attainments were probably typical. A good schoolmaster needed to be a man of good character and he had to be able to teach grammar, so that he must himself have studied the grammar course to at least the level of his highest pupils. But the average English grammar school of the later middle ages required no other qualifications than these. It was not absolutely necessary to be a celibate cleric or a university graduate. A clerk, such as Walter Bradewylle, might be a young man in his early twenties who intended becoming a priest, or a marriageable man whose way of life was largely that of a layman. Only in a few places during our period was anything more demanded. Some of the cathedral chapters confined their schools to graduates in the thirteenth and fourteenth centuries.[13] But when, after the 1350s, it became difficult to get such men to teach, non-graduates were appointed at Lincoln and Salisbury,

[9] Orme, *From Childhood to Chivalry*, pp 20-4.
[10] British Library, MS Harley 3300 f 274ᵛ.
[11] A.F. Leach, *Documents Illustrating Early Education in Worcester*, Worcs. Historical Society, xxxi (1913), pp 76-7.
[12] PRO, C 115/A 3 f 210.
[13] Orme, *English Schools*, p 151.

Canterbury and Worcester, and probably at most other similar places.[14] Towards the end of our period, when endowed schools were being founded with salaried masters, standards began to rise again, and a few such foundations re-introduced the graduation requirement. These, however, were still only a handful in number by 1509, and even among the endowed schools they were a small minority.[15]

Clerical status could also vary widely. The largest group of medieval schools – the fee-paying institutions of the towns – allowed their masters to be priests, clerks, or married laymen, without discrimination. Monasteries, too, appointed men of each category to teach their novices and almonry boys, and so did the principal endowed schools to be founded in the fifteenth and early sixteenth centuries: Eton, Magdalen (Oxford), St Paul's, and Winchester. Certain minster and cathedral foundations – Beverley, Ripon, Wells and York – drew back a little by requiring their schoolmasters to wear a clerical habit and to join the rest of the clergy at their daily office in the choir.[16] Yet this did not involve a vow of celibacy, and the masters remained free to marry later if not then. Only one area of teaching was absolutely restricted to priests, and that was in the small endowed schools. Most of these were also founded as chantries between the 1380s and 1510s and expected their masters to say a daily mass for the soul of the founder; none-the-less they too were only a minority among the English schools, even at their most numerous in the early sixteenth century. All things considered, priests and graduates had the widest range of opportunities, but they never managed to establish a monopoly against non-graduates or laymen. This can be shown from a single region of England: the six counties of the South West. Eighty-nine masters are known to have taught in this area between 1307 and 1509.[17] Forty-six were priests, most of them (thirty) teaching in the endowed chantry schools; the rest were not so described and were probably either laymen or clerks in minor orders. Eleven were definitely graduates and another twenty-three, who were entitled 'master', possibly came into this category, but the vast majority (fifty-five) seem to have had little or no university training. Figures like these confirm that many openings existed for the mere product of the local grammar school, and equally so for the clerk who was barred from entering the priesthood by marriage, deformity, or merely by love of the world.

Getting yourself a school, once you were qualified, usually meant being formally appointed to one. Most of the larger English towns,

[14] *VCH Lincs.*, ii, 423; Orme, *West of England*, p 76; C.E. Woodruff and H.J. Cape, *Schola Regia Cantuariensis* (London, 1908), pp 34–5; Leach, *Early Education in Worcester*, pp 76–7, 90.

[15] To the list in Orme, *English Schools*, p 154 n 1, add Week St Mary, Cornwall (Orme, *West of England*, pp 176–7).

[16] A.F. Leach, *Early Yorkshire Schools*, 2 vols, Yorkshire Archaeological Society, xxvi, xxxiii (1898–1903), i, 18, 21, 82–6; *VCH Yorks.*, i, 431; Orme, *West of England*, pp 82, 86.

[17] Ibid., passim, with one or two additions and corrections.

where the schools were best organized and most continuous, had educational patrons like the patrons of parish churches, who claimed the sole right to appoint the local master.[18] Bishops, archdeacons, cathedral chancellors, monasteries, collegiate churches, parish clergy and members of the lay aristocracy all exercised this kind of patronage in the middle ages. The endowed schools, which began to appear at the end of the fourteenth century, also had their patrons, some of whom belonged to the groups already mentioned while others were newcomers to the field: borough corporations, city companies, guilds of burgesses, and groups of country gentlemen and yeomen. Masters who were waiting for an established school to fall vacant could take employment as submasters or ushers or could try to support themselves in a smaller and less desirable school or town in the neighbourhood, until they got what they wanted. We find William Buntyng teaching at Blofield (Norfolk) in 1350 before moving to Norwich school in 1369.[19] Richard Darcy formerly submaster of Gloucester in 1410 became headmaster of Winchester in 1418,[20] and John Hamundson was appointed to Howden in 1456 en route for York, where he died in 1472.[21] While most schoolmasters probably kept to their native regions, some used their qualifications to travel widely in search of employment. William Pocklington, for example, originated in the diocese of York, tried unsuccessfully for the school of St Mary le Bow (London) in 1383, and ended in charge of Maidstone school a few years later.[22] His contemporary John Sampson, schoolmaster of St Martin le Grand (London) in 1394, was an Irishman.[23] If there were no vacancy at an established school, it was sometimes possible to function in a private capacity where the control of education was not effective or did not exist. London, apart from its authorized schools, supported several private teachers in the later middle ages.[24] York and Bristol had free-lance masters too, apparently without authority,[25] and there were lesser towns lacking schools or patrons where a visiting master could probably set himself up on his own initiative, provided he could find enough pupils to keep him.

Our next task is to consider how attractive a job schoolmastering was. Three factors are involved: the system of tenure, the remuneration and the status of teachers in the community. Tenure in the English schools is

[18] On patronage, see also Orme, *English Schools*, pp 143-50.
[19] Norfolk and Norwich Record Office, Reg./2 Book 4 f 118ᵛ; H.W. Saunders, *A History of the Norwich Grammar School* (Norwich, 1932), p 91.
[20] Orme, *West of England*, pp 62-3.
[21] Leach, *Early Yorkshire Schools*, ii, 87; i, 28.
[22] Lambeth Palace Library, Reg. William Courtenay f 37; Reg. John Morton f 182-ᵛ.
[23] *Calendar of Patent Rolls, 1391-6*, p 459.
[24] Orme, *English Schools*, pp 190, 210-12, 309.
[25] Joann H. Moran, *Education and Learning in the City of York, 1300-1560* (York, Borthwick Papers, lv, 1979), pp 8-13; Orme, *West of England*, pp 37-41.

a difficult subject to penetrate before the fourteenth century. Most of the early masters appear in records only once, which makes it impossible to determine how long they held their posts and whether they left them of their own free will. Then, after 1300, two kinds of tenant become visible. We encounter masters, especially in the smaller towns, whose appearances in records over several years or whose ownership of wives and property suggest that they were professionals who had settled down to teach for long periods.[26] In other places, particularly the cathedral cities, there were frequent successions of masters, some of them traceable to other careers, for whom teaching only represented a limited part of their lives.[27] Evidently schoolmastering had different attractions for different people. Some found it sufficiently rewarding to remain with it, or else failed to obtain anything better. Others taught merely on a temporary basis with some other end in view. Teaching a school was a useful way of filling up a few spare years. It gave support until you were old enough to be ordained, or found a benefice, or saved enough money to go to university. The desirability of a post, however, lies not only in the ability to leave it but in the right to keep it. During the fourteenth century, in particular, many masters must have ceased to teach after a few years, not by choice but through necessity. Urban decline, plague, and parental indifference all threatened the town schoolmaster, depending as he did for his survival on the fees of his pupils. Even when his clientèle sufficed, he was not always free to teach as long as he wished. The university of Oxford, until about the middle of the fourteenth century, prohibited its graduate masters from teaching grammar for more than three years.[28] A similar custom was widespread in the schools of the north of England. Beverley, Hedon, Hexham, Howden, Lincoln, Northallerton, and York all limited their masters to terms of three or five years for at least part of the fourteenth century, and in some cases even later.[29] The tendency was for tenurial conditions to improve as time went on. The Beverley master appointed for three years in 1320 managed to survive for fifteen.[30] At York the dean and chapter were obliged to suspend the three-year rule in 1368 because of the unwillingness of graduates to teach there since the previous plague. The rule continued to operate in theory, but was frequently disregarded in practice.[31] By the fifteenth century most school appointments appear to have lasted during

[26] E.g. Battle (*VCH Sussex*, ii, 397) and Wakefield (J. W. Walker, *Wakefield, its History and People*, 2nd ed. (Wakefield, 1939), pp 363-4).

[27] Woodruff and Cape, *Schola Regia Cantuariensis*, pp 22-33; Saunders, *Norwich Grammar School*, pp 85-102; Leach, *Early Yorkshire Schools*, i, 21-4.

[28] *Statuta Antiqua Universitatis Oxon*, ed. Strickland Gibson (Oxford, 1931), pp 20-3.

[29] Leach, *Early Yorkshire Schools*, i, 23-4, 27, 30, 90; ii, 60-2, 84-6; *Calendar of Patent Rolls, 1340-3*, p 59; J. Raine, *The Priory of Durham*, vol i, Surtees Society, xliv (1864), p lxxix; *VCH Lincs.*, ii, 423.

[30] Leach, *Early Yorkshire Schools*, i, 97-100.

[31] Ibid., pp 23-4, 27-30.

good behaviour, while the foundation of the endowed schools and the growth of masterships in the monasteries provided an increasing number of secure paid posts. By 1509 the tenurial situation, though varying widely, was probably a good deal more favourable to more schoolmasters than it had been in 1307.

Next to security – but even more important – was remuneration. It is not very clear, unfortunately, how much masters earned in the fee-paying schools. School fees can be ascertained but numbers of pupils are rarely recorded. An interesting list of boys at a small country school at Basingwerk (north Wales) in the second half of the fifteenth century, recently discovered, shows that their numbers varied weekly between five and twenty-seven over the course of twelve weeks. As they each paid a penny a week, their master would only have earned about £3.10s. or £4 a year.[32] This sum, of course, would have been larger in a town school, and would also have been increased if the master took in boarders and made a profit out of their keep. We have a guide, however, to the prosperity of fee-earning town schoolmasters in their wills, of which a few survive. A good example from the fourteenth century is that of John Burdon, schoolmaster of Carlisle in 1371.[33] We do not know his age, beyond the fact that he had kept the school for nine years,[34] but the impression is that of an older rather than a younger man, who had been married but whose wife was dead. His monetary wealth enabled him to bequeath £14.13s.4d. in separate legacies. He had about him for his use and comfort six silver spoons, a maple-wood bowl, his books (presumably of grammar), a furred coat with a hood, and a strong box containing jewellery. He was able to pay a priest to say mass for his soul and that of his wife Christiana, and he had a circle of at least seven friends to mourn him, including a canon of the cathedral priory. Much the same characteristics appear, over sixty years later, in the will of John Seward of London, who died in 1435.[35] Seward was the master of a successful private school which he operated for many years, and lived to be seventy-one. Like Burdon he was married, but his wife survived him and they had one child. Four other relations and two friends received bequests in his will. His clothes included a green gown with belts of black and red, he had cauldrons in his kitchen, and bowls, a cup, and silver spoons to lay upon his table. He owned enough beds and chests to be able to give one of each to a friend, besides the residue of his goods which he

[32] D. Thomson, 'Cistercians and Schools in Late Medieval Wales', *Cambridge Medieval Celtic Studies*, iii (1982), pp 76–80.

[33] *Testamenta Karleolensia*, ed. R.S. Ferguson, Cumberland and Westmorland Antiquarian and Architectural Society, ix (1893), p 101.

[34] He was licensed to be schoolmaster of Carlisle on 23 October 1362 (Carlisle, Cumbria Record Office, Reg. Gilbert Welton f 103).

[35] V.H. Galbraith, 'John Seward and his Circle', *Medieval and Renaissance Studies*, i (1941–3), pp 98–9. For Seward's career, see Emden, *BRUO*, iii, 1674–5.

left to his wife. He also resembled Burdon in being an owner of books – some of which, as we shall see, were probably written by himself. Both wills convey an impression of modest comfort: not ostentatious luxury but not grinding poverty either. It is likely that they represent with some accuracy the wealth of the average fee-earning masters in the larger English towns.[36]

The best evidence about schoolmasters' earnings accompanies the foundation of the endowed schools with their regular salaries. The earliest salary recorded, that of the headmaster of Winchester College in 1400, was set at £10 a year with board and lodging.[37] It probably aimed to match and perhaps to exceed the net income of the fee-paying schools, and certainly attracted applicants from such places: Chichester in 1394 and Gloucester in 1418 and 1424.[38] Later endowed schools, of which the majority were founded after 1440, adopted the sum of £10 a year purely and simply, and this became the usual rate for the job until well into the sixteenth century. Not many founders cared to set it higher, though Henry VI offered £16 at Eton in 1443 and John Colet provided the very generous sum of £34 at St. Paul's (London) in 1518. Elsewhere a few of the salaried masters who were clerics managed to hold a parochial benefice as well,[39] but there were not many such instances and in general the rate of £10 predominated. A sum of this kind raised its recipient above the lowest ranks of society, but not unduly high. The easiest comparison to make is with the incomes of the clergy which survive in taxation records. Take, for example, the clerical subsidy list for Oxfordshire in 1526.[40] The best-paid teachers in the county at that time were the master of Banbury school with £14 and his colleague at Magdalen College school whose £10 together with board and lodging probably gave him about the same. Their salaries – which were unusually high for that period – raised them with the upper half of the beneficed clergy (rectors and vicars), of whom about seventy received more than £10 a year and thirty or so more than £14. Below them the master of Ewelme school had the normal salary of £10, which put him above the lower half of the beneficed clergy, another seventy men or so, who got less. Finally came the master of Chipping Norton school with only £6, which grouped him with the poorest of the beneficed clergy and with the crowd of 200 or so assistant curates and chantry priests. A

---

[36] See also the inventory of the goods of Richard Penyngton, late schoolmaster of Ipswich, in 1412-13 (I.E. Gray and W.E. Potter, *Ipswich School, 1400-1950* (Ipswich, 1950), pp 3-4) and the will of John Hamundson, schoolmaster of York, in 1472 (York, Borthwick Institute, Probate Reg. 4 f 85).

[37] T.F. Kirby, *Annals of Winchester College* (London, 1892), pp 486, 497, 499, 510.

[38] Emden, *BRUO*, iii, 1588; *VCH Hants.*, ii, 284.

[39] Orme, *West of England*, pp 164, 183; *VCH Notts.*, ii, 221-2; Emden, *BRUO*, iii, 1754-5 sub John Stanbridge.

[40] *A Subsidy Collected in the Diocese of Lincoln in 1526*, ed. H.E. Salter, Oxford Historical Society, lxiii (1909), pp 249-78.

clerical schoolmaster with £10 could therefore take comfort that he was better off than the majority of the parish clergy, but equally there were rectors and vicars above him whom he could envy, who were getting £5 or £10 a year more than he did, with less apparent effort.

If teaching paid so modestly, could greater gains be made elsewhere? Many masters, as we have already noted, did leave their schools for other work, but those of them whose careers are easiest to trace – the clerics – appear to have done only slightly better as a result. This can be illustrated by two representative biographies, one from the fourteenth and one from the fifteenth century. The first is that of William Wheatley, who was born in about the 1280s, somewhere in the region of the upper Thames valley.[41] He seems to have studied at Paris, and he got his first known benefice, Sulham (Berks.), in 1305. It was not very wealthy, having only been rated at £4 in 1291, but it probably gave him enough money to continue his studies at Oxford, for which he was given three years' leave of absence in 1306. Three years later he resigned Sulham to become master of Stamford school, which ought to have paid him better, and from there he went to Lincoln – one of the major English schools – where he appears as master in 1316. He must have been a good candidate for appointment since he was also a scholar and author whose writings we shall encounter later. Yet when he returned to parochial life as rector of Yatesbury (Wilts.) in 1317, he got a benefice that was only rated at £10, and as far as we know he held it until his death, perhaps in 1331. It was a modest achievement for so talented and travelled a man, yet it was a typical one, and it was not capable of much improvement even 150 years later. This can be seen from our second example, Edward Janyns, who was born in the 1430s or thereabouts.[42] A probable native of the Monmouth area, his first post after his ordination in 1459 was as chantry priest and grammar master of Newland (Gloucs.), four miles from Monmouth and worth about £10. He left it after four years for a succession of livings, each of which lifted his income a little until he emerged as vicar of Newland in 1476, with a stipend of about £18. He also took the opportunity, when he was well enough established, to go to university, probably in 1468, where he got a bachelor's degree in canon law. He ended his life as a respected member of the local clergy, taking his turn as rural dean and dying in about the 1490s. Like Wheatley he did not rise very high, but he seems to have done as well as an ordinary ex-schoolmaster could.

Few others achieved anything better. Of the forty-six west-of-England masters who were priests, at least eighteen are known to have gone on to hold parochial benefices. Yet hardly one of them gained anything really lucrative. Their benefices paid them a few more pounds than their schools had done, but that was all. They stopped well short of

[41] For his biography, see Emden, *BRUO*, iii, 2030-1.
[42] For his career, see Orme, *West of England*, p 162.

the grades that counted: cathedral dignities, canonries and prebends, and wealthy parochial pluralities. Even the most famous schoolmaster of early sixteenth-century England got little more. John Stanbridge, master of Magdalen College School, Oxford (1488-94), and later of Banbury school (1501-10) was the humanist reviser of the common fifteenth-century elementary Latin school-texts. His versions circulated widely by means of the new printing presses, he was patronised by the bishop of Lincoln, and revered after his death. Yet when he died in 1510, the only preferment he possessed, apart from his school, was a rectory in Northamptonshire and an exiguous canonry of Lincoln Cathedral, total income about £25 net per annum.[43] This tells us something about teaching in the later middle ages, and probably gives us a clue to the social origins of teachers. Hardly anyone who had been a schoolmaster reached a high position in the Church or the world, and not all such men can have been quiet or mediocre. Teaching evidently did little to forward their ambitions and may even have done them harm. The only exceptions were the small group of masters who benefited from the brief interest in grammar at the court of Henry VI. John Chedworth (tutor of Robert Lord Hungerford) became bishop of Lincoln, John Somerset (master of Bury St Edmunds and tutor of the king) became chancellor of the exchequer, and William Wainfleet (headmaster of Winchester College) became bishop of Winchester.[44] They were the first beneficiaries of a more favourable attitude to school education, which disappeared with the Wars of the Roses, and gradually emerged again after 1500. Thomas Wolsey began a new series of successes by rising from the schoolmaster's chair of Magdalen College School to the woolsack, and other ex-masters were to reach the privy council and the episcopal bench under Edward VI and Elizabeth.[45] Until then, teaching remained almost uniformly meagre in its rewards, and for this reason it had nothing to attract the well born or the well connected. The masters of the later middle ages must have come from modest burgess families, from the yeomanry of the countryside, or from lower origins. Only at these levels did teaching offer its recruits an equal standard of living, or a better one.

It is not surprising, after reviewing these modest rewards and achievements, to find that the reputation of schoolmasters in society was also a modest one. Teaching failed to make an impact on the public imagination, and the public at all its levels thought little of teachers. They were not so much despised as overlooked, forgotten, and unnoticed. The Crown, for its part, did not involve itself with schoolmasters in general

---

[43] Emden, *BRUO*, iii, 1754-5.

[44] For Chedworth, see ibid., i, 401-2, and Orme, *West of England*, pp 128, 142; for Somerset, see Emden, *BRUO*, iii, 1727-8; and for Wainfleet, see ibid., iii, 2001-3.

[45] George Cavendish, *The Life and Death of Cardinal Wolsey*, ed. R.S. Sylvester, EETS, original series, ccxliii (1959), p 5.

until the Reformation.[46] Education was primarily an ecclesiastical matter in the middle ages, but even the Church paid it little attention compared with later centuries.[47] The ecclesiastical authorities – bishops, archdeacons, and cathedral chancellors – were concerned that a network of schools should operate over the country. They were anxious that masters should only be appointed by the lawful patrons and that once appointed they should not be threatened in their rights by outsiders trying to set up rival, unauthorized schools. The authorities intervened from time to time to appoint a local master, to decide a disputed appointment, or to deal with an unlicensed school. But they did this only at irregular intervals, in times of emergency. It was almost unknown for any ecclesiastical power to interest itself with teachers as a group on any regular basis. Masters were not presented to the bishops for institution, they were not usually expected to appear at visitations, and they hardly ever received directives about their teaching or demeanour. If the Church's leaders were aware of schoolmasters in general, they certainly took them for granted and felt it unnecessary to have any regular relations with them.

The laity appears to have taken the same view. It knew, of course, what a schoolmaster was, and sometimes called him 'master', a title of respect. People had dealings with their local teacher. They gave him their children to teach and they encountered him, like anyone else, in the petty disputes and transactions of everyday life. But they too seem to have been unconscious of schoolmasters as a group or the schoolmaster as a type. Only once do we hear of a confrontation between the laity and the schoolmasters in general. This took place in the Peasants' Revolt of 1381 when the rebels, hot in pursuit of literates and literature – tax-collectors, lawyers and manorial records, are said to have warned schoolmasters not to teach children grammar. The incident, however, is only recorded by one writer (Thomas Walsingham) and must, if it did take place, have been a rather minor feature of the rising.[48] The famous accusation of Jack Cade in Shakespeare's *Henry VI Part II*, 'thou hast most traitorously corrupted the youth of the realm in erecting a grammar school', is in the same tradition as Walsingham's anecdote from which (through Holinshed) it may have been derived.[49] But contemporary support for it is equally lacking and the man accused, James Lord Saye and Sele, never founded a grammar school. Medieval English writers ignored the schoolmaster, too. Chaucer was fully aware of scholars, several of whom he portrayed in the *Canterbury Tales*, from the pupil of a petty

[46] P.L. Hughes and J.F. Larkin, *Tudor Royal Proclamations*, vol i (New Haven & London, 1964), p 231.

[47] Orme, *English Schools*, pp 142-3.

[48] *Chronicon Angliae*, ed. E.M. Thompson (London, Rolls Series, 1874), p 308.

[49] Shakespeare, *The Second Part of King Henry VI*, ed. A.S. Cairncross, 3rd ed. (London, Arden, 1957), p 124 and note.

song school to a well-educated squire and four university clerks. But the only teacher to be included in the *Tales*, was Nero's tutor Seneca; Chaucer had no interest in contemporary schoolmasters.[50] Langland too, despite the immense range of his references in *Piers Plowman*, mentioned schoolmasters only once, and then merely as an example, of men receiving lawful payment for their work.[51] Their whole appearance in medieval English writing is in fact confined to a few school lyrics and school exercises from the fifteenth century.[52] It is a very different story from the age of Elizabeth, when the quarrelsome pedant became a frequent and familiar character of literature, and Shakespeare (to take only one example) was inspired to paint his memorable portrait of Holofernes.

There is little comment about schoolmasters even from the groups with which they were most concerned: their pupils and their pupils' parents. We know that a few of the masters who tutored the great and famous were rewarded for their services. John Paynel, the instructor of Edward III, was raised to be chamberlain of Chester.[53] John Chedworth was given a rectory in Dorset for teaching the grandson of Walter Lord Hungerford.[54] John Rede was made a canon of Newark College, Leicester, after tutoring Prince Arthur.[55] Largesse of this kind implies a gratitude that has not survived in words. Contrariwise we hear of some dissatisfied customers. Robert Buck claimed to have left school at Clitheroe in 1283 because he was so badly beaten.[56] Robert Eliot of Harnhill (Kent) sued his master in 1390 for beating him, alleging damages of £20,[57] and William Skidmor, a London goldsmith, actually had the teacher of his son imprisoned in the 1460s on a similar charge.[58] These, however, were exceptional cases. What is lacking from the middle ages is almost any assertion by any ex-pupil of what he owed (or did not owe) to his schoolmaster. The twelfth century has much more to offer in this respect. Alexander Neckham, Gerald of Wales, and Jocelin of Brakelond are only some of its writers who put on record their affection for their masters or the affection of those they knew.[59] But such acknowledgements disappear during the thirteenth century, and they are rare during the fourteenth. Not until the fifteenth do they begin to increase again. The first major example is that of Thomas Rotherham, archbishop of York, in the foundation charter of the college he founded

[50] Below, chapter 13.
[51] Below, chapter 14.
[52] Orme, *English Schools*, pp 139–41.
[53] *Calendar of Close Rolls, 1327-30*, p 573.
[54] Emden, *BRUO*, i, 405; ii, 985.
[55] Ibid., iii, 1555–6.
[56] *Calendar of Inquisitions Post Mortem*, iv (1913), pp 171–2.
[57] Edith Rickert, *Chaucer's World* (London, 1948), p 118.
[58] Public Record Office, C 1/46/162.
[59] Orme, *English Schools*, p 135.

at Rotherham in 1483. Here he was moved to tell how he passed his early years in the town without a knowledge of letters, until there came 'by God's grace' a wandering teacher of grammar from whom he received his first instruction.[60] This starts the modern series of education reminiscences, which multiply in the sixteenth century and descend in growing numbers to the present day. But they appear too late to cast any light on the relationships of masters and pupils in the period with which we are dealing.

It remains to be asked whether the schoolmasters of the later middle ages deserved the comparative neglect which they received. In some respects, perhaps, they did. Their impact upon many aspects of national life was indisputably weak. Numerically, as we have seen, they were insignificant. Their economic importance was a restricted one. A master's pupils paid him fees and (if they came from a distance) they also spent money locally on board and lodging. But school-fees barely supported the master and his usher; no school can have generated any significant capital, and the money brought into a town by visiting school-boys must have remained a very small part of the town's whole trade. The role of schoolmasters in public life was also modest. We find them being admitted as burgesses or as members of religious guilds, and very occasionally they held municipal offices. Robert Simon was elected town clerk of Henley-on-Thames in 1419.[61] William Hardynge became one of the twelve governors of Beverley in 1446,[62] and John Squire was chosen to be treasurer of Ipswich in 1483.[63] Clerical schoolmasters, too, are sometimes found discharging minor administrative duties. One acts as a papal judge-delegate,[64] another proves a will in the absence of executors,[65] while a third inquires into the vacancy of a parochial benefice.[66]. But these were all peripheral activities. The principal concern of schoolmasters was with the world of learning. Their major activity lay in reading, writing and teaching, not in trade or public administration. It was their literary and educational achievements that mattered, and to which we must turn before a proper judgment can be made of their importance.

The first and most basic function of schoolmasters, and their greatest contribution to medieval civilization, was their teaching. They taught a wide curriculum, from the alphabet through plainsong to the various

---

[60] Leach, *Early Yorkshire Schools*, ii, 110.

[61] *Henry Borough Records*, ed. P.M. Briers, Oxfordshire Record Society, xli (1960), p 28.

[62] Leach, *Early Yorkshire Schools*, i, 104.

[63] Gray and Potter, *Ipswich School*, p 12; *VCH Suffolk*, ii, 327.

[64] Several schoolmasters were appointed as judges-delegate in the thirteenth century (Jane E. Sayers, *Papal Judges Delegate in the Province of Canterbury, 1198-1254* (London, 1971), pp 132-3).

[65] Orme, *West of England*, p 196 n 5.

[66] Ibid., p 163.

branches of Latin: its grammar, its composition, its oratory, and its elementary literature.[67] At their best they introduced their pupils to topics such as literary criticism, logic, and speculative grammar which were also part of the university arts course. They catered for thousands of pupils every year, many times more than studied at Cambridge or Oxford. Their pupils ranged from those who wished merely to read and spell, in order to understand literature in French or English, to those who sought the fluency in Latin that was necessary to enter university. It was these schoolmasters, so unobtrusive otherwise, who taught the scholars and poets of medieval England, the clergy of the parishes and the religious orders, many of the male aristocracy, the common lawyers, some of the merchant elite, certain of the yeomanry, and even a few from the classes below. Alike in the lives of Henry V and Henry VII, Bradwardine and Wycliffe, Chaucer and Langland, the Stonors and the Pastons, there lurks a schoolmaster – a forgotten contributor to the achievements in government and scholarship, literature and administration, of his more famous pupils.

Let us take care then, lest we magnify the pupil at the expense of the master. Medieval teachers were men of obscurity, as we have seen too well, but obscurity does not establish mediocrity. If some masters were unlearned, dishonest and lazy – and we know of such men – others were equally learned and diligent. They were, in the first place, collectors and owners of books: not only of the texts they used in school but of a wide variety of titles and subjects. Already in the middle of the fourteenth century they were able to draw a compliment from the greatest bibliophile of the age. When Richard de Bury completed the *Philobiblon* in 1345, he did not omit from his survey of books and their owners 'the masters of country schools and the instructors of rude boys'. He had even perused their libraries, with profitable results. 'When we had an opportunity, we entered their little plots and gardens, and gathered sweet-smelling flowers from the surface and dug up their roots, obsolete indeed, but still useful to the student'.[68] We do not know what books of theirs he found, but a number of titles survive which belonged to their successors in the fifteenth century. A fine volume of Latin chronicles owned by John Pyke of St Martin le Grand (London) is still preserved in the British Library, with what appear to be his own grammatical notes.[69] William Fellows of Evesham bequeathed St Gregory's *Pastoral Care*, the *Sermons* of St Bernard, and Hugh of St Victor on *Ecclesiastes* to various Oxford libraries.[70] John Hamundson of York had a book of chronicles in

[67] For the grammar course, see Orme, *English Schools*, pp 87-115, and D. Thomson, *A Descriptive Catalogue of Middle English Grammatical Texts* (New York & London, 1979).

[68] Richard de Bury, *Philobiblon*, ed. M. Maclagan (Oxford, 1960), pp 94-5.

[69] BL, Royal MS 13.C.XI f 254ᵛ; Sir G.F. Warner and J.P. Gilson, *Catalogue of Western MSS in the Old Royal and King's Collections, British Museum*, 3 vols (London, 1921), ii, 106-7.

[70] Emden, *BRUO*, ii, 675.

English for his relaxation.[71] Candidates for the degree of master of grammar at Cambridge, most of whom were previous or future schoolmasters, deposited nine books as cautions between 1480 and 1501. They included a breviary, a Latin dictionary, the *Pupilla Oculi*, two books of philosophy, the Bible, an exposition of the Holy Fathers, and the *De Veritate* of Thomas Aquinas.[72] At least one master of the fifteenth century deserves to be noted as a major book-collector. When John Bracebrigge, M.A. of Oxford and master of Lincoln school, entered Syon Abbey as a chaplain after 1420, he gave it a library that included five volumes of grammar, five of philosophy, ten of medicine, and forty-six of theology, canon law, and the liturgy.[73] We cannot regard him as typical, but he certainly enlarges our concept of what a schoolmaster could acquire, given the right conditions.

Next to their reading we have a good deal of writing by schoolmasters. It falls into two categories: textbooks on grammar related to their teaching, and contributions to literature of a more general kind. The latter, which are not numerous, can be dealt with fairly quickly. The relative isolation of most teachers from the main centres of learning and patronage, to say nothing of the demands of their schools, seems to have prevented them making important contributions to scholarship or to imaginative literature, so far as we know. The extent of their activity in these fields is represented, probably accurately, by two of the masters whom we have already met: William Wheatley and John Seward. Wheatley's Latin works, which were written around 1309-16, survive in three manuscripts.[74] They include a commentary on the *De Consolatione Philosophiae* of Boethius, another on his apocryphal *De Disciplina Scholasticorum*, a handful of letters, and two hymns on the life of St Hugh of Lincoln. Seward's effusions, which also reached three manuscripts, include *Arpyilogus* – a commentary on the story of the Harpies in Virgil's *Aeneid, Antelopologia* – a poem on the properties of the antelope addressed to Henry V, some Latin verse *Epigrams*, and other such works.[75] In the field of English literature, John Lelamour, schoolmaster of Hereford, translated a Latin herbal treatise in 1373.[76] Such writings, like those of Wheatley, are interesting to the student of medieval scholarship and minor Latin verse. But they are not, to be truthful, of major importance, and they certainly had no great impact on their authors' own contemporaries.

The one schoolmaster who made his mark on literature did so as a

[71] York, Borthwick Institute, Probate Reg. 4 f 85.

[72] *Grace Book A . . . of the University of Cambridge*, ed. S.M. Leathes (Cambridge, 1897), pp 151, 165-6, 168, 191, 203; *Grace Book B, Part I*, ed. Mary Bateson (Cambridge, 1903), pp 24, 143.

[73] Emden, *BRUO*, i, 239-40; C. Garton, 'A Fifteenth-Century Headmaster's Library', *Lincolnshire History and Archaeology*, xv (1980), pp 29-38.

[74] Emden, *BRUO*, iii, 2030-1.

[75] *Medieval and Renaissance Studies*, i (1941-3), pp 85-104.

[76] British Library, Sloane MS 5 ff 13-57.

publisher rather than a writer. He was that enigmatical and anonymous figure, the schoolmaster-printer of St Albans. Nothing remains of his life beyond the information that he operated a printing and publishing business in the town from about 1479 to 1486 and that he was dead by 1497, when his fellow-printer Wynkyn de Worde described him as a schoolmaster and asked God's mercy on his soul.[77] Eight of the books he published have survived. The first six, which appeared between 1479 and 1483, were university text-books in Latin on various aspects of the arts course, aimed no doubt at the university of Cambridge where no press had yet been established. They do not seem to have been very profitable, and this caused the master to change his tactics. He next attempted to penetrate the wide potential market for books in English of a popular kind. Two such volumes ultimately appeared from his press, both of which he edited personally from earlier writings: *The Chronicles of England* in 1483 and the famous *Book of St Albans* on hunting, hawking, and heraldry in 1486. They were, however, his last productions. Whether he ceased through failure or through death we do not know, but he certainly died too early to reap the rewards he had forseen. These went instead to others. In 1497 Wynkyn de Worde republished the *Chronicles* with greater resources and wider connections. It had a great success; it was reprinted every few years until 1528; and with a shortage of rival volumes, it must have been the major work on English history read by the literate public in England during that period.[78] *The Book of St Albans* fared still better. Also reissued by de Worde in 1496, it outlived even the *Chronicles* to pass through more than twenty new editions, well into the seventeenth century.[79] It is a curious yet memorable fact that the numerous students of heraldry and field sports during the Tudor period owed one of their major sources of information to the enterprise of a late medieval schoolmaster.

The main literary activity of schoolmasters, however, lay in the sphere of their work: the writing of tracts and textbooks on the various branches of Latin grammar. Some of these were advanced discussions of grammatical theory directed at other masters and scholars, but the majority were elementary in their purpose and consisted of simple expositions of Latin accidence and syntax for the use of children. The principal centre of grammatical study in medieval England was Oxford, several of whose schoolmasters produced textbooks during the fourteenth and fifteenth centuries, notably John Cornwall, who operated in the 1340s, and John Leland, 'the flower of grammarians', who

[77] *The Boke of St Albans*, ed. W. Blades (London, 1905), pp 7–23; Rachel Hands, *English Hunting and Hawking in 'The Boke of St Albans'* (London, 1975), pp xv–xvii.
[78] A.W. Pollard & G.R. Redgrave, *A Short Title Catalogue of Books Printed in England, 1475–1640*, 2nd ed., 2 vols (London, 1976–86), nos 9995–10002.
[79] Ibid., nos 3308–3315; *The Boke of St Albans*, ed. Blades, pp 22–3.

flourished from about 1400 until his death in 1425.[80] By the middle of the fifteenth century grammar masters in other parts of England were compiling texts and exercises for their pupils, including a Bristol master (probably Robert Londe) in the late 1420s,[81] and John Drury of Beccles in 1432.[82] Local writing of this kind apparently went on throughout the century. Later still in the 1480s, a revival of activity took place at Oxford, centred upon Magdalen College school, inspired by the renewal of interest in the pagan classical authors and diffused more widely than before by means of the printing press. The chief textbook writers of this period included John Anwykyll, the first known master of the school (*c.*1481-7), his successor John Stanbridge (1488-94), John Holt (usher in the school in 1494-6), and Robert Whittinton, one of their pupils.[83] These men were the vanguard of a wide and active company of grammatical writers in the first half of the sixteenth century, which also included such names as John Colet, William Lily, and Thomas Wolsey.

Most of the school textbooks, from Leland's to Lily's, had major features in common. Their form was based on the *Donet*, the medieval version of the *Ars Minor* of Donatus, who lived in the fourth century. They were often written in English, which made its first appearance in Cornwall's *Speculum Grammaticale* of 1346 and was well established as the language of elementary teaching by the middle of the fifteenth century. They combined the practical teaching of Latin with a strong emphasis on the theory of grammar and grammatical terminology. Finally, they presented their material by means of a series of questions and answers which the master could reproduce in class with his pupils:

What shalt thou do whan thou hast an Englysshe [text] to make in Latyn? I shal reherse myn Englysshe ones, twyes or thryes, and loke out my pryncypal [verb] and aske the questyon 'who?' or 'what?'. And the worde that answereth the questyon shall be the nominatyf case to the verbe, excepte it be a verb impersonall, as in this example. 'The mayster techeth scolers'. 'Techeth' is the verbe. Who techeth? The mayster techeth. This worde 'mayster' answereth to the questyon here, and therefore it shall be the nominatyf case.

This is a passage from the *Long Parvula*, a tract on the translation of English into Latin which exists in several versions, of which this was

[80] R.W. Hunt, 'Oxford Grammar Masters in the Middle Ages', *Oxford Studies Presented to Daniel Callus*, Oxford Historical Society, new series, xvi (1964), pp 163-93; D. Thomson, 'The Oxford Grammar Masters Revisited', *Mediaeval Studies*, xlv (1983), pp 298-310.

[81] Below, chapter 6.

[82] S.B. Meech, 'John Drury and his English Writings', *Speculum*, ix (1934), pp 70-83.

[83] On these masters, see R.S. Stanier, *A History of Magdalen College School, Oxford*, 2nd ed. (Oxford, 1958), and Orme, *English Schools*, pp 107-12.

printed in 1509.[84] Its clarity, simplicity, and orderliness are immediately apparent, and can be appreciated even by a modern audience of hopeless linguists. The method of teaching by questions and answers was supplemented by two other devices. One was the interpolation of mnemonic Latin verses, composed by the author himself or drawn from earlier grammarians. These summarized the rules of grammar or linked together common Latin words in a way that could easily be memorised. The other was the invention of '*vulgaria*' – English sentences which illustrated the rules of grammar in operation and which the pupils were made to translate into Latin as a means of practising their composition. The first known English *vulgaria* date from the early fifteenth century, and they went on being produced well into the sixteenth. They were an educational instrument of much importance and many applications, some of which we shall consider presently.

Textbooks of this kind obviously had an educational impact, helping as they did to instil the rudiments of Latin into generation after generation of pupils. But this was not their only value. They had significant effects on the history of English as well as of Latin, both on the study of language and on the development of literature. It can indeed be said that through their textbooks the medieval schoolmasters made a literary contribution of an indirect kind equal to the writing of many primary works of English prose or poetry. It was they, after all, who first began the study of English grammar. The school textbooks of the fifteenth century, as we have seen, set out to teach Latin through the medium of English. And as Professor S.B. Meech has pointed out this was important for English as well as for Latin.[85] The nature of the effect can be seen in many of the early grammars, like this example, also from the fifteenth century, in a manuscript now at St John's College, Cambridge:

> Qwerby knowyst an adverbe? For he is cast to a verbe and fulfyllyth the significacyon of the verbe. How many degre of comparison hath adverbe? Thre: the posityf, the comparatyf, and the superlatyf. How knowest the posityf degree of adverbe? For he endyth in Englysch most comunly in 'ly', as 'fayrly', 'goodly', 'swetely', and soche othyr. How knowyst the comparatyf degree? For he endyth in Englysch in 'er' or in 'ir' as 'swetter', 'betyr'. How knowyst the superlatyf degre? For he endyth in Englysch in 'est', as 'fayrest', 'fowlest', and soch othyr.[86]

Grammatical writing of this kind had a three-fold influence upon English. In the first place it necessitated the translation of grammatical terms from the original Latin: 'verbe', 'adverbe', 'comparatyf',

[84] *Longe Parvula* (London, Wynkyn de Worde, 1509) (STC 23164) f Aiv. The punctuation and the use of capitals in this and the passages that follow has been modernised.

[85] S.B. Meech, 'Early Application of Latin Grammar to English', *Proceedings of the Modern Language Association of America*, 1 (1935), pp 1012-32.

[86] Ibid., p 1025.

'superlatyf', and so on. Almost all the terms for the parts of speech, the genders and cases of nouns, and the moods and tenses of verbs were probably brought into English by schoolmasters, and certainly established their currency through use in school. Second, by using examples of English words to explain the workings of Latin, the masters were unconsciously dealing with English grammar and reducing it to a series of rules, a century and a half before the first appearance of an English grammar as such by William Bullokar in 1586.[87] Third, their approach to English grammar, like that of Bullokar and his successors, was based on their knowledge of Latin. They supposed the English language to operate on Latin principles, with the same systems of verbs and nouns, and the same kinds of constructions. It was thus the medieval schoolmasters who set the fashion, which endured so long, for treating English as a Latin analogue.

But the textbooks did not only handle words individually. They also set out to teach Latin prose style through the construction of clauses and sentences, and this in turn led them to include passages of English prose, either as explanations of the Latin or as *vulgaria* for translation. And just as the analysis of individual English words had an effect on the study of English grammar, so the invention of English prose passages influenced the development of English prose. Here too, many years before English prose style was formally studied in its own right, it was being taught unconsciously in schools as part of the process of learning to write Latin. The study and translation of *vulgaria* by fifteenth- and early sixteenth-century schoolboys must have been a major influence upon the way they wrote their native language. It is hard to say, of course, whether the school grammars took a lead in the development of English prose style, or whether they merely followed its dominant features at the time. Some of the *vulgaria* passages were over-contrived, in order to deal with complex problems of Latin grammar, and others fall a little flat today. But at its best the English of the school textbooks set a high standard, in which elegance and terseness of manner join together with sincerity of feeling:

> I was very sorry when I herde say that thy brother was dede in this pestilence, for I have lost a gentle frende and a trusty. From our first acquentance, the which was sens we were children, we were companyde togedre in on house and undre onn maister, and lightly we hade onn mynde in every mater. I cannot tell in goode faithe what losse may be comparede with this; the philosopher thought ther was nothynge more to be praisede than a goode frende.[88]

[87] On Bullokar, see *The Dictionary of National Biography*, s.n.
[88] *A Fifteenth Century School Book*, ed. W. Nelson (Oxford, 1956), p 45; cf. below, chapter 8.

As for Robert Whittinton's encomium on his friend Thomas More, a series of sentences in his *Vulgaria* of 1520, it well deserves the fame which it has acquired in modern times:

> Moore is a man of an aungels wyt and syngler lernyng. He is a man of many excellent vertues; yf I shold say as it is, I knowe not his felawe. For where is the man in whome is so many goodly vertues, of that gentylnes, lowlynes, and affabylyte? And, as tyme requyreth, a man of merveylous myrth and pastymes, and somtyme of as sad gravity: as who say, 'a man for all seasons'.[89]

Finally, the writers of the school textbooks can be said to have discovered a major topic of interest in modern English literature: the evocation of childhood. Here too what began as an educational device ended as a literary influence. The schoolmasters of the later middle ages had the same general objective as their modern successors. Their task was to prepare their pupils for adult life, and this they did by introducing into their teaching as many precepts as possible about the ethics and standards required of adults at that time: religious observance, self discipline, obedience, courtesy, and so on. But like their successors today, they found that their teaching was more effective if it made concessions to their pupils and dwelt to some extent on childish things: the everyday life of children, their humour, pleasures, problems, and emotions. Matters of this kind not only held the attention of the class but actively assisted its progress to adulthood. The child who took pleasure in turning a joke into Latin was brought a step nearer to the mastery of the language he would need as an adult cleric or lawyer. The medieval school textbooks therefore included a great many references to childhood in their exercises and examples, and the masters who wrote them descended in doing so from the high study of grammar to view the world through the eyes of their pupils. They thus made the same mental transitions as modern writers for children and those who reminisce about their youth.

The best of these early evocations of childhood is undoubtedly the one in the anonymous collection of *vulgaria* written at Magdalen College in about 1500, and also the best of the whole genre:

> The worlde waxeth worse every day, and all is turnede upside down, contrary to th'olde guyse, for all that was to me a pleasure when I was a childe, from iij yere olde to x (for now I go upon the xij yere), while I was undre my father and mothers kepyng, be tornyde now to tormentes and payne. For than I was wont to lye styll abedde tyll it was forth dais, delitynge myselfe in slepe and ease. The sone sent in his beamys at the wyndowes that gave me lyght instede of a candle. O, what a sporte it was every mornynge when the son was upe to take my lusty pleasur betwixte the sheets, to beholde the rofe, the beamys, and the rafters of

---

[89] *The Vulgaria of John Stanbridge and Robert Whittinton*, ed. Beatrice White, EETS, original series, clxxxvii (1932), pp 64–5.

my chambre, and loke on the clothes that the chambre was hangede with. Ther durste no mann but he were made awake me oute of my slepe upon his owne hede while me list to slepe. At my wyll I arose with intreatese, and whan th'appetite of rest went his way by his owne accorde, than I awoke and callede whom me list to lay my gere redy to me. My brekefaste was brought to my beddys side as ofte as me liste to call therfor, and so many tymes I was first fedde or I were cledde. So I hade many pleasurs mo besides thes, wherof sum be forgoten, sum I do remembre wel, but I have no leysure to reherce them nowe.

But nowe the worlde rennyth upon another whele. For nowe at fyve of the clocke by the monelyght I most go to my booke and lete slepe and slouthe alon, and yff oure maister hape to awake us, he bryngeth a rode stede of a candle. Now I leve pleasurs that I hade sumtyme; here is nought els preferryde but monyshynge and strypys. Brekfastes that were sumtyme brought at my biddynge is dryven oute of contrey and never shall cum agayne. I wolde tell more of my mysfortunes, but thoughe I have leysure to say, yet I have no pleasure, for the reherse of them makyth my mynde more hevy. I sech all the ways I can to lyve ons at myn ease, that I myght rise and go to bede when me liste oute of the fere of betynge.[90]

The author of this passage may have had in his mind (and would certainly have known) the ancient and well-worn comparison between the holy innocence of childhood and the sins and labours of adult life – the theme that is so familiar to us in its expositions by Vaughan and Wordsworth. He may also have drawn upon memories of his own childhood. To this extent he can be said to have anticipated the many modern writers who have recalled the anguish of their transition from home to school. His chief purpose, however, as many other passages in his *vulgaria* make clear, was not only to sympathize with the child he portrayed but to censure and instruct him. In the eyes of the master, the change he described was a necessary and desirable progression from childish sloth, greed, and self indulgence to Christian adulthood with its sustaining virtues of hard work, obedience, and self discipline. The apparent splendour of unfettered childhood, like the apparent splendour of Falstaff's disorders in *Henry IV*, must in the end be rejected, for the sake of both society and the individual, of both body and the soul. Shakespeare and the *vulgaria* author shared a common point of view, and both enclosed their pleasant pictures in a regular dark frame of traditional morality.

Our task is now complete. We have tried to rescue the medieval schoolmasters from their obscurity, with (it is hoped) a little success. We know how it arose. Their lack of numbers, their geographical isolation, and their modest economic importance were all against them. They never managed to develop a national organization, and have hardly done since; even today they are fragmented into half a dozen associations. They stayed secluded in their classrooms while others no better than

---

[90] *A Fifteenth Century School Book*, ed. Nelson, pp 1-2.

themselves – clerics, physicians and lawyers – traversed the world for all to see. The cleric's censures, the physician's poisons, and the lawyer's writs all made their impact upon adults, with memorable results. Schoolmasters, on the other hand, ruled only the powerless and the inarticulate, and suffered accordingly. Yet their obscurity was not their fault. If they had been given more, they might have done better. Like the schoolmasters of any age they taught what their society required with the resources which it provided. As it was, they had some solid achievements. They helped to supply the Church with clerics, the universities with scholars, and the courts with officers and lawyers. The literacy of the laity was in part the result of their efforts. They were inventive as educationalists and they exercised an unseen influence on the development of the English language. The public which ignored them was wrong, as public opinion often is. The schoolmaster's birch touched a lower and less regarded end of the body politic than did the priest, the lawyer, or the physician. Yet it was an end, surely, of fundamental importance.

2 'It falls to Richard, standing up, to oppose (in debate), who lacks the wit of Ralph sitting down' (see p 79). A woodcut of an early-Tudor school, showing the master in a chair clutching his birch, one pupil being examined, and seven others sitting down, two of them with books.

5

EARLY SCHOOL NOTE-BOOKS

There are few older or richer fields in the history of English education than the school curriculum: the topics and methods of the classroom. Since the seventh century AD grammars and reading texts from the Roman Empire can be traced reaching England from abroad, to be followed by the productions of medieval and Renaissance Europe. English teachers in their turn were quick to adapt the Roman and continental grammars and to make their own new treatises, some of which also grew to be standard works. The writing of texts *for* schools was complemented at an early date by literary activity *in* schools, of a more temporary and individual kind. Masters and pupils practised how to write, composed written exercises in prose and verse, made notes and copied extracts from the standard texts. Wooden tablets, covered with wax and written on with styluses, were used for this purpose from at least the twelfth century[1] and were cheap to buy; several pairs bought for the grammar boys of Merton College, Oxford, in 1347-8 cost only 2½d.[2] Parchment was more expensive, but was also sometimes used; it too was purchased for the Merton boys, and in 1365 it was ordered to be provided for the brethren of St Leonard's Hospital, York, when they went to theological lectures.[3] There can be no doubt that writing was practised in schools from their earliest days.

There are plenty of manuscripts of standard school texts – Roman, continental and English – from the Anglo-Saxon period onwards. But it is not until the fifteenth century that written work produced in schools begins to survive, in manuscripts representing the personal working note-books of masters and pupils.[4] There are always reasons for the appearance of new kinds of evidence, and one must be the increasing availability of paper which was used for most of these manuscripts. Paper allowed notes to be kept more durably than on tablets and more cheaply than on parchment; after 1400 a quire of eight sheets (sixteen

---

[1] F. Barlow, *The English Church, 1066-1154* (London and New York, 1979), p 239.
[2] A.F. Leach, *Educational Charters and Documents, 598 to 1909* (Cambridge, 1911), pp 300-1.
[3] Ibid.; Orme, *English Schools*, p 82.
[4] The best account of such works is D. Thomson, *A Descriptive Catalogue of Middle English Grammatical Texts* (New York and London, 1979).

pages) only cost between 1d. and 4d. depending on size and quality.[5] Some paper was also in use in the fourteenth century, however,[6] so there may have been earlier note-books which have been lost. Here another factor may be relevant: the replacement of French by English as the second language in schools in the middle of that century.[7] By 1400, when the last men died who had made their notes in French, their books were of little interest and unlikely to be kept. Even in the fifteenth century, when paper was common and English in use, school note-books did not stand a very good chance of survival. We only possess a few dozen of the hundreds, perhaps thousands, there must once have been. Some writers may have thrown away their notes when their schooldays were over, and even if they kept them till they died, the books needed to contain either useful transcripts or useful blank paper to make it worth the while of other people to preserve them.[8] A further hazard was introduced by the coming of humanism to the English schools between about 1490 and 1520. Like the earlier introduction of English, it rendered many note-books out of date, and must have caused even those of good quality to lose their appeal and fall prey to destruction.

The present chapter and the three which follow are concerned with four early school note-books. They are discussed in roughly chronological order. The first was compiled between 1425 and 1450, probably by a schoolmaster, in Lincoln or the area between that city and the Nottinghamshire border. Its location is defined by the dialect of the English words and passages found in the manuscript.[9] The second began to be written in about 1427 by Thomas Schort (d. 1465), who was a senior pupil or assistant master in the grammar school over the New Gate in Bristol, and later became a chantry priest and rector in Wiltshire.[10] The third was put together at Barlinch Priory (west Somerset), probably by a schoolboy, between about 1480 and 1520,[11] and the fourth was the work of a master or senior pupil at Magdalen College School, Oxford, in the 1510s or 20s.[12] All (except perhaps the

---

[5] J.E.T. Rogers, *A History of Agriculture and Prices in England*, 7 vols (Oxford, 1866-1902), iii, 468-73.

[6] Ibid., ii, 569, 573.

[7] Above, pp 10-11.

[8] For an example of a reused note-book, see Thomson, *Catalogue*, pp 290-315.

[9] University of Yale, Beinecke Library, MS 3 (34), described by Linda Ehrsam Voigts and Barbara A. Shailor, 'The Recovery of a Fifteenth-Century Schoolmaster's Book', *The Yale University Library Gazette*, lx (1985), pp 11-31.

[10] Below, chapter six. It should be added that Schort became chantry priest of Walter Hungerford's chantry in Salisbury Cathedral in 1429, immediately after his ordination (J.M.J. Fletcher, 'The Tomb of Walter Lord Hungerford', *Wiltshire Archaeological and Natural History Magazine*, xlvii (1935-7), p 456). On his note-book, see also now N.R. Ker, *Medieval Manuscripts in British Libraries*, vol iii (Oxford, 1983), pp 630-7.

[11] Below, chapter seven.

[12] Below, chapter eight.

second) are incomplete, and we are lucky to have any of them. The first, which we shall call for brevity the Lincoln note-book (though it may not have come from the city itself), has survived through being used as binding material for the cover of another book – it is not clear when this happened. The Barlinch notes were also put to binding purposes in about 1546, to cover a court-book of the manor of Minehead belonging to the Luttrell family of Dunster Castle, both places near Barlinch. This probably took place not long after the death of the note-book maker, when humanist changes in schools had made his material obsolete. The Magdalen College Book is an incomplete collection of translation exercises, bound up with other Latin tracts, but its subsequent history is also unknown. The best survivor is the Bristol note-book, which was kept long enough to be given in 1612 to an antiquary, John Smith, who was interested in medieval Latin and preserved it.[13] All four note-books represent the work of older better pupils or schoolmasters. This is true even of the worst, the Lincoln and Barlinch examples which contain misspellings and mistranslations and were both consigned to the bookbinder. We do not yet possess books written by younger pupils, dunces or very bad masters, so what we are seeing is the work of late-medieval and Renaissance schools at their best.

Apart from the Magdalen text, which is limited to one sort of material, our note-books accord with other extant examples in containing various kinds of texts in Latin and (often) English. There are whole or partial copies of treatises on Latin grammar and prose composition, vocabularies, Latin poems such as *Cato* which were read and studied in schools, and sentences for translation. Our concern will be mainly with the sentences, which appear in each of our books and are edited with notes as appendices to the chapters about them. Translation sentences are one of the most accessible and appealing genres of school literature in the fifteenth and sixteenth centuries. They indicate the content and level of the curriculum – the grammar, syntax and vocabulary which the master was teaching, and also something of his policy and methods. Medieval and Renaissance schoolmasters used translation sentences to impart wisdom and morality as well as Latin. They set proverbs and wise quotations for translations, and they tried to capture the pupil's interest by choosing topics of humour, school affairs, news and life outside the school. Sometimes we can even glimpse the cycle of the year, as masters gave out topical sentences relevant to the season and its activities.[14] As a result, the sentences preserve a great many general cultural references. They reveal the master himself, his duties and status, the pupils, their families and prospective careers, classroom procedures and customs, common objects and everyday events, and even social problems such as

---

[13] Ker, *Medieval Manuscripts*, iii, 637.
[14] Below, pp 94, 127.

shortage of food, epidemics, crime and war. Some of these topics are recorded elsewhere, but their presence in the schoolroom helps to show their impact on society. Other material like contemporary clichés, scraps of songs and items of children's lore is unique to these note-books and therefore irreplaceable.

Let us begin by considering the history and nature of translation sentences as a genre. The use of short Latin sentences by schoolmasters to demonstrate points of grammar and syntax to their pupils goes back to at least the thirteenth century.[15] The teachers, presumably, dictated and explained the sentences, and the pupils memorised them or wrote them down. Such sentences were called *latinitates* or *latina*, and by the middle of the fourteenth century they were evidently a standard feature of Latin grammar teaching. John Cornwall, the famous schoolmaster of Oxford in the 1340s, is an important name in this respect. His *Speculum Grammaticale* of 1346 is the first surviving grammatical treatise from England to include model *latinitates*, set into the text in order to illustrate the topics under discussion. Like many schoolmasters, Cornwall based his *latinitates* on matters of everyday life to give them greater appeal, such as the wars of Edward III with the French which were going on at the time.[16] His sentences display a further novelty in that some of them are followed by English translations. Cornwall is said to have been the first schoolmaster in England to introduce English into the grammar schools instead of French, as the secondary language used for explaining Latin or for translation work.[17] The *Speculum Grammaticale* confirms his recognition of the English language, and is thus the first text to include both model sentences in Latin alone and ones in Latin and English together.

The growing number of school note-books preserved after 1400 also contain many Latin and English sentences. Sometimes they occur as examples in treatises, as they do in the *Speculum Grammaticale*. Equally often, they stand independently and by themselves. Note-books may contain anything from single isolated sentences to long sequences, suggesting in the latter case that they were being dictated or composed as translation exercises. As well as the term *latinitas*, which went on being used to mean a Latin sentence, an equivalent word in English appears by the 1420s: the noun 'latin'. 'A hard latin to make, my face waxeth black', as a schoolboy is humorously portrayed as complaining.[18] At about the

---

[15] R.W. Hunt, 'Oxford Grammar Masters in the Middle Ages', *Oxford Studies Presented to Daniel Callus*, Oxford Historical Society, new series, xiv (1964), p 175. The Oxford background to this article now needs correction from D. Thomson, 'The Oxford Grammar Masters Revisited', *Mediaeval Studies*, xiv (1983), pp 298-310.

[16] Hunt (above, note 15), pp 174-5.

[17] *Polychronicon Ranulphi Higden*, ed. C. Babington and J.R. Lumby, 9 vols (London, Rolls Series, 1865-86), ii, 158-161.

[18] Below, p 104.

same time, the word 'english' came into use to mean a sentence in English in a school context. It is first found in the treatise of another well-known Oxford schoolmaster, John Leland's *Informacio*, probably written before 1415. 'What shalt thou do', asks Leland, 'when thou hast an english [i.e. an English sentence] to make into Latin?' and then he proceeds to give instructions.[19] By 1465-70 the word 'english' must have been familiar in schools, because it occurs in the morality play *Mankind*, where the irreverent character Nowadays says to the grave confessor Mercy:

> I prey yow hertyly, worschyppull clerke,
> To have this englysh mad in Laten:
> 'I have etun a dyschfull of curdys,
> And I have scheten yowr mowth full of turdys.'
> Now opyn yowr sachell with Laten wordys
> And sey me this in clerycall manere![20]

The first two lines are an evident parody of Leland's *Informacio*, and the next two contain an english, based on the formula 'I have something nice and you have something nasty', which is found elsewhere in the schoolbooks of this period.[21] Later in the century, the word *vulgus* in Latin (plural *vulgaria*, 'vulgar' in English) was also introduced to mean an English sentence in school use. It first occurs in Latin as the title of a collection of English and Latin sentences published at Oxford in 1483, and probably made by John Anwykyll, master of Magdalen College School.[22] The word 'vulgar' in English first survives in the same sense in 1520.[23]

We have now identified a genre of Latin and English sentences in schoolroom use. Sometimes they occur in treatises, sometimes separately; sometimes in Latin alone, and sometimes in Latin with an English translation. The Latin sentences with English translations can be further divided into those where each Latin sentence comes first and its English equivalent second, and the reverse where each English sentence comes first and its Latin equivalent second. There was no special terminology for pairs of sentences in the two languages, in either order.

[19] Thomson, *Catalogue*, pp 189, 288; *An Edition of the Middle English Grammatical Texts* (New York and London, 1984), p 105 (cf. pp 93, 104, 111).

[20] *The Macro Plays*, ed. M. Eccles, EETS, original series, cclxii (1969), p 158 lines 129-34.

[21] Below, pp 116, 119.

[22] *Vulgaria quedam abs Terencio in Anglicam linguam traducta* (Oxford, 1483) (STC 23904).

[23] *The Vulgaria of John Stanbridge and . . . Robert Whittinton*, ed. Beatrice White, EETS, original series, clxxxvii (1932), p 87. Both 'english' and 'vulgar' remained in use throughout the sixteenth and early seventeenth centuries: see for example John Brinsley, *Ludus Literarius or The Grammar Schoole* (London, 1612), p 148.

[24] S.B. Meech, 'John Drury and his English Writings', *Speculum*, ix (1934), pp 82-3; Thomson, *Catalogue*, pp 174-5, 177.

They could be called *latinitates* like sentences purely in Latin, as they are in one manuscript of 1434-5,[24] or *vulgaria*, which is used from 1483 onwards as the title of sentence collections in both English and Latin. When the Latin sentence is placed first, one presumes that it was the starting point and that the following English translation was added to help the master explain the Latin, or was written down by the pupil as an aid to his own understanding. Collections of Latin sentences followed by English translations usually have the latter added in an unsystematic way, that is to say they are appended to some Latin sentences but not others. It would appear that Latin sentences followed by English translations are basically *latinitates* to which the author or scribe has added an English version when he felt some personal need or impulse to do so. Pupils do not seem to have been made to write systematic English translations of Latin sentences; they probably did so orally. The earliest set of Latin sentences to incorporate systematic English translations seems to be the set in the Magdalen College note-book of the early sixteenth century, which is printed in Chapter Twelve.

Let us turn next to the reverse arrangement, in which the English sentences appear first, each followed by a Latin translation. Early examples of these include the Bristol sentences in Thomas Schort's note-book, and others written by John Drury, master of Beccles school (Suffolk) in 1434-5.[25] The sentences in the Lincoln note-book, which apparently date from about 1425-50, also belong to this group. Pairs of sentences with the English first sometimes appear in Latin treatises,[26] but they are much more likely to occur on their own, singly or in sets, with a regular alternation of the two languages – as they do in the note-books just mentioned. Towards the end of the fifteenth century, systematic collections of English and Latin sentences were also printed with the English first, starting with John Anwykyll's *Vulgaria* of 1483. Three other schoolmasters published large collections of this kind in subsequent years: John Stanbridge in 1508, William Horman in 1519, and Robert Whittinton in 1520.[27] Sentence collections with the English first probably represent the stock on which the master drew whenever he wanted to set his pupils a translation exercise. The English was usually the starting point, and the aim was for the pupil to translate it into good Latin. This is a reasonable assumption, given that the English sentences are frequently well-known proverbs or fragments of popular songs

[25] Meech (above, note 24).

[26] E.g. *The Winchester Anthology: A Facsimile of British Library Additional MS 60577*, ed. E. Wilson (Cambridge, 1981), ff 67ᵛ, 73, 74ᵛ, 75ᵛ.

[27] *The Vulgaria of John Stanbridge and . . . Robert Whittinton*, ed. White; William Horman, *Vulgaria* (London, 1519) (STC 13811) (facsimile ed., *The English Experience*, no 745 (Amsterdam, 1977), also ed. M.R. James, Roxburghe Club, 1926). To these should be added the MS *vulgaria* in the British Library, Arundel MS 249, ff 9-61, published as *A Fifteenth Century School Book*, ed. W. Nelson (Oxford, 1956).

which evidently predated the Latin translations. They sometimes centre on problems of English usage, like the need to distinguish 'read' and 'red' in no. 18 of the Lincoln sentences, and sometimes alternative Latin versions are given, as in Lincoln nos. 24 and 26. The Latin translations written beneath the English were usually the master's model versions, but in some of the manuscripts written by pupils they may be the pupils' own productions.

Sometimes in these collections, however, a deliberately inaccurate English sentence is placed before an accurate Latin one. The exercises from John Drury's school include a set of twenty sentences which were studied in Christmas term 1434–5, and are prefixed by the heading *parue latinitates . . . sed non pro forma reddicionis* ('small latins . . . but not in the form to be rendered').[28] They include examples like:

I saw the drunkyn while thu were sobere;
Ego vidi te ebrius dum fuisti sobrius,

which teaches the importance of following Latin word agreement rather than word order. The correct translation is 'I being drunk saw thee while thou was sober'. Another of Drury's false translations,

I saw a nakyd man gaderin stoonys in hys barm,

may have been a classic example of mistranslation from Latin, since it also occurs in Schort's Bristol exercises as

I say a nakyd man bere fyve lovis in hys lappe.[29]

In both cases the Latin requires to be read as 'I being naked saw a man'. The Lincoln sentences include two examples of the same kind:

I standyng seys the wall renyng,

where the Latin means the opposite, and

Syttyng, standyng, rawf, richard, fals to [a]pos, wyt wantyng,

which is a meaningless translation of the Latin word order and should read: 'It falls to Richard, standing up, to oppose [in a debate], who lacks the wit of Ralph sitting down'. In these cases the English cannot be a set piece for translation into Latin. Instead, the Latin is the starting point, even though it comes second, and the English is an example of how not to translate, or to illustrate the different way in which the English language works.

We shall now turn briefly to the 31 sentences in the first of our four note-books: the Lincoln manuscript. The collection is a small one because the manuscript is defective; the sentences occupy two sides of a

[28] Meech (above, note 24), pp 82–3.
[29] Below, p 105. I must withdraw my needless emendation of the Latin, caused by ignorance of the Beccles parallel.

single leaf which was apparently the last part of a larger collection, of which the rest has been lost. English sentences for translation into Latin tend to be shorter, simpler and less ambitious in the schoolbooks of the early and mid fifteenth century than they became in the early Tudor period, and this is true of the Lincoln as of the Beccles and Bristol manuscripts. The largest element is that of wise teaching in the form of proverbs, which accounts for eighteen sentences. Fourteen of these are recorded elsewhere and were therefore in current use (nos. 5-13, 20, 23, 27, 28 and 30), while four others (nos. 4, 14, 20 and 22), though unrecorded, seem to belong to the same genre. Four of the certain proverbs (nos. 7-9 and 28) occur here well before the earliest datings hitherto discovered. The rest of the collection includes five references to life in school, and three to life outside. One is apparently about boys coming late to school (no. 25), another about the master himself being absent (no. 26) and a third about him questioning or 'apposing' a boy (no. 2). Number 19, as already mentioned, features a boy himself apposing (probably debating a grammatical point with a colleague), and no. 24 talks about forgetting what one has learned. Of the non-school allusions, no. 29 refers to a boy's father possessing an enclosed piece of land (perhaps reflecting the more affluent social ranks from which grammar schoolboys came), and nos. 3 and 31 mention domestic animals: a dog and a hen. The dog's name may be Whitefoot and the hen's is certainly 'Copple' meaning 'crested', a hen's name which is also recorded in the fifteenth-century comic poem, *The Tournament of Tottenham*.[30] All the topics in these sentences are predictable, and have parallels among the other collections which we shall study.

The two most interesting of the Lincoln sentences are nos. 1 and 19, which also come closest to providing a humorous element. The first, now mutilated, is a taunting rhyme against the Scots, written in couplets. Reconstructed and modernised, it reads somewhat as follows:

> Rough-footed Scot with a raveling,
> Wast thou at [Verneuil ?] at the wrestling?
> In the crook of the moon went thou thitherward,
> And in the wild waning came thou homeward;
> There wast thou casten in midst of the place,
> That thy neck broke thee through evil grace.[31]

This is a longer version of a poem recorded elsewhere in the fifteenth century. In 1424 the English defeated a mixed force of French and Scots at the battle of Verneuil in Normandy. A few years later a London

---

[30] W.C. Hazlitt, *Remains of Early Popular Poetry in England*, 4 vols (London, 1864-6), iii, 84.

[31] The first two lines have virtually disappeared from the MS. But 'rough-footed' and 'raveling' are likely translations of the Latin *pedem hursute cum coterno*, and often occur in anti-Scottish literature (see the *Oxford English Dictionary* under the words cited). The bottom parts of the letters of the missing word in the second line can just be read in the MS, and they could represent W'nō for Wernon, i.e. Vernoun or Verneuil.

chronicler, describing this event, wrote that 'the victory fell to the Englishmen . . . But the most vengeance fell upon the proud Scots, for they went to dog-wash [died like drowned dogs] the same day, more than 1,700 of coat armours of these proud Scots, so that they may say well

> In the crook of the moon went they thitherward,
> And in the wild waning came they homeward.'[32]

The English traditionally sneered at the Scots because of their rough brogues or 'ravelings' of undressed hide with the hair on (hence 'rough-footed'). The first quarter of the moon, when it was crooked, and the last quarter when it was waning, were both reckoned to be unlucky times.[33] It is possible that the rhyme originated after Verneuil, like the Agincourt song, or it may be an older one rewritten or requoted for the occasion. Whichever of the two, it was certainly familiar to children when the Lincoln sentences were written.

The same is true of sentence no. 19, a tongue-twister roughly stressed and rhymed:

> Three gray greedy geese
> Flying o'er three green greasy furs [i.e. furrows]:
> The geese was gray and greedy,
> The furs was green and greasy.

Here too the note-book writer was borrowing from popular literature, for the words are a version of a rhyme long-known to English children. Four hundred years after the Lincoln sentences were written, the antiquary John Bell (1783-1864) added to his copy of the children's verse-book, *Gammer Gurton's Garland*,

> Three grey geese crossed through a green river;
> Grey was the geese and green was the river,

and as recently as 1952 Mr and Mrs Peter Opie, the folklorists, received from a schoolgirl in Helensburgh (Dunbartonshire) the rhyme

> Twelve grey geese in a green field grazing,
> Grey were the geese and green was the grazing.

The rhyme finally reached print in the Opies' *Oxford Nursery Rhyme Book*

---

[32] *The Brut or The Chronicles of England*, ed. F.W.D. Brie, part ii, EETS, original series, cxxvi (1908), p 440-1; *Chronicles of London*, ed. C.L. Kingsford (Oxford, 1905), pp 75, 129.

[33] *Middle English Dictionary*, ed. H. Kurath and S.M. Kuhn (Ann Arbor, 1954 in progress), sub 'crok'; B.J. Whiting, *Proverbs, Sentences and Proverbial Phrases from English Writings Mainly before 1500* (Cambridge, Mass., and London, 1968) C557, W36.

(1955).[34] It and the Scottish poem are both arguably nursery rhymes, in that they were rhymes current among children and, as we shall see, they have their counterparts in the Bristol note-book. The writers of early school note-books would be surprised to learn that they were, unconsciously, the first collectors of children's rhymes and lore – yet such indeed was the case.

[34] I am grateful to Mrs Opie for these references.

An Edition of the 'Lincoln' Sentences of c. 1425-50 in Beinecke Library MS 3 (34), f 5

The following edition is a corrected version of that previously published in *The Yale University Library Gazette*, lx (1985), pp 54-7. I am grateful to Professors Linda Ehrsam Voigts and Barbara A. Shailor for bringing the MS to my attention, to them and Mr S. Parks of the Beinecke Library for permission to edit the sentences, to Mr M. Benskin of the Middle English Dialect Project for his help in locating the dialect of the MS, and to Professor Norman Davis and the Revd. Dr D. Thomson for their kindness in making corrections and offering advice on editing.

In the edition, the use of capital letters and punctuation follows modern practice. Y and þ (thorn) are distinguished, although in the MS they are indistinguishable. Contractions are expanded in italics, editorial additions are given in brackets, and holes and illegible words are marked by empty brackets. Alterations and cancellations are not noted. For ease of study, the Latin sentences are indented from the English ones, and each pair of sentences has been numbered.

1. [Rough-footed Scot, with a raveling, was] þ[u] at [Wernon?] at þ[e wrast]lyng? In þe cruk on þe mowne went þu thederward, *and* in þe wyyld wen[yng] com þu hamward; þer was þu castyn *in* med*is* on þe plays, þat þi nek brak þe tyl [ev?]yll grays.

   Scotte pede*m* hursute *cum* coterno, fuisti-ne apud deluctacio[nem]? *In* decricione lune illuc accessisti, *in* anatemate domu*m* re[ce]cisti; *in* medio sp*ectaculi prostratus* fuisti supin*us*, *quo* frangiebar*is* collu*m* sorte media p*eruersitatis*.

2. Mast*er* fallyng for to apoys *and* me be hofyng to hanswar, both oppociscion *and* responcion her to be purwyd.

[1] For translation and discussion, see above pp 80-1.
[2] The master befalling to question and I behoving to answer, both opposition and responsion are to be provided.

Magistro existente cui*us* e*st* oppone*re et* me existente que*m* oport*et*
re*s*ponde*re*, *et* oppoci*s*cio et re*s*poncio prouidenda su*nt*.

3. My dog qwyyt feyt lepyd ov*er* þe hek spenfutte.
   Canis me*us* albu*m* pede transluit anticam pedib*us* co*n*iunct*is*.

4. A rok *and* reyl *and* spenyng weyll, my babyll vag*is* neu*er* a deyll.
   Collum, alabru*m et* tornu*m* filiatorium, mi*h*i nulla vatellat pegma.

5. Bett*er* frend i*n* curt *and* pe[nny] i*n* purs.
   Curia que*m* gestat, lo[cu]l*us* qu*am* minime prestat.

6. As þe cok craws þe [chi]kyn herys.
   Vt cantat gall*us* si*c* audit estimo pull*us*.

7. Bornt hand fyr dreyd*is*.
   Igne*m* formid*et* se[mel] adusta m[anus].

8. Was he neu*er* gud swayn þat let hys herand for þe rayn.
   Que*m* retinet stille non e*st* bon*us* armig*er* ille.

9. Schort hos, lang lanʒars.
   Ad curtas caligas, ligulas d*ebet* adde*re* longas.

10. Pep*er* is blak boyt has a gud smak.
    Pip*er* e*st* grossu*m* s*ed* h*abet* bonu*m* preciosu*m*.

11. Far fro þe ee, far fro þe hart.
    No*n* oculo nota, res e*st* a corde remota.

12. Betwyx two stolys fals þe ars down.
    Int*er* scanna duo co*n*cidit an*us* rui*n*a.

13. Qwe*n* þe as well down, hyng vp þi hachytt.
    Cu*m* bene fescisti, sursu*m* tu pe*n*de secura*m*.

14. Qwe*n* þe prasyd prays þe prasar þat þe prasar *and* þe prasayd h[er] lyke.
    Cu*m* ille a quo quis lic*et* ab ill[o] [   ]licabat, tu*n*c qui licebat *et* qui lic*et*
    ad p*ar*[iam] [ind]icant*ur*. [f 5ᵛ]

---

³ My dog Whitefoot (or with white feet) leapt over the heck (lower half of a door) with
linked feet. Heck is translated *antica* in *Promptorium Parvulorum* (1440), ed. A.L. Mayhew,
London, Early English Text Society, original series, cii (1902), col 216.
⁴ A distaff and reel and spinning wheel, my talk wags never a bit. Babul is translated
pegma in *Promptorium Parvulorum*, col 23.
⁵ Better friend in court than penny in purse. Purs is translated *loculus* in *Promptorium
Parvulorum*, col 350. The proverb is recorded in B.J. Whiting, *Proverbs, Sentences and
Proverbial Phrases from English Writings Mainly before 1500* (Cambridge, Mass., and
London, 1968), F633.
⁶ As the cock crows, the chicken hears (Whiting, C347).
⁷ Burnt hand dreads the fire (Whiting, H53). *Semel*: the proverb is translated with this
word in a similar fifteenth-century note-book (BL, Harley MS 1587, f 105ᵛ).
⁸ He was never a good swain that stopped his errand for the rain (Whiting, S920).
⁹ Short hose, longer laces (Whiting, H547).
¹⁰ Pepper is black but has a good smack (Whiting, P139). The proverb also occurs in
The Vulgaria of John Stanbridge and . . . Robert Whittinton, ed. White, p 23.
¹¹ Far from the eye, far from the heart (Whiting, E213).
¹² Betwixt two stools falls the arse down (Whiting, S794).
¹³ When thou hast done well, hang up thy hatchet (Whiting, A251).
¹⁴ When the praised one praises the praiser, then the praiser and the praised are alike.

15. [Iij] gray gredy geys f[li]yng [over] iij greyn gresy furs. Þe geys was gray *and* gredy; þe furs was greyn *and* gresy.

Tres auce elbide *et* auide volebant vltra tres sulcos verides, et auce erant elbide *et* auide *et* sulci erant verdes.

16. I standyng seys þe wall renyng.

Ego stantem vidio murum currens.

17. We ar euyneld.

Nos sumus coequi *et* coetanij.

18. I sal reyd apon þe reyd messebuyk.

Ego legam super missale rubricum.

19. Sittyng, standyng, rawf, richard, fals to [a]pos wyt wantyng.

Sedentis stanti radulfi ricardo inest opponere carenti ingenio.

20. Cum to þe ton pursles *and* peniles, yt sal be metlys *and* drynclys.

Ad villam vento absque bursa *et* pecunijs, posterius cistitur absque cibis et potibus.

21. No langer foster, no langer lemmoun.

Non vltra quam proterius erit quis amasius.

22. At pays is nothyng so wa as heggis and alleluia.

Ad festum pasche nihil ita vsuale sicut oua *et* hec vox alleluia.

23. Þe tong braks bayn *and* self a[s] nown.

Lingua teret ossam *et* inde se nec habet vlla.

24. My lesson forgetyn, i am [to] be blamed for þe forgettyng.

Leccionem meam oblitus, culpandus sum obliuionis vel -ne.

Alio modo sic: Leccione mea oblita, culpandus sum obliuionis vel -ne.

25. Layt resyn *and* leyt comyn, qwam befals to be blamyd yn leyt rysyng *and* leyt commyng?

Terde surecto *et* terdius vento, cuius nisi mea interest vituperari terde surgentis et terdius venientis?

26. Mayster not ȝyt is cumyn in þe scull

Magister non dum est ingressus scolam / A magistro non dum venietur in scola.

---

[15] For discussion, see above, p 81.

[16] I standing sees the wall running. See above, p 79.

[17] We are of equal age.

[18] I shall read upon the red massbook.

[19] Sitting, standing, Ralph, Richard, falls to appose, wit wanting. For discussion, see above, p 79.

[20] Come to the town purseless and penniless, it shall be meatless and drinkless.

[21] No longer provider, no longer loved one (Whiting, F551).

[22] At Easter nothing is so the way as eggs and alleluia.

[23] The tongue breaks bone and itself has none (Whiting, T384).

[24] My lesson forgotten, I am to be blamed for the forgetting.

[25] Late rising and late coming, to whom does it befall to be blamed for late rising and late coming? Compare below, pp 105-6, nos 55-7.

[26] The master is not yet come into the school.

27. Self do, self aff.
    Quod ipse eumpse feceris, ipse tuleris.
28. Be þe summer day neuer so lang, at last coms heyngsang.
    Quam longa fuerit dies estiualis, tandem venit nox et vespere.
29. Þis cloos of my fader is seueryl and noth comon.
    Ista clasura patris mei est apropriata et non communis.
30. I prowd and þu prode, qwa bers þe hasse out?
    Mei superbi et tui superbi, quis portabit seneres?
31. Cop[y]l our heyn þat [springs?] wp vsys to werp hyr hegis þer out.
    Gallina nostra sir[gens?] patitor / solet forisdino ponere oua sua.

[27] Self do, self have (Whiting, S143).

[28] Be the summer day never so long, at last comes evensong (Whiting, D40), also used later in *The Vulgaria of John Stanbridge and . . . Robert Whittinton*, ed. White, p 18.

[29] This enclosed land of my father is private and not common.

[30] I proud and thou proud, who carries the ashes out? (Whiting, A 207).

[31] Copple our hen that [springs?] up is accustomed to lay her eggs out of doors. *Dino*: presumably a mistake for *nido*. For Copple, see above, p 80.

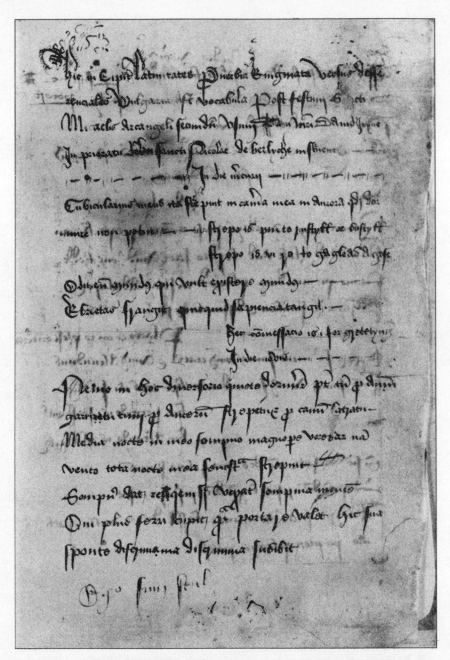

3 A pupil's diary: notes kept during a Michaelmas term, between 1480 and 1520, in a school in the small remote priory of Barlinch (west Somerset). The notes, made on a Wednesday and a Thursday, are transcribed on p 118.

6

A GRAMMATICAL MISCELLANY FROM BRISTOL AND WILTSHIRE

English grammatical miscellanies, of which numerous examples survive from the fourteenth and fifteenth centuries, are a major source of the history of education in later medieval England.[1] We mean, by miscellanies, collections of treatises and exercises relating to the study and teaching of Latin. Works of this kind were compiled for their use by university scholars, members of the religious orders, and the masters and pupils of ordinary grammar schools. The study of such works today, most of whose contents have yet to be printed, adds greatly to our knowledge of medieval English life and thought. The Latin treatises on grammar which they contain reveal the history of the study and usage of Latin in England. They make it possible to reconstruct the grammar curriculum of the English schools and universities, for which other evidence is rarely available. They contain the earliest grammatical treatments of the English language, too, in the form of English glosses and translations of Latin grammatical works, long before the publication of the first definitive grammar of English in 1586. Of wider interest still, the miscellanies contain numerous school exercises which aimed to teach Latin to pupils through references to the speech, activities, and surroundings of everyday life. Such texts are especially valuable, since they preserve many illuminating details of English social history that have not survived elsewhere.

The following article is intended to describe the contents of one such manuscript collection, and to analyse and edit one of the items in particular: a set of English and Latin *vulgaria* or school exercises. The manuscript in question is Lincoln College, Oxford, MS Lat. 129 (E), which is now deposited in the Bodleian Library.[2] A full description of what it contains will be found in Dr. N. R. Ker's *Medieval Manuscripts in British Libraries*, volume III,[3] so that

---

[1] The best modern discussion of late-medieval English grammatical MSS is by D. Thomson, *A Descriptive Catalogue of Middle English Grammatical Texts* (New York & London 1979). It contains a good bibliography. A list of medieval English and European grammatical works is being published by G. L. Bursill-Hall, 'A Check-List of Incipits of Medieval Latin Grammatical Treatises,' *Traditio* 35 (1978) 439–74, and in progress.

[2] I acknowledge gratefully the permission of the rector and fellows of Lincoln College, Oxford, to publish material from the manuscript.

[3] Oxford: Clarendon Press, forthcoming. I am indebted to Dr. Ker for his kindness in communicating his description of the MS to me before publication. The manuscript is also discussed, and item 3a is edited, by Edward Wilson, 'An Unpublished Poem on Plant-

only its most important features need be mentioned here. The volume con-consists of 120 folios, arranged in five quires of paper and parchment, which have been later bound together. It contains 40 items in writing: 28 wholly in Latin, nine in a mixture of Latin and English (items 3b–d, 3f, 4b–c, 5a–b, 5i), and three in English alone (items 3a, 3e, 3i). The principal scribe and compiler of the volume was a certain Thomas Schort, who wrote the earliest dated item in 1427 (item 1f) and who died in 1465. The script is in a variety of styles, and the question arises how much of it is in Schort's hand. Four items are certainly signed by him (items 1f–g, 2b, 2e), and five others relate to episodes in his career (items 2a, 3g–h, 5c, 5j). A further four make up a group of grammatical works which also seem to be connected with Schort's career and were probably copied by him (items 4c, 4e, 5a–b). These thirteen texts are written in a mixture of secretary and anglicana styles which vary considerably. Most of the other contents of the volume are in similar scripts, and even those which seem to be different may also be by Schort, in view of the variations in his probable writings. There is no sign that his pages passed into anyone else's possession during his lifetime, and it is possible that the whole collection was compiled over a long period (1427–65), hence the scriptural variations. The likelihood is that most of the manuscript was copied by Schort, with only a few additions by other hands, notably items 1h, 2a, and perhaps 3e.

Thanks to his manuscript and to the assistance of other records, it is pos-sible to reconstruct the outlines of Schort's life. He was probably born soon after 1400, not later than 1406 in view of the date of his ordination to the priesthood. The circumstances of his later career make it likely that he was born or brought up in Bristol, north Somerset, or northwest Wiltshire. The first dated reference to him occurs in his manuscript on 8 May 1427, when he finished transcribing a Latin tract on the nominative of nouns (item 1f) at Bristol, 'over the new gate' (*super novam portam*).[4] Newgate, or rather the building above it, was the site of a grammar school during the middle of the fifteenth century, taught by a secular chaplain, Robert Londe.[5] Since Schort was at least twenty-one at this time, he must have been an advanced pupil or a schoolmaster, either in the school itself or as a visitor to it. He seems to have stayed in Bristol for the next two years as a layman or a clerk in minor orders,[6] until on 15 January 1430 he secured a 'title' or guarantee of support from the canons of Keynsham Abbey near Bristol, preparatory to receiving

---

Names from Lincoln College, Oxford, MS. Lat. 129 (E.),' *Notes and Queries* NS 26 (1979) 504–8.

[4] Lincoln College, Oxford, MS Lat. 129 (E.) fol. 18.

[5] On Londe and his school see Nicholas Orme, *Education in the West of England, 1066–1548* (Exeter 1976) 38–40.

[6] Since he transcribed item 1g at Bristol on 20 May 1428 (MS fol. 24).

full ordination.[7] He was probably ordained acolyte and subdeacon soon afterwards, but the ordination records of Worcester diocese, in which the greater part of Bristol lay, are missing for the first six months of 1430. They reappear in time to show that he was ordained deacon at Alvechurch on 10 June and priest at Worcester on 23 September.[8] The date of the latter event requires him to be distinguished from a priest or priests of the same name beneficed in north Somerset in 1428, although the parties concerned may have been kinsmen.[9]

Between 1430 and 1436 Schort left Bristol to become chaplain of a chantry in Salisbury Cathedral. The chantry was a new foundation for two priests, with stipends of £8 a year each, which had recently been erected by Walter Lord Hungerford, a major landowner in northeast Somerset and west Wiltshire.[10] The priests were nominated by Walter himself,[11] and if Schort was born in or connected with the areas of Hungerford power, this would explain his migration to Salisbury. The date of his admission to the chantry is not recorded in the chapter act-books of the cathedral, which contain few records of chantry priests, but he was certainly there on 25 March 1436 when he became liable to pay the clerical subsidy granted to the crown in the previous winter.[12] At least one item in the manuscript comes from Schort's Salisbury years: a letter of 1435, not in his handwriting, from the bishop's official to a rural dean in Dorset (item 2a), and two other texts may do so. These are some notes and a prayer (items 3g–h) relating to St. Osmund, first bishop of Salisbury, the campaign for whose canonisation was in progress at this time, before its successful completion in 1456. We do not know how long Schort stayed at Salisbury, but he may have done so until he was admitted on 15 April 1445 to the vicarage of Wootton Bassett in northwest Wiltshire, on the nomination of the abbot and monks of Stanley Abbey.[13] Wootton, which was valued at £11 gross per annum in 1535,[14] was worth much less to Schort since he was obliged to pay £5 a year as a life pension to the previous vicar. Perhaps for this reason he gave up the benefice soon afterwards. On 24 September he ex-

---

[7] MS fol. 120ᵛ.

[8] Worcester, Hereford & Worcester Record Office, Reg. Thomas Polton, fols. 104–5.

[9] *The Register of John Stafford, Bishop of Bath and Wells, 1425–1443*, ed. T. Scott Holmes (Somerset Record Society 31; 1915) I 63, 96, 150.

[10] London, Public Record Office, Exch. KR, Clerical Subsidy Rolls, E 179/52/147.

[11] Salisbury, Dean & Chapter Archives, Reg. Harding, fol. 104ᵛ.

[12] Above, note 10. For the date of the subsidy see *Calendar of Fine Rolls, 1430–7* (London 1936) 269–72.

[13] Trowbridge, Wiltshire Record Office, Reg. William Aiscough, fol. 76.

[14] *Valor Ecclesiasticus tempore Henrici VIII*, ed. J. Caley (London 1810–24) II 130.

changed it with another cleric for the rectory of Bremilham in the same region, two miles west of Malmesbury.[15]

Bremilham, at first sight, seems the exchange of a Simple Jack. It was valued at only £4 9s. 8d. in 1535,[16] and must have been worth far less in the 1440s than the Salisbury chantry, yet Schort held on to it until he died in 1465.[17] Its attraction probably stemmed from its being a small and thinly populated parish (which has since been united with Foxley), whose incumbent did not need to reside permanently. No surprise attaches to the discovery that in 1455, when we next hear of Schort on his appointment by the bishop of Salisbury as one of three penitentiaries to hear the Lenten confessions of the clergy in the rural deanery of Malmesbury, he was described as 'chaplain in the church of St Paul of Malmesbury.'[18] This was the parish church of the town, next to the abbey and now demolished. By this time Schort was probably living in Malmesbury, acting as a chantry priest or assistant curate in the town, and going out to Bremilham merely on Sundays and festivals. Lesser clergy of this kind were generally paid £4 or £5 a year, which together with the profits of Bremilham would have given Schort an annual income of £8 or £9. His appointment as penitentiary shows that he had a good reputation for knowledge or behaviour; his two colleagues were both entitled 'Master.' One item in the manuscript probably dates from his Malmesbury years: a quotation from William of Malmesbury relating to the tomb in the abbey there alleged to belong to the early medieval scholar Johannes Scottus Eriugena (item 5c, fol. 103v).[19]

All that is certain has now been said about Schort's career, but two conjectures are worth mentioning. First, the fact that his miscellany consists so largely of grammatical texts and moral poems of the kind read in fifteenth-century schools, makes it likely that he spent part of his life as a schoolmaster. Both Salisbury and Malmesbury had medieval schools, the masters of which are not known by name when Schort was working there.[20] Second, he may have concluded his life in London, in view of the will of a Thomas Short, chaplain in the city church of St. Mary Abchurch, which survives in the registers of the prerogative court of Canterbury.[21] The will was dated 22 February 1465 and was proved on 27 June of the same year, after the testator's death.

---

[15] Reg. Aiscough, fol. 82v.

[16] *Valor Ecclesiasticus* II 139.

[17] Wiltshire Record Office, Reg. Richard Beauchamp, fol. 119.

[18] *Ibid.* fol. 41.

[19] The quotation is to be found in William of Malmesbury, *De gestis regum Anglorum*, ed. W. Stubbs (Rolls Series; London 1887) I 131–32.

[20] On these schools see Orme (above, note 5) 65–78, 101.

[21] Public Record Office, Probate Court of Canterbury, Registered Copy Wills, Prob 11/5 fol. 69ʳ⁻ᵛ (PCC 9 Godyn).

The evidence for supposing that the two Thomas Shorts are the same is suggestive but not conclusive. The date of the testator's death between February and June accords with the admission of Schort's successor to Bremilham on 10 October 1465,[22] and although the will mentions no other place than St. Mary Abchurch, it would not have been registered in the prerogative court unless the testator had possessed goods in at least one other diocese besides London. It is not impossible that Schort, having already abandoned his parish for Malmesbury, eventually went to work in London as a schoolmaster, curate, or chantry priest. Unfortunately, the will itself fails to settle the matter. It provides for its author's burial in St. Mary Abchurch and leaves tiny sums of money for the upkeep of lights in the building. The rest of the testator's goods (which were not described) were bequeathed to John and William Short, his brothers.

Thomas Schort can therefore be summarised as a secular priest from the west of England, of modest intellectual attainments, who never rose far above the lowest ranks of the clergy but who enjoyed a good reputation with his bishop. Whether or not he was a practising schoolmaster, his collection of transcripts is certainly schoolmasterly in character. Of the forty items within it, the largest group (nineteen) consists of grammatical texts of the level studied in school, and the second largest (nine) of specimens of Latin poetry which also resemble those of the school curriculum. The collection, in short, is that of a schoolmaster rather than a scholar of university level or a man of letters. Those items which are not connected with school education can be dismissed fairly quickly. One or two are autobiographical, such as the copy of Schort's title for ordination (item 5j) and the letter written during his residence at Salisbury from the bishop's official (item 2a). There are a few religious texts: part of a Latin sermon on robbery (item 2f) and the two pieces, already mentioned, referring to St. Osmund (items 3g–h). Three others — a list of the articles of the faith and of the sacraments (item 1e), a list of signs presaging the Day of Judgment (item 4d), and a catalogue in verse of the saints in the Church's calendar (item 5h) — though primarily religious works, were also suitable for use by a schoolmaster, many of whose pupils would aim at becoming clerics. There are also three pieces wholly in English: a rhymed and alliterated poem containing names of plants in alphabetical order (item 3a),[23] Lydgate's verses on the kings of England from William the Conqueror to Henry VI (item 3i), and a set of 34 medical recipes in prose (item 3e), the latter not certainly in Schort's hand. Even these pieces, if authentic, reinforce the picture of a mind more interested in information than in works of the imagination.

---

[22] Above, note 17.
[23] Edited by E. Wilson (above, note 3).

The school texts themselves, as already explained, consist of both grammatical and literary works, mostly in Latin but including a few English glosses
and translations. Five of the grammars are in question-and-answer form in
prose (items 1c, 1f, 2d, 4e, 4g), and others are wholly or partly in verse (items
1f, 2b, 3b–c, 4c, 4f). They do not amount to a complete course of Latin grammar, but cover selected topics which interested the copyist, who, if he were
a schoolmaster, must have had access to other books as well. Six texts deal
with the grammar of nouns, including the nominative case (item 1f), genders
(items 1g, 2b), irregularities (item 2d), Greek nouns (item 4f), and words beginning with S (item 3b). Two are concerned with verbs: one on their grammar in
general (item 1c) and the other on deponent verbs alone (item 3c). Item 2c
is a list of numbers from one to a million, equating the Latin words with the
Roman and Arabic figures. There are three works relating to the use of Latin
in practice: a tract in prose and verse on Latin syntax (item 4e), a set of 115
vulgaria or sentences in English and Latin suitable for translation work (item
5a), and some dialogues in Latin prose about student life in Oxford (item 2e).
The latter illustrate grammatical usages and probably provided training in
the speaking of Latin too. There is also a short tract explaining the terminology used in Latin grammar (item 4g). The pieces of Latin literature are mainly
in verse, but are not easily identifiable with other known works. Most are
complete poems, but item 5g is a collection of extracts from classical and medieval poets including Horace and Theodulus. The poems are largely moralistic.
Some are collections of wise proverbs, such as 5b and 5d, which begin respectively by nothing that 'while your purse rings, people crown you with praise' and
'he is a hostile father unless his son feels the rod.' Others call to mind the wickedness of the world ('I see too many men who speak perversities' — item 5f)
and the insufficiency of human life ('If you are beautiful, great, and strong,
what then?' — item 4a). Their sentiments resemble those of poems such as
the *Cartula*, the *Distichs of Cato* and the proverbs of Alain de Lille, which were
read in medieval schools.[24] A short list of precepts for good behaviour at the
table (item 1a) belongs to another common genre of medieval educational
literature.

Where did Schort's grammatical texts originate, and how was he able to
collect them? The manuscript offers a little guidance on the subject. Two or
three of the works appear to derive from Oxford: the Latin dialogues, which
contain references to scholars in the city (item 2e), some of the moral Latin
verses which are given a heading 'Oxon' (item 5b, fol. 101), and the tract on
the genders of nouns, *De cognitione generum* (item 1g). The latter, which also
occurs in three other manuscripts, is ascribed in two of them to John Leland,

---

[24] On these texts see Nicholas Orme, *English Schools in the Middle Ages* (London 1973)
102–5.

the famous Oxford grammar master and grammatical author who was working there by about 1401 and died in 1428.[25] Oxford was the chief centre of grammatical study and teaching in medieval England, and the influence of Oxford material on a collector in the nearby English shires merely serves to confirm this fact. Leland's tract came to Schort's hands via Bristol, which was probably important as a provincial centre of grammatical learning. Schort transcribed it there in 1428, a year after he had copied the tract *De nominativo casu*, on the nominative of nouns, at Newgate school (item 1f). That work is also preserved in another manuscript, written in northeast Wales.[26] Yet another tract on irregular nouns, *Quot modis fit ethroclisis* (item 2d), is described at the end as 'following the use of Kond,' the letter K being apparently an overelaborate attempt at an L. 'Lond' would be short either for London, indicating a grammatical work used by masters there, or more likely for Robert Londe, the master of Newgate school. Finally, there are headings in four of the tracts relating to 'Wotton' (items 4c, 5a–b) and to 'Chyppnam' (items 4e, 5a–b). These appear to identify material originating from or copied at places in south Gloucestershire or north Wiltshire: Chippenham, which may have possessed a school at this time, and Wootton Bassett or more probably Wotton-under-Edge, the site of an endowed grammar school founded in 1384.[27] In this way the world of Latin study and teaching in which Schort lived is seen to have been a living and developing one. Grammatical works were constantly being rewritten and revised, especially at Oxford, and were making their way from one local school to another.

The part of Schort's manuscript of easiest and most immediate use to the historian of education consists of the *vulgaria* (item 5a, fols. 92–99): 115 sentences and passages in English, each followed by a Latin equivalent, which were probably meant as exercises in translation. Several collections of similar *vulgaria* are preserved in manuscripts and printed schoolbooks of the fifteenth and early sixteenth centuries, and those transcribed by Schort are among the oldest surviving examples.[28] They seem to have come from three sources. Numbers 1–79, which include two references to Bristol in general (nos. 33, 77) and one to Newgate school in particular (no. 20), doubtless originated from that school and probably from Robert Londe, its master. They allude to the arrest of Lollards 'in dyverse scheris,' which best suits the years between 1414 and 1431 (no. 74). Numbers 80–99 are headed by the word 'Wotton' already discussed, and include several sentences which are shorter than those in the Bristol section. They mention a visit by the king to Calais (no. 92), which

---

25 Thomson (above, note 1) 6–8.

26 *Ibid.* 129.

27 On Wotton-under-Edge school see Orme (above, note 5) 190–99.

28 On early *vulgaria* see Orme (above, note 24) 98–100.

must refer to the years 1415–21 or to 1430. Numbers 100–15 are prefaced by the heading 'Chyppnam'; they have no datable references. In general, therefore, the *vulgaria* probably originated among schoolmasters in Bristol and its region, not earlier than the mid-1410s and possibly as late as the early 1430s. They were copied by Schort at any time between the late 1420s and the middle of the fifteenth century.

Vulgaria in general, and these examples are no exceptions, set out to teach pupils how to handle Latin grammar, especially its trickier constructions, and ease the pain of the process by basing the work upon incidents of everyday life and speech which would interest the pupils and amuse them. Most of the sentences in Schort's collection are concerned with problems of syntax, but a few attempt to increase the vocabulary of nouns as well (e.g. nos. 9, 13, 25). On several occasions alternative ways are suggested for translating phrases into Latin (e.g. nos. 3, 9, 20, 22, 40). The matter of the sentences consists of allusions to daily life, scraps of conversation, proverbs, witticisms, and pieces of wise advice. The sequence appears at first sight to be unplanned, but it is not entirely so, since adjoining sentences often deal with the same word or construction: *applaudere* (nos. 14–15), *quanto . . . tanto* (nos. 34–35) and *interest* (nos. 55–56). In the Bristol sentences there seem to be allusions to the passing of time during a single spring. We proceed from Candlemas eve, 1 February (no. 36), via the period before Lent (no. 42), two apparent references to the Lenten confessions (nos. 50, 57), the end of Lent (no. 57), and the coming of spring (no. 59). This progression, which is parallelled in at least one other set of *vulgaria*,[29] may indicate a master devising sentences from day to day for his pupils to translate, during the end of a single winter.

The value of *vulgaria* as a whole lies in the insights they allow into the organisation of schools: their buildings and facilities, their masters and pupils, their curricular and extra-curricular activities. The best-known *vulgaria*, those of the early sixteenth century, were composed at well-organised boarding schools such as Eton College and Magdalen College, Oxford, and portray a school life which was correspondingly well organised. The sentences in Schort's manuscript are rather different. They come from schools a century earlier, whose organisation was more rudimentary. There was a classroom, and some boys may have lodged with the schoolmaster, but most probably lived at home or boarded in private houses (practices hinted at in nos. 7 and 79). The school community was weaker and the school less of a focus of its pupils' lives, which were more involved with the life of the outside world. So there is less about the school itself in Schort's *vulgaria*, and more about life in general. An actual

---

[29] Nicholas Orme, 'An Early-Tudor Oxford Schoolbook,' *Renaissance Quarterly* 34 (1981) 15.; now below p 127.

school (Newgate) is identified only once (no. 20), and its furnishings are not particularised. Nor is the schoolmaster. He is mentioned eight times (nos. 19, 21, 40–41, 68, 80, 108, 111), but he is not clearly described and it is never certain that he himself is speaking. He is a shadowy figure compared with the schoolmasters of the early sixteenth-century *vulgaria*. This is only to be expected. Schoolmasters in the 1410s and '20s were much less conscious of their own identity and importance than were their successors a century later. Robert Londe, the master of Newgate school, was apparently active in Bristol for many years between about 1419 and his death in 1462. Yet nearly all the documentary references to him call him 'chaplain,' not 'schoolmaster,' and although he was buried in St. Peter's church (Bristol) with a brass effigy over his tomb-slab, the inscription too described him merely as a chaplain, and his effigy portrayed him in priestly vestments with no indication of his function as a teacher.[30]

On the subject of the master's pupils the *vulgaria* are a little more informative. The Bristol sentences especially suggest the varieties of boys who attended Newgate school. As in other town schools of the period, they came both from the immediate neighbourhood and from places farther away where schools did not exist. One boy has a father who dwells a mere stone's throw away (no. 79), another is from Devonshire, over fifty miles distant (no. 20), and a third, who has lived in Bristol for only three years or so, must also have come from elsewhere (no. 77). There is a mixture of wealthy and poor. 'Children stond yn a row, sum wel a-rayd, sum evel a-rayd' (no. 65). Some of the poor are assisted to study by patrons, the bishop of St. David's being singled out for praise in this respect (no. 55); others (at Wotton) are reminded to take special heed to their books, since they will have no help in life but their own knowledge (no. 98). At the other extreme there are children of wealthy parents. One has a buttoned wristlet (no. 18), another's father maintains a good household (no. 71), and the boy from Devonshire is a 'gay squyere' (no. 20). Their destinations in life were also varied. Some, like Schort himself if he did study at Newgate school, became priests; others, like the squire who is to be married to the daughter of a Bristolian (no. 20), remained literate laymen. The squire's career was parallelled in real life by that of William Worcester, the antiquary and scholar who was born in Bristol in 1415. He evidently went to school in the town, and since he mentions both Newgate school and Robert Londe in his writings,[31] he may well have been studying there at this very time, in about 1430. Worcester proceeded to Oxford, but took a

---

[30] Orme (above, note 5) 40.
[31] *Itineraria Simonis Simeonis et Willelmi de Worcester*, ed. J. Nasmith (Cambridge 1778) 178.

secular post as secretary to Sir John Fastolf and later married.[32] There must have been others like him at Newgate school, preparing for careers in trade or household administration.

Some indications can also be found of the daily life and organisation of the schools to which the three parts of the *vulgaria* refer. School begins early in the morning, 'at mortyde' (no. 70), which from school records of the early sixteenth century we know to have been at about six o'clock. There is a pause for breakfast at or after the ecclesiastical service of prime (at about eight or nine o'clock by modern reckoning — no. 110), and another for dinner at mid-day (nos. 70, 97). During school the master teaches busily (no. 68), principally no doubt by oral dictation and questioning. The boys consequently imbibe much grammatical material through the ear and commit it to heart, but they also *study* (no 30), implying the perusal of written material, and books are indeed mentioned (no. 98). As well as listening, rehearsing, and studying, they also do exercises, probably both in their heads and in writing on paper or wax. The making of 'latins' (Latin sentences) is mentioned, and can be difficult (no. 43). The study of comparison likewise gives cause for grief (no. 91). An important feature of the lessons is the 'apposing' or questioning and examining of boys by the master, which is mentioned seven times (nos. 4, 19, 35, 80, 107, 111, 115). The boys answer the questions put to them, and try to do so readily (nos. 35, 108). It is bad to be 'concluded': confounded in argument or found wrong in your knowledge (no. 107). Good pupils are praised (nos. 4, 30, 108), but the bad are beaten with a birch-rod or a whip (no. 27). Beating is conceived, here as elsewhere, as a positive aid to education which makes a pupil good and quiet (no. 38). There is some comradeship among the boys; several mentions are made of schoolfellows (e.g. nos. 27, 38, 41, etc.), and they are exhorted to behave well to one another (no. 67). But sometimes there are fights (no. 83), and even murmurings against the master (no. 41). The school year seems to begin at Michaelmas (no. 77), and is varied by holidays, one occupation of which is walking in the fields (no. 16). The number of years spent at school doubtless varied, depending on the extent of knowledge required, but one boy has apparently spent over three years (no. 77). Five or six were usually necessary in medieval schools to master the grammar course.[33]

The attention of Schort's *vulgaria*, however, is not confined to what goes on in school. There are also allusions to life elsewhere, both in the religious and in the secular spheres. Religion was an obvious subject for *vulgaria*, since some pupils were destined to become clerics and all were expected to be trained in Christian knowledge and practices. Schort's *vulgaria* include about eighteen

---

[32] On Worcester's career see A. B. Emden, *A Biographical Register of the University of Oxford to A.D. 1500* (Oxford 1957–59) III 2086–87.

[33] Orme (above, note 24) 133–34.

religious references. Several draw attention to church buildings and what goes on inside them. In church, the clergy occupy the chancel (no. 103), where they perform the daily offices and celebrate mass (no. 89). The parish clerk rings a bell when services are due (no. 110). The laity use the nave (no. 103), where they receive baptism at the font (no. 102) and where the clergy wait for them hooded to hear their confessions (no. 50). Religious controversy intrudes here since the layman is advised to confess to his parish priest, not to a friar, which reflects the rivalry between the two species of clergy over this pastoral work (no. 29). The author of the Bristol *vulgaria*, probably Robert Londe, was evidently a partisan of the secular clergy. Other sentences contain precepts for the good Christian. He should observe the Church's times and seasons; indeed, time itself is sacred, the hours of the day being identified by the daily services (nos. 97, 110), and the course of the year marked out by flesh and fasting days (no. 23) and by the cycle of seasons and festivals: Candlemas, Lent, and Easter. There are encouraging references to fasting (no. 36), receiving the sacrament at Easter (no. 57), going on pilgrimage to Compostella for the remission of one's sins (no. 61), and observing chastity which is rewarded in heaven (no. 113). Heresy is mentioned once, in relation to the arrest of Lollards (no. 74). The Christian teaching in the *vulgaria*, however, cannot be regarded as austere. If fasting is commended, there are also appreciative mentions of food and feasting (nos. 37, 112). So too, the single *vulgare* which praises chastity is outnumbered by those which feature marriage, love, and ladies (nos. 20, 39, 114). In religious terms we are far from the age of the Reformation, and the *vulgaria* reinforce the impression of a school for training laymen as well as clerics, and of a Church with a fairly tolerant ethos for its trainee clergy.

There are also evocations of secular life in the *vulgaria*, especially in the section relating to Bristol. It is a place of much resort. Men come into the town on market days, some riding horses (no. 66), and far more strangers visit it, because of its port, than go to Coventry which is of similar size (no. 33). It is a centre of skilled tradesmen — the mason, the goldsmith, and the manuscript illuminator (no. 52) — and someone, perhaps the master, has ordered a missal from the illuminator to be decorated with blue azure (no. 46). The problem of town life is the price and availability of food, and the Bristol butchers are particularly unpopular in this respect. They sell meat at a high price in the days before Lent (no. 42) and repeat the practice at Easter when fasting is over (no. 8). The Wotton *vulgaria* also mention a bread shortage, when nothing can be had but a loaf the size of a man's fist for a halfpenny, which would scarcely fill one hungry boy at his dinner (no. 94). Food is mentioned several times in the *vulgaria*, doubtless because of its popularity with the pupils. The diet of every day — cabbage stalks, herring (no. 23), and rashers of meat (no. 97) — contrasts with the luxury dishes which were prob-

ably rarely or never available: boar's head and breast of veal (no. 26), meat
with green sauce (no. 37), young geese with garlic (no. 59), and fritters and
pancakes (no. 112). Little is said of the world beyond the immediate vicinity,
but the Bristol *vulgaria* evoke a fair manor house with a moat and drawbridge
(no. 44), while those of Wotton mention the king at Calais (no. 92) and describe
a judicial combat which the narrator has just seen at Westminster (no. 96).

The *vulgaria* in Schort's manuscript, as has been noted, are among the earliest
surviving examples of their kind. In later times the genre was to develop in
scale and sophistication, culminating in the fine specimens written in the early
sixteenth century at Oxford and Eton by masters such as William Horman,
Robert Whittinton, and the anonymous author of Magdalen College School.[34]
Compared with their products, the *vulgaria* of Bristol, Wotton, and 'Chyppnam' look crude and primitive. Their style is matter-of-fact and lacking in
elegance; only once does it reach the epigrammatical level of the early Tudor
examples (no. 31), and the sketches of everyday life are shorter and less ambitious. This contrast, of course, is usually visible between the earlier and later
specimens of a given form, but the later could not have evolved without the
earlier. Moreover, the lack of sophistication of Schort's *vulgaria* has preserved
one thing more freshly than the Tudor authors have done: 'the lore and
language of schoolchildren.' In the Tudor collections, the evocations of
schoolboy life and speech are much more shaped by literary artistry, whereas
those in Schort's manuscript seem to contain, with greater fidelity, actual
scraps of fifteenth-century schoolroom speech and song. Tudor *vulgaria* are
definitely written by schoolmasters; Schort's, at times, could almost be the
work of the boys themselves: 'Lyʒt lefe of þe lynd ley þe dewe a-downe'
(no. 5) sounds very much like a line from a popular lyric; 'Blodles an boneles
stondyth by-hynd þe door' (no. 6) suggests schoolboys frightening one another
with stories of ghosts; 'Þu sc[h]alt have a kast afore, for a botyn of þy poynet'
(no. 18) seems to preserve a real playground transaction in which one boy
offers another a 'go' at casting dice or throwing a missile, in return for a button
of his decorated wristlet; while 'Y say a nakyd man bere fyve lovis in hys
lappe' (no. 49) looks like a riddle, perhaps with the meaning 'hand' or 'foot.'
Finally, there are two snatches of the very simple rhymes that children have
made up and sung in every century. The first,

> Y say a sparw
> Schotte an arow
> By an harow
> Into a barow (no. 25),

---

[34] William Horman, *Vulgaria*, ed. M. R. James (Roxburghe Club 169; Oxford 1926);
The Vulgaria of John Stanbridge and Robert Whittinton, ed. Beatrice White (EETS os 187;
London 1932); *A Fifteenth Century School Book*, ed. W. Nelson (Oxford 1956).

is an early allusion to that sparrowish archery which was later to lead to the death of Cock Robin. The second,

> [One more than] thre and fewer þan fyv[e]
> Y hadde upon my cule [i.e. behind] strokes ful ryve;
>
> [One more than] thre and fewer þan fyve
> Y plokkyd appullys ful ryve (nos. 105–6),

is a very simple riddle, with the answer 'four' in both verses, but it also has the movement of a rhyme for skipping or for counting out. The presence of matter like this in the *vulgaria*, unshaped and unadorned, is another testimony to the importance of fifteenth- and early sixteenth-century school texts. The authors and collectors of these works, in trying to put over Latin to children in an enticing way, descended for the purpose to the level of children's minds and to the subjects which interested them. By doing so, they anticipated the modern interest in childhood, and the many more sophisticated attempts which have since been made to evoke its world and record its folklore.[35]

AN EDITION OF
THE ENGLISH AND LATIN 'VULGARIA'
IN LINCOLN COLLEGE, OXFORD,
MS LAT. 129 (E.), fols. 92–99

The following changes have been made to the original text for the reader's convenience. Each *vulgare* is numbered and the Latin portions are inset to the right (except for nos. 45, 72, 76, 80, and 103–4, where there is only a Latin version). Abbreviations are expanded in italics, and a few omissions are supplied in square brackets. Modern usage is followed with regard to punctuation and capital letters (except for proper nouns, which follow the MS). Word elements written separately in the MS, which are nowadays joined together, are linked by hyphens, and an oblique sign is inserted to separate alternative Latin renderings of the English when these are given. Scribal cancellations, and additions by other hands, are not noted. No other changes have been made to the text, except for four corrections to the English portions of nos. 52, 98, 106, and 114, which are described in the notes.

---

[35] This subject is also touched on by Orme (above, note 24) 137–41, and in 'Schoolmasters, 1307–1509,' *Profession, Vocation and Culture in Medieval England*, ed. C. H. Clough (Liverpool 1982) 236–37; now above pp 69–70, 81–2.

[fol. 92ʳ or p. 187]

1. Schort hors sone y-whyped, lytell mete sone y-flypyd.

   Curtus equus sito strigillatur, et modicus sibus illico liguritur.

2. Hyt ys grete feleny a mon to say a word *and* noun to with-say þe same.

   Inmensum dedecus est hominem dicere verbum in publica audiencia *et* protinus idem dedicere.

3. Þe heyward haþ y-dryue my bestys to pond *and* þerfor crystys corsse make hys chekys fatte!

   Agellarius minauit pecora mea ad inclusorium et

   idio anatema cristi inpinguat males suas / vel saginat buccas

   suas / vel incrasset fauces suas!

4. Y Jon aposyd schalbe preysyd.

   Ego Johannes in opposito laudabor.

5. Lyʒt lefe of þe lynd ley þe dewe a downe.

   Leue folium tilie decucias rorem.

6. Blodles an boneles stondyth by-hynd þe dore.

   Exangue et exarsatum stant pone ostium.

7. Bymyfey, y went to bedde soperelees tonyʒt þat whas, *and* þerfore crystys curs [in] þe botelere-ys chekys!

   Medius fidius, ibam ad lectum insenis nocte elapsa, et idio anatema cristi insit faucibus acaliculis!

8. By ryʒt, bowcherys schold not sylle flesche so dere in þis tyme of ʒer as þey dowyth a-bowte ester.

   Eiure, a macellarijs non venirent carnes tam care illo tempore anni sicut ci[r]citer festum pasche.

9. Y say a goldfynche fedyng hymsylfe apon o þystyl yn [a] þystyly place.

   Vidi vnum cardoelum / vel vnum cardoelem passentem se super cardonem in cardeto.

---

¹ Short hors: B. J. & H. W. Whiting, *Proverbs, Sentences and Proverbial Phrases from English Writings mainly before 1500* (Cambridge, Mass. 1968) H525. Y-whyped: curried. Y-flypyd: the nearest medieval verb recorded is 'flipe' meaning 'to strip.' The Latin form 'liguritur' means 'licked up.'

² Noun: anon.

³ Pond: pound. Inclusorium: is glossed in Latin 'catabulum.'

⁴ Aposyd: questioned or examined in grammar.

⁵ The lightness of the lime-tree leaf occurs as an image in other medieval English writings (Whiting, *Proverbs* L139).

⁶ Exarsatum: *recte* 'exossatum.'

⁷ Bymyfey: added later.

⁸ By ryʒt: added later.

[fol. 92^v or p. 188]

10. Fyr of sponys, love of gromys, ale in a tankerd, al ys weyward.

   Ignis quisquiliar*um*, amor garcion*um*, *et* ceruisia in amphera, semp*er* sunt res fugitiue.

11. Þe ner þe chyrche, þe fer fro god.

   Tanto pr*o*pior ad ecclesiam, tanto remocior a deo.

12. Þys strayte schone wryngeþ heuel my tone.

   Isti stricti sotilares male angunt articulos meos.

13. Hyt ys not secur to goo alone by a þevi place, for þ*er* lotyth þeuys.

   Non e*st* securu*m* p*er*gere solu*m* p*er* cribrifuru*m*, *quonia*m *ibi* latitant cliptes / fures / siue latrones.

14. Þe kyng y-drad *and* louyd w*yche* schal haue mery wordle.

   Rege ente illo que*m* aliqui timent et dilecto nobis bon*us* mu*n*d*us* applaudet, pro rege temito si esset tale.

15. Þes worle ys mony manys.

   Iste mu*n*d*us* pluribus applaudit.

16. We beþ þe childryn þat schal walke y flowry medys *and* yn dylettabyl placys yn holy days.

   Nos sum*us* pu*er*i qui spaciabunt*ur* in ti*m*marijs *et* in locis apricis in dieb*us* festiuis.

17. Y am sclepy for þe wed*er* y[s] slepy.

   Ego su*m* somnolent*us* q*uia* aura e*st* somnefera.

18. Þu sclalt haue a kast afore for a botyn of þy poynet.

   Tu h*a*bebis iactu*m* pr*e*ambulu*m* pr*o* nodulo manicelle tue.

19. Hyt befallyth þe mayst*er* to bete roberd *and* me ȝyf we fayle wan we beþ aposyd yn a lyȝt matyr.

   Int*er*est a magistro vapulare mea et roberti si deficiam*us* cu*m* in mat*er*ia facili nobis apponat*ur*.

20. Sum gay squyere of deuynschere schal wed my dowȝt*er*, þe weche go to schole ap-on þe new ȝate.

---

[10] Sponys: chips. The first two elements of the proverb are recorded elsewhere in the late 15th century (Whiting, *Proverbs* F187).

[11] *Ibid.* C251.

[13] Lotyth: lurk. Cribrifurum: presumably 'a sieve of thieves.'

[14] Wordle: world. Temito: perhaps meant for 'timeto.'

[15] Worl: world.

[16] Timmarijs: presumably 'thymy' from Latin 'timus.'

[18] Kast: presumably a throw at dice or with a missile. Afore: beforehand. Poynet: a poignet (wristlet or bracelet).

[20] Scolatiso: *recte* 'scolatisat.'

Cuidam armigero curioso de comitatu deuanie nubet filia mea /
*ve*l sic: quidam curiosus armiger filiam [fol. 93ʳ or p. 189] meam
ducet in vxorem, qui scolatiso su*per* nouam porta*m*.

21. For soþe j schal preyse þe ȝyf þu spedilych teche me.

Nimiru*m* a me licebis tu si efficaci*ter* docueris me.

22. My fadyr ys a gode housband and kan gode skole of husbandry, *and* my
moder ys a gode houswyffe and can gode skyle on houswyffeschyppe.

Pa*ter* meus e*st* bonus yconom*us* e*t* scit bona*m* racione*m* de yconomia /
*ve*l yconomatu, e*t* mater mea e*st* matrona e*t* scit bona*m* racione*m*
de matroni / *ve*l matronatu.

23. Y had as lefe be se*ru*yd wi*th* a cawlestokke as wi*th* heryng yn flesche day.

Tam acceptu*m* e*st* mi*hi* mi*hi* se*ru*iri cu*m* maguderi quam cu*m* alece
in die carnea.

24. Þis brody henne haþ þe pyppe.

Ista gallina incubosa ha*bet* scream / siue petuitam.

25. Y say a sparw schotte an arow by an harow into a barow.

Vidi passerem sagittare sagittam *per* herpicam in baiulatoriu*m* /
siue in cineuectoriu*m*.

26. Bowchere, how lowys þu þe borys hede, þe spald of motyn, þe brest of
vele *and* loyne of porke, at on word?

Carnifex, qua*n*ti / *ve*l qua*n*to liceris cap*ut* aprinu*m*, spatula*m* ouina*m*,
pectusculu*m* uitilinu*m* e*t* lu*m*bum porcinum, ad vnu*m* verbu*m*?

27. My felow y-bete wi*th* a byrch ȝerd, y ham to be bete wi*th* a whyppe.

Socio meo vapulante cu*m* virga lentiscina, ego sum vapulaturus
cu*m* scutica.

[fol. 93ᵛ or p. 190]

28. My belsyre þe whyche ys totheles byhouyth tender mete, *and* þes sowgyng
chyld þe whyche ys totheles by-houyth pappe.

Auo meo qui est edentat*us* oportun*us* e*st* cibus ten*er*, e*t* huic pusioni
lactenti qui est edentul*us* oportunum e*st* pappatu*m*.

29. Owre parson schal schryve me yn lent, holyist of tymys, *and* not a fryre
noþer non oþer relygyusmon.

Nostro rectori confitebor ego in quadragesma, sanctimo temporu*m*,
e*t* non fratri nec alicui viro religioso.

---

²³ Cawlestokke: cabbage stalk.

²⁴ Pyppe: pip, a respiratory disease of poultry.

²⁶ Lowys: loves. Spald: shoulder. A similar sentence occurs in some 15th-century *vulgaria*
from Winchester: 'Draper, howe louys þu a yerde of þis clothe, þe whiche ys well colowryde?'
(British Library, Add. MS 60577, fol. 73).

²⁸ Belsyre: grandfather. Sowgyng: sucking.

²⁹ Sanctimo: *recte* 'sanctissima.'

30. Jon y-bete hyt befallyt to study yn a hard lessyn, þe whyche y-studyd *and* y-kan, he schal haue myche þonke.

> Joha*nn*is vapulantis e*st* studere in lect*ione* difficili, q*u*a p*er* studiu*m* capta *et* bene scita, multipharias gra*ciarum* accio*n*es reportabit.

31. Conyng ys an hy tre, of þe whyche þe rote ys ful byttyr bot þe fryte ys ful swete. He þat disspysyth þe byttyrnasse of þe rote schal neu*er* tast þe swetenasse of þe fryte.

> Sciencia est arbor altissima, cui*us* radix e*st* amarissima s*ed* fruc*tus* dulcissim*us*, et q*ui* n*e*cligit radici*s* amaritudine*m* fruc*tus* dulcedine*m* nequaq*u*am gustabit.

32. 3yff we suff*er* worn*ges* here yn herþe, for soþe we schal[have]ry3t yn heuen.

> Si toleremu*s* iniuria*m* h*i*c in via, p*ro*fecto h*a*bebim*us* ius in patria.

[fol. 94ʳ or p. 191]

33. To brystow, þe wyche ys an hauyn towne, comyth moo strangerys þan to covyntre, þe wych ys no hauyntowne, notwi*th*stondyng þat boþe beth lyche good.

> Bristoliam, que e*st* possidiuo pag*us*, confluu*n*t plures alienigeni q*u*am couentriam, que non e*st* possidiuo pag*us*, non abstante q*uod* ambo sunt equiformit*er* bone.

34. Þe more a schrewe be sparyd, the more schrewe he ys.

> Quanto mag*is* prauo p*ar*cat*ur*, tanto mag*is* adu*er*sat*ur*.

35. Þe ofter a chyld ys aposyd, þe redyer answerer he schold be by reson.

> Quanto crebreus pu*ero* opponit*ur*, eiure tanto esset promtior respon-salis.

36. For þe blessyd maydys sake y ham to dryng clere wat*er* a candylmasse euyn.

> Intuitu / obtentu / *ve*l p*re*texte beatissime uirginis in vigilia purifi-cacionis ego su*m* hausturus aquam illimam / *ve*l aquam illimem.

37. Mony men had leu*er* be y-seruyd wi*th* grene sewe þan wi*th* vergys oþer vyne-egur, and namelych wan þey beth y-seruyd wi*th* a kalfys hed oþer wi*th* a lomys schuld*er*.

---

³² Worn*ges*: wrongs.

³³ Possidiuo: perhaps intended to mean 'in possession of.' Pagus, 'a district': apparently a mistake for 'portus,' 'a port.'

³⁴ The proverb has not been found in English in this form; the Latin (with an internal rhyme) may be the original.

³⁶ Candylmasse euyn: the day before 2 February. Fasting was encouraged on the eves or vigils of great ecclesiastical feasts.

³⁷ Green sewe: probably the same as 'sauce verte,' a green sauce made with parsley, mint, and other herbs (*Two Fifteenth-Century Cookery-Books*, ed. T. Austin [EETS os 91; London 1888] 77, 110). 'Vergys' (verjuice) and vinegar were other popular constituents of sauces to go with veal or mutton (*ibid*. 13, 72, 110).

Multi homines malunt illis seruiri cum viridi salsa quam cum viridi succo vel vino acri, et precipue quando illis seruitur cum capite vitulino vel spatula agnina.

38. Ʒyf jon my felow were y-bete as ofte as he doþ deseruy hit, with-out dowte he wold be come a gode chyld and an hesy wyth-yn a fewe days.

Si johannes socius meus verberaretur tociens quociens meretur, examussim deueniret bonus puer et equanimus infra paucorum dierum curricula.

[fol. 94ᵛ or p. 192]

39. A gold ryng rychest and precyst of þyngys hyt be-semyth a gentyl womman to were apon þe leche fynger and not vpon þe myddyl fynger.

Anulo aureo ditissime et preciosissime rerum decet generosam feminam vti super medicum et non super verpum.

40. Þe mayster hath yrebukyd me for my defawtys.

Magister affecit me contumelijs / vel verbis contumeliosis propter meos defectus.

41. My felowis haue opynlych ychyd the mayster, þe wych schal turne hem to grete repreff.

Socij mei publice conuiciati sunt magistrum, quod redundabit illis in magnum obprobrium.

42. Bowcherys schal sylle dere flesch ontyl flescholeve, and than þey schal ses by here leue, maygreþ here tethe, ontyl eyster.

Carnificibus venibunt care carnes vsque ad carnipriuium, et tunc cessabunt per licenciam suam, inuitis dentibus suis, vsque ad festum pasche.

43. A hard latyn to make, my face wexyth blakke.

Difficilem latinitatem composituri, facies mea nigrescit.

44. My lord haþ a feyr maner with a mote abowte with a drawȝt brygge.

Dominus meus habet pulcram maneriem cum pereferencia / siue circumferencia cum ponte volubili.

45. Salubrius est esse laxatiuum quam constupatum.

[fol. 95ʳ or p. 193]

46. Þe lempner most by an honce of asyre to lempne my myssal.

Oportet mimogrophum emere onciam asure ad aluminandum meum missale.

---

³⁹ Leche fynger: the fourth or ring finger.

⁴² Flescholeve: perhaps meant for 'flesh-leave,' a literal translation of 'carniprivium,' the beginning of Lent.

⁴³ Latyn: a Latin exercise.

⁴⁵ 'It is healthier to be loose than to be constipated.' Laxatiuum: is glossed in English 'laxatyfe.' Constupatum: is glossed in English 'costy, as a mon þat may not go to sege.'

⁴⁶ Asyre: an ounce and a half of pure azure blue cost 2s. 6d. at Westminster in 1290 (L. F. Salzman, *Building in England down to 1540* [Oxford 1967] 169).

47. Y know not of þy conseyle, ne y kepe not know hit.

Consilium tuum latet me, et volo quod lateat.

48. Prystys schal not know al schwreyd turnys þat men doþ, but god only schal hem.

Presbiteros latebunt multa facinora que homines perpetrant; deum tamen non latebunt / vel sic: a presbiteris abscondentur multa facinora; a deo tamen non abscondentur / siue ignorabuntur.

49. Y say a nakyd man bere fyve lovis in hys lappe.

Ego vidi nudus hominem gerere quinque panes in gremio suo.

50. Prestys walkyth vp and down yn þe bowke of þe cherche y-hodyd, þe whyche hyt be-fallyth to schryue vs.

Presbeteri ambulant susum et iusum in naui ecclesie capiciati, quibus interest confiteri nostra.

51. My felow haþ a spyryte y-close.

Socius meus habet spiritum phitonicum.

52. A mason whyrchyt slylych, a gold-smyth werchyth slyor, but a lympner wyrchyþ slyyst of alle hem.

Latamus operatur subtiliter, aurifaber operatur subtilius, sed mimographus operatur subtilissime omnium illorum.

53. Wham hyt be-fallyth to schryve fyscyus men but men of holy chyrche?

Quibus interest confiteri virorum flagiciosorum nisi viris ecclesiasticis?

[fol. 95ᵛ or p. 194]

54. Grete wel þy fader at þat tokyn þat we dranke a pot of wyne þet oþer day at þe wyne taverne.

Saluta patrem tuum super hoc intersigno quod bibimus altera die vrnam vini in meroteca.

55. Wham hit be-fallyth to vynde pore scolerys to scole but þe byschyp of synt dauyes, holyist of creaturs?

Cuius / vel cuia interest exhibere pauperes scolares ad studia literarum nisi episcopi meneuencis, sanctissime creaturarum?

---

49 Nudus: *recte* nudum.

50 Bowke: the nave of the church, open to the laity. A medieval priest commonly drew his hood over his head and face before hearing confession (John Myrc, *Instructions for Parish Priests*, ed. E. Peacock [EETS os 31; London 1868] 27).

52 Gold-smyth: godl-smyth in MS.

53 Fyscyus: vicious.

55 Þe byschyp of synt dauyes: presumably Benedict Nicholl(s), bishop from 1417 to 1433. For his biography see A. B. Emden, *A Biographical Register of the University of Oxford to A.D. 1500* (Oxford 1959) III 2200–1. He is not known to have had any connection with the Bristol area, but may have taken ship from the city when travelling to his diocese.

56. Wham hyt be-fallyth to bygge al þyng þat longyth to hweshold *and* al
þyng þat longyth to chambur but a grete lord þe whyche [will well arrange for his household and the things of his house?]

> Cui*us* / *ve*l cuia int*er*est comp*ar*are vtencilia *et* supelleccilia ni*si*
> magnat*us* qui vult bene dispon*er*e familie sue et reb*us* dom*us* sue?

57. Eyster nyȝyng and lent a-most y-yendyd, wham hyt be-fallyth to be
clene yn consyans but cristy*n* men, þe whyche worþylych but to reseve
þe wyrschypful sacrament?

> Festo pasche approximante et quadragesima paulomin*us* finita, quo-
> r*um* int*er*est esse pura*rum* consciencijs ni*si* c*r*isticola*rum*, qui digne
> sunt recepturi venerabile sac*r*amentu*m*?

58. What by ryȝt, what by wronge, my wylle y haue y-gete.

> Tu*m* p*er* fas, tu*m* p*er* nefas, mea*m* uoluntate*m* obtinui / *ve*l sic:
> quid p*er* ius, quid p*er* iniuriam, meu*m* velle impetraui.

59. Grene gees schal come hastely yn seson wi*th* þe garlec knocul-depe.

> Anceruli nouit*er* venient i*n* tempestiuitate cu*m* aliato condolotenus.

[fol. 96ʳ or p. 195]

60. My felow ys watt schode or wyne dryonke.

> Socius meus e̦st humide calciatus aut temelent*us*.

61. Me schal goo to seynt jame by þe grete see sory, but me schal come home
glad and soylyd of alle here syn*n*ys.

> It*ur* ad *sanctum* jacobu*m* p*er* occianu*m* contrito / *ve*l contritis, sed
> rediet*ur* domu*m* deo fauente gauisis / *ve*l gauiso absoluto / *ve*l -tis
> ab om*n*ibus peccatis.

62. A mon þat takyt p*art* of al my godys maygreth me, [I] schal neu*er* tryst
to wyle y ham a-lyue.

> Ho*min*i qui p*ar*ticipat bono*rum* meo*rum* / bona mea / *ve*l -is -is me
> inuito, nu*n*quam adhibebo fiduciam vita mi*hi* comite.

63. Jon twlenkelyd a-ponne me ȝere wyle, but y wyst not what he menyd by
hys twlenkelyng.

> Johan*n*es conniuebat sup*er* me vice prius, sed nesciui q*u*id vellet
> innuere p*er* conniuencia[m] suam.

---

⁵⁶ The last part of the English sentence is missing in the MS.

⁵⁷ But: probably for 'buth' (are).

⁵⁹ Grene gees: young geese. Garlic was a recommended ingredient of sauce for a goose (*Two
Fifteenth-Century Cookery-Books*, ed. Austin, 109).

⁶⁰ Watt schode: wet-shod. The *Oxford English Dictionary* records a similar usage of the
term to mean 'drunken' in 1589.

⁶¹ Me: indefinite pronoun (singular or plural) meaning 'one,' 'people.' Seynt jame:
Compostella in northern Spain, for which Bristol was a favourite port of departure. See, for
example, *The Book of Margery Kempe*, edd. S. B. Meech & H. E. Allen (EETS os 212; London
1940) I 108–10, 310.

64. Þe walkyn ys alle ouer-cast.

   Celum obducitur nubibus.

65. Chyldryn stond yn a row, sum wel a-rayd, sum euel a-rayd; dyuers beth þe wyttys.

   Puerorum stantium seriatim quorundam bene apparatorum, quo-rundam vero male, varia sunt ingenia.

66. Men comyth to þis towne yn market days, sum a-pon horssis *and* sum apon mares.

   Homines confluunt ad istam villam in diebus forensibus, quidam super equos quidam vero super equas.

[fol. 96ᵛ or p. 196]

67. Chyldryn þat beth come of good kynd schyld forbere eueryoþer, *and* not chyd euerychon oþer lyke harlotys.

   Pueros qui traxerunt originem de nobili parentela / vel sic: ex illus-tri prosopia / vel sic: de clara stirpe, oportet deferre alterum alteri, et non conuiciari instar scurrarum.

68. Chyldryn þat haveth good wyll to lerne, þe mayster schal besy-lyche enforme and fare feyre with.

   Pueros qui habent deuotum animum addiscendi, magister diligenter informabit honeste-que tractabit.

69. Þe kyng most loue hys lege men.

   Oportet regem diligere suos ligittimos.

70. Me comyth to scole yn þe mortyde sory, but me goyth to dyner mery *and* glad.

   Venitur ad monitorium in diluculo tristi / vel tristibus, sed itur ad iantaculum leto / vel letis.

71. My fadyr holdyth a good howshold; almyȝty god menteyn hym ȝyf h[i]t be hys wylle.

   Pater meus sustinet grande domicium; omnipotens eum manuteneat si sue libuerit voluntati.

72. Quilibet vir sanctus audacter predicaret in adulterum et in desertorem quia adulter et desertor abhominabiles fiunt deo.

73. A quest hath y-quyt hym.

   Duodena fidedignorum acquietauit eum.

---

⁶⁴ Walkyn: welkin.

⁷² 'Any holy man should preach boldly to an adulterer and a deserter [in marriage], because an adulterer and a deserter are abominable to God.'

⁷³ Quest: inquest.

[fol. 97ʳ or p. 197]

74. Þer buth mony lolerdys ytake in dyuerse scheris of þis contrey, as y hyrd say now late of trewmen.

    Multi lollardi sunt capti in diuersis comitatibus istius prouincie, prout ex relacione fidedignorum nuper accepi.

75. He ys not worþy ese þat canoȝt suffry desese.

    Non est dignus prosperitate qui non potest tolerare modicam aduersitatem, vnde boythius de disciplina scolarium: 'Non est vir dignus dulcoris acum[i]ne qui amaritudinis nequit jnuiscari grauamamine'.

76. Nos moderni sumus in sexta ciliade ab origine mundi.

77. Y haue dewllyd att bristow þis þre ȝere, and as myche more as fro myȝel-masse hedyr-to.

    Ego mansi bristolie isto triennio et eo amplius quanto est elapsum festum michaelis vsque in hodiernam diem.

78. Y kan ryde to bathe in a day and als for beȝond for nede.

    Ego scio equitare bathoniam in vna die et eo vltra pro necesse.

79. My fadyr dwellyth a stonys cast hennys.

    Pater meus moratur ab hinc per tantam distanciam quantus est iactus lapidis.

Wotton [*in margin*]

80. Nisi melius et perfectius meo monitori in materia mihi ab illo proposita respondero antequam hinc recedam, timeo mihi acriter verberari.

81. Þis wyne ys new a-broche.

    Istud vinum est de nouo attaminatum.

[fol. 97ᵛ or p. 198]

82. Felow, go þy wey; yc haue noȝt to do with þe.

    Socie, prode viam; nichil michi et tibi. Incassum laboras / frustra / vel in uanum.

---

74 Lolerdys: arrests of Lollards in England reached their peaks after the Lollard risings of 1414 and 1431, but went on intermittently during the 1420s (J. A. F. Thomson, *The Later Lollards, 1414–1520* [London 1965] *passim*).

75 Boythius: *De disciplina scholarium* 4.23, ascribed to Boethius in the Middle Ages (PL 64.1232ʙ), but actually an anonymous work of ca. 1230–40, probably from Paris (Ps.-Boèce, *De disciplina scholarium*, ed. Olga Weijers [Leiden–Cologne 1976] 115). The English proverb is not listed in Whiting, *Proverbs*.

76 'We men of today are in the sixth millennium from the beginning of the world.' Medieval chronologists often dated the creation of the world to 4000 B.C., so that the A.D. 1400s would fall in the sixth millennium. Ciliade: is glossed in Latin 'millinario.'

77 Dewllyd: dwelt.

78 For: far.

80 'Unless I reply better and more perfectly to my master on the matter set by him before I leave here, I fear I shall be severely beaten.'

83. My felow hath crachchyd my face for þe nonys.
     Socius meus rupit faciem meam abintento.
84. Y haue no spendyng money.
     Ego non habeo pecuniam famuliarem.
85. Y haue made convenant with a crupul.
     Ego iniui contractum cum contracto.
86. Þes haþ y-smete me þorowout onware.
     Iste traiecit me incaute.
87. Þis mon ys wyse and whare.
     Iste homo est prouidus ac circumspectus.
88. Hyt is long ago seþ y was soculyng.
     Longum tempus effluxit ex quo fui sububeris / vel suberis.
89. Þe prest hath y-sacryd.
     Sacerdos confecit.
90. Þis hath y-ʒeue vp hys benefyce.
     Iste cessit beneficium suum.
91. For soth we hatyth þe compar[i]sonys, for þey beth hard to vs sowkyng chyldryn.
     Reuera nos odio habemus comparaciones, quia nobis sububeribus sunt valde deficeles.
92. The kyng dwellyth at calyce, a gode toun and famoce.
     Rex moratur calisius, bone ville et famose / vel sic: bona villa et famosa.
93. For godysake, be mery and lette be þu mornyng.
     Letare pro deo, et deduc merorem et sis hilaris et iocundus.
94. Ther ys no bred yn towne to sylle but a lytyl lofe for an halpeny, as myche as a man-ys fust, þe wheche onnethe wold ful an hongry [boy] at hys deynere with-owt beter sowle.
     Nullus panis est venum / vel venalis in villa nisi modicus paximatus pro denario, tantillus quantillus pignus hominis est, qui vix saciaret famelicum pusionem ad iantaculum suum sine edulio meliori.
95. My gowne ys y-steynyd.
     Toga mea est detincta.

---

83 Crachchyd: broken.
85 Crupul: cripple.
86 Y-smete me þorowout onware: smitten me thoroughly unawares.
88 Soculyng: suckling.
89 Y-sacryd: consecrated the bread and wine at mass.
91 Comparisonys: either the morphology and syntax of comparison in Latin, or exercises on the subject.
92 Calyce: Henry V was at Calais in 1415, 1416, and 1421; Henry VI was there in 1430.
94 Onnethe: scarcely. Sowle: sowl, any relish eaten with bread.

96. Y say a pelere *and* a defendere that other day, fyghtyng togad*er* by-sydys westmyst*er* opon tote hulle.

[fol. 98ʳ or p. 199]

Ego vidi vnum antigonistam *et* vnum agonisetam alt*er*a die, pignan-tes ad inuicem sup*er* p*ro*montorium iux*ta* westmonasterium.

97. Y smothe flynt w*ith* the smytyng yr*n* and ther fel a sp*a*rkyl yn-to tyndyr where-of y tend the lygh yn the chylle, whyle þe sone hath rostyd a colop to h*i*s nonemete.

P*er*cussi scilicem cu*m* fugullo *et* scintilla cecidit in naptam vnde ac-cendi crucibolum in crucibolario, du*m* filiolus assauit carbonellam ad merendam.

98. Pore scolares schold bysilych ta*n* hede to here bokys, the whyche byth not y-ware of none other help but of here one konnyng.

Paup*er*es scolares suis libris officiosissime insudarent, qui non con-siderati sunt de aliquo alio auxilio ni*si* de sua sciencia.

99. Y haue a pykyd staff.

Ego h*a*beo baculu*m* rostratu*m* / cuspidatu*m* / *et* ferratu*m*.

Chyppnam

100. Nomore prys þan oþer halff pond cost my browdyd gowne.

Nulli*us* maior*is* precii / *v*el nullo maiori p*re*cio libra *et* alt*er*ius dimi-dia constabat mea toga polomita.

101. Hayle felew, wel y-mette; helfe me þis hachett.

Aue socie, b*e*ne ti*b*i obuiato; manica / *v*el manubria mi*hi* ist*am* securicul*am*.

102. Y see my modyr y-crystenyd yn þis holy font, þe wych hath y-brow3t me in-to þis world suffryng mony tribulac*i*onys.

Ego video matr*em* mea*m* baptisati in isto sacro fonte, que p*ro*fudit me in hunc mond*um* multas t*ri*bulaci*o*nes pacientem.

103. Int*er*est claricor*um* in cancello stare, s*ed* int*er*est laicor*um* *v*el laicar*um* stare in naui ecclesie.

---

⁹⁶ A peler and a defender: the parties in a law-suit which was being settled through trial by battle (Sir W. S. Holdsworth, *A History of English Law* [5th ed.; London 1931] I 308–10, 678–79). Tote hulle: Tothill, the area west of Westminster Abbey, part of which (Tothil] Field) was open ground (John Stow, *A Survey of London*, ed. C. L. Kingsford [Oxford 1908] II 123). It was still used as a place for trial by battle in 1571 (Holdsworth, *op. cit.* 310).

⁹⁷ Lygh: light. Chylle: chelle (lamp vessel). Colop: a slice of meat, e.g. bacon.

⁹⁸ Schold: schlod in MS.

¹⁰² Baptisati: *recte* baptisari.

¹⁰³ ' It belongs to the clergy to stand in the chancel, but to laymen and laywomen to stand in the nave of the church.' Naui: is glossed in English 'bowke.'

104. Tua generositas est inualida.

105. On feler þen thre *and* fewer þan fyvy, y hadde vpon my cule strokes ful ryve.

> Vno plures tribus *et* pauciores quinque, habui super anum ictus copiose.

106. On feler þen thre *and* fe[w]er þan fyve, y plokkyd appullys ful ryve.

> Vno plura tribus et paciora quinque, excirpsi poma copiose.

[fol. 98ᵛ or p. 200]

107. Euery of my felowys yposyd *and* non of ham y-concludyd, god forbede me to be concludyd of eny *and* namelych in lyȝt materys, y-contyd wysyst of grammyre of hem alle.

> Cuilibet sociorum meorum opposito *et* nulli eorum concluso, absit mihi ab aliquo concludi *et* precipue in materiis facilibus, reputato sapientissimo gramatice omnium illorum.

108. Y and my felow, þe wyche buth y-sette in þe scole þe best answerer *and* the best lerner, hyt befallyth þe mayster to preyse.

> Mei *et* socij mei, a quibus sedetur in scola melioris responsalis *et* melioris adiscentis, jnterest a magistro licere.

109. An hors a beste þe wyche y haue yhured for fowre pannys a day ys wery [of] hys iorney, *and* had leuer a fowle stabul than a feyre way.

> Animal equus quod conduxi pro iiijor denariis diurnis est fessum itinere suo, *et* mallet habere turpe stabulum quam pulcram viam.

110. Me hys yn þe scole euery day fastyng tyl neryng prime of þe horlage clercke, þe wych hyt be-fallyt to besy in rynggyng owrys of þe day.

> Cistitur in scola ieiuno / vel ieiunis cotidie donec pulsetur ad horam primam ab horespice, cuius interest esse assidui in pulsando ad horas canonicas diei.

111. All my felowys aposyd but y, þe mayster thenkyt noȝt apon me.

> Omnibus consortibus meis opposito preterquam mihi, magister non meminit mei me / siue me.

---

104 'Your courtesy is weak.' Generositas: is glossed in English 'cortesy.' Inualida: is glossed in Latin 'non valet.'

105 Feler: more. Cule: bottom.

106 Fewer: feler in MS.

107 Y-concludyd: confuted or overcome in argument.

110 Prime: the third of the eight daily services or 'hours,' said at about 7:00 or 8:00 A.M. The association here with breaking one's fast is also found at Exeter Cathedral, where the choristers seem to have had breakfast when prime was over (*Ordinale Exon*, ed. J. N. Dalton [HBS 37; London 1909] I 7; G. Oliver, *Lives of the Bishops of Exeter* [Exeter 1861] 228). Horlage clercke: the clerk of a church responsible for keeping time and ringing to announce the approaching times of services.

112. Y haue noȝt ete half my fulle of pankakys *and* of fryturys, *and* þerfor
onthonke haue owre koke þe wych schold haue a-rayd ynowȝt, hauyng
flowre *and* whyte grece y-nowȝt redy wyth hym y þe kechyn.

Ego non commedi semisufficienciam laganor*um* et frixurar*um*, *et*
ideo dem*er*itum habeat n*oste*r fullinari*us* q*ui* parauisset sufficient*er*,
h*a*bens sat*is* suminis *et* similaginis p*r*esto secum in coquina.

113. That man des*er*uyth exellent mede to be reward[ed] in heuene, þe wyche
in þ*is* worle may lyue vnd*er* þe mantel of chastyte.

[fol. 99ʳ or p. 201]

Ille homo p*r*omeret*ur* exellenti p*r*emio recompensari in celo, qui
in valle mis*er*ie potest viuere sub pallio castitat*is*.

114. A mayd þe qwych by-fore alle cryat*ur*ys lyuyng in þ*is* worl y sum tyme
louyd, a man today schal wedde þe wyche for sothe me ruyth hugylych.

Puella quam pre om*n*ibus craturis in hoc mu*n*do quandam amabam,
ho*mi*ni ista die nubet cui*us* me reuera mis*er*et vehement*er*.

115. Alle my felowys y-posyd, y þe wyche grete desyre haue to lerne, god
forbede to be spared.

Omnibus soci*j*s meis opposito, m*ihi* cui magnu*m* desideriu*m* est
addyscere, absit p*ar*ci.

---

[112] Flowre and whyte grece: flour and lard. The Latin equivalents 'similaginis' and 'suminis' are in the wrong order.
[113] Worle: world.
[114] Worl: world. Y sum tyme: sum y tyme in MS.

A SCHOOL NOTE-BOOK FROM BARLINCH PRIORY

Barlinch Priory near Dulverton was one of the poorest, remotest monasteries of medieval Somerset. At the time of its dissolution it had an income of only £98.00, and its previous internal history, like that of so many small religious houses, is virtually unknown.[1] The discovery of a note-book written by a schoolboy in the priory in the early Tudor period is consequently of some interest, not only casting further light upon the monastery and revealing a hitherto unknown Somerset school, but supplying the oldest full evidence of what was taught in any of the county's grammar schools.[2] The evidence is contained in one of the Luttrell MSS now deposited in the Somerset Record Office: a mid-Tudor court-book of the manor of Minehead, 1546–1560.[3] The covers of this book are roughly made up from odds and ends of older parchment and paper, including a leaf from a thirteenth- or fourteenth-century Vulgate and three pages from a fifteenth-century choir-book.[4] The rest of the binding material consists of sheets from the Barlinch school note-book.

The note-book was a paper volume, measuring about 19½–21 × 14 cms. in size. We do not know how many leaves it originally contained, since only some were apparently used in the binding and several of these have now disintegrated into illegible scraps. Fortunately, about a dozen pages are more or less complete, all written in an anglicana hand showing secretary influence, dating from the late fifteenth or early sixteenth centuries. The provenance is clear, since the material in the note-book is twice said to follow 'the usage of Master David Juyne' who is identified as 'teaching in the priory of St Nicholas, Barlinch'. The author of the note-book was not the master himself but one of his pupils, possibly William Nicolas whose name occurs twice among scribbles on a waste page. This is borne out by the character of the notes, which reflect the needs and work of a learner not of a teacher and are marred by the kinds of mistakes and obscurities committed by someone struggling with an unfamiliar language. The date of the note-book is roughly indicated by the style of the handwriting and by the watermarks on the paper: a Gothic P with flower, and a quadruped, probably a unicorn. Neither mark can be parallelled absolutely, but they resemble ones in use from the 1480s onwards, and especially after about 1500.[5] The contents of the note-book point in the same direction. The use of the term *vulgaria*,

I am grateful to the Revd. Dr. D. Thomson for his expert knowledge and suggestions in editing the Barlinch note-book.

1   On the history of the priory, see F. W. Weaver, 'Barlinch Priory', *Somerset Archaeological and Natural History Society*, liv (1908), pp 79–106 and *Victoria County History of Somerset*, ed. W. Page, vol ii (London, 1911), pp 132–4. Dr. R. W. Dunning kindly informs me that the priory was dissolved in February 1536 (Public Record Office, SC6/Henry VIII/7298.)
2   The school must be added to those listed in the present author's previous survey of Somerset schools: *Education in the West of England, 1066–1548* (Exeter, 1976).
3   Somerset Record Office DD/L/ P29/29. I am grateful to Dr. R. Bowers for bringing the MS to my attention.
4   The choir-book is edited by R. Bowers, *Early Music History*, iii (1983), pp 156–730.
5   For the unicorn, see C. M. Briquet, *Les Filigranes*, 2nd ed., 4 vols (Leipzig, 1923), iii, 1012–30, 10216 (*c.* 1498–1519) and for the P with flower, ibid., 8622 (1480s) and G. Piccard, *Wasserzeichen Buchstabe P*, 3 vols (Stüttgart, 1977) 471–1113 (1490–1540, mainly after 1500).

meaning English sentences with Latin translations, makes likely a date after 1483 when this term is first clearly found in use,[6] while the presence of Alain de Lille's moral verses, the *Liber Parabolarum*, suggests a date before 1520, since this work was not printed in England after 1510 and probably fell out of popularity during the following decade.[7] On the whole, the evidence suggests a date between about 1480 and 1520, with a slightly greater probability after 1500 than before.

The priory was a small community of Augustinian canons, usually numbering a prior and seven or eight brethren during the late fifteenth and early sixteenth centuries. Nothing else is known at present about the schoolmaster David Juyne, though his surname is often encountered in the west of England, but he is unlikely to have been one of the canons, since we have a virtually complete list of their names from records of ordinations and the elections of priors, and his does not appear among them. He did not hold a parochial benefice in either of the two adjoining counties of Devon and Somerset, which makes it likely that he was either a professional schoolmaster or a poor chaplain at the level of a chantry priest or hired curate. His status in the priory may have been either official or unofficial. Since 1339 the papal constitution *Ad Decorem Ecclesie* had laid down that all Augustinian monasteries should maintain a schoolmaster to instruct their canons in grammar, logic and philosophy. The master was allowed to be a member of the order or an outsider, and had to be paid a salary.[8] Not all the monasteries obeyed the rule consistently, especially small houses like Barlinch with limited resources and few members, but from time to time they experienced visitations from the local bishop or the leaders of their order, and any educational deficiencies which came to light were commanded to be remedied. Barlinch itself was visited by Augustinian commissioners, probably in 1510, who enjoined that someone should be made ready (*preparetur*) as soon as practicable to instruct the canons in grammar,[9] and this is a possible date and explanation for Juyne and his school. Equally, however, Juyne may simply have been a private schoolmaster, teaching in the priory on his own initiative and with the canons' permission, as a convenient place for holding a school in that area.

The master's pupils are likely to have been much the same, whatever his status. Barlinch usually contained a novice or two: young men in their late teens and early twenties, for the ordination records of the bishops of Bath and Wells show that the house sent up between one and four such canons to be ordained each decade during the late fifteenth and early sixteenth centuries.[10] These novices were prime candidates to be sent to the local schoolmaster. The priory probably housed some younger boys as well, who would have benefited from schooling. Large religious houses before the Reformation supported groups of almonry boys and choristers to help with worship, and even Barlinch, small as it was, appears to have had a few boys of this kind since the visitation of 1510 allowed each canon to keep one servant or boy, but only one.[11] There may have been secular boys in the monastery too, boarding with the prior or coming in daily from outside, and being paid for by their parents, so that Juyne may easily have gathered a dozen or two dozen assorted boys and young men under his care. The pupil who kept the note-book could have belonged to any of these categories. Two features point to the novices. At one point in his notes, the pupil talks of the need to learn *normula*, a word meaning 'rules', often in the sense of 'monastic rules'. At another he says that by next Michaelmas he will go to Wells to receive holy orders,

6   The term is used in [John Anwykyll,] *Vulgaria quedam abs Terencio in Anglicam linguam traducta* (Oxford, 1483).
7   A. W. Pollard and G. R. Redgrave, *A Short Title Catalogue of Books Printed in England* (London, 1946), nos. 252–4.
8   C. Coquelines, *Bullarum Privilegiorum ac Diplomatum Romanorum Pontificum Collectio*, 6 vols (Rome, 1739–62), iii, part ii, 264–86.
9   *The Triennial Chapters of the Augustinian Canons*, ed. H. E. Salter, Oxford Historical Soc., lxxiv (Oxford, 1920), p 184.
10 In 1479 four, unusually, were ordained, but this seems a little early for Juyne's school (Somerset Record Office, Reg. Robert Stillington, *ff*. 202–v).
11 Above, note 9.

something that was regularly done by the young canons. On the other hand, there is nothing monastic about the character of the note-book. It could have been written in any medieval school, and the simple nature and schoolboyish humour of its contents fit equally well a younger almonry boy or a boy from outside who intended to be ordained as a secular priest, rather than take vows as a canon.

A number of similar school-books survive from the fifteenth century onwards, often identifiable with known schools, so the Barlinch one is not unique, though it is the first to be traced to Somerset.[12] It contains two kinds of material: first, copies of a grammatical text and literary works which were used in many other contemporary schools, and secondly notes and exercises which pertained to the pupil himself and his own work. The contents show that Juyne's school was no casual or elementary operation but an organised grammar school, teaching Latin in the same way and to the same standard as schools in major towns like Bristol and Exeter. The teaching was organised in terms and the note-book includes the pupil's work in two of these: Michaelmas and Christmas. Within each term, he recorded the days of the week on which he made his notes or did his exercises — a practice which is parallelled in another west-country school note-book from Devon (probably Exeter) in the fifteenth century.[13] Not every day of the week is recorded in the Barlinch case. There are no Sundays, because the school was probably suspended that day, no Saturdays, and only one week has a complete sequence of days from Monday to Friday. Normally only two or three days are listed in each week, Monday appearing most often. This may reflect a pattern either of attendance or of teaching. The pupil may not have gone to school every day, or the lessons may only have included on certain days the kind of material which he wrote down in his note-book.

The pupil learnt the basic rules of Latin grammar orally from the master or visually from written texts, portions of which he might copy into his note-book. His first surviving transcript is a prose description of the forms of the verbs *sum*, *possum*, *volo* and *nolo*. His daily notes and exercises show how the process of learning Latin went on in practice. The teaching was done at least partly in English, and the pupil often wrote down the English translations of the words he learnt. Each term's notes begin with a title explaining that they contain Master Juyne's *latinitates*, *versus differenciales*, *vulgaria* and *vocabula*. *Latinitates* or 'latins' were Latin sentences dictated by the master to illustrate points of grammar and syntax, or composed by the pupil as exercises in writing. The *versus differenciales* were Latin verses, also originating from the master, explaining homonyms, homophones and synonyms — words of similar spelling, sound or meaning. Being in verse they were easy to keep in one's memory. One of them centres on *mundus*, which can either mean 'the world' or 'pure' in a moral sense; another points out that *tibia* signifies both the shin-bone and a musical instrument. *Vulgaria* or 'vulgars' were sentences in English which the pupil had to translate into Latin. Large collections of these appear in some contemporary school-books, but there are only two or three among the Barlinch exercises. *Vocabula* were vocabulary lists. Several of the dictated latins and verses introduced the pupil to new words and he sometimes responded to this by writing the latter out separately underneath, along with their principal parts and their meaning in English. He was also introduced to Latin poetry of a fairly simple kind, chiefly medieval in origin because this was before the re-emphasis on classical Latin poetry in the early sixteenth century. Three of these poems he copied out in part or in whole, all of them texts which were very popular in contemporary schools: the *Parvus Cato*, a series of moral admonitions; the *Liber Parabolarum* of Alain de Lille, a collection of proverbs and wise observations; and *Stans Puer ad Mensam* by Robert Grosseteste which deals with children's behaviour when serving or eating at table. The pupil thus emerged

12   The best survey of such exercises is that of D. Thomson, *A Descriptive Catalogue of Middle English Grammatical Texts* (New York and London, 1979).
13   Ibid., pp 301, 310.

from his schooling with a fund of morality and etiquette, as well as a knowledge of Latin grammar. He became familiar with verse (though it is not clear whether he composed it himself) and the process of copying out his notes helped him to write in a legible way and to master the abbreviations with which Latin was written, many of which he used in his transcripts.

The grammar-text of *sum* and *possum* and the three well-known school poems in the Barlinch note-book signify the school's and the pupil's involvement in the general adult culture of pre-Renaissance England and Europe. The daily exercises which the master dictated and the pupil composed are more orientated towards children and Barlinch itself. Like those in other contemporary school-books, they try to appeal to the pupil by dwelling on the classroom environment with which he was familiar and on jokes and riddles which would amuse him and keep up his interest. As a result they tell us something about the school, its pupils and what they thought about. Lessons in school began early, probably by 6.00 a.m. and in one sentence the boy asserts that he has been there since 5.30. The relationship between pupil and master is treated humorously. 'I stand before the master like an image on a wall', says the pupil, 'for he speaks not to me nor I to him', and the following sentence may be the master's riposte: 'I'll spoil your portrait, said the the painter to his image'! Elsewhere it is noted wryly that a master who teaches pupils day in and day out becomes very irritable. Food and play are other topics of the exercises. No doubt the hours between meals were long and the food when it came (perhaps) not very plentiful so eating was always a popular subject. One sentence asks to have breakfast early, another points out sardonically that he who eats little at supper, lunch, dinner and breakfast has no spirit left in him and a third reports with satisfaction that the writer has filled his belly to sufficiency with bacon and eggs. It would be pleasant to think that the Barlinch boys went bathing in the summer in the nearby River Exe, since one sentence appears to mean 'we are all going to the swimming place (*piscinam*). Another, which declares that 'he can swim well whose chin is held up by another' is unfortunately less relevant here; it was a common proverb of the day.[14]

The humour in the exercises is schoolboyish, and includes the ruderies which boys enjoy in every era. In one sentence someone else is compared with a sow who suckles twelve piglets; in another, the Latin is the translation of a taunting English rhyme:

> I will have the whip and you will have the pip;[15]
> I will have a rose and you will have a running nose.

Two of the exercises include excretory and sexual references: one that a strong man should not give his powers to prostitutes, and another that the wind has changed nine times in the space that it takes to make water (the contemporary English term for this was 'a pissing while'). Frankness about such matters is typical of medieval school literature, and indicates a lack of demarcation between children and adults not a laxity in morals and manners, which the poems by Alain de Lille and Robert Grosseteste show was taken seriously. Nothing is said about the priory directly and little about the world in general, but Barlinch cannot have been so remote if a sentence could allude to being in London four days previously. The exercises do recall, however, a few of the sounds which floated into the schoolroom by day or vexed the sleep of its inmates during the night. The chamberlain enters at dawn, making a noise in the room; poultry cluck and dogs bark; a bell rings; the wind rattles the window. These sounds are precious for they are haunting reminders, like the note-book as a whole, of the time when Barlinch in its deep wooded valley was no ruin, but a living community of people: worshipping, studying and doing the work of everyday life.

14   B. J. Whiting, *Proverbs, Sentences and Proverbial Phrases from English Writings Mainly before* 1500, Cambridge, Mass., & London, 1968, C232.
15   'Pip' (*petuitam*) in the sense of the disease. There is an identical translation of the Latin word in this sense in some 15th-century school exercises from Bristol: N. Orme, 'A Grammatical Miscellany of 1427–65 from Bristol and Wiltshire', *Traditio*, xxxviii (1982), p. 316.

A DESCRIPTION OF SOMERSET RECORD OFFICE, MS DD/L P 29/29 (binding fragments)

All the material which follows is in Latin, unless otherwise stated. In the transcripts, capital letters and punctuation have been modernised, abbreviations expanded in italics, and editorial additions placed within square brackets. Gaps and holes are indicated by empty square brackets. Erasures and corrections in the MS are not generally noted. It is impossible wholly to reconstruct the sequence of contents, so the following list is not necessarily fully in the original order.

(1) On one complete folio and two scraps:

> [S]Vm es fui esse -di -do -dum supinus caret . . .
> . . . vnicum participium trahitur ab hoc verbo neutro et anormalo presentis temporis tantum vt nolens; futuro caret.

The conjugations of the verbs sum, possum, volo and nolo in prose form, with one or two English equivalents, *e.g.* 'eram, y was'. Common in grammatical MSS, where it usually also includes fero, edo and malo (Thomson, *Middle English Grammatical Texts*, p. 109).

(2) On the recto of a complete folio; the beginning of the text is probably lost:

> [Dum manducatis . . . ,] Vultus hylares habeatis/Sal cultello capiatis/ Quid edendum sit ne petatis/Non depositum capiatis/ Rixas murium fugiatis/Mensa recte sedeatis/Mappam mundam teneatis/Ne scalpatis caueatis/Aliis partem tribuatis/Morsus non ren[un]ciatis/ Modicum sed crebro vivatis/Grates christo referatis.
> Explicit documentum brevissimum de regimine mense.

Precepts in rhyme about eating at table. Similar (not identical) versions, usually of 12–14 lines, are common in MSS and two have been printed: J. Morawski, *Le Facet en Françoys*, Poznan, 1923, p. 125, and S. Gieben in *Vivarium*, v (1967), p. 52. For a similar text from Devon, see Thomson, *Middle English Grammatical Texts*, p. 291.

(3) Immediately following, on the recto and verso of the same folio and the recto of another, a virtually complete text:

> Caue puer ad mensam domini dogmata discas
> *   *   *
> Presul et ille fuit cui fexil [*sic*] det deus omen.
> Explicit. Finis adest mete mercedem quero diete.

Robert Grosseteste's poem on table-manners, *Stans puer ad mensam*, common in schoolbooks; the text is printed by S. Gieben in *Vivarium*, v (1967), pp 57–8. The Barlinch version (of 52 lines) is unusual in beginning 'Caue' rather than 'Stans', and like some other MSS has certain lines in inverted order. The sequence of lines, compared with Gieben's standard text, is 1–7, 9, 8, 10–11, 13, 12, 14–27, 30–38, 44, 46–8 and 50–52.

(4a) Immediately following, on the rest of the recto and the verso, without any title:

> Ad corpus sanctus, ad mentem pertinet almus;
> Vir sacer est ille qui sacra celebrare solet.
> *   *   *
> Versus amor mundi caput est siue bestia terre.

End of folio; 33 lines of verse, seven of them fragmentary.

(4b) On the recto and verso of another folio, the same or a similar text, without any title:

> Dat cano laudare, dat scribere vaticinare
> *   *   *
> Si doceas stultum, non letum dat tibi vultum;
> Odit te multum, uellet te scire scepultum.

Ends half-way down the verso, without any mark of conclusion; 35 lines of verse.

Both 4a and 4b are probably *versus differenciales*, a fifteenth-century term (used in this MS, below, section 7) for verses teaching pupils to distinguish homonyms, homophones and synonyms. They often occur in schoolbooks (Thomson, *Middle English Grammatical Texts*, pp 26, 175, 223–4, 243, 304–5) and the Barlinch examples may well have been collected and partly invented by Juyne himself. Several of the lines were also copied out, day by day, in the pupil's daily notes and exercises (below, section 7). The following line is typical:

> Non capo cauponem commedit, sed cavpo caponem.

One couplet appears to include a list of word-elements with a mnemonic to remember them:

> Al pi pen ca bas tot habet quot habet trus:
> Pica habet tot albas pennas quot habet grus.

Intermingled with the grammatical material are humorous or riddling lines:

> Siquis amat ranam, ranam putat esse dianam,

and moral and proverbial ones:

> Viuat ut edas, non sed edas vt uiuas.

Several of the lines are well-known proverbs or quotations recorded elsewhere and are listed in H. Walther, *Initia Carminum ac Versuum Medii Aevi Posterioris Latinorum*, Göttingen, 1969 [hereafter C] and *Proverbia Sententiaeque Latinitatis Medii ac Recentioris Aevi*, 5 vols., Göttingen, 1963–7; 2nd ed., 1982–3, in progress [hereafter P]. These include 4a lines 11–12 (P 28, 318), 14

(P 24, 256), 16 (C 2,559), 26 (C 436), 31 (C 4,333), 33 (P 33,183) and 4b lines 6 (P 30,626a),
9 (C 9,278), 15 (P 37,690a), 17 (P 27,684), 20–1 (P 28,311), 22 (C 2,052), 24 (C 11,136), 27–8
(P 38, 498c2), 29–30 (C 4, 539), 31 (C 17,913; P 28,967) and 34–5 (P 28,443).
(5)   On the recto of a fragment:
      Impetus est fuluis et vasta leonibus ira
                                     *   *   *
      Post noctam sperare diem, post nubula sol[em];
      3 lines of verse. On the verso:
      Phebus ab occasu rursus raptatur ad ortum
                                     *   *   *
      Non possunt habitare simul contraria cum sint;
      9 lines of verse. On the recto and verso of another folio, after two fragmentary lines:
      Sic iuuenis dum tempus habet sudaribus aptum
                                     *   *   *
      Cum videant illos carpere lucis iter;
      48 lines of verse, of which four are fragmentary. All come from Alain de Lille, *Liber Parabolarum*,
      book i, lines 105–7, book ii, lines 13–21, 37–84, printed in J. P. Migne, *Patrologia Latina*, vol.
      ccx, Paris, 1855, cols. 584–5. This work, a collection of proverbs and wise observations in verse,
      was a popular school text and is frequently found in school MSS.
(6)   On the recto and verso of a folio:
      [C]vm animadverterem quam plurimos homines errare grauiter in via morum . . .   . . .
      Libenter amore ferto. Explicit. Finis adest mete mercedem quero diete.
      The *Parvus Cato*, or prose prologue to the *Distichs of Cato*, printed by M. Boas and H. J.
      Botschuyver, *Disticha Catonis*, Amsterdam, 1952. The *Parvus Cato* which consists of 58 prose
      admonitions, beginning 'Itaque deo supplica/Parentes ama/Cognatos cole', etc., was one of the
      most popular of all school texts throughout the middle ages and the Renaissance.
(7)   On the recto and verso of five folios, part of them in scraps, the pupil's daily notes and exercises,
      of which the following is a complete transcript:

      On the recto of the left-hand of two joined folios:
            Hic incipit latinitates, prouerbia, enigmata, versus defferenciales, vulgaria ast vocabula
      post festum sancti Micaelis arcangeli, secundum vsum Magistri Dauid Juyne in prioratu
      sancti Nicolai de Berlyche inst[r]uentis.
                              In die mercurij
      Cubicularius meus ita strepuit in camera mea in aurora quod dormire non potui.
            Strepo, -is, -pui, to rustyll or bustyll.
            Strepo, -is, -vi, -re, to gagle as a gose.
      Odit eum mundus qui vult existere mundus.
      Ebrietas frangit quicquid sapiencia tangit.
            Hec commescacio, -is, for gret etyng.
                              In die iovis
      Nemo in hoc diuersorio quiete dormire potest, tum pro auium garriretu tum pro
      ancerum strepitu et pro canum latratu.
      Media nocte in meo sompno magnopere verebar nam vento tota nocte mea fenestra
      strepuit.
      Sompnus dat reliquiem sed vexant sompnia mentem.
      Qui plus ferri cupit quam portare valet hic sua sponte discrimina subibit.
      On the verso:
                              In die veneris
      Stultior est stulto qui plus ferre presumit quam sustinere potest.
            Viuo, inspiro, to be, lyve.
      Non viuas vt edis sed edas vt viuas.
      Qui cenam, merendam, prandium et iantaculum est ieiunus stratum non petit, ni insit
      sibi demon.
                              In die lune
      No man may nowadays plese or content excepte he can flatyr and glose and ber' to
      faces vnder one hodde.
      Nemo potest nunc dierum placere ni sciat adulari et palpare et simulare et dissimulare.
            Placeo, -es, -cui, to please or to content.
      Ego et frater meus sumus vnius etatis et vnius altitudinis sed non sumus vnius forti-
      tudinis.
            Hec etas, -is, for age.
            Hec fortitudo, -is for strenth.
            Hec altitudo, -is, for heyth.
      Si sis vri [*i.e.* vir] fortis non des tua robora scortis.
      Buxus dum crescit buxum dum crescere nescit.
      Ille qui suas normulas basso dicit nullo pacto nostro preceptori placere potest.
      On the recto of the right-hand folio:
                              In die iovis
      Media nocte magnam exclamacionem inter anseres, gallos, capones, gallinas et pullos
      audiui; credo quod vulpes interfuit illis.
      Non capo cavponem commedit sed caupo caponem.
            Hic gallus, -i, for a coke.
            Hec gallina, -e, for a hen.
            Hec pullus, -i, for a chyke.

Hec ancer, -ris, for a gander.
Hec vulpes, for a fox.
Hic capo, -is, for a chapon.

In die lune

Hodie ad scolam per circuitum veniebam vbi propriorem viam potui habere.
Disce, puer, dum tempus habes etate iuuinili,
Ne doleas cum pauca scias etate senili.

In die mercurii

Ista aura est apta ad ranas incubandum.
Ista phebe fuit valde ventosa, ymbrosa, procellosa et vltra modum pluuiosa.
Tibia dat sonitum sed portat tibia totum.
Siquis amat ranam, ranam putat esse dianam.

In die veneris

Ego hic in scola hodie [dimedia *cancelled;* semi *inserted*] hora ante horam sextam fui.
Bene potest nare cuius mentum sustinet alter.
Nolo scolam exire absque potestate preceptoris nam si exiero verberabor procul dubio.
Ante festum sancti Michaelis Welliam equitabo ad sacros ordines recipiendum, gracia diuina.

On the verso:

In die lune

Ista aura est mutabilis instar mentis muliebris, qua in tempore quo quis mingere potest novies mutatur.
Vaspa meam manum suo pugione pupigit.

In die martis

Te amo sed tuum consorcium minime amo, nam turpiloquio detraccione et scandalo plenus es.
Si doceas stultum non letum dat tibi vultum;
Odit te multum, vellet te scire sepultum.

In die mercurij

Plus, magis requirunt genitiuum qualitatiue,
Et ablatiuum tibi dabunt quantitatiue.

Hoc subligar, -ris, for a garter.

In die lune

Preceptor qui cotidie tirunculos informat aliquam cum re et aliquam ab re irascitur.
Dico sequor pedibus sed moribus dic imitari.

Deleo, -les, -ui, to put owte.

In die martis

Tu vero mirabiliter degeneras nam non pratrisas neque matrisas.
Ego sto coram preceptore instar ymaginis in pariete depicte, nam me non alloquitur neque ego ipsum alloquor.
Ego pravo tuam effigiem, dixit pictor ad suam ymaginem.

In die mercurij

Ego reperi heri numellam equi in orto dum mei.

On the recto of another folio:

Ego reperi heri numellam equi in orto dum mei [*repeated*].
Est compes furis sed equi datur esse numella.
Esto manus manica uult uetere bona quam colla.
O prauas et peruersas illorum dissipulorum condiciones qui sponte nolunt disce⌐.

In die jouis

Pape tuos mores qui mihi in quantum vales; semper et verbo et opere aduersaris pape interieccio; anglice y wondor, mervell.

In die veneris

Ego habebo scuticam, tu habebis petuitam; ego habebo rosam [?] et tu habebis catarrum. Y woll have the wypp.

In die lune

Preceptor noster bis hodie soluit ientaculum.
Preceptor noster bis hodie soluit ientaculum suum.
Jantamus mane jantaculum dicimus inde.

In die vineres [*sic*]

Campana quam audio non est tinnula neque bene arguta.
Vestris nostra damus; pro nostris vestra rogamus.

In die lune

Collega, scis tu quis hos tris pullos in mea zeta me ignorante conclusit?
Est thalamus zeta sic thome passio monstrat.

On the verso:

In die martis [*cancelled*]
In die marcurij

Nos diu scole abfuimus et ideo fore nostrarum regularum (vel nostras regulas) obliti sumus.

In die veneris

I hawe ete my belyfull of coloppes and egges today.
Ego hodie carbonellas et oua vsque adsaturitatem ventris mei edi.
Ego [   ] nunquam ante hunc diem cibum ederas.

Tu es instar suis que duodecim porcellos vberelactat.
Cum porcum tibi do, saccum reser[a]re memento.
Qui non vult dum quit, dum vellet forte nequibit.
 Reserro, -as, -ui, -re, to opun.
  In die lune
Ego sedeo in scola qui (vel que) est locus discendi.
Legere et scribere faciunt scolarem peritum.
Non vadit peritum [peryse *above*] qui vult audire peritum [wyse *above*].
  In die martis
Frater, loquere sapienter aut taceas nam de stultiloquio et ideo verbo ocioso in die
iudicij redenda est racio.
On the recto of another folio, whose verso is blank :
 Hic incipiunt latinitates, prouerbia, enigmata, versus differenciales, vulgaria ast vo-
cabula post festum natiuitatis dominice, secundum vsum Magistri Dauid Juyne in prioratu
sancti Nicholai de Berlyche instruent[is].
  In die [*lost*]
Noster preceptor inuen[it?] et docet nos nouellos gramaticastros gramaticam, sub-
[stanciam?] omnium scienciarum.
  In die martis
Ve mihi qui hodie tardu[s] ad scolam veniebam.
Ego sciscitabor Johannem socium meum heri rumores, et ipse nullos mihi voluit
narrare.
 Hic rumor, -ris, for a tydyng.
 In modio [ ] ola plena sciendi.
 [ ] sum, n, to inquier.
 N[arro, -ris, ?] to telle.
Ego narrabo preceptori quod [ ] sum sedere in pacem pro te.
  In die [*lost*]
Tria sunt qui nullo mod[o] [ ] haberi possunt, que tria in versibus subscriptis[ ].
 Latinum fari bene scr[ ]
 Hec tria nullus habet [ ]
  In die mercurij
Ego qui sto coram precept[ore] pretimor[   ]

On the recto of another folio:
 Omnibus nobis eundeum [*sic*] est ad piscinum [*or* pistinum?].
 Hic quadrans, -tis, -ti, anglice for a diall.
 Parco, -is, -si vel peperci, -re, anglice spare.
 Placeo, -es, -cui, -cere, anglice plese.
 Noceo, -es, -cui, -cere, anglice to hurte or noy.
 Respondeo, -es, -re, anglice anser.
 Precipio, -is, -re, anglice to command.
Infirmos medici querunt, comiuia mimi;
Funera presbiteri querunt, cadauera corui.
  In die mercurij
 Arbitror, -aris, -tus sum, n, to be cuntyd.
 Oppono, -is, -re, anglice to appose.
 Supplico, -es, -cui, -re, anglice to beseche.
 Subuenio, -is, -i, -re, anglice to helpe.
 Propicior, -aris, -tus sum, anglice to haue merci.
 Hec marra, -e, -e, anglice for a mattocke.
Quamuis ego sim inops et tu diues, tum me non dirideas . . .

On the verso:
  In die iouis
Quam plures [*word faded*] puer[i?] ob nutricis amorem osculantur.
Scribe ti[*word faded*] si vis vrbanus haberi.
 Hoc capicium, -i, -o, anglice a hood.
 Hic calx, -cis, anglice a hele.
 Hic calx, -cis, anglice for lyme.
 Sublestus, -a, um, anglice sore.
Osculare calcem meum, nam meum os est sublestum.
Osculare meam aurem cum lac littera.
  In die veneris
 Hec ocrea, anglice botte.
 No [mionativ?]o: calciatus, -a, u[m], anglice for wetsed.
 N[minativ?]o: somnolatus, -a, u[m], anglice for slepi.
 [ ]a me cecidit in cenum exopposito.

On another scrap:
 [Thi]s day fowr' days y was at London.
 [ ] quartus fui Londonijs.

(8) On the recto of a folio:
 (i) Ad corpus sanctus, ad mentem pertinet almus;
  Vir sacer est ille qui sacra celebrare solet;

see above, section 4a.
        Sanct*us*, -a, -um, for holy in body.
        Alm*us*, -a, -u*m*, for holy in mynd.
        Sac*er*, -a, -u*m*, for hym p*at* halowyth holy thyng*es*.
    (ii) Dies dominic*us*, for sonday ... ... In die sabbati, on saturday.
Two lists of days of the week, one nominative one ablative, in Latin and English.
    (iii) Hoc frewment*um*, -ti, -to, for whete.

(9) There are various other lines and scribbles throughout the MS, of which the chief are:
    (i) Memorit*er*, anglice wit*h*out boke.
    (ii) Hoc pandoxatorium, for a bruhosse.
        Hoc brasium, malte.
        Hoc promtuario, for a buttri.
    (iii) Ego sum stul[tus].
        Ego sum bonus pu*er* [several times].
        Ego sum bonus pu*er* quem zelat Altissimus.
        Ego sum alt*us* pu*er* puem zelat Altissim*us*.
    (iv) Est sine carne veru dicas cu*m* carne verutum;
        Est similis stulti qui p*r*edicat infatuo. Ame*n* dicant om*n*es.
    (v) Pargas in pace.
    (vi) Wylle*lmus* Nicolas [*also* Nycolas].

8

AN EARLY-TUDOR OXFORD SCHOOLBOOK

O N E of the most attractive genres of educational literature consists of the sets of Latin and English prose passages written by
English schoolmasters during the fifteenth and sixteenth centuries to
exercise their pupils in Latin. Some of the exercises were in Latin alone,
intended as examples or models of Latin grammar and syntax. Others,
which contemporaries called "vulgars" (Latin *vulgaria*), comprised
passages in English for the pupils to translate into Latin, with model
Latin versions for comparison.[1] What distinguishes the school exercises of this period and makes them so interesting today is the masters'
concern to appeal to their pupils by choosing subjects based on episodes of daily life and speech, especially those familiar to children. The
exercise books are consequently treasure houses of typical English
scenes, proverbs, quotations and colloquial dialogue which preserve
many details, both of life in general and schools in particular, which are
not easily to be found elsewhere. Many of these exercises survive in
manuscripts or in printed editions of the early sixteenth century, the
most interesting and sophisticated being the English and Latin *vulgaria*
of Arundel MS 249 in the British Library, which were composed by
one of the schoolmasters or fellows of Magdalen College, Oxford in
about 1500, and brought to light by the late Professor William Nelson
in his charming edition of them: *A Fifteenth Century School Book*.[2] The
present article is concerned with another set of exercises, similar to
those of the Arundel manuscript and originating from the same college
in the same period, but hitherto unprinted. They share the features of
other contemporary schoolbooks; they also adopt the attractive
method of teaching Latin through describing everyday scenes and
events, and they add much to our knowledge of the ideas, methods and
problems of English school education in the early sixteenth century.

The exercises in question are preserved in Royal MS 12.B.xx in the
British Library, a collection of five items from the late fifteenth and
sixteenth centuries, the others being a set of Latin medical notes and

---

[1] On *vulgaria* see Nicholas Orme, *English Schools in the Middle Ages* (London, 1973),
pp. 98–100.
[2] William Nelson, *A Fifteenth Century School Book* (Oxford, 1956).

three Latin tracts on mnemonics, one of them printed.³ It is not clear when the five came to be bound together. The school exercises are the fourth item in the collection (fols. 35–49), and cover fifteen paper folios measuring 14.5 × 21.5 centimeters. The paper bears two watermarks: a hat (fol. 35) and an erect hand with open thumb and closed fingers, surmounted by a star or flower (fols. 45–46). Watermarks which are fairly similar can be dated between about 1473 and 1530.⁴ The text is written in a hand of the same period, different from the other hands in the volume. It consists of 87 passages of Latin prose each followed by an English translation, the Latin being inset by about 1.5 centimeters to the right of the English. The text is not preceded by a title or any explicit sign that the present starting point was the original one, but this is probably the case since the first passage (fol. 35) commences "God help us at our beginning," which is very similar to the opening of William Horman's *Vulgaria*, published in 1519.⁵ The last extant folio, however, was certainly not the last originally, since it concludes (fol. 95ᵛ) with an eighty-eighth passage in Latin, the English version of which must have followed on another folio, now lost. It is impossible to tell how many folios have disappeared, but the number may have been high. The exercises in Arundel MS 249, which are similar in character, total 387 passages covering 53 folios, four or five times as long as the fragment in the Royal manuscript.

In content, the Latin and English passages of the Royal author resemble other contemporary collections of *vulgaria*, but in arrangement they do not. *Vulgaria*, as a rule, were presented with the English passage first and the Latin equivalent afterwards, but the Royal manuscript reverses this order. The Royal exercises, therefore, may not be true *vulgaria*, intended for pupils to translate into Latin, but a set of Latin passages illustrating different usages of grammar, to which a schoolmaster or pupil has added an English translation for his own purposes. The English is certainly slipshod at times, leaving out neces-

³ The MS is described in G. F. Warner and J. P. Gilson, *British Museum: Catalogue of Western Manuscripts in the Old Royal and King's Collections*, vol. ii (London, 1921), p. 18.

⁴ The hat is closest to C. M. Briquet, *Les Filigranes: Dictionnaire Historique des Marques du Papier*, 2nd ed., 4 vols. (Leipzig, 1923), nos. 3396 and 3406, dated respectively 1473–85 and 1524–25. The hand resembles Briquet's nos. 11152, 11154 and 11165, dated respectively 1473, 1479–82 and 1505, and *Monumenta Chartae Papyraceae*, vol. i: *Watermarks mainly of the 17th and 18th Centuries*, ed. E. Heawood (Hilversum, Netherlands, 1950), nos. 2470–82, dated 1508–1530.

⁵ William Horman, *Vulgaria*, ed. M. R. James (Oxford, 1926), p. 13.

sary letters and sometimes whole words, and this may strengthen the theory. The exercises feature the life and work of a grammar school, its master and his pupils. The school concerned can be easily identified. At one point the master declares that he would rather teach anywhere in the world than "here at Oxford" (passage 72); a speaker elsewhere compares Oxford with another town in which he is now living (81), and there are two mentions of "the university" (22, 78). The location is therefore undoubtedly Oxford. The school is open to day–boys from the town (34), boarders from elsewhere (22–23, 66), and it, its master and at least some of its boarders belong to an organized body, described as "our house" (22–23) and "our hall" (66), the members of which withdraw to the countryside in times of sickness (78, 81). After they have finished learning grammar the pupils go on to study logic (28). All this points clearly to Magdalen College School, Oxford, founded by William Wainfleet in 1478–80 and closely attached to the college itself.[6] The school was staffed by a master and an usher, who were paid stipends of £10 and £5 respectively, in return for teaching grammar without charge to all comers.

The pupils of the school included the choristers, demies (or under-graduate scholars) and commoners (or fee-paying undergraduates) of Magdalen College, pupils boarding elsewhere in Oxford, and sons of Oxford citizens. The demies went on to learn logic after they had mastered grammar, and the collegiate body frequently moved into the countryside when sickness raged in Oxford. The Latin base of the exercises was evidently composed by one of the schoolmasters, or by another member of the college for his use. Magdalen College School was one of the leading educational institutions of early Tudor England, and several schoolbooks were written by its masters or former pupils. Collections of Latin and English exercises in particular are associated with the names of John Anwykyll (master c. 1481–87), John Stan-bridge (master 1488–94) and Robert Whittinton (pupil c. 1494), as well as the anonymous one in the Arundel manuscript.[7] The Royal school-book is yet another example of the activity and inventiveness which characterized the school at this time, and as we shall see, some of its passages bear close resemblances to those in the Arundel collection.

---

[6] On the history of the school see R. S. Stanier, *Magdalen School*, 2nd ed. (Oxford, 1958).

[7] *Ibid.*, pp. 29–41; Nelson (above, note 2), pp. vii–xv.

The date of the Royal exercises is more difficult to establish. They cannot be earlier than the foundation of the school in 1478–80, or later than about 1549, in view of their Catholic notion of confession, contrition and satisfaction (16). Greater precision is hard to achieve. References to Greek being studied in England (77), to scholars travelling abroad to Italy (*ibid.*), and to the outbreak of sickness (22–23, etc.) could all have been made at any time during the reigns of Henry VII or VIII. The most helpful indicator is probably the mention of war and the exposure of English seaports to attacks by enemy ships (37). England was at war with France, or was in fear of attack from the sea, in 1489–97, 1512–14, 1522–27, 1539 and 1543–46. Of these dates, the 1490s seem a little too early. The Royal author stresses the importance of classical Latin authors, several of whom he names; he seems to despise pre-humanist Latin (47), and he is very conscious of the importance of his vocation (41, 48–50). In all these matters he is more emphatic, and therefore presumably later, than the author of the Arundel manuscript, who wrote in about 1500. Equally, the 1530s and 40s seem rather too late, in view of the watermarks and the absence from the text of any of the distinctive flavor of the Reformation period. On the whole the evidence, though not conclusive, points to the work as having been written during the French wars of 1512–14 or 1522–27.

The Royal exercises can be divided into two kinds, each with its own distinctive purpose. The first consists of those which allude to everyday surroundings, speech, or events and seek to arouse the pupil's interest by describing scenes with which he is familiar. The second comprises those which centre on moral advice and warnings, designed to inculcate virtue and to repress idleness and vice. Both kinds of passages have a common aim to widen the pupil's vocabulary, the one in concrete and the other in abstract words, and to teach him to use the Latin language fluently in speech and elegantly in written prose. The exercises are variously written as monologues in the first person, addresses to second persons, and statements about third parties. Sometimes the speaker is the master, sometimes the pupil, and sometimes he is not particularized. Only one passage (31) adopts dialogue form between two people, but in several other cases a statement by one person is followed by an answer from somebody else. Eighteen passages are arranged in pairs, the second being either a reply or a sequel to the first (17–19, 20–21, 22–23, 30–31, 35–36, 49–50, 58–59,

69–70, 71–72). Some of the exercises contain references to the times and seasons of the year, and these may indicate the length of time during which the work was composed. The passages start at the beginning of the year with the return to school after the Christmas holidays (2), and proceed via Lent (15–16) and the second Monday after Easter (27) to the summer or autumn (46). Later we are again in Lent (67), followed by further references to spring or summer (81) and to the season of soft fruit (87). All this suggests that the part of the work which survives was written during the space of eighteen months. There are similar indications of the seasons in the Arundel exercises, but there the pattern is irregular, and it is much less clear that the manuscript order reflects the calendar during which the author worked.

In other respects the relationship between the Royal exercises and those in the Arundel manuscript is a close one. The two authors were both writing for the same school within much the same period. Both aimed their work at the same level: that of advanced rather than elementary pupils, who were able to read Latin authors and aimed to proceed, as soon as they could, to the study of logic. Many of the same topics and situations, as might be expected, are dealt with in both texts, but there is particular significance in the fact that four of the passages appear in closely similar (though not identical) forms in both.[8] Clearly, one author has either read the other or else a source used by him. These resemblances are balanced by some differences of emphasis. The Royal exercises are more uniform in design than the Arundel ones. They contain fewer very short or very long passages; they are less concerned to increase the vocabulary of nouns, and hence exhibit less virtuosity in devising situations in which unusual nouns can be featured. The Royal text also makes far less use of the dialogue form which is so popular with the Arundel author. In general, the compiler of the Royal exercises is more sober and less playful or fanciful than his Arundel counterpart. For that reason the Royal manuscript, in its present form, is likely to be less appealing to a modern reader, though it remains a very interesting and instructive document for the historian.

We can now proceed from the text itself to the world of the master, school, and pupils it describes. The Royal exercises add further useful

---

[8] Royal 12 and Arundel 164; Royal 40 and Arundel 189; Royal 45 and Arundel 195; Royal 50 and Arundel 56. For other parallels see the notes to the text, below, pp. 37–39.

information to what is known about education in general and Magdalen College School in particular, during the early sixteenth century. The principal member of the school, the master, appears in many of the exercises. He is characterized as both wise and stern, sometimes giving encouragement (44) but more frequently admonitions (2, 4, 13, etc.), which can escalate into reprimands (64), threats (8), and the promise of punishment (72). Beating, however, which features prominently in other schoolbooks, is strangely underemphasized. The master is a single man, since there is no reference to his wife or family, and this accords with what we know of his real-life Magdalen counterparts, most of whom were either priests or unmarried clerks. He sometimes finds teaching in Oxford tiresome, because of the criticism he gets from others who think they know his business better than he does himself (72), but he is represented as a diligent teacher (56) and a sober citizen out of school hours, taking his recreation by gentle walking (84) and by dining out with a friend (53). The Royal author is much more conscious than the Arundel one of the importance of schoolmastering as a vocation. He rejects the extreme suggestion that children owe more to their masters than to their parents (49), but he considers that masters have a crucial role nonetheless (50). He likens them to parent birds, gathering small rules and Latin exercises to feed their pupils, just as birds do for their young (48). A master teaches his scholars learning, by which they can gain a living in adulthood, and precepts to lead them to virtue and the love of God (49). The author asserts it to be "an honest labour to teach" and one which both pleases God and benefits society, "for Tully saith what greater or better gift may we bring to a commonwealth than if we teach and inform young men" (41). These sentiments accord with a rise in the status of contemporary schoolmasters, and with a growth in their self-consciousness. The increasing number of endowed grammar schools like that of Magdalen, compared with the older type of school in which the master depended on fees, was giving their occupants more certain remuneration and better security of tenure.[9] The degree registers of Oxford and Cambridge in the early sixteenth century show many practising or intending schoolmasters taking degrees in arts or in grammar, with the

---

[9] On the status and remuneration of schoolmasters up to 1509 see Nicholas Orme, "Schoolmasters," in *Profession, Vocation and Culture in Medieval England*, ed. C. H. Clough (Liverpool, 1981); now above pp 49-71.

evident hope that graduation would improve their qualifications, status, and chance of promotion.[10] Magdalen College School was a particularly influential foundation in its day, owing to the wide circulation of its masters' textbooks, and one of its recent teachers, Thomas Wolsey, was rising during the 1510s and 1520s to become the greatest personage in England next to the king himself. No wonder, in this situation, that the Royal author should have looked on the status of schoolmasters with pride and complacency.

The boys whom the master taught included the children of Oxford citizens (34) and boarders from elsewhere, the latter, who are mentioned far more often (5, 28, 55, 57, 60, 67), being probably in the majority. Boys were supported at school by their fathers (58), widowed mothers (57) or other "friends" (55, 60), who provided them with food, drink, clothes, and masters (50). Some of those who boarded lived in Magdalen College itself or in the adjoining Magdalen Hall (22, 66), but others probably lodged elsewhere in Oxford. The latter group, and possibly some of the former as well, lived with tutors or "creansers" (Latin *creditores*), appointed by their parents to look after them. The creanser was a senior member of the university who controlled the boy's money, regulated his behavior (5), and supervised his progress through learning (28). In one case the creanser decides that a boy is not yet ready to proceed from the study of grammar to that of logic (28); in another example, a boy falls victim to a clash of authority between the creanser and the schoolmaster about when he should arrive at school in the mornings (5). The pupils' ages are not specified in the Royal exercises, but twelve is mentioned in the Arundel text,[11] and in reality the boys of Magdalen College School probably ranged from about ten to about eighteen. The length of time they spent there varied from pupil to pupil. One boy, whose father has sent him to Magdalen believing that two years or three at the uttermost would suffice, complains that he has studied grammar for two years and scarcely seems able to understand the first principles (58). He is told, apparently, to take extra lessons from a crammer (59). Others are

---

[10] On Oxford, pending a new edition of the "Register of Congregation" after 1505, see A. B. Emden, *A Biographical Register of the University of Oxford, A.D. 1501 to 1540* (Oxford, 1974), *passim*, and on Cambridge, *Grace Book Γ containing the Records of the University of Cambridge for the years 1501–1542*, ed. W. S. Searle (Cambridge, 1903), entries indexed on pp. 443 and 448.

[11] Nelson (above, note 2), p. 1.

judged to be competent after three or four years, by which time they are able to go on to higher studies (28).

The school day began early. The Arundel author mentions five o'clock as the time to start;[12] six was common in English schools of the early sixteenth century,[13] and a boy arriving at seven is much too late (5). The grammar curriculum included several stages and activities, and the boys in the school were consequently engaged in different tasks. The elementary stage of Latin involved the mastering of "small rules" and Latin examples, which the master prepared and expounded in a simple way (48). Rules could be studied from a written text, but were also committed to memory and learnt by heart "without book" (56). These "first principles" had to be understood before the pupil went on to more difficult matters (4, 88). Once he had learnt his elementary grammar, he was made to practise using words together. Boys in early Tudor grammar schools did prose composition in Latin, though this is not actually mentioned in the Royal exercises. They learnt to write Latin verses, which are depicted being scrutinized for false quantities and stuck up on a post for all to read (71–72). They were also expected to acquire fluency in speaking Latin by using it as often as possible for everyday purposes. "If thou cannest not express the conceits of the mind in Latin," declares the master, "this is the cause and none else, that thou art wont more to thy mother tongue than to Latin, which thing hurts greatly not only thee but also thy school fellows" (13). Eloquence, the speaking of Latin formally and by rules, was also highly prized (20–21), and schoolmasters organized formal speeches and disputations among their pupils, which helped to prepare them for logic and other university studies in which the method of disputation was employed.[14] The only disputation mentioned in the exercises, however, is an informal one between two boys on their own initiative (47). Finally, the grammar curriculum included the reading of good Latin literature, which meant after 1500 the pagan classical authors. Exactly what was read in Magdalen College School we do not know, but the classical quotations in the Royal exercises give some idea of the likely authors: Cicero, Horace, Martial, Ovid, Sallust, Terence, and Virgil.[15]

---

[12] *Ibid.*, p. 2.
[13] Orme (above, note 1), p. 124.
[14] *Ibid.*, pp. 98, 130–131.
[15] The earliest known lists of authors and texts studied in Tudor schools are those of

It was the schoolmaster's task to teach virtue as well as learning. As with many moralists, the Royal author felt that the youth of his day was especially in need of such teaching: "in our times . . . all young men for the most part give themselves more to pleasure than to learning" (41). Like others of his contemporaries—the Arundel author and the royal minister Edmund Dudley—he placed much of the blame for disorderly youth on the indulgence of parents, particularly mothers.[16] Just as the Arundel text depicts a boy being given his breakfast in bed and having his clothes warmed for him before he deigns to get up,[17] so the Royal exercises feature a pupil who misses school because his mother will not allow him to be wakened even when he has overslept. An implicit condemnation lurks within both episodes. It is the duty of the school and its master to correct this situation by good precepts, work, and discipline. "Cease, thou wanton boy!" roars the exasperated master at one of his fractious pupils, "though thou have been brought up here afore with thy mother, wantonly, yet I counsel thee to put out of thy mind that wantonness here!" Each boy is accordingly told of his duties to God, to his neighbors, and to himself. Without the help of God no one can be perfect (1). He must obey God's law (10), observe His holy times and seasons (16), and respect His messengers, the priesthood (74). He is reminded of his obligations to his parents who have given him life and support (50), and of his duty to work hard at school as they would wish (57, 85). He is instructed in the value of friends, who will listen to his troubles (40) and help him in need (25, 29). His pity is aroused, when he is cold, for the worse condition of those who lie in wards and prisons "which have neither fire nor covering to their bodies" (3). Finally, he is urged to be true to himself. He should aim to be virtuous all his life (17), to avoid the sins of anger (7), covetousness (42), and the chief temptations of the schoolboy: wasting time and the inordinate love of play (9, 11, 57, 85). For these and all his sins he must do penance (16). The Royal author is concerned with the ethics of behavior rather than the forms and has

---

Eton and Winchester in 1530 (A. F. Leach, "Winchester College," *Victoria County History of Hampshire*, vol. ii (Westminister, 1903), pp. 298–299; "Eton College," *Victoria County History of Buckinghamshire*, vol. ii (London, 1908), p. 179; *Educational Charters and Documents, 598 to 1909* Cambridge, 1911), pp. 448–451.

[16] For references see below, p. 38, note 34.

[17] Nelson (above, note 2), pp. 1–2.

little to say about etiquette and manners; he does, however, urge the need for decorum in speech (45, 69).

The work of the school, at Magdalen as elsewhere, was subject to many interruptions. School hours and terms were less standardized than they are today. The master could go off to dine at midday in such a leisurely fashion that he found, on returning, that his scholars had all gone home (53). In the Arundel text he can even be anticipated closing the school for a day or two in order to rest in the country.[18] Irregular holidays of this kind—remedies as they were called—were not greatly approved of by parents or those who supervized schools,[19] but regular ones took place quite lawfully at Christmas, Easter, on other high feast days, and in the summer, and these are mentioned four times by the Royal author (2, 54, 63, 72). Holiday tasks could be set (72), but the author felt little optimism that they would be done, and seems to have regarded holidays as an institution of doubtful benefit, eroding much of the knowledge his pupils had gained hitherto (54). Yet holidays at least could be predicted and were of limited duration; far worse were the disruptions caused to Tudor schools by visitations of plague and sickness. The threat of disease and its consequences is never far away from our author's mind. The chief thing that he and his contemporaries are anxious to know about the future is whether or not it will be a year of health or of sickness (36). "God give grace that it [the sickness] begin not again this year" (55). There is an apt illustration of the fear which the sickness inspired. Two scholars fall ill at the same time, one of them possibly merely through eating a rotten herring (22). At once an epidemic is suspected; several boys are withdrawn from the school, and when the two scholars make a quick recovery, it is necessary for the master to send out reassuring messages to persuade the absent to return (23).

The author's concern with the sickness reflected a real situation. Oxford was constantly visited and disrupted by sicknesses of one kind or another during the early sixteenth century. The prevention favored by organized bodies such as the colleges was for the whole community to withdraw to the countryside until the outbreak was over. The members of Magdalen were dispersed to Brailes and Witney in 1500, Witney and Wallingford in 1502 and Highworth in 1507, to name only a

---

[18] *Ibid.*, p. 30.
[19] Orme (above, note 1), p. 133.

few examples.[20] They lodged in farms and cottages, wherever places could be found, and the school went with them. All this is faithfully reproduced by our author, who varies his Oxford setting with scenes of rural life and portrays the difficulties caused by makeshift accommodation away from home. "When we last [went] forth from the university for sickness we had a foul slutty kitchen for our school, but now we be provided of a place a little more honest, how be it is but a stable" (78). Life in the country seems dull at first, compared with the pleasures of Oxford, but in time the refugees come to appreciate what it offers and are quite content to stay there until the summer is over (81). Not everyone, however, was able or qualified to follow the school to the country, and for the unlucky, sickness and its disruptions dealt a serious blow at their studies. "I was from school a great part of this last year," complains one scholar, "by the reason of sickness that continued here in the town." If it break out again, he declares, "I shall shortly go hence, for my friends have determined to send me away to another place where they think I may go to school with less jeopardy" (55). The predicament of scholars who had to change school through these outbreaks of sickness was one motive for the decision of the convocation of Canterbury in 1530 to introduce a uniform Latin grammar for the whole of England, a measure eventually made effective by Henry VIII in 1540.[21] The adoption by individual schools of different grammars, several competing versions of which were printed during the early sixteenth century, seemed to offer a real impediment to pupils whom sickness was forcing to move from one school to another.

Compared with his valuable glimpses of the contemporary school and its problems, the Royal author has little to say about the world outside and much less than his Arundel counterpart. National events impinge on him only when war breaks out (37), and his conversation, like that of Englishmen in general, centers much upon the weather (3, 15, 35, 46). The many delightful vignettes of Tudor life in the Arundel manuscript are not entirely absent, but they are few in number: men shooting for wagers at a hen buried in the ground (14), the women of a parish capturing men on Hock Monday to extract donations for the church (27), and most dramatic of all, the account of a mugging in

---

[20] W. D. Macray, *A Register of the Members of St. Mary Magdalen College, Oxford*, new series, vol. i (London, 1894), pp. 21–68 *passim*.

[21] Orme (above, note 1), pp. 254–257.

Oxford at 8:00 P.M., when one of the scholars was set upon by three villains who beat him and stole his purse (66). Yet if the Royal author fails to reach the heights of the Arundel master, his work remains a good example of its genre and better than some of the others. It attempts to fulfill several tasks and succeeds by no means badly. It conveys Christian values, teaches fluency in Latin both written and spoken, and introduces its readers to classical literature. It tries to reach their minds by means of ideas and situations familiar to them and to which they can respond. It is another monument to a period in which educationists worked hard to convey the best things in the best way, with an ambition and ingenuity equal, perhaps, to any of their successors.

TEXT

The text is that of the English passages in British Library, MS Royal 12 B xx, fols. 35–49. Punctuation, sentence division, and the use of capital letters follow modern practice, except for proper nouns which are capitalized (or not) as in the original. Words or word elements which appear separately in the manuscript, but which are generally written together today, have been joined by hyphens. All abbreviations have been expanded and omissions supplied, the former in italics and the latter within square brackets. Finally, a number has been added to each passage for purposes of reference, and the notes refer to these numbers.

[fol. 35]

1. God helpe us at owre begynny*ng*, with-owt whos helpe we can not *pro*fet, for likewise as *the* bowes of trees if *the* be cut vp from *the* royttes sone wether and wanysshe a-waie, so we if we lacke *the* helpe and grace of god son fall and come to nowght.

2. Me semeth it is tyme to leue owre plays, sport*es* and mery conseitt*es* *tha*t we haue fullyd your mynd*es* with this cristinmes holidays, *and* to fall in hand a-nother while with mate*r* of sadnes, for and if we giue your

selfe styll a-pease to maters of sport, it wilbe long or we cum to con-
nyng wich must be gotten with grett labour and diligence.

3. For all my clothis iet I am often tymes a-cold. I mervell in what case
the be that be kept in wardes and prison this cold season, wich haue
nother fier nother covering to ther bodis. In a veri evill case me semeth
the be.

[fol. 35ᵛ]
4. I thinke that ye can not profet, your furst principulles not knowen.
Therfor first of all se that ye knowe them, wiche knowne ye sholle son
a-wae with other thinges.

5. He that hath the rule of me will not be content that I shold go furthe
before hit be sevin of the clocke strekyn, therfor I can not tell what y
may do, wether I shuld do after him or eles the scole master, wich will
for-bede me the scole except I vse to comme soner in the mornyng.

6. I ma wyet all the wrong that I haue sufferd to the and to no body eles,
for and if I hade not folowid the cownsell that thu dides gyue me, I
shold neuer haue be in dawnger of this wronge. Therfor me semeth I
did folisshely to do after thy cownsell.

7. He semeth a weri demure felow but and thu shuldyth continew with
hym as many yeres as I haue don, thu woldist say that ther wer not an
angraer mane in the world, for he wilbe angre at the waggynge of a
straw, wich thyng makyth me often tymes werie of his cumpany.

[fol. 36]
8. My maister did thretyn me yester-nyght whan I wente to bedde,
whos thretyng be-cause y was grettly aferd of, y dyd rise today oon
owre soner then I was wont to do and conveyd miselfe owte off the
dore priuilye, trustyng to gett, or y cum in his sight a-gayne, sum-
bodye to entrett hym to for-gyue me.

9. Me semet I haue had no smale lose of tyme that haue discontinuyd
scole this iiijor or v yere, gyuyng no maner of heyd in the world to
good lernyng. It greuthe me now to remember how vngraciosly and
how wrechedly I haue spend my tyme.

10. I determynyd rather to dye then to folo thi consell. Thu art the
[most] vnresonable man that euer y was wit. Thinkist thu that thu
cannist cause me to do that is a-genst bothe the laue of man and of god?

*Th*u *ca*nust not ma, therfor do not *con*sell me this. Go get suche as be of thi appetiet, for I will neu*er* agre wnto the.

[fol. 36ᵛ]

11. It is pity to spare an vnthrifti trewand as *th*u art. *Th*u hath no *con*sideration how *th*u spend*es* thi tyme so that *th*u maist haue thi belie full of plaie, but p*a*rawent*er* *th*u shallt oons repent the lesyng of thi tyme.

12. Su*m* men haue so redi witt*es* in thing*es* to be don *that* for all *the* weyghtenes of them yet ther ys nothyng to sech w*ith* them, but as for me I am of a cleyn *con*trary disposition, w*ich* as oft as I haue any mat*er* of weyght to be don, am so vnredy that I c*an* not tel in *the* worlde whether to turne me.

13. If *th*u cannyst not exprese *the* conseyt*es* of thi mynd in latyn, this is the cause *and* noon el*es*, *that* *th*u art wont more to thi mother tong than to latyn, w*ich* thyng hurt*es* gretly not only the but also thi scole felow-is.

[fol. 37]

14. As I walkyd yest*er*day in the feld*es* I sawe a henne set vpe to shoit at ix strid*es*, soo that *the* hed only shulde a-pere owt, all the remnand of the bodi hide vnd*er* the gronde, *and* ther was no man lett shott at hir but suche only as wold promisse *that* as oft as the faylyd of the hedde the wold lese so many pense.

15. Iff this ferwent cold *con*tynewe as hit hath begonne, it will make an ende of me or this lent *cum* to a nende, for I c*an* nother a wey with hunger nor w*ith* colde.

16. This holy tyme *that* is callynd lent requirith all true cristyen me*n* to do penance for ther synnes and returne in to fau*er* with allmyghty god, for true penance is that thing *that* maketh gode m*er*cifull to sinners, w*ich* penance no ma*n* c*an* do well except he will *con*fese and be sori and do sat*is*faction.

[fol. 37ᵛ]

17. This day senett oon of my bretheren that I lovid best of any ma*n* in the world died upon a *con*sumption, whose deth thawght it c*an* be bot hevines to me, yet be-cause I eu*er* knew hym vertuose in all his lyffe, I am more glad of his vertuosnes than I am hevy for his dethe.

18. Hit is for a wise man to take no gretter burden apon hym than he maye a-way with, w*ich* thing me semythe orasse techith vs well wher he seith, take ye *that* writt a mater equall to your streynketh *and* consider wel what ye ma a-wa w*ith* and what ye ma not. Therefor as for this mater as su*m* me*n* do cownsell the to take in hand, or *th*u begyn it loke well what thi strenketh ma do. If *th*u thenke *that* *th*u art able to performe it, take hit in hand; if not, it wer wisedom to refuse hit.

19. How be it *th*is mater semeth hard to the and gretter then I may ma away with, yet by-cause hit is pot vnto me of suche a ma*n* as I lowe well *and* also *that* I percewe loweith me right well, therfor I am a-visyd to sa what I can do rather then vtterly to refuse hit. Paraventer hit semeth harder to the then to me, for ther is no thyng hard to a ma*n* that lowith, as tully weneth.

[fol. 38]
20. Eliquens is a gay thing be the w*ich* a ma*n* ma expresse all the consetes of his mynd w*ith* grett abu*n*dance *and* diuersite of speche, but yet me semeth eloqua[ns] w*ith*owt wisdom doth a man but lityll good, for wisdom is the fu*n*dation of eloque*n*s as it is of all other thyng*es*.

21. He that desirithe to be eloque*n*t had nede to go to philosophie, for w*ith*owt hit as tully seyt no ma*n* can be mayd eloque*n*t, for of it cum*m*yth all the abu[n]dant of ornat spech w*ith*owt *the* w*ich* can be seid and expressid noo thyng wisely, no thyng excellently, no thyng abun-dantly.

22. Ther be tow scolers in owre howse *that* be veri sike in ther stomakes, of *the* wiche oon wyt*es* all his disease to *the* etyng of a heryng, the other knowis not *the* cause of his disease. God grant the both scape ther siknes *and* recouer, for an if fortune them to die ther deth will make not only vs but many other to fle from *the* vniuersite.

[fol. 38ᵛ]
23. Owre scolars *that* we toke so gret hevynes for the last day be recoverd, thankyd be god, *and* therfor se *that* when *th*u cum*m*yst agayne *th*u bryng thi scole felowis as many as be lefte at home w*ith* [the] to scole, for her is no iuperti to be a-frayd of.

24. If *th*u wer suche a ma*n* as y dyd take *the* for, it shold not a grevid the to do this *that* I haue desiryd of *the*, I can not tell how ofte it shuld not a byne, as *th*u knowist as well for my profet as for thyn, but I know

not suche a-nother as *th*u art, for *th*u art nother good to thyselfe nother to any other body.

25. I haue sped all my besines *tha*t I had to do at London wi*th* a mervelos spede and wi*th* as good a spede, con mater and noo mo except, wi*ch* bi-cause I cowde not bryng to passe af*t*er my mynd bi-fore my depa*r*tyng from thense, I pot hit to a good frend of myne wi*ch*, if he gyue *th*e diligens in hit as he p*r*omisid me, can not sped a-mysse.

[fol. 39]
26. If ther shalbe any thyng *tha*t ye thinke *tha*t [I] can do you good yn, cum vnto me when ye will; ye shall lacke nother my duty nother my diligens in suche thing*es* as I thynke shalbe for your profet.

27. As I went hes*t*erday to sant mari church *th*er cam a grett meny of wemen a-bowte me and be-gane to stope me of my gate, so *tha*t [I] cowde nother go forwarde nother backewarde for them. And when I axid them what *th*e ment thei answerd *tha*t it was the gyys to let no ma*n* pase *tha*t day but *th*ei would haue sumwhat of hym, *and* so wether I wold or no I was fayne to giue them sumwhat. *And* I dyd se after-ward *tha*t I was not se*r*uid soo onli but many other me*n* wher so se*r*uid as well as y, for ther was no ma*n* passid by them but the got sumwhat of hym other by hocke or by crocke.

28. Ther were viij of owre scole felose takyn from vs the last weke wi*ch* had ben at gramare iij or iiij yere *and* wer judged able to go to sophistice, *and* I shold haue gone to sophistir too if my crea*n*ser wold a byn co*n*tent, but he wold fayne haue me to here a lity*n* more gramer ar I be takyn from hense.

[fol. 39ᵛ]
29. I am both fatherles and mother-less and [have] no kynseman to take succor of except you. Therfor I pray you for the loue *tha*t was sumtyme be-twene my father *and* you to se to me and help me, for if ye for-sake me I am vt*t*erly lost.

30. To se as tesipho seyth in terence, I am a-fraid to prace *th*e to *th*i face leste *th*u thinke *tha*t I do it more to flat*t*er the than to say as I thinke. Therfor *th*u shalt loke for no preis of me but sho[r]tly I will showe *th*e what is my mynd. Me semeth *th*u shot*es* well, *th*u rides well, *th*u pleis at

tenesse well, *and* to make a short talk *and* se as phedra seyth in ouyd, what su*meuer th*u doyst it pleasit well my seght.

[fol. 40]
31. When *th*u dyd se so oft *that* I dyd all thing well, I was a-frayd lest at *the* last *th*u woldyste haue pleayd w*ith* me as the se me*r*cial playd w*ith* attalus. How plead marshall w*ith* attalus? Tel me a good feloschippe. I wold tell if I had lesur, but and if *th*u redde *the* epigrame that folowithe thu shalt vnde*r*stand by thi selfe.

32. I can not be in rest her for your antony, w*ich* dyd bete me a-bowt *the* hede *and* a-bowt *the* face yesterda w*ith* his fiste*s*, so that for ache this nyght y cauld be no mane*r* a menys fayl a-slepe. Ye ma se how my hede is fowle, how blacke *and* blew my cheke*s* be, *and* if ye fynd not remedi for this mate*r* it is tyme for me to goo hense for good and all.

33. Ther is a co*m*panion of myne that sayth *that* ther is [no] mete so hevi but it ma be digestid in a daye and a nyght. He seyth ther is so grett heyt in eue*r*ybody, but I ca*n* not pe*r*cewe suche a heit in my body, for it fortunyd me this day tre days to ete henys mette w*ich* as moche as I ca*n* percewe is not yet all digestyd; therfor I haue a me*r*velu*s* cold stomake.

[fol. 40ᵛ]
34. I wakyd a grett part of *th*is nyght *and* abowte day I begane to fall fast *and* heuy a-slepe, *and* so thawghe the owre *that* was a-powntyd me to to go to scole in was cu*mm*e, yet my mother co*m*mandyd *that* ther shuld no noyse be mayd *and* wold not let me be callyd vp. Therfor my mother is *the* cause of my late co*m*yng *and* not I, for if I had wakynd my selfe or el*es* anny other body had wakynd me, y wold haue ben glad to a comyn hether at *the* owr *that* was a-powyntyd to me.

35. This day 6 days I was in *the* contrey to make me mery, *and* when I had pu*r*posid yerly in *the* mornyng to take my iorney from thense hitherward, ther was a husbanma*n* cownsellyd to me leue my iorne as for *that* day, thought *the* wether apperyd very faire to me, for he seyd *that* he knew by ce*r*tyn tokynys *that* hit schold be a ranny day. So after muche commu*n*ication had w*ith* hym y folowyd his cownsell *and* taryd ther that day, in *the* w*ich* ther was y wene more rayne then was any other day this yere. I was in hand w*ith* the felow after that, [fol. 41] wyllyng fayne to know how he knew afore *that* this shold be, w*ich* answeryd me *that* he knew oft tyms not only when rayne sholde be but

also many other thyng*es* be notyng *the* risyng*es*, the goyng*es* doyn *and the* mowyng*es* of *the* sun and of *the* moyne and other synn*es* of sterres.

36. I wold god *thu* had axid *that* feloue, *that* maid hym-selfe so wise of thing*es* to c*um*, what he p*er*cevid of this yere: whether he thowggt it shuld be a yere of helth or of syknes. How be it I wene it be bett*er* for a man to hold his peace than to axe suche man*er* of q*ue*stions, for schall no man m[a]ke me to beleue *that* any ma*n* ma know what is to cum except god put hit in hys mynd, yet I do not deny but many thing*es* ma be *con*iecterid of suche me*n* as note diligently the p*ro*fis of thyng*es*.

37. Suche men as dwell in *the* town*es that* be a-pon *the* seye syde, *and* especiall suche townes as lyes open to *the* prayes of *the* stuner*es* of *the* sea, be fayn to kepe wache both nyggt *and* day this ware tyme, lest ther enimys c*um* apon them vnware *and* distroe ther lond*es and* the[r] tow-n*es*, and other take them prisoun*er*es *and* cari them awai wi*th* them or el*es* vtt*er*ly kyll them.

[fol. 41ᵛ]

38. My scole felow hathe complaynd of me to yow wraunfully, wher-for I pray you to gyue noo *cr*edans to his complant*es* tyll the trewith be browggt owt. Y wil bryng for my wittnes tow or thre sad men w*i*ch shall p*ro*ve *and* be opun tokyn*es* showe *that* I am fawetles in *thi*s as y am accusid yn.

39. Tully, if a grett cause had not lat hym, wold a left noo place of philosophie but he wold a mad hit lyght by latyn, w*i*ch thyng if he had don he shold a doyne a grett ease to them that studie both philosophie *and* eloqu*en*s.

40. It is not only a pleasur but it is very p*ro*fitable for the to haue suche a frend *that thu* mayst be bold to comm*en* everie thyng w*ith* as *thu* wylst w*ith* thi-selfe, for in suche a frend*es* communication *thu* mayst put a-wey all troble *and* vexacion, but and if *thu* be so cloyse *that thu* wylt make no ma*n* of *thi* knolege thow shallt ofte tym*es* hurt thi-selfe.

[fol. 42]

41. It is an honest labor to teche, and suche a labor *that* a ma*n* ma both please God in *and* do muche good to *the* commonewelth, for tully seith what grett*er* or bett*er* gyfte ma we bryng to a comenwelth than if we teche and informe yong men, *and* especially now in owre tym*es* in *the*

wyche all yong men for *the* most p*ar*t gyue them-selfe more to pleasur than to lernyng.

42. My father hath riches a-nowghe but for all his riches yet he is alweis nedi. In good soeth me semeth he hath *the* properti of a cowetos ma*n* for, as horase sayth, *the* cowetys man ys alweys nedy *and* to his mynd agreyt also saluste, seyng covetosnes is eu*er* withowt ende *and* vnsaciable *and* his minishid nother in plenty nother in powerti.

43. Hit wer a folishe thing for me *that* haue a-nowghe to do of my owne mat*er*s to imbesy me in thine, for hit can not be chosin but that oon shall lett the other *that* bothe ca*n* not be don well. Wherfor I pra *the* put *th*i mat*er*s to su*m* other body to do, who so eu*er* *thu* wylt.

[fol. 42ᵛ]

44. If *thu* haste a good witt, giwe suche heyd styll a-pece as *thu* hast, be ground *thu* wylt growe shortly to grett con*n*yng, but *and* if *thu* gyve no labur but trust to moche apon thy witt, the laukyth *thu* wilt be deceuyd *and* the shall pass the that haue but dowle wittis.

45. If *thu* woldyst refrayn thi-self fro*m* the fowle communicacion *that* *thu* vsist dayly, ther shold be no man in the world *that* I wold desire to cu*m*pany wit more. If *thu* dydist vnd*er*stande how euyll hit be com-*m*yng the and *thu* grettly *thu* dost a-myse w*ith* *th*i spekyng in *that* faschon, y dowte not but *thu* woldyst refrane from all suche comunica-cion.

46. I wene *the* wynd *that* was hest*er*day hath cast don applys, peris, wardens *and* many suche other frut*es*. I wene also *that* it hat layd done suche corne as is to rancke, for y remember not *that* eu*er* y hard grett*er* blast*es* seth I was borne.

[fol. 43]

47. I had moche a-do yest*er*da w*ith* a rewde gramarion w*i*ch dispisid al good lernyng laten, and prasuse only his barbarusnes. We wer at bate for many thyng*es* that we spoke, wiche me thought wer far from good latyn. Y wold god *thu* haddist byn by, for we lacked a jugge to ende *the* stref *that* was betwen vs.

48. Lykewise as brid*es* gether mete in ther mowght*es* *and* part it a-mong *the* yong whan *the* be lityn oons and not able to helpe them selfe, *and* after *the* be waxid bige or rype go a-for them and teche them to cu*m*

owt of ther neyst*es* a lityl and so to fli a-bowte vntyll the be able to get ther oon mete, so good techer*es* gather small*e* rules *and* latyns *and* part them a-monge *the* yong scolar*es*, and as the go forward a lityll and a lityl*l* expownde vnto them all the best author*es*, and sease not teching them vntyll *the* be able to rede them selfe and to vnd*er*stand that as they rede *and* to gether out of that as the vnd*er*stande all thing*es* as be most profitable for them.

[fol. 43ᵛ]

49. Me semeth I ame more bownd to my maisters than to my father or my mother, for as for my fat*her and* mo*ther* to se as sent bornard seid make me as a damnyd body or y was borne in-to *the* world. Sinn*er*s brought furth a sinn*er* in ther syne, wrechys brought furth a wreche in-to this wrechid world; of them I haue nothing but wrecheydnes, syne and *thi*s corruptable body. But as for my masters wiche, when I was nother lernyd nother manerd, toke in hand to bryng me to lernyng and man*er*, went a-bowt dilygently to bryng me vp *and* informe me not only in lernyng by *the* w*ich* y myght be able to lyve by but also in precept*es* bi *the* w*ich* I myght cum to vertu and to *the* lowe of god by, therfor to these me semeth I am most bownde.

50. Ther is no man I wene but he thynk*es that* *th*u art much bownd to thi ma[s]t*er*s, but me semeth it is a-cordyng *that* *th*u knolege thi-selfe more bownd to thi fat*her* and mo*ther*, for thay the for god*es* sake how browght the furthe in-to *the* world, how norischyd the aft*er* *th*u was brought in-to the world, how prouydyd *the* mast*er*s aft*er* *th*u was nori-shyd vp to whom *th*u was sette as son as it was possible for thi age, how fownd the meite and drynke and cloith so long as *th*u gettest conyng. For-sueth thi father *and* thi mo*ther and* no-bodi el*es* fownd *the* abun-dantly all this, therfor me semeth it is a-cordyng *that* *th*u knolege thi-selfe most bownd vnto them, howbeit I say not na bot *th*u art bownd to both.

[fol. 44]

51. Hit can not be sayd how gretely this lytyll discontinuaunce hathe hurt you, for hit hath maid you not only to forget many things but also hit hath pluckyd your mynd*es* from studi. Therfor I advise you to leve all man*er* of plays *and* record suche thyngh*s* as ye haue lernyd, lest parauent*er* ye repent this discon*tinuaunce* hereafter.

52. This boye playd the lord yester-day a-mong his companyonce,

a-poyntyng eu*er*y man his office. Oon he mayd his carver, an-other his butlere, an-other his porter, an-other bi-cause he wold not do as he commandyd hym he toke and [made] all to bete hyme, and to make and ende at few word*es*, lykewyse as Cyrus pleyd oons *the* kyng of boyes so he begane to play *the* kyng of his companiouns, how be it I trow in an un-lyke chaunce, for as cyrus was a noble man borne and at *the* last he cam to *the* riallthe of a kyng in veri dede, but as for this is a knawe borne and be lykelyhode wyll playe the knawe all *the* remnant of his lyffe, except he mend his vnhappy man*er*s betyme.

[fol. 44ᵛ]

53. I went I to *the* towne yesterday to dyner, desiryd of an honest man, *and* after dinar I ryde my-selfe from thens as quychely as y cold to *that* attendance to you as y aught, but aft*er* I came hither a-gane I fonde noo mane her for me to teche. Tell ther-for att whose comm*an*menth ye went hense. Thynke ye *that* ye ma do her withowt punyscment what sone eu*er* ye lest? Na, na, ye be deceuyd if ye do thynke so, for except ye haue *the* bett*er* excuse ther shall not as moche as oon of you scape vnpunyschid.

54. Now *that* the holy days be past I advise you to renve *the* studes *that* ye haue discontynyd. I fere me lest this discontinuaunce hath hurt grettly and su*m* of you and especiall *the* wich, as long as *th*u haste ben a-wa, I dare swere thu loked*est* not as moche as oons apon thi boke, wich thyng p*ar*avent*er th*u wylt repent her-aft*er*.

55. I was from scole a grett part of this last yere *and that* be *the* reason of sykenes *that* c*on*tynyd her in the towne. God gyue grace *that* it be-gyne not a-gen this here, for and if it do I shall shortly go hense, for my frynd*es* haue det*er*mynd to send me a-wa to an-other place wher the thinke I ma go to scole withe less iup*er*ty.

[fol. 45]

56. I sholl haue no lesser a-fore dyner to declare suche thing*es* to you as hit was my mynd to do, for by-cause thys for-nowne for *the* more p*ar*te [I am busy] aboute techyng thys boie. After dinar we shall fynd a tyme more conveniant; the meane season, do you recorde *and* can withowt boke suche thyng*es* as wer thaugh[t]e hest*er*day.

57. If thi mother wich only now *that* thi fat*her* ys deyd fynd*es* the exhibic*i*on to scole did know thi disposition well, I wene she wold not

let *the* continue long her, for *thu* canst neu*er* a-dell how lytyll *thu* profet
in lernyng so *that thu* myast passe other thi tyme w*ith* pleyng and
sportyng, and *that* w*ith*owt beatyng.

58. My fat*her* send me hether to lerne gramm*er* wenyng *that* ij yere or at
the vtt*er*-must iij yere suffices for me sped *that* mather, but I haue bene
at gram*m*are this ij yere *and* me semeth *that* a-neyth I vnd*er*stand the
furst princi[p]les of hit, therfor I c*a*n not tell in *the* world how I shall
content my fathers opinion.

59. This mather requirith both more tyme and labor than *thu* wenst *that*
it doth; therfor for I desire *the* hartely, put it not to me the w*i*ch haue
a-nowghe to do of my*n* oon mat*er*s. *Th*u shalt fynd other e-now *that*
wylbe glad to take it in hand, if *thu* p*ro*misse to reward them w*ith* mone
accordyng to ther labor.

[fol. 45ᵛ]
60. Ther is nother shamefastnes that c*a*n fere *the* from filthenes, nother
shopnes of punyschment from vnythryftines, and ther-for as sone as I
may speke w*ith* thy frynd*es* I wyl desire them to take [the] hense, for
her ther is no mane I dare say but he is wery of thi abominable condi-
tionce.

61. Me semeth all meyth waxith owt of season now except hene w*i*ch is
pleasaunt, yet so *that* it be tend*er* and sawsid w*ith* th*e* joyse of an orage
w*ith* sugure and a lityll ging*er* put to.

62. I dyd take ij of owr scolar*es* iettyng *the* last nyght at suche a season
as it was more meyt for men *that* kept good rule to be *that* rest*es* in ther
bed*es* than to wagge a-bowt in *the* strett*es*. If I schold tell you who *the*
be, p*ar*avent*er* you wold gyue but lytyll c*re*dance to my word*es*, for the
seyme to demure *and* to gentyll to geytt in *the* nyght tyme *and* to go
a-bowt anny schrowyd turne, but and [ye] had sene them as I dyd ye
wold haue sayd *that* the had been more lyke ravenyng wolfys then
demure *and* gentyll yong men.

[fol. 46]
63. Ye had your liberte now a grette whill to play at dise, at card*es*, at
tabl*es*, at chest*es*, to syng, to daunce, to drynke, to reuell and to do
suche thyng*es* as ye thowght p*er*tynyd to *the* pleasur of mynde. Now
this day begyng*es* in another man*er* of lernyng *that* requirith other

manor*es*. It is yo*ur* parte therfor to go a-bowght other thynges, *that* is
to say go se a-nother whyll your bok*es and* renew your studis *that* haue
ben discontinuyd and set yo*ur* mynd*es* to them, for *and* you begynne all
to pla styll a-pece ye shall neu*er cum* to *the* lernyng *that* ye desire.

64. Sese, *thu* wanton boy, complayn no mor of this cause *that thu* art in
here! *Thu* art in bett*er* case here then *thu* art worthi to be. Thoughte *thu*
haue ben brought vp here afore w*ith* thi mother wantonly, yet y co*n*sell
the to put owt of thi mynd *that* wantones here, for *and* if *thu* do not *thu*
shall sa here-after *that thu* hast a grett caus to complayn.

65. I haue solde my boke for an noble w*i*ch was neu*er* bought vnder a
riall. Thought I had lost in *the* sellyng of hit yet I am glade *that* I haue
sold hit, for hit is so corrupe *that* I hade neu*er* pleasur to loke on hitt.

[fol. 46ᵛ]
66. Ther ys a scolar in owr hall that had a lytyll besines to doe in the
towne *the* laste weke. He went owt to do hit in *the* euynyng vnhappaly,
w*ith* whome thre goynge lyke scolares—but the were theuys in very
deyde—meyt hym abowght viijt of *the* cloke as he was comyng hom
agayne. One of them steppyd to hym *and* stoppyd his moyth w*ith* one
of his hand*es* leset he shold crye owt, and w*ith* the tother hand he
pomelyd hym a-bowth the payte to make hym a-masyd. The meyne
whyll *the* secunde pluckyd a-way his pur*es and* all *the* mone *that* was in
hit. The iijde stode a good way of, wachyng lest any shold *cum* a-pon
them sodenly. What and thes feloys had ben taken, as the myght sone
haue bene, and if *the* mater had ben craftely handelyd what and if the
had ben hangyde w*ith* them *that* were hangyd yesterday for stelyng. I
wene ther hys no mane bot the wold say *that* the hadbene well saruyd,
but the be a-lyue yet *and* shall lyue a-monge vs, ye and if *the* had done a
more greuose myschefe, for suche men as schuld especiall serche owt
suche me*n* take no heyd in *the* world, therfor it ys no wond*er* if the haue
boldnes to do grett*er* myschefe her-after.

67. My father sende me fygges *and* resyns in *the* begynnyng of lent, *the*
w*i*ch I layd vp in my cofer thinkyng not to take them w*ith*-owt tyll
werey neyde compellyd me, but sum-body hath cumyn—I ca*n* not tel
who—*that* hath broken vp *the* loke and emptyd my cofer clene *and* lefte
[fol. 47] nother fyge nor resyng for me. If he had taken p*ar*te, who so
eu*er* he was, I wold haue ben content, but to haue all takyn a-wa I ca*n*
do no no*ther* wise but be discontent.

68. Hit is told me ye fowght yesterda hand to hand; let me se *th*is day *wi*ch of you dar feght *with* me hand to hand. I am cu*m* here owt to feght *with* one of you *wi*ch su*m*euer he be, *th*erfore let on what su*m*euer he be cu*m* owt to assa what his ma*n*lynes ca*n* doo. If he haue *th*e bett*er* of me let hy*m* pu*n*yse me to *th*e vttermost—I be-shrowe hym if he spare—but and if he fortune to haue the worse a shrinke, let hym be ware, let hym not trust to skape vnpunysshid.

69. When *th*u dydest speke I toke hede *and* held my peise, but now when I speke in the mydest of my tale *th*u tak*est* it owt of my mow-the, *th*u bringyst me owt of hit and troblest all my communicacion. Therfor I neu*er* kepe to haue commu*n*yca*ci*on *with* a babler, as I perceue *th*u art, *and* if *th*u hadd*est* any shame *th*u owghtyst to be ashamyd of *th*i bablynge.

70. Well, go to! I wyll do nomore, so tell forth *that that* is behynd. *Th*er is no remedy bot I must hold my pease, for I se wel *that* a litell thyng ma bryng you owt of yo*ur* talke, wherfore tell you haue done I wyll speke neu*er* a word at all.

71. Who styckyd vp all thes v*er*sus apon this post? Who-so-eu*er* he was me semeth he was not dylygent enowght in s*er*chyng vp eu*er*i sinable, but ther is no thyng *that* I wyll say in thys [fol. 47ᵛ] mat*er*. Ther be *th*at wyll both answere to them and correcke to *th*e vtter-most the fawtys if ther be any funde in them.

72. I hade leuer teche in any place in *th*e wor[l]de then her at oxford, wher I ca*n* teche nothyng *that* I thanke profitable for my scolar*es* bot su*m* be agenst yt; I ca*n* consell nothyng but the co*n*sele *th*e contrarie. I consellyd you to make u*er*sis thes holydays [and] when ye had mayde them to sett them vp apon this post. Ye bega*n* and ther was no mane *that* was wise but he prasyd you for yo*ur* begynny[n]g. I merwell grettly for what case ye seasyd from yo*ur* purpose. Who conseled or feryd you from hit? I wene *that* hare brane feryd you *that* set vp v*er*sus here *and* presumptuosly comman-dyd to silens. In good feith if [I] knewe for a surty *that* you wer a-frayd for hym I wold sharpely punyse you eu*er*yon. Be-ware *th*er-fore lest any man fere you hereaft*er*. If other *that* felow or anny trowbyll you, se *that* you make all to-gether insurreccion age[n]st hym, in *th*e *wi*ch if my cownsell ca*n* do you any good you shall not

lacke it. Therfor be wise, play *the* man hereaf*ter and* not *the* boys, as ye haue don in this mather.

73. *Thu* didest call apon me yes*ter*-nyght at that tyme *that* I cold not tary. Now me seameth we have leasure con*u*enient bot for *the* to tell *and* me to here, therfore say *thi* mynd. I am redy [to] here those thyng*es* that *thu* shalt say.

[fol. 48]

74. Me semyth a prest office passith all other offic*is* in *the* world, for p*re*ist*es* be callyd in *the* holy scripture *the* mesynger[s] of all-myghty god, *ther*fore he had neyd to be very p*er*fett *that* inte[n]des to take apon hym to execut *that* office lest he be iuged vnworthi of hit.

75. Nature hath gyuyn to dyu*er*es me*n* dyu*er*s appet*ites*: su*m* desire for horsis, su*m* for dogg*es*, su*m* for gold *and* su*m* for honor. As for me I set lityll by all thes thyng*es* and only haue a desire to get con*n*yng, wich if [I] had oons get I wyl thynke my-selfe as riche as he *that* hath all *the* thyng*es that* I spake of be-fore.

76. I am indiffere*nt* other to goo wi*th* the if *thu* wilt or to tary if it be neid. If *thu* thynke it shalbe more p*ro*fett by taryng then by goyng wi*th* the, I wyll a-bydde *and* prouyd for *thi* absens suche thyng*es* as shalbe thought most for *thi* p*ro*fet.

77. I am p*ur*posid to leue my cu*n*tre *and* go in-to italie *and* that oonly for *the* desire of latyn and greke, for thought I ca*n* fynd here in ynglonde that ca*n* thech me, yet by-cause I thynke I can lerne bet*ter ther* than her I haue a gret desire to goo thether.

78. When we last [went] fo[r]the from *the* vniu*er*site for sikenes we had a fole slutty kechyn for owr scole, but now we be p*ro*uydyd of a place a litylmore honest, how be it is but a stable, wich thought be not p*ar*aventure for you*rr* appetyte yet ther is no remedy but we must be content wi*th* it, for we must remember *that* we be not at home at owr owne howse but in a-nother ma*n*s hoyse [fol. 48ᵛ] wher we may not loke for all thyng*es* af*ter* our appetytes, but we must be contentyd to take such thing*es* as be proferde.

79. *Thu* remembrist not *the* comunica*tion that* I had yesterda with *the*, *and* if *thu* haddyst other regardyd thi one p*ro*fett or *thi* frend*es* honeste *thu* wold*es* not a for-gotton them so son. *Thu* art a lyght felow *and* as

muche as I perceve a lowe, wherfor if all thi frendes for-sake the I mind neuer a deyll.

80. I pray God I be ded if euer I other said or thought this thynge that is layd a-genste me. Sum men haue a good sport to ymagene and go a-bouggt that thyng that the wene the may trowble me in, but paraventure I will disapoynte them of ther purpose this oons, for I wyll bryng iij or iiij wittnes that [shall] shew clerly that I am in no fawte in that as the accuse me in.

81. When I cam furst to this towne it greuyd me to lacke the pleasures that I had at oxforth, but now I perceve ther is so many pleasures here that I kepe not to change place a-gayn this somer season, except I myght goo in-to my cuntray wher I shold haue parauenture more pleasures in a day then here ar at Oxforde in a whole yere.

[fol. 49]
82. My mayster is so dawngerus in maners that I had leuer serue any mane in the world then hym. Other wyles he wull haue this and other wyls he wyll haue that verse of horase. That as he desiryse [be-]for he settes nawght by, and that as he settes nowggt by a lityll by-fore now he desirus for agayne. I wold to god thu weneth sum other body that were bowne to serue hyme, for ther is nothing that I can please hyme in. Except I know hym better manerd her-after, I wylt not a-byd with hym if he wold gyue me an honnderd ponde in the yere.

83. The shepe I wene be the profitables[t] best that be vpon the gronde, for the do not only bryng forth lames and bere the flessis of woole that we make owr raimentes of, but also the gyue mylke that chese is mayde of and of ther bodys we haue flese that is owr mete eueryday, so ther is nothyng fond vnprofitable in them—not as muche as the donge, for the that be experte in housbandre say that ther is nothyng more profitable to dong the land then the dong of them.

84. Ther is a long row of treis as men go owt of the towns end wher the maister is oftym to walke vp and downe, therfor I desire the that watyst apon hym to send me worde when he goyth next ther, for I haue many thyng to common with hyme and a more conueniant place to speake with hyme in I thynke ther be non.

[fol. 49ᵛ]

85. *Thu* carist nother wether *thi* father lyue or die so *that thu* maist get liberty to do what *thu* wylt, but when so eu*er* it shall fortune hym to dye *thu* shalt be the furst *that* shall repent his dethe, for *thu* hast nother wit to rule thy selfte nother to kepe suche thyng*es* as he p*ur*posith to be-quethe vnto *the* when he deys.

86. *Thu* sayste *thu* doist nothyng but syppe, but w*ith* thi sippyng *thu* riddist a-wa clene all *the* drynke *that* is set a-fore vs. If *thu* kepe thi owld gyse, *thu* wylt not sease thy sippyng tyll *thu* haue thi bely full of drynke. Me semeth [thu hast] *the* properti of an horse lech, for lykwese as horase sayth as a horse leche wyll not go fro *the* skyne tyll he be full of blode, so *thu* wylt neu*er* leue *the* cupp*es* except *thu* be ful of drynke.

87. Straberes, both thes *that* grow in gardens *and* also those *that* grow apon hyls, waxe out of season now and *that* ame I sory for, for I p*er*cewe *that* the haue done [my] weke body muche good, but when straberus be ons goon cherys wyll wax in season, w*ich* thougg *the* be not so holsu*m* as *the* straberes be, yet su*m* me*n* thynke *that* the be good bothe to quenche *the* thurst and to cole *the* body.

88. [Are you ready to begin the book of Maro which the rest of your school-fellows are ready to begin? You seem to me not at all ready to hear it. First of all, you do not yet understand the rudiments of grammar, of which being ignorant you will not be able to make progress either in this or in any work of the poets.]

NOTES TO THE TEXT

1. Compare the opening of Horman's *Vulgaria*: "There is no thynge in the worlde so conuenient to a man as to be holy and to loue god and worshyppe hym" (William Horman, *Vulgaria*, ed. M. R. James [Oxford, 1926], p. 13).

3. Compare no. 15 and William Nelson, *A Fifteenth Century School Book* (Oxford, 1956), nos. 3, 8.

5. "He that hath the rule of me": i.e. the boy's creanser. Compare Nelson, no. 140.

7. "Angre at the waggynge of a straw": compare *The Oxford Dictionary of English Proverbs*, ed. F. P. Wilson, 3rd ed. (Oxford, 1970), p. 446.

12. Compare Nelson, no. 164.

13. Compare Nelson, no. 87. Complaints that members of Magdalen College were negligent in speaking Latin occur in 1507 and 1520 (W. D. Macray, *A Register of the Members of St. Mary Magdalen College, Oxford*, new series, vol. i [London, 1894], pp. 46–47, 73).

15. See above, note 3.

18. "Orasse techith": Horace, *Ars Poetica*, lines 38–40.

19. "As tully weneth": Cicero, *Orator*, x (or 33).

21. "As tully seyt": *ibid.*, iv (or 14).

22. "Etyng of a heryng": a good deal of fish was eaten at Magdalen College, some of which indeed became putrid (Macray [above, note 13], pp. 57, 66, 69–71).

23. "Iuperti": jeopardy.

24. Compare Nelson, no. 206.

25. "Sant mari church": the church either of St. Mary the Virgin or of St. Mary Magdalen, Oxford. "A grett meny of women": a reference to the gathering of money at Hocktide (the Monday and Tuesday of the second week after Easter). On the Monday (mentioned here) the women of a parish tried to capture the men and on the Tuesday the reverse, the captives being released on payment of money which went to the funds of the church (J. C. Cox, *Churchwardens' Accounts* [London, 1913], pp. 261–263). "By hocke or by crocke": a phrase already long current (*The Oxford Dictionary of English Proverbs*, p. 383).

28. Compare Nelson, nos. 75–77.

30. "As tesipho seyth": Terence, *Adelphoe*, act iv, scene i, lines 19–20. "Me semeth thu shotes well": this sentence is modelled on Martial's epigram referred to below in note 31. "As phedra seyth": Ovid, *Heroides*, iv, line 84.

31. "Mercial playd with attalus": Martial, *Epigrams*, book ii, no. 7. The Latin passage includes the epigram.

32. The name Antony also appears in Nelson, no. 332.

34. "My mother": criticism of the indulgence of mothers to their children also occurs below in no. 64, in Nelson, no. 52, and in the contemporary work of Edmund Dudley, *The Tree of the Commonwealth*, ed. D. M. Brodie (Cambridge, 1948), p. 68.

37. "This ware tyme": the possible dates of the war concerned are discussed above, p. 14.

39. "If a grett cause had not lat hym": presumably Cicero's involvement and death in the Roman civil war of 44–43 B.C.

40. Compare Nelson, no. 189. There are similar sentiments in Cicero, *De Amicitia*, xv (or 55) and xxi (or 80).

41. "Tully seith": Cicero, *De Divinatio*, book ii, ii (or 4); compare also *De Officiis*, book i, xliv (or 155).

42. "Horase seyth": Horace, *Epistles*, book i, no. 2, line 56. "Agreyt also saluste": Sallust, *Catilina*, xi, line 3.

45. Compare Nelson, no. 145.

46. "The wynd": bad storms are mentioned in Magdalen College records in 1509 (Macray [above, note 13], p. 66).

47. "Rewde gramarion": presumably an adherent of pre-humanist Latin. Compare Nelson, no. 78, which takes a more favorable view of the old Latin.

48. "Latyns": Latin examples, extracts or exercises.

49. "Sent bornard": *Meditationes Piissimae de Cognitione Humanae Conditionis*, chapter 2, opening lines (J. P. Migne, *Patrologiae Cursus Completus*, vol. clxxxiv [Paris, 1854], col. 487). The ascription of this work to St. Bernard is now doubted (*Dictionnaire de Spiritualité*, ed. M. Viller, vol. i [Paris, 1937], col. 1500). Compare Nelson, no. 135.

50. Compare Nelson, no. 56.

51. Compare below, no. 54, and Nelson, nos. 107–108.

52. "Cyrus pleyd oons the kyng of boyes": the story occurs in Herodotus, *Histories*, book i, chapter 114. It was known in medieval England and is told in Ranulph Higden, *Polychronicon*, vol. iii, ed. J. R. Lumby (London, Rolls Series, 1871), pp. 140–143.

54. See above, note 51.

58. Compare Nelson, nos. 85–86.

61. "Hene . . . with the joyse of an orage (Latin *malum assyrium*)": sweet sauces were

popular with chicken in Tudor England. A similar recipe, "to boyle a capon with orenges," occurs in Thomas Dawson, *The Good Hus-Wives Jewell*, 2 parts (London, 1596–7), part ii, pp. 2–3.

62. "Iettyng": jetting, i.e. vaunting themselves with evil intent. Compare Nelson, no. 221.

63. "Dise, cardes": both were frequently played (but frowned on) at Magdalen College in the early sixteenth century (Macray [above, note 13], pp. 43, 45–46, 49, 60, 93). "Tables": backgammon. "Chestes" (Latin *calculis*): presumably chess.

64. See above, note 34.

65. The coins mentioned varied in value during the early sixteenth century, the ryal being valued at 10s.–11s. 3d. and the noble at 6s. 8d.–10s. (C. E. Challis, *The Tudor Coinage* [Manchester, 1978], pp. 68, 222).

66. Compare Nelson, nos. 220, 387.

67. "Broken up the loke": the barber of Magdalen College was accused of forging a lock in 1507 (Macray [above, note 13], p. 39). Compare also Nelson, no. 64.

71 "Sinable": syllable.

72. "Hare brane" (Latin *cerebrosus*): harebrain. The episode is obscure; presumably "harebrain" is a member of Magdalen College who has criticized the work of the schoolboys during the master's absence.

74. "The mesyngers (Latin *angeli*) of all-myghty god": the biblical source is Malachi, chapter 2, verse 7. For the discussion of the idea by medieval commentators see Cornelius a Lapide, *Commentarii in Scripturam Sacram*, 10 vols. (Lyon and Paris, 1875), vol. vii, pp. 821–822. Compare also Horman, *Vulgaria*, pp. 17, 35.

77. "In-to italie": Englishmen had been visiting Italy for study since the 1440s (R. W. Weiss, *Humanism in England during the Fifteenth Century*, 2nd ed. [Oxford, 1957], pp. 84–127).

86. "Horase sayth": Horace, *Ars Poetica*, line 476. Compare also Nelson, no. 35.

88. "Maro": Virgil.

4 An early fifteenth-century French miniature of Aristotle teaching Alexander the Great, probably as in the real school of a royal or noble household. The prince is accompanied by other noble boys, all are richly dressed and each has a schoolbook — well before the coming of printing.

9

THE EDUCATION OF THE COURTIER

'The king's household is the chief academy for the nobility of England.
It provides schooling in athletics, moral integrity and good manners,
through which the kingdom flourishes, acquires honour and is protected against invaders.' The words are those of Sir John Fortescue in
the 1460s,[1] but they could equally well have been written one or two
hundred years earlier. Throughout the later middle ages, the court
and household of the kings of England were important centres of
education and of educated people. First, the king's household and the
ancillary establishments of the queen and the royal children were in
part schools for the training of young aristocratic men and women.
The royal children were brought up there; so were many orphan heirs
in the king's wardship, and so were other noble children sent or
gathered for the purpose. Secondly, the king's court was a meeting
place of adult noblemen and women, educated in other great households, schools and universities. The manners and accomplishments
which children learnt and adults practised at court made up a code of
behaviour, 'courtesy', which formed a model for the aristocracy as a
whole. In the following pages we shall attempt to reconstruct the
education of the lay aristocracy of later medieval England: the dominant group among both those who staffed the royal household and
those who visited the king's court. By 'aristocracy' we mean the whole
of the medieval 'second estate' of society: the royal family, peers and
great magnates, knights, esquires and ordinary gentlemen, both male

---

1. 'In ea [domus regia] gignasium supremum sit nobilitatis regni, scola quoque stren-
uitatis probitatis et morum quibus regnum honoratur et florebit, ac contra irruentes
securatur': Sir John Fortescue, *De Laudibus Legum Anglie*, ed. S. B. Chrimes (Cambridge, 1942), 110–11.

and female. It was the education of this estate which came nearest to embodying courtly education in England during the period.

Few laws prescribed how medieval boys and girls should be educated. The command of the church that everyone must be baptised, confirmed and taught to pray, constituted the only major directive about the matter.[2] There was no attempt in medieval England, as there was in Scotland in 1496, to impose a statutory obligation upon the aristocracy to send their sons to school.[3] Yet if stated laws were few, many other invisible forces shaped the form which aristocratic education took. The church again, by preaching a code of belief, worship and behaviour, stimulated the teaching of children in prayer and confession, deportment in church, and Christian ethics. Law and custom, which required the male aristocracy to govern and defend the realm, necessitated boys being taught to read, in order to understand administrative and legal documents, and to be trained in military techniques. Aristocratic wealth and possessions indicated the preparation of boys and girls for adult life of a certain style. Future knights and ladies needed to learn how to behave to one another and how to follow the occupations of civilised life: music, embroidery, dancing, and exercises such as archery and hunting. The emphasis placed on these different elements may have differed from household to household, but there is unlikely to have been wide variation. Aristocratic families were interrelated, and the standards of one were influenced and regulated by others. The institution of feudal wardship took fatherless children away from their mothers to be educated in the households of their superior lords. Travel and social intercourse, most notably through attending the court itself, also diffused a common code of values and accomplishments. Medieval England was a nation, not a group of tribes, and the education of aristocratic boys and girls is likely to have aimed at similar objectives in most places.

Literature was another shaping force. Throughout the later middle ages, many writings circulated among the aristocracy and their servants which helped to establish common standards and techniques in education. First, there was the great corpus of religious and moral literature which gave knowledge of God, narrated Christian history, taught virtues and censored sins. Most of it was addressed to mankind as a whole, rather than to children in particular, but by moulding the attitudes of parents and teachers it reached the young as well, albeit indirectly. A second genre of literature, related to the first, consisted of works of advice to kings and princes specifically, on how to govern

2. *Manuale ad Vsum Sarisburiensis*, ed. A. Jefferies Collins (Henry Bradshaw Soc., XCI, 1958), 32, 37–8.

3. *The Acts of the Parliaments of Scotland, 1124–1707*, ed. T. Thomson & others, 12 vols. (Edinburgh, 1814–75), II, 238.

themselves and their subjects. Historians have called such writings 'mirrors of princes'. One of the most famous, the *Secretum Secretorum*, was the translation of an Arabic text allegedly containing the counsel of Aristotle to Alexander the Great.[4] Others were original works by French and English scholars and poets, of which a long series was produced from the twelfth century onwards, including (in England) Hoccleve's *Regement of Princes*, Fortescue's *De Laudibus Legum Anglie* and Skelton's *Speculum Principis*.[5] Both the *Secretum* and several others of the 'mirrors' circulated in later medieval England in Latin, French and English versions, and though written primarily for kings or their sons, they are frequently to be found in the possession of the nobility. This shows that the aristocracy shared the interest of their rulers in statecraft, and suggests that the 'mirrors' in consequence may also have influenced the education of aristocratic children. A third supply of educational ideas came from imaginative secular literature: romances and chansons de geste. These works, even at their most sensational, were not wholly confined to fictional happenings but portrayed knights and ladies who typified the virtues of real society and set standards of behaviour which their readers could imitate. Many stories went further than this, since they began by describing how their heroes and heroines were brought up, thus providing models for the educational process itself. Medieval parents and children must have absorbed something about standards and techniques in education as they read about the ideal upbringings of Guy of Warwick and Felise, Paris and Vienne, Chaucer's Squire, and Virginia in his 'Physician's Tale'.[6]

The concern of most medieval literature with the education of children, however, can only be rated as secondary. Generally, the educational message was addressed to mankind as a whole; often, as in works of fiction, it competed with the aim to entertain. Medieval England was short of books which discussed the education of young people as a primary theme. There was nothing so relevant or so widely diffused as *The Governor* by Sir Thomas Elyot or Henry Peacham's *Compleat Gentleman* in the sixteenth and seventeenth centuries. The absence of texts does not mean that education was not practised among the medieval aristocracy; many records prove the contrary, as we shall

4. *Secretum Secretorum: Nine English Versions*, ed. M. A. Manzalaoui, I: Text, *EETS* OS 276 (1977); George Cary, *The Medieval Alexander*, ed. D. J. A. Ross (Cambridge, 1956), especially 105–10, 250–1, 287–90, 344–5.

5. For a good recent survey of the genre see *Four English Political Tracts of the Later Middle Ages*, ed. J.-P. Genet, Camden Society, fourth series, XVIII (1977), ix–xix.

6. *The Romance of Guy of Warwick*, ed. J. Zupitza, *EETS* ES 25–6 (1875–6), 3–5; ibid., 42 (1883), 6–7; *Paris and Vienne*, ed. M. Leach, *EETS* OS 234 (1957), 1–2; *Canterbury Tales*, ed. Robinson, General Prologue, lines 79–100; Physician's Tale, lines 30–66.

see. The lack was one of educational consciousness. Most medieval thinkers and writers failed to distinguish children as a separate group, or education as a process separate from human life in general. Works which discussed the training of the young were few, and most of them dealt with the subject as part of wider studies of mankind, rather than in its own right. The principal discussions of children's education which circulated in medieval England owed their birth or their popularity to the rise of the universities and the friars in the thirteenth century. First, there was Aristotle's *Politics*, the seventh and eighth books of which contain an extended discussion of the training proper to the aristocracy. It has not yet been ascertained that any noble household contained a copy of the *Politics*, either in Latin or in the fourteenth-century French translation by Nicholas Oresme, but the work was studied in the English universities and must have been known to the graduate friars and secular clergy who mingled with the aristocracy and advised them.[7] Next should be mentioned the encyclopaedia of the English Franciscan scholar, Bartholomew Glanville, *De Proprietatibus Rerum*, compiled in the mid-thirteenth century. This work includes several chapters, descriptive rather than instructive, about the duties of parents and nurses and the care of young children from birth until the age of seven. It circulated widely in medieval England in the original Latin, was translated into French in 1372 and into English by John Trevisa in 1398.[8] Thirdly, there was the great work of the Italian Augustinian friar, Giles of Rome, *De Regimine Principum*, composed for the young Philip the Fair of France in the 1270s. This treatise, as well as providing one of the most complete and coherent accounts of the duties of kings, contained a section of twenty-one chapters on the education of aristocratic boys and girls. It was well-known in late-medieval England in Latin; several of the aristocracy are known to have possessed French translations, and a single copy even survives of an English version, made in about 1400.[9]

7. On the knowledge of Aristotle's *Politics* in later medieval England see S. H. Thomson, 'Walter Burley's commentary on the *Politics* of Aristotle', *Mélanges Auguste Pelzer* (Louvain, 1947), 557–78.

8. On the author see A. B. Emden, *A Biographical Register of the University of Oxford to A.D. 1500*, 3 vols (Oxford, 1957–9), II, 771–72, and on the French translation, *Dictionnaire des Lettres Françaises*, I: *Le Moyen Age*, ed. R. Bossuat & others (Paris, 1964), 57–8. The English translation has been edited: *On the Properties of Things. John Trevisa's Translation of Bartholomaeus Anglicus De Proprietatibus Rerum*, ed. M. C. Seymour & others, 2 vols. (Oxford, 1975).

9. The only available modern edition is of the 13th-century French translation by Henri de Gauchy: Giles of Rome, *Li Livres du Gouvernement des Rois*, ed. S. P. Molenaer (New York & London, 1899). The English translation, possibly by John Trevisa, is discussed in John Trevisa, *Dialogus inter Militem et Clericum*, ed. A. J. Perry, *EETS* OS 167 (1925), xcviii–c. For some references to the work's popularity in later medieval England see R. H. Jones, *The Royal Policy of Richard II: Absolutism in the Later Middle Ages* (Oxford, 1968), 154–63.

The translations of Bartholomew and Giles have a particular interest for the historian of education. They show that the works concerned, though academic in nature, were coming to attract the interest of the lay aristocracy as well: the owners and readers of books in French and English. Among the many matters that the treatises contained, their noble readers must have learnt something about education and its theory. This learning had a sequel, since a few of the medieval aristocracy were moved to write about the subject themselves. As early as the mid thirteenth century, Walter of Bibbesworth, a knight of Essex, wrote a treatise which explained, *inter alia*, how to bring up babies and how to teach noble boys the French vocabulary they would need in adult life to organise the husbandry of their estates.[10] A century later Geoffroy de la Tour Landry, a knight of Anjou, compiled the *Book of the Knight of the Tower* in the 1370s. This was a prose collection of moral stories and observations in French, intended to educate his daughters in the absence (through death) of their mother. It reached England in French during the fifteenth century and two English translations were made, one of them by Caxton who also printed it.[11] Notable too is Peter Idley, lord of the manor of Drayton in Oxfordshire and controller of the king's works under Henry VI, who produced in about the 1450s, a long verse treatise of 'Instructions' for his son. The work, adapted and translated from various earlier moral works by Albertano da Brescia, Robert Mannyng and John Lydgate, achieved a modest circulation and survives in seven manuscripts.[12] None of these authors can be rated highly as educational theorists. The works of Idley and La Tour Landry in particular draw heavily on other authors; they are not very orderly, and their models are literary rather than academic. Nevertheless they all possess a very great importance in the social history of education. Like the translations of Bartholomew and Giles, their writings show that educational literature had ceased to be the preserve of clerical intellectuals. It was becoming a matter of interest to the lay aristocracy.

The educational writers of the middle ages all agreed that the basic responsibility for bringing up children belonged to their fathers and mothers. 'A man loueth his childe,' declares John Trevisa in his translation of Bartholomew in 1398,

and fedith and noriscith him, and settith him at his owne bord whenne he is i-wenyed, and techith him in his youth with speche and with

10. *Le Traité de Walter de Bibbesworth sur la langue française*, ed. A. Owen (Paris, 1929), especially 43–70.

11. *The Book of the Knight of the Tower*, ed. M. Y. Offord, *EETS* SS2 (1971).

12 *Peter Idley's Instructions to his Son*, ed. Charlotte D'Evelyn (Boston and London, Modern Language Association of America, Monograph Series, VI, 1935), especially 1–35.

wordis, and chastith him with beting, and settith and puttith him to lore vndir warde and kepinge of wardeynes and tutours. And the fadir schewith him no glad chere lest he worthe proude. And a . . . yeueth to his childeren clothinge and mete and drinke as here age askith, and purchasith lond and heritage for his children alwey and maketh it more and more.[13]

This admirably summarises the duties which the noble father was expected to bear in mind. He should maintain the child with food, drink and clothing. He should teach the child, or appoint tutors to do so instead. Finally, he should provide the child with an endowment or career. The ethic of parental responsibility can also be traced in practice. The household accounts of noble and gentle families record expenditure on children's food and clothes, and sometimes indicate the presence of nurses, guardians and schoolmasters. Wills, enfeoffments and marriage contracts reveal the disposition of property by parents to support their offspring. By the second half of the fifteenth century, letter collections like those of the Pastons, the Plumptons and the Stonors record some of the personal relationships within the families of the lesser aristocracy. The letters have a special value in illuminating the role of women in the educational process. Mothers emerge as powerful auxiliaries during their husbands' lifetimes and as substitutes for them after they died. Agnes, the widow of William Paston I, held sway over her children following his death in 1444. She wrote to her son Edmund, a student at the inns of court, that he should think each day of his father's injunction to learn the law; she bullied her daughter Elizabeth until she was married, and urged the tutor of her youngest son Clement, then aged sixteen, that he 'trewly belash him' if he had not done well.[14] Margaret, the wife of John Paston I and a milder woman, interceded for her eldest son John II when he displeased his father, but broke into fury when her daughter Margery fell in love with the family's bailiff, Richard Calle, and ended by forbidding her the house.[15] Parental interventions could be dramatic; as in Margery's case, they were not always effective.

The responsibilities of aristocratic parents for their offspring, however, were not discharged in person all the time. Parental dignity and business made it necessary to entrust at least part of the everyday care and training of the children to others, who had more time or expertise for the purpose. This process began at birth, since it was common if not universal for aristocratic mothers to depute the feeding of their babies to a wet nurse possessing, in the opinion of Giles of

13. *On the Properties of Things*, book VI, chapter 14.
14. *Paston Letters and Papers of the Fifteenth Century*, ed. N. Davis, 2 vols. (Oxford, 1971–6), I, 27, 41; II, 32.
15. Ibid., I, 289–90, 293, 341–3.

Rome, as many as possible of their own physical characteristics.[16] The nurse's duties are described by Bartholomew.[17] She suckles the baby, kisses, cleans and washes it, gives it medicines and dances it up and down. She whistles or sings the child to sleep, swathes it in sheets and clouts, and stretches out its limbs with cradle bonds lest they should grow awry. At a later stage she weans the child by feeding it food chewed in her own mouth, and teaches it words by saying them over and over, in a gentle voice. The social status of those employed as nurses is not clear, but we may guess them to have been the wives of yeomen, grooms or other men of free status in their masters' service. Their breast-feeding duties lasted for about two years, after which they may have remained with their charges as servants. The best-recorded nurses, those of the royal children, were well paid for their work with grants and annuities, and in one or two cases the benefits were redoubled at a later date when the former baby ascended the throne as king.[18]

Medieval theorists divided childhood into three parts: *infancia* from birth to the age of seven, *puericia* from seven to fourteen, and *adolescencia* from fourteen to twenty-one or later.[19] Both Aristotle and Giles regarded *infancia* as a period in which food, play and exercise should take precedence over formal training, though Aristotle proposed that boys should become onlookers at the training of their elders when they were five.[20] Most aristocratic children of both sexes apparently remained under the government of women when they left their wet-nurses, until they were seven. Among the lesser aristocracy they were probably supervised by their mother and her household women, but in the families of the king and of some great magnates, where the mother was not available for this duty, we find the care of the young children being deputed to a mistress of the nursery. Unlike the nurse, the mistress was a noble- or gentlewoman. Her tasks would have been to supervise the nurse and the children's other servants, to provide the nursery with food and clothes, and probably also to help the children to speak and to learn good manners. We find Elizabeth of St Omer acting as mistress of the four year-old Black Prince and his younger sisters in 1334,[21] and Maria Hervy of the six year-old Henry

16. Giles of Rome, *De Regimine Principum* book II, part II, chapter 15.
17. *On the Properties of Things*, book VI, chapter 9.
18. There are references to royal nurses throughout the *Calendars of Patent Rolls, 1216–1509* (London, 1891–1916).
19. *On the Properties of Things*, book VI, chapter 1.
20. Aristotle, *Politics*, book VII, chapter 17; Giles of Rome, *De Regimine Principum*, book II, part II, chapter 15.
21. T. F. Tout, *Chapters in the Administrative History of Mediaeval England* (Manchester, 1920–33), V, 319–20.

V and his younger brothers and sister in 1393.[22] Lady Alice Butler, who was appointed to teach courtesy and 'nurture' to the two year-old Henry VI in 1424, doubtless fulfilled a similar role.[23] Some light is thrown on the duties of these ladies by an indenture of 1502 between Robert Turberville, treasurer of the household of Edward Stafford, duke of Buckingham, and Margaret Hexstall, gentlewoman.[24] It arranged for Margaret to attend on the duke's heir, the nine month-old Lord Henry Stafford and his elder sisters, in the ducal manor of Blechingley. She was not to remove the children without the permission of one of the duke's councillors, and was to provide food for her charges and their servants, to a total number of seventeen. Finally, she was to choose the menus and see that the children were served each day with four or five dishes of flesh and fish. The indenture does not mention educational duties, but these may well have been taken for granted.

In the seventh year, or at the age of seven, the training of boys and girls began to diverge. According to the theorists, boys of this age were ready to undergo instruction and discipline from men, or, as John Trevisa expressed it, to be 'put and sette to lore vndir tutours and compelled to fonge [i.e. undergo] lore and chastisinge'.[25] So too in practice Henry VI, discharging the mistress of his six and a half year-old son Edward in 1460, explained that he was sufficiently grown 'to be committed to the rules and teachings of wise and strenuous men, and to understand the arts and manners of a man, rather than to stay further under the keeping and governance of women'.[26] The arrangements for providing the tutors of aristocratic boys are difficult to reconstruct, since they are badly recorded and may have varied from family to family according to wealth and status. In the best-known cases, those of the heirs to the throne, the boy was entrusted to a senior knight or nobleman who was entitled his master (*magister*) or tutor (*pedagogus*).[27] Edward I was tutored by Sir Hugh Giffard, Henry VI by the earl of Warwick, and Edward V by Earl Rivers. Richard II had three such masters: Sir Richard Abberbury, Sir Guiscard D'Angle and Sir Simon Burley. The knightly tutor probably exercised a general oversight of his royal pupil, saw to his manners, taught him to ride, and supervised his training in arms when he grew older. Literary

22. PRO, Duchy of Lancaster, Accounts Various, DL 28/1/4–5; J. H. Wylie, *History of England under Henry the Fourth*, 4 vols. (London, 1884–98), IV, 163, 171.

23. *Proceedings and Ordinances of the Privy Council*, ed. N. H. Nicolas, 7 vols, (London, Record Commission, 1834–7), III, 143.

24. *A Relation . . . of the Island of England, 1500*, ed. Charlotte A. Sneyd, Camden Soc., XXXVII (1847), 75–6.

25. *On the Properties of Things*, book VI, chapter 5.

26. *CPR, 1452–61*, 567.

27. Nicholas Orme, *English Schools in the Middle Ages* (London, 1973), 22 and note 5.

studies were entrusted to a separate clerk or schoolmaster, Edward III being taught by John Peynel, Henry VI by John Somerset, and Edward V by John Giles.[28] It is possible that this diarchy of knightly tutor and clerical schoolmaster was also imposed on the younger sons of the king and the sons of the great magnates, though the evidence for it is difficult to find. Among the lesser baronial and knightly families, however, where unoccupied knights were harder to come by, a cleric may have acted alone as tutor, giving general supervision as well as literary instruction. During the 1430s and 40s Robert Hungerford and John Tiptoft, both heirs to baronies, each spent some time at Oxford under the care of a graduate cleric,[29] and Edmund and Jasper Tudor are said to have been entrusted to virtuous priests for teaching and for guidance in good living and behaviour.[30] Sometimes a domestic chaplain may have undertaken this task, as John Still appears to have done in the Paston family in 1468.[31] The appointment of a cleric alone as tutor need not have meant that military and athletic training was absolutely neglected. Most medieval clergy were used to riding, some were only too fond of hunting, and others had been present at battles and knew something about fighting. It was not a knight but a precentor of Salisbury Cathedral, Nicholas Upton, who wrote the chief English treatise of the fifteenth century on heraldry and the laws of war.[32]

Aristocratic girls, unlike their brothers, remained under female supervision throughout the periods of *puericia* and *adolescencia*, until they became married. The system by which they were governed was also subject to variations, depending on the importance and wealth of their families. Among the lesser aristocracy, the care of the older girls like that of the nursery children probably fell to the lot of their mother. Life in a small household brought mothers and daughters closely together, while resources for paying a special governess were limited. Most mothers must have been capable of teaching behaviour, deportment, dancing, embroidery and even language and reading.[33] What they lacked in religious and literary expertise could be easily supplied by a chaplain or friar. In the families of the king and the greater magnates, however, where mothers and daughters spent more of their lives apart, there developed during the later middle ages the office of mistress, the female equivalent of the boys' master or tutor. Like the mistress of the nursery, the mistress of the royal or noble girl was

28. *CCR, 1327–30*, 573; *CPR, 1429–36*, 241; ibid., *1467–77*, 592.

29. Emden, II, 985; III, 1877.

30. *Henry the Sixth: a Reprint of John Blacman's Memoir*, ed. M. R. James (Cambridge, 1919), 8–9, 30–1.

31. *Paston Letters*, ed. Davis, I, 540.

32. Emden, III, 1933–4.

33. On mothers as teachers see *The Book of the Knight of the Tower*, 3–4, 13.

herself a lady of aristocratic rank. The best known of them all, Katherine Swynford, mistress of the daughters of John of Gaunt in the 1370s (and also to Gaunt himself), was a knight's daughter married to a knight in her master's retinue.[34] Katherine Waterton, mistress of Henry IV's daughter Philippa in the first decade of the fifteenth century, was also the wife of a knight in her lord's service.[35] The existence of mistresses in the households of the great magnates was sufficiently common at the end of the fourteenth century to attract the attention of Chaucer himself. In his 'Physician's Tale', which opens with an evocation of the virtues of Virginia, a noble girl of ideal qualities, Chaucer breaks into the narrative with an exhortation to 'maistresses ... that lordes doghtres han in governaunce'.[36] He asserts that they fall into two kinds: those who are well known for their honesty and those who, though they have fallen into frailty (evidently of a sexual kind), have reformed themselves and gained a reputation for experience. He ends by urging them to keep a close guard on their charges and not to slacken in teaching them virtuous things. Like the mothers and the tutor, the mistress probably taught a wide range of accomplishments in an informal way, presumably helped when necessary by a cleric in the spheres of religious and literary studies.

In what has already been said, we have assumed that aristocratic children were brought up in the households of their own parents. This is not wholly true. Their education began at home, indeed, and involved the arrangements that have been described, but it is probable that most of them also left home during the course of their childhood and got part of their training elsewhere. Departure from home could take place at any time, and by accident as well as by design. In the first case a father might die or fall into disfavour, causing his children to be removed into the wardship of his feudal superior or that of the king. Alternatively, parents might lay deliberate plans for their children to spend their *puericia* or *adolescencia* in the household of a greater magnate, or in a specialised institution such as a school or university. There were good reasons for such a move. Boys and girls alike stood to benefit from widening their experience of life in another environment, and could gain useful patronage from the lords and ladies with whom they were boarded, leading to service or marriage in adult life. Boys who aimed at careers involving special skills were likely to gain a better understanding of fighting by living with a famous knight, religion with a prelate, or scholarship in a university. Educationists approved the sending of children away from home. William Worcester

34. *John of Gaunt's Register, 1379–83*, ed. Eleanor C. Lodge & R. Somerville, vol. II, Camden Society, third series, LVII (1937), 302–3, 93.
35. Wylie, *England under Henry the Fourth*, IV, 222, 241.
36. Ed. Robinson, lines 72–82.

and Sir John Fortescue, writing in the third quarter of the fifteenth century, both praised the placing of youths in the households of the king and the magnates, as a means by which they would receive more expert and disinterested supervision and become more proficient in arms and noble behaviour.[37] Some commentators believed that parents, in contrast, were too indulgent. The children of most rich men 'be loste nowadais in ther youghe at home, and that with ther fathers and mothers'. So wrote the author of a set of school exercises at Magdalen College, Oxford, in about 1500.[38] He went on to censure mothers for playing with their children as if they were dolls, allowing them to use bad language, and being unwilling to put them to any discipline. When the children arrived at adulthood, he asserted, they had no shame, were bold to do evil, and showed every probability of ending their lives on the block or on the gallows.

There is no need to quarrel with Fortescue's view that the pre-eminent place to which aristocratic children could be sent in the later middle ages was the royal household. Here, in the household itself, or in those of the queen and the royal children, could be found orphan sons of the tenants-in-chief, some of them heirs to earldoms and baronies. Here too were sons with fathers still alive, who were important enough to gain the privilege of court attendance during their youth or early manhood. Already by 1318, the date of the Household Ordinance of York, 'the children who lie in the king's ward' were a regular charge on the household, taking wages and liveries after their degree.[39] The heirs to the throne were often brought up alongside these wards, in less seclusion than their Hanoverian and Victorian successors. In 1301 the future Edward II, then aged sixteen, was accompanied by ten wards in his household, including Gilbert de Clare later earl of Gloucester and the notorious Piers Gaveston.[40] Every boy except Gaveston had his own master with him. In 1425 the privy council of the four year-old Henry VI commanded that all the heirs of baronies in the king's wardship, the keeping of whom had apparently become dispersed, should return to dwell in the royal household, each with at least one master to be paid for at the king's expense.[41] During the course of the fifteenth century the educational arrangements in the king's household became increasingly formalised. By about 1449 there

37. *The Boke of Noblesse*, ed. J. G. Nichols (London, Roxburghe Club, 1860), 76–7; Fortescue, *De Laudibus Legum Anglie*, ed. Chrimes, 110–11.
38. *A Fifteenth Century School Book*, ed. W. Nelson (Oxford, 1956), 13–14. Compare Edmund Dudley, *The Tree of the Commonwealth*, ed. D. M. Brodie (Cambridge, 1948), 45, 68.
39. T. F. Tout, *The Place of the Reign of Edward II in English History* (Manchester, 1914), 280.
40. Tout, *Chapters*, II, 172.
41. *Proceedings and Ordinances of the Privy Council*, ed. Nicolas, III, 170.

was a grammar master to teach 'the noble boys brought up in the king's household', an office which continued on a regular basis during the following hundred years.[42] By the reign of Edward IV the 'Black Book of the Household', compiled between 1467 and 1477, mentions not only the king's wards but a separate category of noble youths called 'henchmen', six in number or more 'as hit shall please the king'.[43] The henchmen were sometimes wards and sometimes not. It was recorded on the tomb of Thomas Howard, second duke of Norfolk who died in 1524, that he was henchman to Edward IV: at a time when his father, Sir John Howard, was still alive.[44] The henchmen, and perhaps the wards as well, were under the supervision of a 'master of the henchmen' with the rank of a squire, who was charged with teaching them courtesy, languages, music, riding and feats of arms.[45] Instruction in grammar was given by the grammar master.[46] The assembly of noble youths in the household thus evolved into an organised school with a defined curriculum and professional teachers. But not all court education was so formal. It was also possible for a young man to be sent to court and to stay there at his father's expense on the peripheries, awaiting recognition and a permanent place, like the nineteen year-old John Paston II, reputedly too shy in 1461 'to put forthe hym-selfe' and gain advancement.[47] This kind of attendance could also be educative, bringing as it did a young squire into contact with great men, formal life, and the latest fashions in cultural accomplishments.

The educational function of the king's household was paralleled in those of the great lay magnates. Here too we find frequent references to boys, and also girls, as wards, pages and paying guests, formally or informally undergoing education. The best-known example of a page is that of Chaucer himself, son of a London merchant and vintner, who first appears in historical records in the household of the countess of Ulster in 1357, when he was in his teens.[48] Education through wardship is typified by the future Henry VII, born earl of Richmond in 1457, but deprived of his title by Edward IV five years later. He spent the next seven years of his life as a ward in the household of William Lord Herbert at various places in Wales, including Raglan.[49] Since Edward Haseley, dean of Warwick, is described in 1495 as

42. *Liber Regie Capelle*, ed. W. Ullmann, Henry Bradshaw Soc., XCII 1961), 57; Orme, *English Schools in the Middle Ages*, 218–19.

43. A. R. Myers, *The Household of Edward IV* (Manchester, 1959), 126.

44. J. Weever, *Ancient Funerall Monuments* (London, 1631), 834; (London, 1767), 554.

45. Myers, *Household of Edward IV*, 126.

46. Ibid., 137–8.

47. *Paston Letters*, ed. Davis, I, 199–200.

48. *Chaucer Life-Records*, ed. M. M. Crow & C. C. Olson (Oxford, 1966), 13–18.

49. S. B. Chrimes, *Henry VII* (London, 1972), 14–17.

'instructor to the king in his tender age', it looks as though the amenities of the Herbert household included a schoolmaster.[50] Certainly by the early sixteenth century, several great magnates had come to institute bodies of henchmen, wards and grammar masters in their households, on the lines of the royal ones.[51] The sending away of girls in a similar manner is well illustrated in the Paston Letters. Elizabeth, daughter of William Paston I, was boarding with Lady Pole in 1458 when her mother sent her some money and urged her to accustom herself to work readily like other gentlewomen.[52] A decade later John I's wife Margaret did her best to place their elder daughter Margery with Lady Oxford or Lady Bedford in 1469, to forestall her love affair with the bailiff.[53] Anne, the younger daughter, also lived away from home with the wife of Sir William Calthrop until about 1470 when Sir William asked for her removal, on the grounds that he had to reduce his household.[54] A mother who sent her own daughters to board elsewhere might equally well receive strange girls herself. Margaret's cousin, Sir John Hevingham thought so in the early 1460s, at any rate, when he asked her to take in a girl called Agnes Loveday at his own expense. She was not at her ease in her present situation, he said, and all his efforts to place her with another family had failed.[55]

The education of the aristocracy was not confined to secular households; many examples occur of boys and girls being trained in those of the clergy. There was, of course, much in common between the establishment of a prelate and that of a lay magnate. Each provided similar opportunities to gain patronage, meet other people, acquire good manners and be trained in special techniques. We find William, son and heir of James Lord Berkeley, in the household of Cardinal Beaufort in 1437–8 at the age of twelve;[56] Thomas More, son of Sir William More, in that of Cardinal Morton in about 1491, when he was thirteen;[57] and Henry Percy, son and heir of the earl of Northumberland, in that of Cardinal Wolsey in 1522, at the age of twenty.[58] Recourse could also be had to a religious house for the same purpose. In the case of male foundations, this meant joining the abbot's retinue and staying in his private lodging, rather than dwelling among the

50. *CPR, 1485–94*, 332.
51. For examples and references see Orme, *English Schools in the Middle Ages*, 321–2.
52. *Paston Letters*, ed. Davis, I, 42.
53. Ibid., 339.
54. Ibid., 339, 348.
55. Ibid., 350–1.
56. J. Smyth, *The Lives of the Berkeleys*, ed. Sir J. Maclean, 2 vols (Gloucester, 1883), II, 100.
57. Emden, II, 1305–6.
58. George Cavendish, *The Life and Death of Cardinal Wolsey*, ed. R. S. Sylvester, *EETS* OS 243 (1959), 29–30.

monks themselves. John Hertford, abbot of St Albans (1235–63), was remembered long afterwards as a man to whom the nobility of England had sent their children to be educated.[59] The abbot of Hyde at Winchester had eight noble boys lodging with him in order to study in about 1450,[60] and Woburn Abbey, in the 1530s, housed three young gentlemen commoners and their own schoolmaster.[61] Nunneries, on the other hand, opened themselves fully for the reception and training of children, to an extent well beyond that of the orders of men.[62] It is significant that Chaucer, when he described the Prioress, sketched a portrait of which nearly half was a list of educational accomplishments, such as a nun might teach or a girl absorb: French of the Anglo-Norman dialect, deportment, careful speech and good table manners.[63] Bishops visiting nunneries throughout the later middle ages found them boarding children on a large scale, of both sexes and of all ages, some of them sleeping in the nuns' own dormitories. Rules were often laid down to control these practices. Children were ordered to be banished from the dormitories; nuns were to receive only one child each, or only children licenced by the bishop; boys were not to remain after a certain age, variously fixed from five to eleven, or girls after twelve to fourteen. The need for regulation testifies to the great popularity of nunneries as centres of education.

There remains one other group of institutions to which aristocratic boys were sent to be trained. These were the specialised centres of education: schools and universities, joined in the fifteenth century by the inns of court. Throughout the later middle ages sons of the nobility and gentry went away from home to one or other of these institutions in order to gain specialised knowledge which the household could not provide: advanced grammar, the liberal arts, theology, and the various kinds of law. Until about 1400, however, departure to school or university was probably mainly confined to aristocratic boys intended for ecclesiastical careers. Those who anticipated remaining in secular life could learn enough grammar for their needs in the household, though some of the lesser aristocracy who had no tutor at hand may have sent such boys to a local school instead. There was always the possibility, of course, that ecclesiastical trainees might revert to secular life in adulthood, either through lack of vocation or the unforeseen inherit-

59. *Gesta Abbatum Monasterii Sancti Albani*, ed. H. T. Riley, 3 vols (London, Rolls Series, 1867–9), I, 397.

60. T. Warton, *History of English Poetry*, ed. W. C. Hazlitt, 4 vols (London, 1871), IV, 9.

61. *Calendar of Letters and Papers, Foreign and Domestic, Henry VIII*, XIII, part I, 361.

62. On education in nunneries see Eileen Power, *Medieval English Nunneries, c. 1275–1535* (Cambridge, 1922), 237–84, 568–81.

63. *Canterbury Tales*, General Prologue, lines 118–41.

ance of family property. John Balliol, a fourth son who was at school at Durham in the 1260s, survived to inherit the Balliol lands and become king of Scotland.[64] William Beauchamp, another fourth son, began to study at Oxford in 1358–61, when the death of his elder brothers caused his diversion into a military and political career which ended in his elevation to a barony in 1392.[65] By the early fifteenth century, however, the sending of boys away to school or university was becoming extended from those who would or might become ecclesiastics to those who were definitely intended to remain seculars. We have already mentioned the nine year-old Robert Hungerford, who stayed for three terms in University College, Oxford, in 1437–8, and John Tiptoft who spent a longer period of three or four years in the same college in 1440–4, during his early teens.[66] Cambridge likewise reveals Henry Holland, son of the earl of Huntingdon, as a commoner of the King's Hall in 1440–2,[67] and the less exalted John Paston I at Trinity Hall and Peterhouse at about the same time.[68] All four youths were the eldest sons and heirs of their families, and there can be no doubt that their presence in university towns were aimed at enhancing their adult careers as landowners and men of affairs, rather than training them to enter the Church. It is an interesting development, but it should not be overestimated. The boys concerned need not have studied more than grammar and elementary logic, and they were not apparently followed by many others of their kind during the fifteenth century. Visiting heirs of the aristocracy could easily escape record, but it still seems true to say that the universities did not become widely popular as training centres for such youths until the second half of the sixteenth century.[69]

More important much earlier was the role of the inns of court and chancery in London. Here too institutions originally concerned with training professionals were infiltrated by nobility and gentry merely intent on acquiring a general education for aristocratic life. But whereas comparatively few such boys can be traced at the late-medieval universities, the inns were already attracting significant numbers by the second half of the fifteenth century. Fortescue's famous account of English legal education, written between 1468 and 1471, states that knights, barons and other magnates and noblemen were placing their

64. *Historiae Dunelmensis Scriptores Tres*, ed. J. Raine, London & Edinburgh, Surtees Soc., IX, (1839), 74.

65. Emden, I, 138–9.

66. Above, note 29.

67. A. B. Emden, *A Biographical Register of the University of Cambridge to 1500* (Cambridge, 1963), 321.

68. *Paston Letters*, ed. Davis, I, 215; II, 21.

69. A. B. Emden, *A Biographical Register of the University of Oxford A.D. 1501–1540* (Oxford, 1974), xxiii–xxiv.

sons at the inns not in order be trained as lawyers, nor in order to practise law for a living, but to prepare them for a life based on independent means.[70] In fact, the surviving registers of the inns before the Reformation do not suggest that many sons of peers entered them to study.[71] Aristocratic admissions are dominated by the sons of knights and gentlemen, for whom the study of law conferred real advantages in running the affairs of a small landed family. Like William Paston I their fathers knew that 'ho so euer schuld dwelle at Paston schulde have nede to conne defende hymselfe'.[72] The practical use of the study of law was one obvious reason for the early popularity of the inns with the aristocracy as against the universities, but there were other reasons too. At a time when facilities for gentlemen commoners in Oxford and Cambridge were still undeveloped, the inns provided accommodation in chambers, sociable meals in hall, and at least a modicum of moral supervision. The early registers of Lincoln's Inn reveal the enforcement of rules against women, dice and cards, which must have been a favourable factor with parents.[73] For those who wished to study there was access to the public law-courts in term time and to the lectures and moots provided by the inns during vacations. For those who did not there were most of the recreations proper to the aristocracy. Fortescue mentions reading, singing, dancing and the playing of games similar to those which were practised in the royal household itself. Here too the inns surpassed the clerical, provincial universities in their closeness to the fashions of court and capital.

The educational system which we have just described seems to have been applied to the individual child with a good deal of flexibility. The practice common in earlier times by which parents vowed a boy or girl at an early age to a life as a monk, friar or nun was unusual after 1300.[74] Parents must have made plans for their sons and daughters to become knights, clerics, wives or nuns in adult life, but these plans were not and could not be decisive absolutely. Deaths among children, and the aptitudes they displayed as they grew up, frequently altered the situation with which each parent had to deal. Many fathers and mothers were careful to keep their options open. When Richard, earl of Arundel made his will in 1393, he thought it likely that his sons Richard and Thomas would both marry, if they lived, but he also provided that a church living should be kept available in case either

70. Fortescue, *De Laudibus Legum Anglie*, ed. Chrimes, 116–21.
71. E.g. *The Records of the Honorable Society of Lincoln's Inn*, I: *Admissions, 1420–1799*, ed. W. P. Baildon (London, 1896), 10–44.
72. *Paston Letters*, ed. Davis, I, 27.
73. *The Records of the Honorable Society of Lincoln's Inn: the Black Books*, I: *1422–1586*, ed. W. P. Baildon (London, 1897), 68, 71, 74, 79, 103.
74. For an example of 1411 see *Calendar of Papal Letters*, VI: *1404–15*, 223–4.

of them wished to become a cleric.[75] So too Margaret Paston, when her teenage son Walter went off to Oxford in the early 1470s, advised him 'that he be not to hasty of takyng of orderes that schuld bynd hym, till that he be of xxiiij yere of agee or more'. She would love him better, she said, as a good secular man than as a lewd priest.[76] It followed that educational specialisation – the separation of some children to be trained as laity and others as clergy – was unwise, at least until the teens, and is unlikely to have been practised inflexibly. Until about fourteen most children probably followed a common curriculum, modified only by sex, and even afterwards a child being trained as a cleric had to bear in mind the possibility of diversion to a secular career. All this goes far to explain the secularism of so many adult clergy. Their inclinations towards hunting, warfare, extravagant clothes, and even the making of love, were not necessarily manifestations of evil natures. They could also have resulted from years of secular education in childhood, which those concerned found hard to shake off when they entered the Church.

The range of studies and pursuits in which aristocratic children were trained was a wide one, including three principal areas: the intellectual, the artistic and the physical. Children begin their intellectual development with the acquisition of language, and for medieval aristocratic children this meant two languages: English and French. Professor Rothwell has recently argued that English was the true vernacular of the aristocracy in England as early as 1150 or 1200, in that it was the language which they absorbed first and naturally from their nurses, household servants, and all the other speakers of English whom they would meet as they grew up.[77] French by the same period, he suggests, was already a taught language which was learnt with a degree of formality from parents, tutors and clergy who knew and used it. John Trevisa in a famous passage of the 1380s noted a decline in the learning of French by the aristocracy:'gentil men habbeth now moche yleft for to teche here childern Frensch'.[78] Notwithstanding this remark, however, it is likely that many and perhaps most aristocratic children went on learning some French throughout the fifteenth century. Despite the increasing use of English for official and literary purposes between 1350 and 1420, French remained the language of most of the books possessed by the aristocracy until Caxton's time in the 1470s, and survived in written and in spoken forms among the common lawyers throughout the century. Concerning the gentry, we

75. *Testamenta Vetusta*, ed. N. H. Nicolas, 2 vols. (London, 1826), I, 131–2.

76. *Paston Letters*, ed. Davis, I, 370.

77. See W. Rothwell, 'The role of French in thirteenth-century England', *Bulletin of the John Rylands University Library of Manchester*, LVIII (1975–6), 445–66.

78. *Polychronicon Ranulphi Higden*, ed. C. Babington & J. R. Lumby, 9 vols. (London, Rolls Series, 1865–86), II, 159.

find it said of Margaret, the four year-old daughter of the Yorkshire esquire William Plumpton in 1463, that she 'speaketh prattely and french, and hath near hand learned her sawter'.[79] In the royal family, Prince Arthur and Henry VIII both had a French master, Giles Dewes, in about 1500,[80] and when Katherine of Aragon was about to leave Spain in 1498 to marry Arthur, she was advised to learn French and be able to converse in it when she reached England.[81] The nature of the French which the English learnt and spoke must always have varied. The children of the great magnates, whose parents and household retainers had travelled in France, could have acquired the French of Paris. Those who lacked such contacts, on the other hand, would have deviated into Anglo-Norman or law French, permeated by English usages. As late as 1535 it was noted that the nuns of Lacock understood a French which was not like the language of France, but resembled that of the English common law.[82]

The teaching of reading and writing was based on a third language: Latin, rather than French or English. Medieval children, when they learnt to read, learnt the alphabet in Latin; when they first practised recognising and pronouncing words, the texts were also in Latin, so that every literate child was a minimal reader and speaker of that language. Literacy, and the elementary knowledge of Latin it involved, were probably universal among the later medieval English aristocracy of both sexes. This is suggested by their involvement in keeping and using written records, in getting and sending letters, in owning books, and in a few cases even in writing them.[83] Learning to read could begin at an early age. Philippa and Blanche, the daughters of Henry IV (then earl of Derby), were three and five respectively when copies of the ABC were bought for them in 1397.[84] Margaret Plumpton, as has been mentioned, was learning the psalter at the age of four in 1463, and Edward V had a schoolmaster when he was five in 1476.[85] Arthur and Henry VIII were being taught at similar ages twenty years later.[86] After assimilating the Latin alphabet, children proceeded to study liturgical texts like the psalter and the antiphonal, learning how to spell the words, how to pronounce them, and how to sing them to the rules of ecclesiastical music. Everyone who reached

79. *Plumpton Correspondence*, ed. T. Stapledon, Camden Soc., IV, (1839), 8.
80. *Dictionary of National Biography*, s.v. Giles Dewes.
81. *Calendar of State Papers, Spanish*, I; *1485–1509*, 156.
82. *Letters & Papers, Foreign & Domestic, Henry VIII*, IX, 47.
83. For recent surveys of aristocratic literacy see M. B. Parkes, 'The literacy of the laity', in *The Medieval World*, ed. D. Daiches & A. K. Thorlby, vol. II, (London, 1973), 555–77; Orme, *English Schools in the Middle Ages*, 21–36; and M. T. Clanchy, *From Memory to Written Record: England 1066–1307* (London, 1979), especially 175–201.
84. PRO, DL 28/1/6 fol. 36.
85. Above, notes 79, 28.
86. Orme, *English Schools in the Middle Ages*, 27–9.

this far, and it seems likely that everyone did, would have been able to pronounce (though not to understand) the words of a Latin text and use a prayer book in church. Furthermore they had acquired knowledge which could serve as the basis for understanding texts in the languages they spoke: English and French.

From this point onwards, the intellectual training of children seems to have diverged according to sex. We do not find much evidence of girls or women practising literary skills beyond those which have just been mentioned, until the early sixteenth century. Many records suggest, on the other hand, that even by the fourteenth century boys usually proceeded to learn grammar: the formations and meanings of Latin words, and the methods of using them in speech, prose writing and verse. Thomas of Woodstock was studying grammar in 1366 at the age of eleven;[87] his great-nephew Henry V had books of grammar bought for him in 1396 when he was eight,[88] and a Donatus or elementary Latin grammar was purchased for Henry's brother John, later duke of Bedford, in 1398.[89] Those of the aristocracy who trained to be clerics and went to university must have become fluent Latinists. The abilities of their brothers who remained as laymen are more difficult to summarise. A few may have achieved the fluency of the clergy. Henry IV was able to spend an afternoon reading in the library of Bardney Abbey in 1406,[90] and Humphrey duke of Gloucester and John Tiptoft earl of Worcester were notable patrons of Latin scholars and collectors of Latin books.[91] Even Peter Idley was able to make his educational translations from the Latin version of Albertano da Brescia.[92] For most such people, however, it seems likely that the use of Latin was confined to practical purposes: the use of prayer books in church and the reading of statutes and legal instruments, most of which followed a regular form. For ease and pleasure, as we know from their books and letters, they preferred to read and write in French or English. True, many noblemen possessed books in Latin, but they also had clerics at hand who could translate and interpret the contents on their behalf.

The learning of language and letters had a religious as well as a literary dimension. The Church's commandment that children should learn the Paternoster, the Ave Maria and the Apostle's Creed[93] was echoed by moralists and educationists. Kings and princes, said Giles

---

87. F. Devon, *Issues of the Exchequer* (London, 1837), 189.
88. Wylie, *England under Henry the Fourth*, IV, 172.
89. PRO, DL 28/1/6 fol. 42.
90. J. Leland, *Collectanea*, ed. T. Hearne, 2nd ed., 6 vols (Oxford, 1770), VI, 300–1.
91. R. Weiss, *Humanism in England during the Fifteenth Century*, 2nd ed. (Oxford, 1957), 39–70, 112–22.
92. *Peter Idley's Instructions to his Son*, ed. D'Evelyn, 36–8.
93. Above, note 2.

of Rome, should teach their children the articles of the faith, because faith cannot be proved rationally and is especially suitable for the young who do not seek for reason.[94] Reading, as has just been noticed, began with the study of religious texts, and the first pages which a young child had to learn contained the three basic prayers, followed by the psalms, hymns and antiphons of the liturgy. Once literacy had been mastered, a child could read or be read to from adult collections of religious stories and admonitory literature. Every household had its chaplains and friars who could convey this material in oral form as well. Children were also introduced to religious surroundings and observances. The nine year-old Isabella, daughter of Edward III, and her eight year-old sister Joan are both recorded listening to a sermon by a Dominican friar on Palm Sunday 1341.[95] Henry IV took his teenage sons with him to Bardney Abbey in 1406,[96] and the twelve year-old Henry VI prayed at the shrine of St Edmund at Bury when he spent Christmas there in 1433.[97] The familiarity of noble children with religious practices did not ensure, of course, that they all grew into devout or well-behaved adults. Thomas Brinton thought the opposite as true in 1375. When noble children are young and under a master, he said, they attend services, recite litanies, and have a conscience to put away their vices. But when they are lords they sleep until terce (the middle of the morning), and treat divine worship with scorn.[98]

Spiritual and mental improvement was only one side of medieval education. Teaching and upbringing also placed an emphasis on the care and use of the body in a decorous way. The closeness of cleanliness to godliness was recognised even in the middle ages. From the twelfth century onwards there were written guides to personal hygiene and social behaviour, in Latin at first, in French by the thirteenth century, and in English by the fifteenth.[99] They explained such matters as how to keep oneself clean, how to avoid habits unpleasant to others, when and how to speak in public, and the etiquette of waiting at table. Aristocratic youths in great households were expected to do certain symbolic acts of service to their fathers or lords: to carve meat, serve drinks, hold lights, and bring water for washing the hands. When

---

94. Giles of Rome, *De Regimine Principum*, book II, part II, chapter 5.

95. PRO, Exch. KR, Accounts Various, E 101/389/11.

96. Above, note 90.

97. Sir W. Dugdale, *Monasticon Anglicanum*, ed. J. Caley & others, 6 vols in 8 (London, 1817–30), III, 113.

98. *The Sermons of Thomas Brinton, Bishop of Rochester*, ed. Mary A. Devlin, I, Camden Society, third series, LXXXV (1954), 217.

99. On the genre see S. Gieben, 'Robert Grosseteste and medieval courtesy books', *Vivarium*, V (1967), 47–74; H. Rosamond Parsons, 'Anglo-Norman Books of Courtesy and Nurture', *PMLA*, XLIV (1929), 383–455; and F. J. Furnivall, *Manners and Meals in Olden Time: The Babees Book*, EETS OS 32 (1868).

meals were over, children were encouraged to practise the arts of leisure: music and dancing. Here the sexes were equal. Chaucer not only describes a Squire who knows how to dance, flute, sing and compose songs, but a princess, Canacee, who can dance, and a noble maiden of Troy who has composed a song of love which Antigone, another lady of the city, is able to sing.[100] The sexual equality to which the poet paid tribute really existed. If Henry IV was described by a contemporary as a 'sparkling' musician,[101] his first wife Mary Bohun also had three dozen strings bought for her harp in 1387–8 when she was in her late teens.[102] Likewise, a century later, the young Henry VIII who could dance, set songs, and play the flute and virginals by the time he was nineteen, did not display a male superiority in doing so.[103] His sisters Margaret and Mary also danced well and performed on the lute and the clavichord at similar ages.[104] Indeed, the education of girls had an artistic dimension lacking from that of boys, since they alone were exercised in the decorative arts of tapestry and embroidery. Work of this kind was highly commended by moralists as a means of keeping ladies from idleness and, when it involved the making of vestments for clerics, contributing to the well-being of society.[105] Here too girls were taught an art in childhood which they brought to perfection as women.

The third area of aristocratic education was the physical one. Common sense dictated that all children should be encouraged to take exercise, irrespective of age and sex; both Aristotle and Giles of Rome, as we have seen, urged the need for play and movement up to the age of seven.[106] The peripatetic nature of aristocratic life, in which families moved from one house to another and children sent away from home went to and fro on visits, necessitated the learning of riding by boys and girls alike. Hunting, hawking and shooting with bows were also common to both sexes in adulthood, and there are occasional references to the involvement of children in these pastimes. Prince Arthur had a bow bought for his use in 1492 when he was five and a half,[107] and his fourteen year-old sister Margaret, on her way to be married to

100. *Canterbury Tales*, General Prologue, lines 91–100; Squire's Tale, line 277; *Troilus and Criseyde*, book II, lines 876–82.
101. BL, Additional MS 35295, fol. 262.
102. Wylie, *England under Henry the Fourth*, IV, 159.
103. Edward Hall, *Chronicle Containing the History of England* (London, 1809), 515.
104. BL, MS Cotton Vespasian C. xii, fol. 283v; Leland, *Collectanea*, ed. Hearne, V, 361; N. H. Nicolas, *Privy Purse Expenses of Elizabeth of York* (London, 1830), 29; S. Bentley, *Excerpta Historica* (London, 1831), 125, 133.
105. For references to the practice of these arts by aristocratic women see Giles of Rome, *De Regimine Principum,* book II, part II, chapter 20; William Langland, *Piers Plowman*, B. Text, passus VI, lines 7–16; Chaucer, *The Legend of Good Women*, lines 2350–8.
106. Above, note 20.
107. S. Bentley, *Excerpta Historica*, 88.

James IV of Scotland in 1503, succeeded in shooting a buck while hunting in Alnwick deerpark.[108] It is fair to say that the physical training of girls, however, remained circumscribed compared with that of boys. Aristocratic women required exercise, but their menfolk were a military estate. Even if they did not aspire to knighthood and service in war, they were bound by law to possess arms,[109] and prudence directed that they should know how to use them to guard their property and keep order in their districts. The basic textbook of military training in medieval England was the fourth-century work of Vegetius, the *Epitoma Rei Militaris*, originally intended as a training manual for the whole Roman army but interpreted in medieval times as a guide for the aristocracy in particular.[110] The work was translated into French in 1284, into English prose in 1408, and paraphrased into English verse during the 1450s.[111] It was also drawn upon extensively by Giles of Rome and many writers on chivalry. Vegetius, like Aristotle, indicated *adolescencia*, the years from fourteen to twenty-one, as the period for military training. The activities he recommended included running, throwing weights, casting spears, jousting on foot at the quintain, riding, jousting on horseback, and swimming. Most of these feats can be paralleled in later medieval practice. Edward the Black Prince was only sixteen when he took part in the real battle of Crécy in 1346. John Hastings, earl of Pembroke, was mortally wounded in 1389 at the age of seventeen, as he tilted with an older knight under his master's supervision.[112] An equally ill-fated boy, Edward son of Henry VI, is described by Fortescue in the late 1460s, when he was in his mid teens, giving himself almost entirely to martial exercises: riding, fighting with swords and other weapons, and learning the rules of military discipline.[113] He too experienced battle and death soon afterwards, at Tewkesbury in 1471.

It will now be apparent that the shortage of specialised treatises on aristocratic education in medieval England did not reflect a want of education itself. There might have been little theory but there was much practice. What separated the fourteenth- and fifteenth-century aristocracy from their Tudor and Stuart successors was not a lack of

108. Leland, *Collectanea*, ed. Hearne, IV, 278.

109. On this subject see M. Powicke, *Military Obligation in Medieval England* (Oxford, 1962).

110. For a survey of the history and influence of the work see J.-A. Wisman, 'L'E-pitoma rei militaris de Végèce et sa fortune au Moyen Age', *Le Moyen Age*, LXXXV, fourth series, XXXIV (1979), 13–31.

111. The English prose translation has not yet been printed. It is discussed in John Trevisa, *Dialogus inter Militem et Clericum*, ed. Perry, xciv–viii. The English verse paraphrase is *Knyghthode and Bataile*, ed. R. Dyboski & Z. M. Arend, *EETS* OS 201 (1936).

112. *Polychronicon Ranulphi Higden*, ed. Babington & Lumby, IX, 219–20.

113. Fortescue, *De Laudibus Legum Anglie*, ed. Chrimes, 2–3.

education but a lack of consciousness about it. This arose from the nature of medieval education, which was less distinct from life in general than it has since become. In the great household, the chief location of aristocratic upbringing, education was only one of many activities. Most of those who provided it – parents, nurses, clergy and even some tutors – were not specially trained to do so, and often had other duties and interests. Specialised schools and universities existed from the twelfth century onwards, and so did professional masters and mistresses, but their influence, as far as the aristocracy was concerned, only gradually developed during the later middle ages and the sixteenth century. The evolution of a specialised literature of education was complementary to this process; education had to become a distinct process before it could stimulate a distinct genre of writing. It would be difficult to establish that the informal and unspecialised system of education in medieval times was inferior by nature, or served society less well, than the more formal and specialised systems that have succeeded it. As we have seen, the aristocratic curriculum was a wide one. Much of it was common to both sexes. Girls and boys alike were schooled in religion, literacy, deportment, music, dancing, and outdoor exercises. If men were privileged to learn grammar and military techniques, this merely reflected the greater role in government and business which they played in adult life. Ladies were denied this role, but they had something equally distinctive of their own in the cult of the decorative arts. Well-educated noblemen and women came to the court with an experience which encompassed people and places, as well as pursuits. How they fared when they got there, of course, depended on many other factors besides education: personality, family connections, and the circumstances they encountered. But that is another story.

5 Hugh Oldham, bishop of Exeter (d. 1519), stares boldly from his tomb in Exeter Cathedral, a typical prelate of the pre-Reformation era and educational benefactor. He endowed Manchester Grammar School, helped found Corpus Christi College (Oxford), and tried to improve the learning of his cathedral clergy.

10

THE EDUCATION OF EDWARD V

THE CHILDHOOD and education of Edward V necessarily make up the whole of his biography, for he was only twelve when he was overthrown as king in 1483 and died, almost certainly, before he was thirteen. They are also worth studying, however, because of the careful and well-recorded arrangements which were made by his father, Edward IV, for bringing him up. The education of previous heirs to the English throne, of course, had been careful too. Special households were organized for them to live in; nurses, mistresses and masters were assigned to care for them and teach them; and they were trained in a wide range of knowledge, skills and activities.[1] The education of Edward V conformed to this tradition, but seems to have differed in being more deliberately and formally planned in advance. Written ordinances were drawn up to regulate the prince's education in 1473 when he was nearly three, and reissued ten years later with appropriate revisions as he entered upon his adolescence.[2] It is in the formulation of these ordinances, where hitherto princely education had been mainly informal, that the particular interest of Edward's childhood lies. The article which follows is centred on discussing them and placing them in context.

Edward V was born at Westminster on 2 December 1470. As he was the fourth child of his parents (there were three older girls) and the queen had been regularly giving birth to children every sixteen to eighteen months, he probably started his life in a pre-existing nursery establishment along with his elder sisters. Elizabeth Darcy, lady mistress of the king's nursery, was rewarded for good service to the prince in 1481,[3] and doubtless supervised his babyhood with the help of a domestic staff of nurses and female rockers. We also know the name of Edward's nurse (probably his wet-nurse): Avice Welles, a married woman who was granted a tun of red wine annually soon after the prince's second birthday in November 1472, perhaps at about the time that he was weaned and no longer required her services.[4] Deliberate plans for Edward's education were drawn up in the autumn of 1473, as he approached the age of three. First, on 27 September the ordinances for his upbringing were issued, committing the care of his person to the queen's brother, Anthony Lord Rivers, and the charge of his household to the bishop of Rochester, John Alcock. Secondly, on 10 November Rivers was formally appointed as 'governor' and 'ruler' of the prince, and Alcock as his 'teacher' and president of his council.[5] The appointment of Rivers was in a long

[1] On this subject see N. Orme, *From Childhood to Chivalry: the education of the English kings and aristocracy, 1066–1530* (1984), ch. i.

[2] Printed below, document 2.

[3] *Calendar of Patent Rolls 1477–85*, p. 241.

[4] *Cal. Pat. Rolls 1467–77*, p. 358.

[5] Public Record Office, Patent Rolls, C 66/532 m. 15, summarized in *Cal. Pat. Rolls 1467–77* pp. 401, 417.

tradition, for similar 'masters' of young kings and heirs to the throne can be traced back in the royal family of England to the time of the Norman Conquest. Up to the fifteenth century, however, these masters were invariably knights rather than members of the peerage, though one of them, Sir Guichard d'Angle the master of Richard II, did rise to be earl of Huntingdon on his pupil's accession in 1377. Their status too was rather informal. No documents survive appointing them, and they are known to us only through casual references in chronicles or documents.

The early fifteenth century saw changes to this system, both with respect to the type of person appointed to care for the heir to the throne and the manner in which he was appointed. In 1422 Henry V, in his last will, nominated his uncle Thomas Beaufort, duke of Exeter, to govern the person of his son Henry VI: the first appointment of a peer to this function and the first (so far as we know) to be made in writing.[6] Beaufort died at the end of 1426, and shortly afterwards in June 1428 another peer, the earl of Warwick, was formally given the duty of looking after the young king's person and supervising his education.[7] The appointment of Rivers, a peer and kinsman of the king, maintained the upgrading of the rank of prince's master, and the putting of the appointment into writing reflected the crystallizing of the master's functions into what was now described as an 'office'. The use of the titles 'governor' and 'ruler' was new, and probably arose because the ancient one of 'master' was coming in the fifteenth century to be associated with schoolmasters, men of a lowlier kind. No other breach with tradition seems to have been envisaged, however, and Rivers's appointment gave him the same power that had belonged 'to any other man in days past'. The assignment of Bishop Alcock to be Edward's 'teacher' was also new, for although earlier princes may well have had some informal instruction from bishops or other great clerics, no such person had even been designated in this way. In the outcome, Alcock's role appears to have centred on ruling the prince's household rather than instructing the prince, and Edward's teaching was probably deputed to specialized tutors of lesser rank. Thus in grammar, Edward was taught from about the age of four by John Giles, a professional schoolmaster,[8] and Alcock probably did little more than supervise the process.

The remaining novelty about the arrangements for Edward's education was the embodiment of them in a set of written ordinances. True, in the case of Henry VI, the appointments of the mistress of his nursery in 1424 and of the earl of Warwick as his master in 1428 were both accompanied by statements of the powers they were to hold and rather vague indications of what they should teach: good manners, letters, languages, nurture and courtesy.[9] The ordinances for Edward, on the other hand, not only lay down the powers of Rivers and Alcock and some of the matters to be taught, but do so in the framework of a regular daily timetable, explaining the order (and in one or two cases the hours) that things should take place. They are consequently among the earliest modern timetables in the history of English education. In this respect they reflect a characteristic development of English life in the fifteenth century: the growth of a more precise system of measuring time and a more sophisticated concept of using it. Again, this is not to deny that boys and girls had previously been

---

    [6] B. P. Wolffe, *Henry VI* (1981), p. 29.

    [7] *Proceedings and Ordinances of the Privy Council of England*, ed. N. H. Nicolas (7 vols., 1834–7), iii. 143, 296–300; cf. iv. 134–7.

    [8] *Cal. Pat. Rolls 1467–77*, p. 592.

    [9] *Proceedings and Ordinances*, iii. 143, 296–300.

brought up in regular daily routines of activities. The novices of monasteries and the choristers of cathedrals had long been trained in the framework of the daily cycle of prayers and observances carried out by their elders. Schools and universities probably had their customary daily patterns of starting, changing and finishing their work as early as the twelfth century, though little or nothing of these patterns has been recorded.[10] Among the aristocracy, the view of life in a noble household presented in romances like *Sir Gawain and the Green Knight* suggests a parallel sequence of religious devotions, recreations and meals, which must have shaped the education of the children who were brought up in such places. In the fifteenth century, however, a greater concern with daily times and routines appears to have grown in English society, marked by the proliferation of mechanical clocks in churches, noble households and town communities.[11] Clocks demonstrate the wish of their users to follow daily routines in some detail with small seasonal variations, and consequently to observe each day in the same way. Their advent in fifteenth-century England has not received much notice from historians, but their impact on the way of life of adults and children alike was evidently important and has left many traces in records. In schools the first clear evidence of routines timed by the clock comes from the foundation statutes of endowed schools from the fourteen-forties onwards.[12] At the universities the statutes issued for colleges in the fifteenth century gradually begin to fix the house at which business should take place and lectures be given.[13] By the reign of Edward IV the household ordinances of the king and his brother Clarence lay down specific times for meals, meetings of officers, attendance on the king and the opening and shutting of gates.[14] In a more private capacity, Edward's mother Cecily, duchess of York (d. 1495), and Henry VII's, Lady Margaret Beaufort (d. 1509), are both known to have followed carefully timed routines of business, meals and prayers in units as brief as a quarter of an hour.[15] The ordinances for Edward V involve the application of the same principles to the bringing up of a royal child.

They were not, however, quite the first of their kind. As early as the fourteen-thirties a set of ordinances had been drawn up which anticipate those of Edward V in several respects, though they are very little known as they occur only as a stray document in the registers of the former priory of Lanthony near Gloucester, and have never been printed.[16] These ordinances refer to the upbringing of John Mowbray II (1415–61), who succeeded his father as duke of

---

[10] E.g. the 13th-century pseudo-Boethius, *De Disciplina Scolarium*, ed. O. Weijers (1976), pp. 126–8, discusses the best parts of the day for scholars to learn and be taught.

[11] For the increasing evidence of church clocks in the 15th century see C. F. C. Beeson, *English Church Clocks, 1280–1850* (1971), pp. 22–4.

[12] N. Orme, *English Schools in the Middle Ages* (1973), p. 124.

[13] The statutes of New College, Oxford, 1389–94, prescribe no hours for any activity (*Statutes of the Colleges of Oxford* (3 vols., London and Oxford, 1853), i, e.g. pp. 24, 40–2, 56, 67, 102). Specific hours begin to be mentioned at Oxford in the statutes of All Souls, 1443 (*ibid.*, p. 13); Lincoln, 1480 (*ibid.*, p. 15); Magdalen, 1487 (*ibid.*, ii. 47, 69); and Corpus Christi, 1517 (*ibid.*, pp. 42, 48, 96).

[14] A. R. Myers, *The Household of Edward IV* (Manchester, 1959), pp. 201–4, 208, 214, 218–20; *A Collection of Ordinances and Regulations for the Government of the Royal Household* (Soc. Antiq. London, 1790), pp. 89–105.

[15] For Cecily's timetable see P.R.O., Lord Steward's Department, Miscellaneous Books, LS 13/280 fos. 284–6, printed in *A Collection of Ordinances*, pp. *37–9, and discussed by C. A. J. Armstrong, 'The piety of Cecily, duchess of York', in *For Hilaire Belloc*, ed. D. Woodruff (1942), pp. 73–94. For Lady Margaret Beaufort, see *The English Works of John Fisher*, ed. J. E. B. Mayor, part i (Early English Text Soc., extra ser., xxvii, 1876), pp. 294–5.

[16] P.R.O., Chancery Masters' Exhibits, C 115/K2/6682 fo. 251, printed below, document 1.

Norfolk at the age of seventeen in 1432 and thereby passed into the wardship of the king until he reached the age of twenty-one in 1436.[17] They are not dated, but are probably to be assigned to the year 1435 when the duke was nineteen or twenty. A reference to proceedings in 'the last parlement' which took place on 3 November 1433[18] shows that the text was drawn up between then and the end of the next parliament on 6 December 1435, and it is placed in the register between documents of August and September in that year. It was unprecedented (as far as we know) to design ordinances for the governance of individual wards, and those for Norfolk were clearly the outcome of an abnormal situation, caused by the duke's unsatisfactory behaviour. Although he had taken an oath in 1435, along with the other lords of parliament, not to receive any robbers, manslayers or criminals into his household or to 'maintain' such folk elsewhere,[19] he had evidently acquired unsuitable men in his retinue and was personally living in a disorderly way. The council of the young king Henry VI was forced to take action. Norfolk was summoned before the council, with the king present, and made to promise to follow a new 'rewle' of behaviour. Some of his retainers were removed, and fresh esquires were assigned to serve him. They were charged to accompany him when he went about, encourage him to virtue, and report any vice in his household to the council. Finally, a daily plan was drawn up to regulate the time that he rose in the morning, his attendance at prayers, his bedtime at night and his general demeanour, all of which were enshrined in the ordinances. It is not clear whether they represent a draft scheme or one that was actually put into effect. The contemporary records of the king's council are completely silent about the Norfolk episode, and the ordinances have come down to us only in the unofficial context of the Lanthony registers.

The ordinances for Edward V represent an advance on those for Norfolk, in that they were not provoked by a crisis but represent a development of educational consciousness in which the normal education of a boy was seen as needing to be individually planned. They are, indeed, the principal evidence that the royal family of York perceived the importance of education as much as their predecessors, the Lancastrians, had done. The ordinances consist of two parts: a personal regimen for the prince himself, and a set of directions for the conduct of his household, in which he was to live (like earlier royal princes) separately from the households of his parents. The prince's household was formed on the lines of that of the king or of a leading adult magnate. Already on 20 February 1473 he had been provided with twenty-five councillors to administer his affairs and possessions: a wide and varied body of people.[20] They included the queen, the archbishop of Canterbury, the king's brothers Clarence and Gloucester, Earl Rivers and Lord Hastings, as well as lesser men like Sir Thomas Vaughan, the prince's chamberlain,[21] who actually stayed with him and organized his routine affairs. The household was financed from the revenues of the duchy of Cornwall, the principality of Wales and the earldom of Chester which the prince had been granted as heir to the throne.[22] Our knowledge of its staffing is incomplete, since the ordinances were not concerned to list its members, but its size can be

---

[17] On Mowbray see *The Complete Peerage*, comp. G. E. Cokayne and others (13 vols., 1910–59), ix. 607–8.
[18] *Rotuli Parliamentorum*, iv. 421–2.
[19] *Ibid.*
[20] *Cal. Pat. Rolls 1467–77*, p. 366.
[21] Thomas Vaughan was formally appointed the prince's chamberlain in 1474 (*ibid.*, p. 414).
[22] *Ibid.*, pp. 361, 365.

estimated from the contemporary 'Black Book of the Royal Household' of 1471–3, which advises that the prince of Wales should have a retinue of fifty.[23] The ordinances refer to three chief officers in the household: the chamberlain, treasurer and controller, and to the prince's personal physician and his surgeon (one of whom, John Argentine, was one of the last to see the prince alive in the Tower of London).[24] They also mention a religious establishment, including an almoner, two chaplains and a group of boy-choristers singing in the prince's chapel. More dimly we are made aware of a cadre of esquires, ushers, clerical staff and a household below stairs. Interestingly, the household contained a number of 'sonnes of nobles, lords and gentlemen' who were undergoing education in grammar, music and other exercises. It was evidently intended that Edward, like earlier heirs to the throne, should be brought up in the company of other noble youths and not kept in seclusion. We know the name of one of these youths: Edmund Audley, son of Lord Audley, who died as a young man in about 1478. His family evidently considered his membership of the prince's household as a signal honour, for they had it inscribed on his tomb, alongside his other distinctions, that he had been the prince's sword-bearer and 'henchman' or noble retainer.[25]

With regard to the prince himself, the ordinances provide a careful sequence of activities lasting throughout his waking hours: rising, prayers, breakfast, learning, dinner, more learning, sports and exercises, evening prayers, supper, recreation and finally bed by eight p.m. The plan is concerned with the prince's way of life, rather than with the skills he was to learn, but it points us to the four main dimensions which his education possessed. First, he was taught to be a good Christian, primarily in the sense of following religious observances. Like the adult aristocracy of his day, he was brought up to observe regular daily prayer, including mattins and evensong in his chamber and mass in his private chapel. Secondly, he was entertained with 'noble storyes as behoveth to a prynce to understand': stories which probably centred on the deeds of great kings and warriors to make him courageous, and fables of a moral kind to make him wise. Lord Rivers himself translated the collection of wise precepts called *The Dicts or Sayings of the Philosophers* for Edward's benefit,[26] and Caxton dedicated his translation of *The Historie of Jason* to the prince in 1477 so that he might 'begynne to lerne rede Englissh' from it, no doubt assimilating its noble deeds as he did so.[27] Thirdly, the prince spent time at 'learning', which probably included French and certainly Latin grammar, which we know he was taught by John Giles. Domenico Mancini believed in 1483 that Edward was well learned in literature and could both pronounce and fully understand any work of verse or prose that came into his hands, 'unless it were from among the more abstruse authors'.[28] Unfortunately, Mancini does not make it clear which authors he means, and though Edward must have studied a good deal of Latin, we do not know precisely what level he reached and whether he read the traditional medieval school authors or any of the classical Latin writers who were studied in

[23] Myers, p. 94.

[24] D. Mancini, *The Usurpation of Richard III*, ed. C. A. J. Armstrong (2nd edn., Oxford, 1969), pp. 92–3. For Argentine's career see A. B. Emden, *A Biographical Register of the University of Cambridge to 1500* (Cambridge, 1963), pp. 15–16.

[25] Oxford, Bodleian Library, MS. Ashmole 1137 fo. 152v.

[26] Anthony Wydeville, *The Dictes or Sayengis of the Philosophhres* (Westminster, 1477), prologue.

[27] *The Prologues and Epilogues of William Caxton*, ed. W. J. B. Crotch (E.E.T.S., original ser., clxxvi, 1928), p. 34.

[28] Mancini, pp. 92–3.

the fourteen-nineties by the children of Henry VII.[29] Finally, the prince was introduced to 'such convenient disports and exercises as behoveth his age to have experience in'. These are likely to have included music (both singing and the playing of instruments) and dancing, which we know were learnt by the aristocratic boys in the royal household at this date.[30] Certainly, Edward practised athletic skills. Mancini tells us that the prince 'devoted himself to horses and dogs and other youthful exercises to invigorate his body',[31] and shooting with a bow and arrows formed one of the pastimes of his last sad days in the Tower in the summer of 1483.[32]

The ordinances of 1473 had a sequel. Nearly ten years later, on 25 February 1483, Edward IV emphasized his concern for the prince's upbringing by issuing a revised version, suitable for his son's approaching adolescence.[33] In general, this revision repeated the form of the 1473 ordinances, but it also introduced some detailed changes of significance. First, it supplies the names of the prince's chief household officers in 1483: Alcock, now bishop of Worcester, still president of the council; Richard Martyn, bishop of St. Davids, chancellor;[34] Sir Richard Grey, councillor; Earl Rivers, governor; Sir Thomas Vaughan, chamberlain; Sir William Stanley, steward; Sir Richard Crofte, treasurer; and Richard Haut, esquire, controller. These names reveal the increase of the influence of the queen's family upon the prince and his affairs since 1473. Rivers was the queen's brother, Grey her second son, and Haut a cousin of the queen and Grey.[35] Grey had not been a member of the prince's original council, and he has recently been judged as a personality of Edward IV's reign rather than a power.[36] The 1483 ordinances make it clear, on the contrary, that he had come to possess considerable importance within the prince's household. No mere rank-and-file councillor, he enjoyed equal status with Rivers and Alcock in advising on the prince's affairs and reporting on the prince's behaviour to the king and queen. The original broad-based council of the prince had become eclipsed by a narrow Wydeville interest, by no means popular in the country at large. Herein lay trouble for the future.

The 1483 ordinances also provide a complement to the usual view of Edward V as the pathetic child victim of his uncle, with little of his own personality. In 1483 the section on the prince's personal regimen was enlarged by three new clauses.[37] He was to be accompanied by at least two 'discrete and convenyent persons' at every moment of his day, from getting up until going to bed. He was not to order anything to be done without the advice of Alcock, Grey or Rivers, and none of his servants was to encourage him to do anything against the ordinances. If he did break the latter, or acted in an unprincely way, the three men were to warn him personally and to tell the king and queen if he refused to amend. These clauses are significant because they appear to reflect the experience of organizing the education of the twelve-year-old prince, as opposed to the theory of planning it when he was two. They can have been necessary only if

[29] *Memorials of Henry VII*, ed. J. Gairdner (Rolls Ser., 1858), p. 43.

[30] Myers, pp. 126–7.

[31] Mancini, pp. 70–1.

[32] *Ibid.*, p. 127.

[33] British Library, Sloane MS. 3479 (hereafter cited as Sloane MS.) fos. 53v–58.

[34] For his biography see A. B. Emden, *A Biographical Register of the University of Oxford to A.D. 1500* (3 vols., Oxford, 1957–9), iii. 1236–7.

[35] C. D. Ross, *Richard III* (1981), p. 107.

[36] 'He was never given any important office or appointment' (C. D. Ross, *Edward IV* (1974), p. 96).

[37] Printed below, document 3.

Edward did, at times, assert himself and chafe against his tutelage. There is nothing surprising in that. Henry VI had 'grucched' or complained at the discipline he received from his master, the earl of Warwick,[38] and Norfolk, as we have seen, had broken away from constraint in his late teens. Yet both men survived to live reasonably normal adult lives, and there is no reason why Edward V should not have done so too. He was probably an ordinary lively boy, like his equally lively and ill-fated predecessor, Edward son of Henry VI.[39]

The arrangements of Edward IV for his son look paradoxical today. They brought an almost unprecedented formality to the prince's education, yet they allowed him to become too closely associated with a single group of important, yet unpopular men. This had not been true of the upbringing of earlier royal princes, to nearly such an extent. Their household officers had usually been lesser men uninvolved in high politics, or respected men holding equable relationships with the royal uncles and other great magnates. Henry VII, in the bringing up of his own two sons, was to revert to this older less dangerous tradition.[40] In the case of Edward V, his close association with the Wydevilles and the Greys proved disastrous. Their unpopularity stimulated and enabled Richard III to seize and remove them from power, and then left Edward V as a defenceless remnant of their party. Richard could hardly feel safe after robbing Edward of men so close to him, and to whom he was probably sincerely attached: the removal of Rivers and Grey must have helped to dictate the elimination of Edward. Sadly, the education which was intended to build him into a great king became, instead, a principal element of his downfall.

1. *Public Record Office, Chancery Masters' Exhibits, C 115/K2/6682 fo. 251*[41]
   [Ordinances for John Mowbray, duke of Norfolk, c. 1435]

For the good rewle and governaunce of my lord of Northfolk beyng in the kynges ward, it semeth expedient that he as wele as tho that shall be a boute hys person kepe and observe as hit towcheth hem severally the rewle comprised in particles undir wryton.

Furst, for as mykell as all good governaunce, wisdom and vertues growen and ar roted in the love and drede of God, that the said my lord of N. dispose hym entierlye wyth all his hert from hens forth to love and drede God and to serve hym, and that he so do as it suteth every cristen man and namely theym which be sette in grete estate for worshippes and wordly goodes whych they receyve of our lord to fore other in lower degree and for mony other causes and resons.

Item, that he ryse from his bedde at morowe dayle by twyxt vi and vii of the clok, and say wyth his chapeleyn or som other honeste person matyns of ower Lady wyth prime and houres.

Item, that he be waytyng upon the kyng in the mornyng and go with hym to his messe, and there abyde and here the same messe.

Item, in like wyse that he go wyth the kyng to the hiegh messe whan he gooth and here the sayd messe.

Item, that he say also daylye evensong of our Lady wyth such a person as above.

Item, that he go to his reste every nyght atte lattest be x of the clok.

---

[38] *Proceedings and Ordinances*, iv. 134–7.

[39] Sir John Fortescue, *De Laudibus Legum Anglie*, ed. S. B. Chrimes (Cambridge, 1942), pp. 1–2.

[40] On this matter see Orme, *From Childhood to Chivalry*, ch. i.

[41] In the texts which follow, punctuation and the use of capital letters have been modernized and standard abbreviations have been expanded. The use of 'u' and 'v', and 'i' and 'j' has been standardized, and þ and ʒ have been rendered by their typographical equivalents. Otherwise, spelling is as in the original.

Item, whan he shall passe the place of the kynges loggynges that he have oon atte leest of thesquiers assigned to hym of new by the kynges consell.

Item, that in such thynges as shall touch the governaunce of his person he be advised be thesquiers to for said, or such of hem as shal be abowte his person, and sue here advise and consell.

Item, that he receyve not her aftyr to his compaygnie, familiarite or service abowte his person the persones appoynted by the kynges consell to be removed from hym, ner by hem or eny of hem be advised or conselled toward the governaunce of his sayd person.

Item, that he have bysilie in his mynde and for kepyng of his honour observe in all poyntes tharticle assured as wele by hym as other lordes and estates of this land in the kynges hande at the last parlement holden at Westm',[42] which is as in substance that no lord ner other person receyve, cheryssh, hold in houshold ne maigtene pillours, robbours, oppressours of the peple, mansleers, felons, owtlawes, ravissheres of wommen, brekers of parkes or warennes, or eny other open mysdoor or eny openly named or famed for such till his innocencie be declared, and that no man take eny other mennes cause or querell in favour or meyntenaunce as be word, by writyng or message to officer, juge, jure or partie be colour of eny feffement.

Item, that thesquiers assigned to be aboute his person consell the said my lord of Northfolk and induce in the best wyse that God woll yeve hem grace and in esy and gentill wyse to serve God and to be of good rewle and good governaunce, and to kepe this articles above wryten and soffre not the contrarie in as mykell as they shulle mowe, which so to do and to kepe they shull make feyth in my lordes hand of Warwykes.

Item, if the seyd esquieres or eny of hem have knowleche of eni man beyng for the time aboute his person which be noysed or famed of eny ryot or misgovernaunce or elles that laboreth to breke the advise and ordinaunce appoynted by the kynges consell, or consell hym to every misgovernaunce or confort or cherysch hym ther in, they shull in all goodly hast certefie the kynges consell of her persones and names.

Item, that if my lord said of Northfolk estrange hym and utterlye refuse to sue the-advise and consell of the seid esquiers or of eni of thaym beyng a bowte hym for the tyme, which is not to suppose for as moch as he hath promitted to the kyng beyng presente his consell to obeye what rewle he wold put to hym, the said esquieres shall sue to the kynges consell for there discharge and licence for to departe from hym.

Item, that all other persons beyng in the service of my said lord of N. aboute his person be assured and make feyth to obeye to the said esquiers and to hym of theym which for the tyme shall be aboute hym in such thyng that shall touche the governaunce and rewle of his person, and never to sture hym to do the contrarie of her consell and advises, nether to favour, supporte, confort or cherysh hym in word or dede in enimysgovernaunce, but to lette hym in such caas in all that they shull mowe.

2. *Public Record Office, Lord Steward's Department, Misc. Books, LS 13/280 fos. 277–279v*
[Ordinances for Edward, prince of Wales, 27 September 1473, first printed in *A Collection of Ordinances*, pp. *27–33]

[*fo. 277*] Edward by the grace of God, kinge of Englande and lord of Irelande, to the right reverende father in God the bushop of Rochester and to our right trustye and welbeloved the Earle Ryvers and to every of you, greetinge. Wyte yee that wee, aswell for the vertuous guydinge of the person of our deereste first begotten sonne Edward, prince of Wales, duke of Cornewalle and earle of Chester, as for the pollytique, sadde and good rule of his houshoulde to be sett upp and begunne at the feaste of Snt. Michaell the archangell next followinge, have stablished theise statutes and ordynaunces hereafter partyculerly ensueinge, by us made at Westminster the xxviith daye of September, the xiiith yeare of our raigne, which statutes and ordynaunces we commaunde and will that ye see them and every of them to be firmely observed and kepte, as farre as in you is.

---

[42] A reference to the oath taken by the peers in parliament on 3 Nov. 1433, of which the following lines are a direct quotation (*Rotuli Parliamentorum*, iv. 421–2).

[i]

Ordinances concerninge the guidinge of our sayde sonnes person, which wee comitte unto the sayde Earle Ryvers.

Firste, we will that our sayde first begotten sonne shall arise every morninge at a convenyent hower accordinge unto his adge, and tyll he be readye noe man be suffired to entre into his chamber except our right trustye and wellbeloved the Earle Ryvers, his chamberlayne and his chapleynes, or such other as shalbe thoughte by the said Earle Ryvers convenyent for the same season, which chaplins[43] shall say mattyns in his presence; and when he is ready and the mattins sayde, forthwith to goe into his chappell or closett to here his masse there, and in noe wise in his chamber without a cause reasonable, and noe man to interupte him duringe his masse tyme.

Item, we wyll that our sayd sonne heere every holyday all[44] the devine service of the daye[45] in his chappell or closett, and that he offer afore the alter accordinge[46] to the custome.

Item, we will that upon principall feastes and usuall dayes of predycation sermons to be sayd before our sayde sonne, and that all his servantes be there that may conveniently be spared from their offices.

[*fo. 277v*] Item, we will that our sayd sonne have his breakfaste imediatly after his masse and betwene that and his meate to be occupyed in such vertuous learninge as his adge shall nowe suffyce to receave,[46] and that he be at his dynner at a convenyent howre and thereat to be honorablye served and his dishes borne by worshipfull folkes[47] and esquires bearinge our lyverye, and that all other offycers and servantes give theyre due attendance accordinge to theyre offyces.

Item, that noe man sytt at his boarde but such as shalbe thought by the discretyon of the sayd Earle Ryvers and that then be reade before him such noble storyes as behoveth to a prynce to understande and knowe, that the comunicatyon at all tymes in his presence be of vertu, honor, cuninge, wisdome and deedes of worshippe, and of nothinge that should move or styrre him to vyces.

Item, we will that after his meate in eschewinge of idlenes he be occupyed about his learninge,[48] and after in his presence to be shewed all such convenient disportes and exercyses as behoveth his estate to have experience in.

Item, we will that our sayd sonne goe to his evensonge at a convenyent howre, and that sone after done to be ere at his supper and thereat to be served accordinglie as before.

Item, we will that after his supper he have all such honeste disportes as may be convenyentlye devised for his recreation.

Item, we will that our sayd sonne be in his chamber and for all nighte lyverye[49] to be sette, the traverse[50] drawne, anone upon eight[51] of the clocke, and all persons from thence to be avoyded excepte such as be deputed and apointed to give theire attendance uppon him all nighte, and that they inforce themselves to make him joyouxe and merry towardes his bedde.[52]

Item, we will that yt be seene by his councellours and offecers that sure and good watche be nightly had about his person and duely kepte for the safeguarde of the same.[53]

[43] For *which chaplins* the 1483 text reads *one of the said chapelleyns* (Sloane MS. fo. 53v).

[44] 1483 text omits *all* (*ibid.* fo. 54).

[45] The full ecclesiastical service of the day or 'divine office', as opposed to the short office of Our Lady.

[46] For *in such . . . to receave*, 1483 text reads *an houre at his scole before he goe to meate* (Sloane MS. fo. 54).

[47] 1483 text adds *henchmen* (*ibid.*).

[48] For *about his learninge*, 1483 text reads *twoe houres at his scole* (*ibid.*).

[49] Food and drink, e.g. bread and wine.

[50] A curtain or screen, either of the bed or the bed-chamber.

[51] For *eight*, 1483 text reads *ix* (Sloane MS. fo. 54v).

[52] 1483 text adds *in all vertue* (*ibid.*).

[53] 1483 text adds three further articles after this, printed below, document 3.

[ii]

[*fo. 278*] Ordinances concerninge of his houshoulde, which we committe unto the said bushoppe of Rochester and Earle Rivers.

Item, we will that every day be sayde masse in the hall for the offycers of houshoulde, to begin at sixe of the clocke in the morninge, and at vii mattins to begin in the chappell, and at nine a masse by note with children.[54]

Item, we will that our sayde sonne have the chaplins one of them to be his almoner, and that he will truelye, discreetelye and dilligentlye gether and distribute our said sonnes almes to poore people, and that the said almoner be confessor to the houshoulde and the other twoe chapleynes to saye masse and devyne servyce before our sayde sonne.[55]

Item, we wyll that noe person, man nor woman, beinge within our sayd sonnes houshoulde be customable swearer, brawler, backbyter, comen hasorder, adventorer[56] and use wordes of rybauldrye, and spetyally in the presence of our sayd sonne.

Item, we will that the sonnes of nobles, lords and gentlemen beinge in houshoulde with our sayde sonne arise at a convenyent hower and here theire masse, and be vertuously brought uppe and taughte in grammer, musicke and other cuninge and excercises of humanitye accordinge to theire byrthes and after theire adges, and in noe wise to be suffred in idlenesse or in unvertuous occupacion.

Item, we wyll that daylie, excepte fastinge dayes, the houshoulde of our sayde sonne be at the first dynner[57] by tenne of the clocke and at supper by fower, and every fasting daye to goe to their dynner by eleven.

Item, we wyll that the hall be ordynately served and strangers served and cherished accordinge to their haveures.[58]

Item, we will that noe person of what estate or condicion he be have any servyce of the courte at mealetimes to theire chambers or out of the gates, but that they keepe our sayde sonnes chamber or his hall.

[*fo. 278v*] Item, we will that none of our saide sonnes councell, tresorer, comptroller or other offycer accomptante, nor none of our sayde sonnes houshoulde, lodge out of his courte without a reasonable cause shewed, and that the ushers make theire lodginges as neere together as they conveniently may.

Item, we will that our saide sonnes porters give good and dilligente attendance to the sure kepinge of the gates, soe that he be not at any tyme destitute of one of them, and they from the feaste of Michelmasse unto the firste daye of May be shutt at nyne of the clocke in the eveninge and opened in the morninge betwene six and seaven, and from the firste daye of Maye unto Michellmasse the sayde gates to be shutt by ten of the clocke at night and to be opened betwene five and sixe in the morninge, and that the saide porters shall not open the sayde gates after nor afore none of the sayd howers lymited without a cause reasonable and lycense of some of his counsayle. And that they suffre noe man to entre the sayd gates with weapon, but that they be lefte at the same, and noe dishonest or unknowne person to come in without his cause be well understood and knowne, nor that they suffree any stuffe to be imbezelled out of the sayde gates.[59]

Item, we will that noe person of our sayde sonnes houshoulde, of what estate or condicion he be, mayntaine any false quarrell or doe any extorcion to any of our leidge people, nor that any of his purveyors take any stuffe without true contentacion or paymente for the same.

[54] In this clause, 1483 text prescribes that mass be said *in the chapell of the officers of the houshold* beginning at 6.00, and that mattins, a second mass, evensong and all other divine services are to be done in the chapel at convenient hours (Sloane MS. fo. 55).

[55] 1483 text omits that the almoner is confessor to the household and that the other chaplains say mass and divine service before the prince (*ibid.*).

[56] Hasorder and adventorer are both terms for gamblers.

[57] The preliminary dinner of the household servants before the main dinner, the latter probably taking place at about 11.00 a.m. (cf. *A Collection of Ordinances*, p. *38).

[58] Rank or wealth.

[59] 1483 text adds a prohibition that no servant shall be admitted within the gates at meal-times, unless he is entered on the list of the household staff (Sloane MS. fo. 56).

Item, we will that yf any person strike another within the house that he be punished accordinge to the statutes of our houshoulde, and if he drawe any weapon within our sayde sonnes house in vyolence, the firste tyme to be sett in the stockes and there to sytte as longe as shalbe thought behoofefull by our saide sonnes councell, and at the second tyme to lose his service.[60]

Item, we will that the tresorer and comptroller take every Saterday particulerlye the accompte of every offyce of the expence and [*fo. 279*] changes of the houshoulde for the weeke paste, and that at the monthes ende they to make an whole accompte and declaracion thereof to our sayde sonnes councell.

Item, we will that the clerke of the cheques[61] trulye execute his offyce, and he nightlye unto the comptroller or tresorer deliver the names of all those that be absente.[62]

Item, we will that our sayde sonnes councell shall deliver writinges to the cheife and principall in every office, aswell such ordynaunces and statutes as we have stablished concerninge their offyce as other such as we hereafter shall devise for the worshippe and profitte of our sayd sonne and his houshoulde, to that intente that they shall notte nowe excuse themselves by ignorance, and that they indent with the sayd counsayle for all suche stuffe as shalbe delivered unto them for theyre offyces.

Item, we will that our sayde sonnes councell ordeyne and see that there be contynually in our sayd sonnes houshoulde a phisycion and a surgeon, suffyciente and cuninge.

Item, we will that the principall offycers in every offyce see that theyre offyces be well excercised and kepte to our sayde sonnes honnor, and noe brybery or unfittinge rule to be suffred in the same.[63]

Item, we will that every man beinge of the houshoulde of our sayd sonne give his due and true attendance and obedyentlye excercise theyre offyces, and at all tymes be furnished with horse and harneys accordinge to theyre degrees, and not to be absent without suffycient lycense, and such as shall have servantes that they be personable and able to stand in a mans stead and noe children.

Item, we will that the generall receavor of the dutchie of Cornewall, the chamberlayne of Chester and Flynte, the chamberlayne of Northwales, the chamberlayne of Southwales, at dayes and tymes due and accustomed bringe in all such sommes of money as then shalbe due unto our sayd sonne, and to deliver yt unto his counsayle attendinge upon him, and the sayde money to be put into a cheste under three keyes: our dereste wife the queene to have one, the bishopp of Rochester and the Earle Ryvers to have theother [*fo. 279v*] twoe, and alwaye the receyte of the same moneye to be entred in a booke and in likewise the payment of all such charges as of necessytie muste needes be borne for our sayde sonne, and that our sayde sonnes signette be put into the sayde coffree and not to be occupyed but by the advise of his counsayle.[64]

Item, for the weale, suretye and profytte of our sayde sonne we will and by theise presentes give authorytie and power unto the right reverend father in God, John byshoppe of Rochester, and to our right trustie and welbeloved Anthony Earle Ryvers, to remove at all tymes the same our sonne as the case shall require unto such places as shalbe

[60] 1483 text adds to this clause three new ones, forbidding meals to be taken privately in any department of the household, especially the pantry, buttery and cellar; ordering every officer to 'brefe' or record the goods in his care and account for them; and forbidding any officer to take any fee other than what is allowed by the counting-house (*ibid.*).

[61] The clerk who kept lists of the household retainers, noting which were present and therefore entitled to their daily wages and allowances.

[62] 1483 text follows this clause by another new one, ordering all the offices in the household to be shut at night (*ibid.*).

[63] 1483 text adds that no man may have a servant at meals with him in the household who is not on the chequer-roll (Sloane MS. fo. 57).

[64] 1483 text omits this clause and replaces it by two others. The first orders all the revenues of the prince's lands to be delivered to Master Thomas Bowde and entered into the 'book of the counseil'; Bowde is then to deliver money to the household as necessary, on receipt of a warrant signed by Alcock, Grey and Rivers. The second allows the three men, on receipt of a royal warrant, to order Bowde to make account of all foreign expenses.

thought by their discretions necessarye for the season.[65] And over, that for the sure accomplishment of theise statutes and ordynaunces they have like authorytie to put them and every of them in executyon accordinglye, to theffecte and intent of the sayde articles and the premisses above expressed and rehersed, and to punishe the breaker of the same. In witnesse of our whole pleasure in this behaulfe we haue signed theise premisses with our owne hand, &c.

3. *British Library, Sloane MS. 3479 fos. 54v–55*[66]
   [Additional ordinances for Edward, prince of Wales, 25 February 1483]

[*fo. 54v*] Item, that discrete and convenyent persons bee appoynted to give theire attendance upon his person from his risinge unto his goinge to bedde, so that allwaies and in everie season he be accompanyed with some of them: ii atte leste.

Item, we wil that our said sonne observe and kepe theis articles before written touchinge his person, and that he ne take upon him to give, write, sende or commande any thinge withoute thavise of the said bishop, lord Richard and Erle Rivieres, and that none of his servantes presume nor bee so bold to move, stere or caus him to doe to the contrary of theis ordinaunces uppon payne of grevous punyshement and loosinge his service.

Item, wee charge the said bisshop, lord Richard and Erl Rivieres that if they understond our said sonne of any unprincely demeaning or to dele [*fo. 55*] contrarie to theis ordinances that then they forthwith shewe it in good manner unto him selfe to bee refourmed, and if he will not amend therby then the said bisshop, lord Richard and Erle Rivieres, or one of them, shewe it unto us and to our moost dere wief the quene or unto one of us in all goodlie haste, as they will aunsuere it at theire perill and avoid our grevous displeasour.

[65] Cf. *Proceedings and Ordinances*, iii. 300.
[66] Printed by permission of the Trustees of the British Library board.

11

EDUCATION AND LEARNING AT AN ENGLISH CATHEDRAL

During the last hundred years our knowledge of the educational institutions of medieval England has steadily increased, both of schools and universities. We know a good deal about what they taught, how they were organised and where they were sited. The next stage is to identify their relationship with the society which they existed to serve. Whom did they train, to what standards and for what ends? These questions pose problems. They cannot be answered from the constitutional and curricular records which tell us about the structure of educational institutions. Instead, they require a knowledge of the people—the pupils and scholars—who went to the medieval schools and universities. We need to recover their names, to compile their biographies and thereby to establish their origins, careers and attainments. If this can be done on a large enough scale, the impact of education on society will become clearer. In the case of the universities, the materials for this task are available and well known. Thanks to the late Dr A. B. Emden, most of the surviving names of the alumni of Oxford and Cambridge have been collected and published, together with a great many biographical records about them.[1] For the schools, on the other hand, where most boys had their literary education if they had one at all, such data are not available. Except for Winchester and Eton,[2] we do not possess lists of the pupils of schools until the middle of the sixteenth century, and there is no way to remedy the deficiency.

The student of medieval school education must consequently approach his objective by another route. The information which he seeks exists, but

[1] A. B. Emden, *A Biographical Register of the University of Cambridge to 1500*, Cambridge 1963 (hereafter cited as *BRUC*); idem., *A Biographical Register of the University of Oxford to 1500*, 3 vols, Oxford 1957–9 (hereafter cited as *BRUO*, i–iii); idem., *A Biographical Register of the University of Oxford, 1501–40*, Oxford 1974 (hereafter cited as *BRUO*, iv).

[2] T. F. Kirby, *Winchester Scholars*, London & Winchester 1888; Sir W. Sterry, *The Eton College Register, 1441–1698*, Eton 1943.

it relates to other entities than schools. These entities are of several kinds: social or vocational groups such as the aristocracy or the clergy, local communities such as a city or a county, and institutions or groups of institutions such as cathedrals or monasteries. Examples of all these bodies in the Middle Ages can be found which furnish evidence about the relationship of education with society. In the first place their records, unlike those of schools, often preserve large numbers of their members' names. Next, when the names have been listed, educational data can frequently be gathered about their owners: bequests of money for schooling, possession of books, authorship of documents and involvement in tasks necessitating literacy. These data, scanty for each individual, become more plentiful the more individuals are studied. Added together, they can give us an idea of educational needs and attainments, in at least some sections of medieval society, to an extent that cannot be matched from the records of schools alone.

The present study is an attempt to show what can be done in this field. It centres upon a single institution: Exeter Cathedral, one of the nine such bodies in medieval England staffed by secular clergy. The community at Exeter during the later Middle Ages consisted of a dean and 8 other dignitaries, 24 canons (some of them also dignitaries), 24 vicars (reduced to 20 after the Black Death), about 16 to 18 chantry priests called 'annuellars', 12 secondary clerks (mostly adolescents) and 14 boy choristers.[3] Among the English secular cathedrals as a group, Exeter counted as one of the smallest and least wealthy. It lay in the second rank along with Chichester and Hereford, well behind the giants of the species such as Lincoln, St Paul's, Salisbury and York. It was also remote geographically, commanding a diocese which covered the two isolated counties of Devon and Cornwall and exerting little influence on the development of cathedrals elsewhere. Constitutionally speaking, its chief distinction was that only the dignitaries had separate endowments: the bishop, dean, sub-dean, precentor, chancellor, treasurer and four archdeacons. The canons did not possess their own prebendal estates, as was customary elsewhere; instead they each received a small fixed annual stipend of £4, and the rest of the chapter income was shared equally between those who were resident.[4] This practice encouraged the canons to reside and discouraged (though it did not preclude) the conferment of the office on absentee protégés of the bishop, king, or pope. The surviving records of the cathedral are plentiful, and in preserving the identities of her medieval staff Exeter yields little or nothing to her eight sisters. Over 1,500 of her personnel are known by name during the later Middle Ages, the vast majority of them being recorded between 1380 and the refor-

[3] *Ordinale Exon*, ed. J. N. Dalton, i (Henry Bradshaw Soc., xxxvii, 1909), 2–6; K. Edwards, *The English Secular Cathedrals in the Middle Ages*, 2nd edn, Manchester 1967, passim.

[4] A. M. Erskine, 'The medieval financial records of the cathedral church of Exeter', *Journ. of the Society of Archivists*, ii. no. 6 (1962), 254–66.

mation of the cathedral in 1547–8.[5] The present study is consequently based upon this period. Within these years the names survive of 301 canons, 265 vicars, and 231 annuellars: nearly the whole complement, with insignificant exceptions. We also possess those of 410 secondaries, perhaps two-thirds of the total. Only the choristers, with a mere 39 names out of several hundreds, have largely disappeared without trace. Having identified these names, what can we learn about the education, literacy and learning of their owners and the role of the cathedral as a centre of these things?

The first point to consider, since the cathedral clergy were not born to its service but came from elsewhere, is their origins, both geographical and social. In respect of the former, which are much the easier to discover, there was a difference between the major clergy (dignitaries and canons) and the minor (vicars, annuellars, secondaries and choristers). The majority of the first group had geographical connections outside the west of England. Most of the bishops of Exeter in the later Middle Ages came to the see from other parts of the kingdom and filled the canonries with a good many of their relatives, friends and dependants who also originated from elsewhere in England. Other outsiders, recommended by the king or by powerful magnates, became canons in the same way. An analysis of 144 graduate canons and dignitaries between 1380 and 1540, whose origins and early careers are reasonably clear, suggests that 86 came from outside the borders of Devon and Cornwall compared with 58 from inside.[6] Since most of the canons, as we shall see, were university graduates, even those who were born in the diocese had travelled beyond it in order to study, and some had served the king or bishops elsewhere. The canons in general, therefore, had strong national associations as well as the local ones with which they were born or acquired on coming to Exeter. Exactly the reverse was true of the minor clergy. Their origins and connections lay almost wholly within Devon and Cornwall. This can be seen from their surnames which include a wide selection of local place-names, from their being tonsured in youth by bishops on journeys around the diocese and from their receiving 'titles' or pledges of support from local monasteries when they came to be ordained in adult life. Only a small minority seem to have studied at university or to have held previous employment outside the west of England, and their horizons must have been local far more often than they were national. The social origins of the cathedral clergy still remain to be established, through long and arduous biographical research. Excluding a few dignitaries and canons (largely non-resident) of noble or knightly parentage, the rest probably originated from a variety of ranks, including the gentry, prosperous urban families and (in the case of the minor clergy) ordinary

[5] Lists of the canons and dignitaries are printed in J. Le Neve, *Fasti Ecclesiae Anglicanae, 1300–1541*: ix, *Exeter Diocese*, ed. J. M. Horn, London 1964, and those of the other clergy in N. Orme, *The Minor Clergy of Exeter Cathedral, 1300–1548*, Exeter 1980.

[6] These statistics are based on the names in Le Neve, *Fasti Ecclesiae*.

husbandmen and artisans. The only information readily available, concerning the choristers in the 1530s and 40s, shows that two were the sons of gentlemen (one an illegitimate child), one of a merchant, two of yeomen, five of husbandmen and one each of a brewer, a miller, a weaver and a widow.[7] This may be representative of the social origins of the minor clergy throughout the later Middle Ages.

Let us now pass from the origins of the clergy to their careers at Exeter Cathedral, beginning with the two groups of children and adolescents in special need of education: the choristers and the secondaries. The choristers, as usual elsewhere, were boys below the age of puberty whose voices had not yet broken and who probably ranged between seven and fourteen years old. Unfortunately, the disappearance of virtually all their names makes them much the hardest group to penetrate. Even the details of their organisation during the later Middle Ages must largely be inferred from what is known to have been the case on the eve of the Reformation, when most of their records survive. There is no doubt, however, that the cathedral authorities acknowledged a duty to maintain and educate the choristers, and that they provided amenities for this purpose. Every chorister received food, money and accommodation. He slept in a house opposite the west front of the cathedral, under the supervision of the succentor, and he was accredited to one of the senior canons in residence for the receipt of daily meals from the canon's own kitchen.[8] He also collected a number of small monetary payments from the chapter, amounting by the 1540s to about £1 6s. a year.[9] A choristership was therefore analogous to a scholarship or exhibition and offered a valuable means of support in an ecclesiastical and educational environment to boys who lacked their own resources for the purpose. As well as being maintained, the Exeter choristers received an education in the cathedral song school next to their dormitory. 'Song' comprised two activities: reading and singing. Reading meant learning to recognise and pronounce Latin words from liturgical textbooks, such as the psalter or hymnal. We cannot be sure that the Latin words were translated or understood, though a boy who could pronounce Latin words must be presumed able to read and understand English. Singing included plainsong and, to an increasing extent during the later Middle Ages, pricksong or polyphony. What we know of the names of the song-school masters suggest that, in the long term, the school kept pace with developments in English church music elsewhere, since it was taught in the early sixteenth century by men of good quality.[10] Of the three known

[7] Exeter Cathedral Archives, Dean and Chapter (hereafter cited as D&C) 4721/1–33 (Choristers' releases).

[8] D&C 2433; 3551 fo. 46v; 3552 fo. 33v.

[9] This figure is based on a number of small endowments, too complex to be listed here, and includes payments for attending obit masses.

[10] On the song school and its masters, see N. Orme, 'The early musicians of Exeter Cathedral', *Music & Letters*, lix (1978), 395–410.

masters in the 1520s and 30s, two were profession-conscious musicians who had taken the degree of B.Mus. at Oxford and were both composers of polyphony whose works survive.[11] The third, before coming to Exeter, had been master of the choristers of Magdalen College, Oxford.[12] Besides their work in this school, the boys took turns in assisting the adult clergy with the daily services in the choir and with those in honour of the Virgin Mary in the Lady chapel.[13] They thus acquired a familiarity with the liturgy which would stand them in good stead if they chose to become priests in later life. Whether they learnt grammar, meaning an understanding of Latin, is obscure. The cathedral did not maintain a grammar master of its own, and we do not hear in records that the choristers were sent to the city grammar school or 'high school' in the High Street. Their counterparts at the two neighbouring cathedrals of Salisbury and Wells, on the other hand, are known to have studied grammar,[14] and in 1338 Bishop Grandisson made similar arrangements for the choristers of his collegiate church at Ottery St Mary which was closely modelled upon Exeter Cathedral.[15] Nevertheless, the exact grammatical knowledge of the boys at Exeter remains uncertain and, as we shall see in the case of the other clergy, it may have varied widely.

A chorister whose voice had broken became eligible for promotion as a secondary. This is first recorded as happening in 1413,[16] but it was probably a much older practice, and in 1517 Bishop Oldham laid down that ex-choristers should be always preferred to outsiders when secondaries were appointed.[17] The cathedral statutes required the secondaries to be in the holy orders of acolyte, subdeacon and deacon,[18] indicating an age-range from the mid or late teens to 24—the age of promotion as a priest—and this was probably true of most holders of the office during the later Middle Ages. A few secondaries, on the other hand, held their posts well beyond their mid twenties, with the consent of the chapter, in order to discharge minor administrative duties about the cathedral. With these exceptions, the group consisted of adolescents and young adults who were still making their way and were educable like the choristers. Like the latter, they received maintenance in the form of daily meals, each being assigned to a senior canon for this purpose, as well as monetary payments from the chapter which totalled about £2 a year by the 1540s.[19] They did not possess a common dwelling house, and must either have lodged with

[11] John Derke and James Northbroke (ibid., 405–6).

[12] Nicholas Toker (ibid., 406).

[13] *Ordinale Exon*, i. 6, 7; G. Oliver, *Monasticon Dioecesis Exoniensis*, Exeter & London 1846, 55–6, where the date should be 1236 (D&C 600).

[14] N. Orme, *Education in the West of England, 1066–1548*, Exeter 1976, 72, 81.

[15] J. N. Dalton, *The Collegiate Church of Ottery St. Mary*, Cambridge 1917, 93.

[16] D&C 2595/1.

[17] D&C 2415.

[18] D&C 3625 fo. 15; *Ordinale Exon*, i. 2.

[19] This total, like that of the choristers (above note 9), is based on calculations too complicated to be summarised.

their canons or rented chambers by themselves in some of the multi-tenanted houses within the cathedral close. In their education the secondaries were expected to have reached a certain standard before their admission. By 1390 candidates are recorded being examined in reading and song[20] which, as with the choristers, implies the ability to recognise Latin and pronounce it correctly, but, as we shall see, not necessarily to understand it grammatically. Like the choristers, too, the secondaries were expected to attend the daily offices in the choir and to take turns at those in the Lady chapel.[21] These duties, by increasing their familiarity with the music, texts and ritual of the liturgy, provided a further useful training for a priestly career in adult life.

The secondaries, therefore, did not have to know grammar, but there are signs that several of them were intelligent enough to study it and indeed did so during their spare time. The offices of such men can consequently be seen as scholarships no less than those of the choristers, providing support during the process of education. In 1412, for example, we find Thomas Fyllecombe (secondary 1406–13) being bequeathed £6 13s. 4d. by one of the canons to attend 'school' which in view of his age and the sum involved, implies at least a grammar school and possibly a university.[22] His contemporary Richard Maister (secondary c. 1409–20) must have learnt grammar during his term of office since he became master of the city grammar school almost immediately afterwards,[23] and the same was probably true of John Boryngton (secondary c. 1425–8), who succeeded him as grammar master within another short period.[24] During the fifteenth century a handful of secondaries can be traced to Oxford: Hugh Bresey, John Clere, Stephen Colshyll, William Holcombe and John Lyndon,[25] who must also have been good Latinists while they served the cathedral, or potentially good ones at least. That only a few reached Oxford, which seems likely, was doubtless due to lack of means as much as to lack of ability or of ambition. Many of those who became choristers and secondaries must have found the posts attractive because their own resources were insufficient for their education. Service to the cathedral helped in this respect, but the chapter did not provide university exhibitions as such, though individual canons sometimes helped in the matter from personal charity. The career of John Boryngton in particular suggests the plight of a young man whose ambition to attend university was long frustrated by lack of money.[26] After ceasing to be a secondary in 1428, he passed nine years of his life, chiefly as master of the city grammar

---

[20] D&C 3550 fos. 67, 69.

[21] G. Oliver, *Lives of the Bishops of Exeter and a History of the Cathedral,* Exeter 1861, 473–4; Oliver, *Monasticon Dioecesis Exoniensis,* 55–6.

[22] Lambeth Palace Library, Reg. Thomas Arundel, ii. fo. 168.

[23] Orme, *Education in the West of England,* 56.

[24] Ibid.

[25] Emden, *BRUO,* i. 289, 434–5; ii. 945, 1191.

[26] Orme, *Education in the West of England,* 56.

school, until he received a rectory in the gift of the chapter: St Mary Major, Exeter, in 1437. Only then did he have sufficient financial resources to apply for and receive the bishop's licence to study for two years at Oxford, by which time he was at least in his late twenties and possibly older. Even so his means did not allow him the time to follow the whole arts course, and as far as we know he never graduated. Similar difficulties must have blighted the ambitions of many of his colleagues.

In the early sixteenth century the education of the secondaries in grammar began to be recognised and encouraged by the cathedral authorities. In 1511 Bishop Oldham conceded to them the right to be absent from the choir in order to attend the (city) grammar school or the (cathedral) song school,[27] and this can be traced in practice during the following decades. In 1529 it is mentioned that the secondaries were paying fees of 6d. each per term to the grammar master,[28] and a year later the chapter ruled that the money should be automatically docked from their stipends, with the evident motive of stimulating them all to attend school.[29] This does not mean that all the secondaries became good grammarians, even in the Tudor era. Henry Bant (secondary 1526–7) is recorded in 1561, when he had become a beneficed cleric, as 'studiosus' but 'non Latine doctus', apparently signifying that he could and did read English but was not learned in Latin.[30] In 1528 two of his successors, Robert Johnson and William Parlabeyn, were sharply reprimanded by the chapter because they gave their time neither to grammar, song, nor the cathedral church.[31] They both lost their clerical dress and emoluments for a month as a penalty. In 1547, when Edward VI's commissioners issued new injunctions for the cathedral, they asserted that although the secondaries were bound by statute to attend the grammar or the song school, 'the great number of them do not apply their study in the same but live dissolutely and idly, no fruit coming of them'.[32] In short, there must always have been a range of attainments even within so small and apparently uniform a group as these twelve young men. The least competent had merely the ability to recognise and pronounce Latin words, and profited little from the facilities for learning grammar even when these were made readily available. The best, in contrast, managed to acquire a good enough knowledge of Latin to become local schoolmasters or attend university.[33] We shall encounter similar variations among the other minor clergy.

[27] Oliver, *Lives of the Bishops of Exeter*, 465.

[28] D&C 3551 fo. 55v.

[29] Ibid., fo. 62.

[30] Bishop William Alley's survey of clergy in Exeter diocese, 1561 (Cambridge, Corpus Christi College, MS 97 (hereafter cited as CCCC), p. 20).

[31] D&C 3551 fo. 51.

[32] D&C 3674 p. 55.

[33] In addition to the examples mentioned above, note Hugh Deane (secondary 1540–1), who occurs teaching grammar at Crediton school in 1560–1 (Devon Record Office, Crediton Governors, 1660 A/21).

The next two groups of the cathedral staff, in rising order of rank, were the annuellars (or chantry priests) and vicars choral, whom we may call collectively the adult minor clergy. All were aged at least 24 since all were expected to be priests and, if not already so at their admission, were invariably ordained at the earliest opportunity afterwards. Since literacy was a necessary qualification to be ordained, all of them ought to have undergone more than one scrutiny to establish their competence to read during their progress through holy orders, but the cathedral authorities also conducted their own examination for would-be vicars, though not apparently for annuellars. Two vicars are recorded being examined in 1393–4, one in song and the other without specification. It was also noted as being the custom in the second case that every candidate for a vicarship should sing the mass of the Virgin in the Lady chapel and read the gospel at the following high mass in the choir before he was admitted.[34] This custom, which was still in force in 1416,[35] ensured that holders of the office were able at least to sing and read correctly and intelligibly, and there is no reason to believe that any less was expected of the annuellars. In this respect the adult minor clergy resembled the secondaries. Their power to read did not necessarily imply a grammatical knowledge of Latin and some may have had very little. Others, as we shall see, were Latinists and could use the intervals between their liturgical duties to practise or improve their understanding of the language. Like the secondaries, the adult minor clergy were encouraged by the cathedral authorities to study in their spare time, and two facilities were offered to them for this purpose—both, however, requiring a previous knowledge of Latin. These facilities were the chancellor's lectures and the cathedral library.

Ever since 1283 the chancellor of Exeter stood bound to reside and to deliver regular lectures in Latin to the local clergy on theology or canon law.[36] The lectures were still being given in 1395[37] and it is quite possible that they continued for most of the rest of the Middle Ages. During this period the chancellors were nearly all resident graduates of canon law or theology, and two of them seem to have given similar lectures at other cathedrals before they came to Exeter;[38] the duty was still considered to be statutory at the time of the Reformation. The cathedral library, consisting of volumes also in Latin, was originally established by Bishop Leofric in the eleventh century.[39] By the fourteenth, its academic section—as opposed to the liturgical books used in the choir—was kept in the cathedral exchequer along with other valuable possessions of the

[34] D&C 3550 fos. 89v, 92.

[35] Ibid., fo. 138v.

[36] Orme, *Education in the West of England*, 52–3.

[37] *The Register of Edmund Stafford [Bishop of Exeter]*, ed. F. C. Hingeston-Randolph, London & Exeter 1886, 32.

[38] John Orum (Emden, *BRUO*, ii. 1406) and Richard Rotherham (ibid., iii. 1593).

[39] F. Barlow et al., *Leofric of Exeter*, Exeter 1972, 32–55; L. J. Lloyd, *The Library of Exeter Cathedral*, Exeter 1967, passim.

church, loans being made from time to time in return for caution money.[40] The increase in the·number or use of the volumes gradually made this arrangement unsatisfactory, and in 1388 Bishop Brantingham ordered the provision of a proper library, meaning a special room 'to which the ministers of the church, as often as they shall cry to do so, may have easy access'.[41] This order was not immediately effective. It was still unfulfilled in 1410 when Chancellor Robert Rygge bequeathed two volumes to the cathedral and stipulated the establishment of the library within two years of his death, 'in which these and other books may be chained for the convenience of the clergy of the church'.[42] The library room, however, was finally constructed shortly afterwards in 1412, above the east range of the cloisters, and by 1434 had a keeper to look after it, who was generally one of the annuellars.[43] In 1506, when an inventory of its contents survives, it housed nearly 400 volumes, chained or lying upon eleven desks, including all the standard works on the liturgy, the liberal arts, history, civil law, canon law and theology proper to be found in an ecclesiastical library of the period.[44] Besides the library itself, a smaller collection of volumes was kept within the cathedral church, chained to the walls of the choir. In 1415 Canon Thomas Barton bequeathed two books to this location and mentioned two others already there; he also laid down that the clergy in general should be given reasonable access to read them.[45] By 1506 there were 45 volumes in and around the choir, apart from liturgical books, including texts of civil and canon law, the Bible, theological commentaries and some practical guides to confession and other priestly duties. The *Catholicon* or Latin dictionary of John of Genoa was also provided.[46] The references by Brantingham and Rygge to the library room seem to envisage its use by all the cathedral clergy, not merely by the canons. What was indeed the practice is not known, but the chaining of books in well-frequented places around the choir suggests that these volumes were certainly available to the minor clergy, even if the latter were barred from the library room itself.[47]

It is one thing to describe educational facilities and another to determine whether they were used. We have indeed no certain knowledge that any vicar or annuellar benefited from either the chancellor's lectures or the cathedral library, and our understanding of their educational

[40] D&C 3550 fos. 79, 92.

[41] *The Register of Thomas de Brantyngham, Bishop of Exeter*, ed. F. C. Hingeston-Randolph, ii, London & Exeter 1906, 663.

[42] Public Record Office, Prob 11/2A fo. 161–v.

[43] D&C 2668, 2686; J. W. Clark, 'On the work done to the library of Exeter Cathedral in 1412 and 1413', *Proc. Cambridge Antiquarian Soc.*, xli (1901), 294–313.

[44] Oliver, *Lives of the Bishops of Exeter*, 366–75.

[45] *Register of Edmund Stafford*, 412.

[46] Oliver, *Lives of the Bishops of Exeter*, 334, 359–60.

[47] A room called the library is also mentioned in 1462 in the vicars' own college of residential buildings in the close, but no information is forthcoming about its contents (Exeter Cathedral Archives, Vicars Choral, 3347–9).

qualifications and interests has to be gained from other sources. These are of three kinds. First, we know that a handful of the adult minor clergy were university graduates: men like Thomas David, Stephen Edward, William Glover, Edward Gurgoyne, and William Rode.[48] Most of these men occur in the early sixteenth century, and it is worth noting that in about 1541 Canon William Horsey thought it feasible to found a chantry of two priests in the cathedral confined to graduates of arts or law.[49] Men of this rank can never have been common, but there were generally one or two in the choir after the end of the fifteenth century. Second, we know that many vicars and annuellars were involved in literary tasks additional to those of the choral services. The routine administration of the cathedral, under the supervision of the chapter, was carried out by a number of minor officers chosen from the adult minor clergy, who did the work part-time for small extra stipends. Five of these officers—the clerk of the bread chest, clerk and sub-clerk of the exchequer, clerk of the works and collector of chapter rents in Exeter—were concerned with the keeping and presentation of written records and accounts, usually in Latin, and must have been literate and numerate to that extent.[50] About fifty adult minor clergy are known to have held these posts between 1380 and 1548,[51] besides many others unrecorded, and when we consider that two of the vicars were also chosen each year to administer their body's own extensive endowments,[52] it is manifest that accountancy must have been a common accomplishment.

The third kind of evidence about the learning of these clergy concerns their possession of books. It is not easy to find, since only two or three of their wills survive, but a few volumes are recorded as having been given by them to the cathedral, and others occur as bequests to them in the more plentiful wills of the canons and dignitaries.[53] Together these sources record the names of 21 vicars and annuellars between 1404 and 1506 who possessed books before or during their terms of office. Seventeen of them owned at least one volume, 2 at least two, and 2 at least three. The vast majority of titles mentioned (twenty) were breviaries, psalters or missals related to the everyday work of the clergy in the cathedral. Five were works of pastoral or practical theology, including the *Manual*, the *Pupilla Oculi*,[54] or sermons; one was a text of canon law and one of academic theology. The non-liturgical categories increase, however, if we consider books possessed by minor clergy after they left their cathedral posts. We then find one of them in 1461 with the sermons of *Parisiensis*, another in 1472 with a Bible and a quire concerning miracles and, best of all, an

[48] Emden, *BRUO*, i. 628; ii. 775; iv. 162, 251, 489.   [49] D&C 2924.

[50] On these accounts see Erskine, 'Medieval financial records of Exeter', 254–66.

[51] Orme, *Minor Clergy of Exeter*.

[52] Vicars Choral/Books I, fo. 5–6, 12v–13.

[53] For the sources of these statistics see below, notes 60–1.

[54] A handbook of theology and law for parish priests, by John de Burgh, *fl*. 1370–98 (Emden, *BRUC*, 107).

Exeter rector in 1428 with three scholarly and practical works: the *Pupilla Oculi*, a volume of *Decreta*, and a *Veritas Theologie*.[55] The possession of books after the period of cathedral service does not prove that the owners were Latinists while they were minor clergy, but the likelihood exists, and their eventual Latinity certainly implies intelligence and inclination to scholarship during their earlier years.

The result of this evidence is to suggest that the vicars and annuellars, like the secondaries, ranged widely in their abilities. Their basic duty was simply to read and sing the liturgy with proper elocution, and doubtless some were never able to do more. Even their books, if they had any, were most likely to be the liturgical texts they needed for this work. Above this level, however, there were undoubtedly men who understood Latin grammatically. These were the owners of books on pastoral theology, who evidently hoped to become parish priests, and the holders of administrative offices involving the use of Latin. Some of these people may well have been able to use the cathedral's books or to attend the chancellor's lectures, if they so wished. Highest of all, the small elite of university graduates were certainly competent Latinists by virtue of their previous studies. This range of abilities is confirmed at the end of our period by a survey of the beneficed clergy of Exeter diocese carried out by Bishop Alley in 1561.[56] Among the information it sought to record was an estimate of their educational standards. Nine former vicars and annuellars who had held office before 1548 feature in the survey—all or most of them non-graduates. Two appear in the lowest educational category: 'studiosus' but 'non Latine doctus'.[57] As in the case of Henry Bant already mentioned, this suggests that they could read and understand English, but do little more with Latin than pronounce it. Three others were placed in the medial and commonest category. 'mediocriter doctus', meaning that they were moderately learned in Latin: presumably able to understand it in part, but not great scholars.[58] Finally, 3 others were assigned to the highest category, 'satis doctus'–sufficiently or well learned–and a fourth, described merely as 'doctus' but also as a preacher, probably belonged with them.[59] Since the term 'satis doctus' was also used to describe graduates, it evidently denoted a very good command of Latin indeed. Its application to some former non-graduate members of the cathedral choir serves to confirm the presence there of capable and intelligent men who lacked the means rather than the ability to attend university, or to take a degree.

---

[55] *The Register of Edmund Lacy, Bishop of Exeter: Registrum Commune*, ed. G. R. Dunstan, iv (Canterbury & York Soc., lxiii. 1971), 12–14.

[56] CCCC, 55 pp.

[57] Walter Walker and William Mogryge (ibid., pp. 3, 15).

[58] Richard Growdon, Robert Butston and Peter Holwill *alias* Hopkyns (ibid., pp. 9, 48, 54).

[59] Oliver Loveley, John Wright and Richard Gyll (ibid., pp. 3, 9, 11). William Tanner (ibid., 15) was 'doctus'.

With the canons and dignitaries we reach the elite of the cathedral community, in learning as in other things. Their intellectual attainments were not only higher than those of most of the minor clergy, but they have left more traces and are easier to ascertain. The relevant information comes from two main sources: the canons' possession of university degrees and the records of their books. The statistics of their degrees, which are set out in Table I reveal that the vast majority of the canons

Table I

University degrees of canons and dignitaries of Exeter Cathedral[60]

University degrees	Dates of admission to office				Total	%
	1380–1400	1400–1450	1450–1500	1500–1541		
Unrecorded	18	25	7	3	53	17.6
Univ. study, B.A., 'Mag'.	7	17	15	17	56	18.6
M.A.	2	—	6	7	15	5.0
Lic. and B. Can. and or C.L.	8	27	20	11	66	22.0
Lic. and B. Theol.	—	6	9	2	17	6.6
D. Med.	—	2	—	4	6	2.0
D. Can. and or C.L.	8	8	21	19	56	18.6
D. Theol.	1	7	13	11	22	10.6
Total	44	92	91	74	301	100.0

and dignitaries had studied at a university, shown by other evidence to have been chiefly Oxford with a small contingent from Cambridge. The proportion of university men, or at any rate of recorded ones, grew as time passed, and amounted during the whole of the later Middle Ages to more than 80 per cent. Most had succeeded in graduating, and a good many had done so more than once since almost one in three was a doctor. Among the studies represented, canon and civil law were the most popular, with 40.6 per cent, followed by arts with 23.6 per cent, and theology with 16.3 per cent. Graduates in medicine, as usual everywhere, were uncommon.

The evidence of the recorded degrees can be supplemented by data about the numbers and titles of books possessed by the canons. For this purpose only men likely to have been resident at Exeter will be considered, omitting those whose connections were apparently nominal. Our knowledge of their books derives from three principal sources: wills,[61] records of bequests to the cathedral,[62] and the miscellaneous

[60] The statistics are based on an analysis of the canons and dignitaries listed by Le Neve, (*Fasti Ecclesiae*) collated with Emden's biographical registers (*BRUC & BRUO*).

[61] The evidence from wills is based on those of men who died while apparently resident canons or dignitaries (but not bishops). All the relevant wills have been consulted in the Public Record Office, the registers of the archbishops of Canterbury at Lambeth Palace Library and the registers of the bishops of Exeter in the Devon Record Office, Exeter.

[62] Oliver, *Lives of the Bishops of Exeter*, 320–76.

Table II

Numbers of books recorded in the possession of resident canons and dignitaries of Exeter Cathedral, 1380–1506

Number of books recorded	Number of owners	Number of books recorded	Number of owners
1	11	8	4
2	5	10	4
3	7	12	1
4	10	15	2
5	5	17	1
6	7	24	1
7	3		

Total of owners: 61   Total of books: 325

references collected by Dr A. B. Emden in his biographical registers. Since there are very few sources for the early sixteenth century, the survey is concluded at 1506. In Tables II and III, titles divided into more than one volume have been counted as one work, and so have volumes containing several tracts. A book which passed from one owner to another, on the other hand, has been counted once for each person to whom it belonged. Naturally, statistics of this kind are incomplete. All the sources record book-ownership selectively or by chance, and even wills often fail to mention volumes which we know their authors possessed. The figures are nevertheless of value in showing that the canons and dignitaries did possess their own volumes, as well as using those in the cathedral library, and that the ownership of several books was common; the total of volumes divided by the number of owners gives an average of five each. Better still, it is possible to analyse the kinds of books on the canons' shelves and thus to acquire an idea of their literary needs and tastes. This is done in Table III. As with the minor clergy, liturgical works were the most common—a matter of no surprise, considering that canons like all clerics were obliged to say the divine office each day. Nearly every one of them mentioned as owning a book possessed his personal breviary for the purpose and often other such texts. The next largest category, that of civil and canon law, accords with the predominance of degrees in these

Table III

Subjects of books recorded in the possession of resident canons and dignitaries of Exeter Cathedral, 1380–1506

Choir liturgy	124	Arts course and similar	14
Manuals	5	Medicine	5
Pupilla Oculi	10	Canon and civil law	64
Sermons	16	Academic theology	33
Lives of Christ and of the saints	8	Bibles	14
History and geography	5	Uncertain	27
		Total	325

disciplines and signifies the involvement of many of the canons in the administration of the cathedral and the diocese.[63] Of the other groups worth mentioning, that of academic theology reflects the presence of many theological graduates, that of sermons the probable interest of some canons in preaching, and that of handbooks like the *Pupilla Oculi*, clerical pluralism. Many canons held parochial benefices along with their stalls and must have found such guides to their rights and duties to be useful.

The special value of the academic and bibliographical evidence lies in its revelation of the mentality of the canons and dignitaries as a group. Their chief preoccupations are seen to have been the liturgy, the law of the Church and the study of theology as a means of improving their religious life, probably in that order of priority. The books they acquired were mainly chosen with these aims in mind. Some of the canons may have read some history and literature for recreation, always in Latin, but they did not apparently concern themselves with romantic fiction in French or English. As with the godly clergy of the *Canterbury Tales*, stories for them meant sermons and lives of saints. Their interest in learning was not merely self-centred; they had a concept of 'the republic of letters' and were often generous in spreading the written word among their friends and dependants. We encounter them, for example, lending and borrowing books. Canon John Lydford lent the *Decretals* in 1407 to one of his younger relations,[64] Canon Richard Martyn the sermons of *Parisiensis* in 1461 to the vicar of Sidbury[65] and Dean Henry Webber those of James de Voragine in 1472 to Canon John Evelyn.[66] When they died they often left a breviary or a missal to a parish church of which they had been incumbent and an academic book or two to the cathedral library or that of their old university college. They were also interested in the education of the young. Canon Thomas Barton left 40s. in 1415 to a poor clerk studying at Oxford, Archdeacon William Hunden £10 in 1416 to his cousin 'to put him to school', and Archdeacon Richard Penels £5 in 1418 for three years to another young man for the same purpose.[67] Though many of them had taught at Oxford as well as studying there, they were ex-academics by the time they reached Exeter and did not involve themselves to any great extent in formal teaching or research. Only the chancellor had a statutory duty to lecture, and, although at least three holders of this office in the fifteenth century are known to have published academic works, the writing was done in every case before the authors came to Devon.[68] We know of no significant project of research or

[63] See below, pp. 281–2.
[64] Emden, *BRUO*, ii. 1184.
[65] Devon Record Office, Exeter, Reg. George Neville, fo. 137v.
[66] Emden, *BRUO*, i. 653.
[67] *Register of Edmund Stafford*, 408–10, 411–14, 420–1.
[68] The three were John Orum, Richard Rotherham and Richard Snetisham (Emden, *BRUO*, ii. 1406, iii. 1593, 1725).

authorship carried out at Exeter itself during the period under review. Nevertheless, if they were not academics the canons were well-educated men by contemporary standards. They had read the basic works of medieval scholarship, they probably went on reading them, and they could hold learned conversations with likeminded people. When the antiquary William Worcester visited Exeter in 1478, he met and talked with Dr Owen Lloyd, a canon from Wales whose interests are best known to us through the twenty-four books (mostly on canon law and theology) which he bequeathed to Hereford Cathedral.[69] Worcester elicited, however, that Lloyd was also the owner of the *Itinerary through Wales* by Giraldus Cambrensis and spent part of his visit transcribing from it the description of Anglesey.[70] Here is a rare and pleasant glimpse of scholarly intercourse, timeless in character, within this late-medieval community.

It remains to consider what was the impact of the literacy and learning of the cathedral clergy, major and minor, upon the world beyond their gates. For the cathedral was not an entirely self-contained community. All its members were involved, to a greater or lesser degree, with the wider Church and society of Devon and Cornwall, and this involvement took literary and educational forms as well as social and economic ones. We have seen that the cathedral recruited boys and youths to its service from many places in Devon and Cornwall. Most of these boys, after experiencing the teaching and training which the cathedral gave them, passed back into the society from which they had come, taking with them the knowledge and abilities they had acquired. In the case of the secondaries this process can be followed through the study of their careers. Until the Reformation, most of them appear to have stayed in the ranks of the clergy when they reached adult life. Of the 127 recorded as having held office between 1406 and 1442, at least 52 (40 per cent) are known to have been ordained to the celibate orders of sub-deacon, deacon and priest, or to have held benefices which required these orders. The same is true of 27 (45 per cent) of the 59 who can be traced as secondaries between 1512 and 1530. There must have been several others whose record of ordination has not survived, who were ordained in other dioceses, who took religious vows, or who died on the verge of manhood. If all these categories were added, the proportion of secondaries who became adult clergy would undoubtedly exceed half the total and possibly rise towards two-thirds. The choristers and secondaries of Exeter were thus an important source of recruits for the medieval Church, and this was equally true of their counterparts elsewhere. Some, on completing their education, were promoted to be adult members of the cathedral staff. We know of 29 secondaries between 1380 and 1548 who became annuellars and 32 who rose to be vicars. A further 23, on the other hand,

[69] Ibid., ii. 1154.
[70] William Worcester, *Itineraries*, ed. J. H. Harvey, Oxford 1969, 116–19.

are recorded as chantry priests, curates and beneficed clergy elsewhere in Devon and Cornwall, and there must have been many more than these. In this respect the cathedral provided not only itself but the diocese with adult clergy. Furthermore, although the majority of secondaries during the later Middle Ages became priests, a minority evidently concluded as laymen instead. It is easy to imagine the circumstances which caused them to do so: marriage, crime, loss of vocation and the inheritance of property. Men of this kind, able to read and often well-trained in the liturgy, augmented the fund of lay literacy and possibly even lay devotion when they returned to a secular way of life.

This image of the cathedral sending into the world the men it had trained is confirmed when we turn to the annuellars and vicars. They too by no means limited their careers to the boundaries of the close. Many of them can be traced not only as staff of the cathedral but as the occupants of rectories and vicarages in the diocese at large. Some managed to hold a parochial benefice in plurality with their cathedral posts, a practice originally frowned on by the bishops of Exeter, but increasingly tolerated after 1400. Of the 265 recorded vicars between 1380 and 1548, 53 are known to have held such pluralities, and of the 231 annuellars, 14. Some of the benefices involved were small parishes in the city of Exeter and were probably served in person; others lay a good distance away and must have been deputed to curates. Even more common than this practice was the departure of vicars and annuellars from the cathedral into the sole incumbency of a parochial benefice. The dean and chapter had many of these in their gift and the hope of promotion to a rectory or vicarage with better status and emoluments than the cathedral provided must have been a strong motive for those who entered its service. Seventy-three vicars and 45 annuellars are known to have left Exeter for a parochial benefice during the period under consideration, a total of 118 or not less than 23 per cent of both groups together. They brought to their parishes an experience of life beyond that of a cleric whose background was merely a parish or a grammar school. At the cathedral they had taken part, day by day and year by year, in religious services of a complex and sophisticated nature, with all the accompaniments of ritual, ornaments and music used in the medieval Church. They knew how the liturgy should be properly performed, and the diffusion of new observances and more elaborate music into parish churches during the later Middle Ages may have owed something to them. Whether their cathedral service improved their pastoral abilities as confessors and preachers is less certain. A few minor clergy, as we have seen, possessed books of sermons and pastoral guides, but in Bishop Alley's survey of 1561 only 2 of the 9 former vicars and annuellars were thought worth describing as preachers.[71] On the whole, the adult minor clergy, when they went into parishes, probably accorded with the liturgical and devotional bias of the late-medieval Church, rather than with its instructive and evangelical side.

[71] William Tanner and John Wright, CCCC, pp. 15, 9.

The impact of the canons and dignitaries on the outside world took differerent forms from those we have just encountered. A resident canon, once he acquired his stall, usually held it for life and rarely left the cathedral for a parochial benefice. He often held such benefices in plurality with his canonry, but the cathedral remained the chief sphere of his activities, and his parishes were generally relinquished to deputies. His relations with the outside world were therefore largely based upon Exeter; they also reflected his superior academic qualifications. The canons had two main forms of relationship with the diocese in which education played a part: preaching and administration. In 1337 Bishop Grandisson ordered a sermon to be preached to the populace in the cathedral every Sunday from Advent to Septuagesima,[72] and similar winter sermons were still being given in the 1530s.[73] The evidence about those who preached relates only to outsiders: visiting Oxford scholars and friars from the nearby Dominican convent,[74] but it is hard to believe that the canons did not also take their turn in the pulpit, especially those who possessed volumes of sermons and presumably studied them. Dr John Snetisham, who became chancellor in 1439, was praised in particular on his appointment as a man possessing 'a sonorous voice for holy preaching which does not grow hoarse while showing the people their sins'.[75] Sermons by the canons outside the cathedral are also recorded, though they may not have been common before the sixteenth century: only one canon, Dr John Rygge, is known to have been licensed to preach in the diocese during the entire episcopate of Bishop Lacy (1420–55).[76] Later, with the onset of the Reformation, the activity may have become more frequent. In 1527 Dr Peter Carslegh is reported delivering 'a goodly sermon' at Tiverton at the funeral of the countess of Devon,[77] and in 1545 the chapter agreed that canons preaching outside Exeter in churches appropriated to the cathedral could qualify for emoluments as though they were resident.[78] A year or two later we hear of Dr Richard Crispin criticising Luther from the pulpit at Marldon in south Devon,[79] and another conservative canon, Dr John Moreman, being sent to the Tower for preaching in the south-west against the interests of the Edwardian government.[80] It was chiefly through administration rather than preach-

[72] *Ordinale Exon*, ed. Dalton, i. 294.

[73] *Calendar of Letters and Papers, Foreign and Domestic, Henry VIII*, vii. no. 260 (pp. 107–8).

[74] In 1528 the chapter decided that visiting Oxford scholars who preached in the cathedral should be paid 6s. 8d. (D&C 3551 fo. 48v). For the friars see above note 73.

[75] *Epistolae Academicae Oxon*, ed. H. Anstey, i (Oxford Historical Soc., xxxv. 1898), 174–5.

[76] *The Register of Edmund Lacy: Registrum Commune,* ed. G. R. Dunstan, iii (Canterbury & York Soc., lxii. 1967), 53.

[77] London, College of Arms, MS I/11 fo. 24. The text of the sermon was 'Manus Domini tetigit me' (*Job*, xix. 21).

[78] D&C 3552 fo. 40.

[79] F. Rose-Troup, *The Western Rebellion of 1549*, London 1913, 104–7.

[80] Ibid.; P.R.O., State Paper Office, SP 10/9 no. 48.

ing, however, that the dignitaries and canons of Exeter applied their educational skills to the neighbouring region. The four archdeacons of the diocese were all dignitaries, and the bishop's own administrative and judicial officers were frequently rewarded with canonries or recruited from those already holding them. Under Bishop Lacy, for example, the vicar general, Thomas Hendeman, was a canon, and so were the two occupants of the post of commissary general of the diocese: James Carslegh and Henry Webber. In the consistory court both Carslegh and Webber served as presidents, and three other canons—John Floure, Richard Martyn and John Udy—as commissaries general of the court.[81] The role of a diocesan administrator had its pastoral and instructive sides like that of a preacher, and such offices gave many opportunities for their graduate holders to use the knowledge they had gained of theology or canon law.

It is now possible to summarise what we have learnt from the study of Exeter Cathedral as an educational community. The first lesson has been the variety of literary attainments among its medieval clergy. It is very unlikely that any of them was so illiterate that he could not even pronounce the letters of a written Latin text. All were literate in that most basic sense, but their literacy ranged from the mere ability to pronounce Latin words to a mastery of the language in writing, speech and thought. The standard of attainment varied not only between the different ranks of the cathedral staff but among the members within each rank. If clergy who were otherwise so uniform in their status, emoluments and duties differed so greatly in their learning, we must expect that equal variations existed in other religious houses such as monasteries and collegiate churches. How much greater, then, must educational variations have been among the parish clergy, who in all respects were so diverse and unequal. Simple assertions about clerical literacy in the Middle Ages must evidently be avoided. The existence of clergy who could do little more than pronounce Latin words gives some support to the frequent statements of anti-clerical writers that such men existed. These statements, however, remain open to criticism because most of them were vague and indiscriminate. They too often failed to distinguish between learned and unlearned clergy, they rarely recognised the barriers which we have seen beset so many who may have wished for education, and they made no allowance for qualities such as devoutness, experience and commonsense which compensate for limitations in reading. Indeed, the study of Exeter Cathedral does something to answer the attacks upon clerical knowledge made by the clergy's critics. It shows the cathedral as an important educational agency, supplementing the work of schools and universities in training the clergy and even (in the case of certain secondaries) generating literate laymen. The cathedral recruited local boys, youths and some adult chaplains into its service. It provided them with educational amenities and opportunities: maintenance, schooling, practice in the liturgy and the use of books. Finally it sent them out again, trained and experienced, as ministers and administrators of the local Church. Since there is no reason to think that Exeter was unique, we shall do well to re-assess our opinion of all the late-medieval secular cathedrals in this respect. Their educational function in the twelfth century is well known; the study we have undertaken suggests that this function went on being discharged, albeit in different ways, throughout the later Middle Ages.

6 An eighteenth-century print of All Saints Church, Bristol, showing (right) buildings erected on the shoulders of the church. These are an altered version of the house and library of the guild of Kalendars, which occupied the same site in the fifteenth century.

12

A BRISTOL LIBRARY FOR THE CLERGY

It is a truism to say that the rise of the universities concentrated the teaching of higher studies – arts, canon and civil law and theology – in two English towns. It is also not quite true. Though ever afterwards these subjects were most fully pursued in universities, there remained a demand for the teaching of canon law and theology in particular, which Oxford and Cambridge could not satisfy. Thousands of friars, monks and secular clergy existed all over England who were either unable or unfitted to study at university, and needed to follow the higher subjects (if at all) at a simpler level nearer home. During the thirteenth century various arrangements were made to provide them with teaching locally. The friars developed systems of schools of arts, philosophy and theology based on individual friaries. Some major monasteries organised lectures within their own walls for their own members. The nine secular cathedrals (Lincoln, St Paul's, Salisbury, York and so on) offered similar but more public facilities. A member of the cathedral chapter, usually the chancellor, was given the duty of lecturing once or twice a week, without taking fees and apparently for the benefit of any local clerics who wished to attend.[1]

The history of this teaching, though probably intermittent in any one place, was remarkably long-lived in general. Bishops sometimes complained that lectures were not being given, but they intervened to revive them and the tradition never completely died out. At Exeter, for example, though the practice of lecturing is not mentioned for many years after 1400, it was again going on in the 1530s and 40s, when Robert Tregonwell and Nicholas Weston read divinity lectures in the charnel chapel outside the cathedral – Tregonwell even making gestures in Luther's favour.[2] Moreover in the fifteenth century, John Carpenter, bishop of Worcester, founded two new institutions to organise similar lectures. One, the Carnary library at Worcester, has already been mentioned;[3] the other, the Kalendars' library at Bristol, is the subject of the following chapter. The two Carpenter foundations are interesting because they combine the old tradition of providing lectures for the

---

[1] Orme, *English Schools*, pp 79–86, 226–42.
[2] Exeter, Devon Record Office, Exeter City Archives, Book 51, ff 345, 346ᵛ.
[3] Above, pp 36–7.

clergy with a newer one of establishing libraries. Wealthy literate clergy had long bequeathed volumes to the libraries of university colleges and collegiate churches, but by the fifteenth century such bequests were spreading further to parish churches and other places open to the secular clergy as a whole. Churches like Boston (Lincs.) and Scarborough (Yorks.) are known to have possessed collections of learned works, suitable for clerical use, and many others had odd volumes.[4] In about 1425 another John Carpenter, clerk to the corporation of London, took a leading part in opening the Guildhall library in London, a library chiefly of theology, kept by two priests, and open to the public.[5] The bishop knew his namesake the clerk, and seems to have based his libraries at Bristol and Worcester on the Guildhall model. A further foundation at Norwich, apparently connected with the rest, was planned in 1462 but failed to materialise.[6]

The bishop's educational interests can be traced through most of his life. From Oxford where he was doctor of theology, provost of Oriel College and chancellor of the university, Carpenter rose to be master of St Anthony's Hospital, London (1433-44) and then bishop of Worcester (1444-76).[7] At St Anthony's he was responsible for setting up the first free grammar school in London, by securing in 1441 the revenues of a nearby city church to maintain a master teaching grammar gratis to all comers.[8] St Anthony's school was extremely successful, and remained one of the leading schools in the capital until well into the sixteenth century.[9] On being made a bishop, Carpenter discovered fresh scope for educational schemes in his new diocese. Worcester, with its monastic

[4] W.H.St J. Hope, 'Inventory of the Parish Church of St Mary, Scarborough, 1434', *Archaeologia*, li (1888), pp 61-7. For examples of individual books bequeathed to churches in Devon, see *The Register of Edmund Lacy, Bishop of Exeter: Registrum Commune*, ed. G.R. Dunstan, vol iv, Devon and Cornwall Record Society, new series, xvi (1971), pp 28, 60, and in Yorkshire, Joann H. Moran, *The Growth of English Schooling, 1340-1548* (Princeton, 1985), pp 190, 210.

[5] Orme, *English Schools*, pp 83-4.

[6] John Leystofte, vicar of St Stephen's, Norwich, bequeathed a book called 'Repyngton' (probably the Latin *Sermones* of Philip Repyngton) in 1462, if a library were begun in Norwich within two years after his death (N.P. Tanner, *The Church in Late Medieval Norwich, 1370-1532* (Toronto, 1984), p 35). A connection between this project and Carpenter's is suggested by the fact that Walter Lyhert was then bishop of Norwich. Lyhert and Carpenter were fellows together at Oriel College, Lyhert following Carpenter as provost of Oriel and then as master of St Anthony's hospital, London (Emden, *BRUO*, ii, 1187-8).

[7] On Carpenter's career, see ibid., i, 360-1; R.M. Haines, 'Aspects of the Episcopate of John Carpenter, Bishop of Worcester, 1444-76', *Journal of Ecclesiastical History*, xix (1968), pp 11-40; and M.J. Morgan, 'John Carpenter, Bishop of Worcester 1444-76' (University of Birmingham, MA thesis, 1960).

[8] Orme, *English Schools*, p 212.

[9] John Stow, *A Survey of London*, ed. C.L. Kingsford, 2 vols (Oxford, 1908), i, 173-45, 185.

cathedral, did not possess a public lecturer in theology, and the bishop duly made good the lack with the Carnary library and lecturer in 1464. Bristol, the largest city in the diocese, presented another challenge. It was the second or third biggest town in England after London, with a great potential for good or evil in religious terms, yet it had no cathedral and indeed ignored the diocesan structure. The main part of the city lay in Worcester diocese, but the southern suburbs were in Bath and Wells. The bishops of Worcester had long recognised the city's importance and sought to extend their influence there. At Westbury-on-Trym nearby they had established a collegiate church under their own patronage, and at Henbury they had a manor house where they sometimes stayed. Their knowledge of events in Bristol can be illustrated by the visit of Margery Kempe the mystic to the city in 1417, en route to Compostella. On her disturbing the place by her usual emotional outbursts, the news soon reached the bishop at Henbury, who calmed the situation by asking her out to dinner![10]

In the fifteenth century Bristol gave cause for disquiet as a centre of Lollard heresy. It sent the largest single contingent to the Lollard rising of January 1414 – some forty laymen and six chaplains, and even after that débacle Lollards were discovered every ten years or so, for most of the fifteenth century. The first of these discoveries after Carpenter's arrival was in 1448, when the examination of a Gloucester Lollard, William Fuer, revealed yet another group of heretics in Bristol. Most of them dwelt in the suburbs in the diocese of Wells, but one of the leaders, William Smith who was later burnt for his opinions, lived on the north edge outside Lawford's Gate in Worcester diocese.[11] Carpenter responded to the problem which Bristol presented. At Westbury-on-Trym he reorganised the old collegiate church, established resident graduate clergy there and opened a free grammar school for the locality.[12] In Bristol itself he set up a library and a system of lectures, parallel to those at Worcester. For this purpose he chose to reorganise an existing institution, the guild of Kalendars, rather than found a new one. It was cheaper to do so, and perhaps in accordance with Carpenter's taste. All four educational schemes with which he was concerned at Bristol, London, Westbury and Worcester involved adding educational functions to non-educational institutions: a guild, a hospital, a collegiate

[10] *The Book of Margery Kempe*, ed. S.B. Meech and Hope E. Allen, EETS, original series, ccxii (1940), pp 109–10.
[11] On Lollardy in Bristol, see K.B. McFarlane, *John Wycliffe and the Beginnings of English Nonconformity* (London, 1952), pp 154, 176, and J.A.F. Thomson, *The Later Lollards, 1414-1520* (London, 1965), pp 20–47.
[12] *VCH Gloucs.*, ii, 106–8; Orme, *West of England*, pp 182–4.

church and a charnel chapel. He was one of the first to make this moderate kind of reform, which was widely imitated later on, especially by patrons of chantries and guilds, in the decades leading up to the Reformation.

The guild of Kalendars was a brotherhood of clergy, laymen and women in Bristol, dating back to at least the early thirteenth century and in its own belief to Saxon times.[13] Its function was to provide prayers and charity for its members. Every brother and sister had to say thirteen paternosters and ave marias every day for the souls of the others living and dead. Every month the living met in the church of All Saints at the centre of the city on the kalends or first day, hence their name. They celebrated a mass of requiem for their dead colleagues, and were prayed for in turn when they died. A common chest was kept for donations, from which sick members were supported, and when anyone died the rest attended the funeral. Gradually, the guild acquired property, premises and permanent staff. The property included various tenements in Bristol and its suburbs, given by members, and produced an income of about £30 a year. The premises consisted of a house on the north side of All Saints church, its upper stories projecting into the church like those of the similar later building which occupies the site today. The income of the property supported four chantry priests who lived in the house, the senior of whom was called the prior. He and his colleagues ran the guild affairs by the later middle ages, subject to the supervision of the mayor of Bristol who was regarded as the patron of the institution. There is no doubt that the reorganisation of the guild was due to Carpenter's initiative. The Kalendar brethren and the mayor acquiesced in the work and helped to carry it out, but the idea must have come from the bishop, together with the money necessary to establish the library.

Carpenter's reform of the Kalendars' guild, like that of the Carnary chapel, was formally carried out in 1464, but the intention was clearly in his mind as early as 1451, not very long after the Lollard discovery of 1448. The first sign is the appointment of John Hemming, a priest and Oxford master of arts, as prior of the guild in September 1451. Traditionally, the prior like the other chantry priests had been an ordinary non-graduate secular priest, so that Hemming's appointment marks a change of policy. Moreover, though he was nominated by the guild and presented to the bishop by the mayor in the accustomed way, the relevant documents were copied into the bishop's register at much greater length than usual, a sign of Carpenter's close interest.[14] Three years later in 1454 the bishop gave Hemming permission to live away

---

[13] On the early history of the guild, see N.I. Orme, 'The Guild of Kalendars, Bristol', *Bristol and Gloucestershire Archaeological Society Transactions*, xcvi (1979), pp 32-52, of which this chapter is an abbreviated version.

[14] Worcester, Hereford and Worcester Record Office (hereafter HWRO), Reg. Carpenter, vol i, f 103-^{v}.

from Bristol in order to study at Oxford.[15] The course of study is not mentioned but it is most likely to have been theology, since Hemming had already completed the arts course, and a stipulation that the prior should be a student of theology was eventually made by the bishop in 1464. The intention was evidently to train Hemming for the new role of a preacher and lecturer which Carpenter had in mind. Plans for the guild to run a public library appear at much the same time. On 30 July 1455 William Oakbourne, the dean of Carpenter's other reformed foundation at Westbury, bequeathed a book in his will 'to the new library to be built in Bristol'. The work, entitled *Parisiensis*, was in two volumes, and although an exact identification is no longer possible, it was evidently in Latin and probably theological.[16] No doubt Hemming, once qualified, was meant to return to Bristol to open the new foundation, but he died in Oxford in the summer of 1457 and Carpenter had to find a substitute. He discovered one in John Harlow, an Oxford bachelor of theology, whom the guild and the mayor obligingly presented for institution in April 1458.[17] Harlow was a 'good catch', due to unusual circumstances. While studying theology at Oxford he had fallen under the influence of Reynold Peacock, bishop of Chichester, the rational theologian who was unfortunately and unjustly convicted of heresy in November 1457. Peacock's disgrace soon spread to his followers. A royal letter was despatched to Oxford naming Harlow as a supporter of the bishop's heresies and ordering the university to search for copies of Peacock's books alleged to be in Harlow's possession. Worse still the authorities were warned not to admit Harlow to the degree of doctor of theology, thereby ruining what remained of his academic career.[18] In earlier days, however, Carpenter and Peacock had been fellows together at Oriel College, and the bishop of Worcester's immediate patronage of Harlow after Peacock's downfall suggests that he did not share the prevailing hostility towards the two men. Instead, he gained in Harlow an able graduate, more highly qualified than Hemming, who remained in his service at Bristol for over twenty years.

By 1464 Carpenter was ready to give final legal form to his plans for reforming the guild. Ordinances to this effect were issued by him on 5 April and approved by the prior, his brethren and the mayor of Britol twelve days later.[19] The ordinances did not alter the guild's traditional functions, but made two major additions. First, Carpenter enlarged the office of prior from one of a chantry priest into that of a well-educated evangelist. Each future prior was to be a bachelor of theology, or at least

---

[15] Emden, *BRUO*, ii, 906.

[16] PRO, Prob 11/4 (PCC 3 Stokton).

[17] HWRO, Reg. Carpenter, vol i, f 145ᵛ.

[18] Oxford, Bodleian Library, MS Ashmole 789, f 324. For Harlow's career, see Emden, *BRUO*, ii, 906.

[19] HWRO, Reg. Carpenter, vol i, ff 197-8.

a master of arts who had studied theology. He was to be adequately instructed in both the Old and the New Testaments and able to preach. His duties were to administer the public library, and to deliver a public lecture there once a week. He was also expected to preach in the city when possible, and to ask his audience when he did so to pray for Carpenter's soul and the good estate of the mayor of Bristol. On 20 October 1466, following a benefaction of money to the Kalendars by John and Edith Chancellor of Keynsham near Bristol, the prior was further required to preach four annual sermons in perpetuity. Two were to take place at Keynsham, one at St Augustine's Abbey, Bristol, or at the cross nearby, and the fourth at the church of St Mary Redcliffe.[20] In order to make the prior's office sufficiently attractive to graduate clergy, the salary was set at £10 which was probably higher than it had been hitherto. Carpenter did not provide any new endowments for this purpose, and the necessary income seems to have been found by suppressing one of the four guild chantries which was done in about 1453.[21] Henceforth the guild supported only two priests besides the prior. Since even £10 a year was not much to tempt theology graduates, successive priors were allowed to hold the office in plurality with a parish church in the neighbourhood. Harlow himself was rector of Marksbury (Somerset) and St Stephen, Bristol, and several later priors held benefices in a similar way.

The other major innovation of 1464 was the public library. It seems to have been housed in an attic of the guild house above the north aisle of All Saints, an attic reconstructed in 1443 before Carpenter's time.[22] Since the ordinances state that the bishop had newly built the library at his own expense,[23] he probably modified the structure for his needs and provided the appropriate fittings. The library was to stand open every weekday, for two hours in the morning and two in the afternoon, for anyone who wished to enter for the purpose of study.[24] The prior had to remain in attendance to explain uncertain and obscure points of holy scripture. An inventory was to be kept of the library books, copies of which were to be held by the prior, the mayor and the rural dean of Bristol. New accessions were to be chained in the library under their supervision and recorded in the inventory with a note of their value. Every autumn between Michaelmas and All Saints' Day the prior, the dean and a representative of the mayor were to compare the books with the inventory, and the prior was bound to replace any volume which had left

[20] Ibid., ff 206-7[v].
[21] Thomas Halleway, the last known occupant of this fourth chantry, vacated it *c.* 1453 (Bristol Record Office (hereafter BRO), All Saints City, Deeds, CS A 24 (225)).
[22] Orme (above, note 13), p 38.
[23] *propriis nostris sumptibus noviter edificate* (HWRO, Reg. Carpenter, vol i, ff 197-8).
[24] *per duas horas ante nonam et duas post nonam* (ibid.). For the translation of *nonam* as noon, see above, p 36 note 19.

the library through his negligence. Unfortunately, we know almost nothing about the books themselves. The only ones to be described by contemporaries are the volumes of *Parisiensis*, already mentioned, and a Latin chronicle, probably in the library, noted by William Worcester in 1480.[25] The church of All Saints also still possesses eight books which have traditionally been regarded as survivors from the Kalendars' time.[26] Four are manuscripts and the remainder printed books dating from between 1481 and 1501. Seven are Latin works of theology and the eighth is the *Catholicon* of John of Genoa – the standard Latin dictionary of the later middle ages. They represent the kinds of books which the library may have contained, they date from the right period and they survive in the right place. On the other hand they contain no evidence, such as press marks or inscriptions, explicitly linking them with the library. Their connection with it, though possible, must be regarded as unproven.[27]

In the absence of a reliable list of books we can only determine the nature of the library and its founder's intentions by comparison with similar institutions. The Guildhall library books were mainly theological in content and appear to have been primarily intended for the use and instruction of London clergy. The two known volumes in the Carnary library were both in Latin, one of canon law and the other probably of theology. It seems that all three 'Carpenter' libraries centred on Latin works of a scholarly kind. This in turn suggests the people for whom the institutions were intended. They were not libraries of a modern kind for the general public, but for the local clergy – the rectors, vicars and chaplains of nearby churches and chapels. An exceptional layman, as we shall see, may have wished to consult the books and been allowed to do so, but the laity as a whole, even those who were literate, were not expected to come in. If they had been, these libraries would have contained devotional, mystical and moral treatises in English, such as the laity read. Instead, the Kalendars' library and its sisters reflect traditional methods of evangelism. They set out to improve the education of the clergy, making them better able to preach, hear confessions and give spiritual advice. The laity benefited at second hand, through the teaching they gained from the clergy.

The libraries at London and Worcester continued to function until the Reformation. The subsequent history of the Bristol foundation, on the other hand, is full of mystery. When John Leland the antiquary visited Bristol in about 1540, when the guild of Kalendars still existed, he noted that 'the antiquities of the Kalendars were for the most part burnt by

[25] *Itineraria Simonis Simeonis et Willelmi de Worcestre*, ed. J. Nasmith (Cambridge, 1778), p 229.

[26] T.W. Williams, 'Gloucestershire Medieval Libraries', *Bristol and Gloucestershire Archaeological Society Transactions*, xxxi (1908), pp 87-90.

[27] N.R. Ker, *Medieval Libraries of Great Britain*, 2nd ed. (London, 1964), p 13.

chance', and it has sometimes been supposed that the library came to grief in the same way.[28] Some writers have actually dated the conflagration to 1463-4 when the records of All Saints church refer to a fire as having destroyed two houses next to the church steeple.[29] The church records, however, make no mention of a fire in the Kalendars' own property, and the destruction of the library is hardly conceivable in the very year that Carpenter formally set it up. On the contrary, the writings of William Worcester suggest that the Kalendars' books were still extant in 1480. In that year he mentions finding an abridgement of the Latin chronicle of Marianus Scotus 'in the library of All Saints',[30] which is more likely to mean the Kalendars' library than the library of the parish church, whose inventories survive and are restricted to liturgical books.[31] Even in Leland's time there existed 'a little book of the antiquities of the house of Kalendars',[32] and there was still a chamber in the house called the library when the Kalendars' guild was dissolved in 1548.[33] On the whole, it is less likely that the library suffered from a dramatic conflagration than from lack of care by its keepers and a lack of interest among the clergy for whom it was intended. A decline in the qualifications and activities of the priors of the guild is noticeable in the early sixteenth century, and this may have been accompanied by the decay of the library and lectures.

For the first fifty years after the refoundation of 1464 Carpenter's ordinances appear to have been observed, at least in the attainments of the priors.[34] Harlow's retirement in 1480 brought in John Burton, a Londoner, fellow of Balliol College and bachelor of theology.[35] He held the priorship together with the vicarage of St Nicholas, Bristol, a necessary plurality because at first Burton received only £2 of the prior's salary, the rest having been allocated to Harlow as a pension (Harlow died in 1486). Like his predecessor, Burton was a good scholar. In 1483 he made an adventurous journey abroad to study theology at Bologna, from which he returned with a doctor's degree, and then remained prior until his death in the winter of 1498-9. His will, dated 21 December 1498, arranged for his burial at London in St Margaret's, Bridge Street, and he instructed his executors to dispose of certain books and other goods for the benefit of the 'college' of Kalendars and two parish churches of which he was incumbent.[36] Burton was followed in 1499 by John Vaughan, an

[28] John Leland, *Itinerary*, ed. Lucy Toulmin Smith, 5 vols (London, 1910), v, 91-2.
[29] BRO, All Saints City, Church Book, pp 381, 539.
[30] *Itineraria . . . Willelmi de Worcestre*, ed. Nasmith, p 229.
[31] BRO, All Saints City, Church Book, pp 315, 333.
[32] Leland, *Itinerary*, v, 91-2.
[33] BRO, All Saints City, Deeds, CS B 7 (324).
[34] For the list of priors, see Orme (above, note 13), pp 46-7.
[35] For his career, see Emden, *BRUO*, i, 319, omitting the last paragraph which is not applicable.
[36] PRO, Prob 11/11 (PCC 37 Horne).

Oxford master of arts who stayed for only five months,[37] and later in the year by Richard Eastmond, sometime fellow of All Souls College and junior proctor of Oxford University. He too was well qualified, being also a doctor of theology, and held a Wiltshire benefice throughout his tenure of the priorship.[38] Eastmond died in 1503, and was succeeded by another distinguished man, Thomas Harper, a native of Axbridge (Somerset), fellow of Merton College and doctor of theology.[39] In 1507 Harper was elected warden of Merton, but it was at Bristol that he died in the following year, and in 1509 twenty-eight of his books were brought from there to Merton to be distributed among the fellows in accordance with his will. He also left some small bequests to the Kalendars' guild and its brethren, to be paid with money owing to him there.[40]

Harlow, Burton, Eastmond and Harper were all scholars of distinction whose presence must have strengthened the work of the parish clergy in late medieval Bristol. The first suggestion of a departure from Carpenter's ordinances comes with Harper's retention of the priorship after his election as warden of Merton; the two offices were not truly compatible. Real evidence of decline comes with the priorship of Harper's successor, William Cross, appointed in 1509. Cross was the first prior of the new foundation, apart from the short-lived Vaughan, to be a mere master of arts.[41] He was a middle-aged man at his appointment, probably in his late fifties, and for the last thirty years had been simply the vicar of the Bristol church of St Leonard. He did not enjoy good health, and in the spring of 1512 he was licensed to reside away from the guild on account of his age and infirmities.[42] In the following years Cross seems to have done little to fulfil the duties of his office, so little that in 1520 John Bell, the bishop of Worcester's vicar-general, commanded him to observe certain basic duties on pain of suspension from his benefice. He was ordered to visit All Saints church every day to pray for the founders and benefactors of the guild, to celebrate mass there once a week, and to be present in the choir on Sundays and festivals at mattins, mass and vespers. Bell's injunction gives a distinct impression that Cross was an unsatisfactory prior, and not merely an incapacitated one.[43]

Cross vacated his office between 1520 and 1525 – it is not known why – and with his successor Roger Edgeworth the guild again acquired a

---

[37] For his career, see *BRUO*, iii, 1941.

[38] For his career, see ibid., ii, 650.

[39] For his career, see ibid., ii, 878-9.

[40] PRO, Prob 11/16 (PCC 10 Bennett).

[41] He was vicar of St Leonard, Bristol, instituted 3 January 1480, still in 1515 (HWRO, Reg. Alcock, ff 61ᵛ-2; Reg. S. de Gigli, f 99ᵛ). For other details, see *BRUO*, i, 518-19.

[42] HWRO, Reg. S. de Gigli, f 78.

[43] BRO, All Saints City, Deeds, NA 57 (262).

distinguished theologian as its head.[44] Born at Holt Castle in Denbigh, Edgeworth became a fellow of Oriel College, a doctor of theology and a preacher of some note whose sermons were later printed.[45] A strong supporter of Catholicism when the Reformation came, he was one of the first prebendaries of Bristol Cathedral, and after his death in 1560 was buried at Wells. Edgeworth, however, vacated the priorship in 1528 after only a few years, and the next two priors, Francis Pollard (instituted 1528)[46] and John Pinnock (instituted 1530),[47] exhibit a further decline of qualifications. Neither appears to have been a master of arts, thus making an absolute breach of Carpenter's ordinances. Pinnock was one of the Bonshommes of Edington (Wiltshire), who were regular canons of the order of St Augustine. He is first encountered in 1518 as titular bishop of Syene, and from then until 1535 he acted as a suffragan bishop in the diocese of Salisbury where he held a succession of canonries and other benefices. He can hardly have been very active in Bristol during his five years as prior, which he terminated by resignation in 1535, shortly before his death. The last two priors before the dissolution, John Flook (instituted 1535)[48] and Thomas Silk (instituted 1540),[49] were somewhat better qualified. They were both Oxford masters of arts and both resided in Bristol, but neither is known to have studied theology. On the whole, the priors after 1509, with the brief exception of Edgeworth, failed to reach the standard of their predecessors, and for most of the period from 1509 to 1535 the guild appears to have been led by poorly qualified men, two of whom were not always resident.

With the coming of the Reformation the guild of Kalendars shared the fate of chantries and religious guilds in general. A survey of its property was made under Henry VIII in 1546,[50] and again under Edward VI in the early months of 1548.[51] The foundation was dissolved by order of the crown at Easter in that year, and the prior and chantry priests were awarded pensions.[52] The Kalendars' property was confiscated, and sold by the crown on the following 3 October.[53] The records of this process

[44] For his career, see *BRUO*, iv, 184–5.

[45] They are discussed by J.W. Blench, *Preaching in England in the Late Fifteenth and Sixteenth Centuries* (Oxford and New York, 1964).

[46] The son of John Pollard, mercer, and his wife Maud of the parish of St Nicholas, Bristol, he was in priest's orders by 1521 (see her will dated 2 May 1521 in PRO, Prob 11/20 (PCC 15 Maynwaryng)). For the rest of his career, see *BRUO*, iv, 455.

[47] For his career, see Orme (above, note 13), p 47.

[48] For his career, see *BRUO*, iv, 207–8.

[49] For his career, see ibid., p 552.

[50] PRO, E 301/21 no 65.

[51] Ibid., E 301/22 no 12; Sir J. Maclean, 'Chantry Certificates, Gloucestershire', *Bristol and Gloucestershire Archaeological Society Transactions*, viii (1883–4), pp 246–7.

[52] PRO, E 318/1845, ff 12–13.

[53] *Calendar of Patent Rolls, 1548–9*, pp 105–6; BRO, All Saints City, Deeds, CS B 7 (324).

give us an insight into the state of the guild during its last years. The net income of the endowments was estimated at £33.5s. in 1535, and the gross income at about £39 in the 1540s. The latter figure, however, included the endowments of Richard White's chantry in St Stephen's church, Bristol, of which the Kalendars were trustees. The survey of 1546 reported that the property of the guild was 'in great decay', but no mention of this was made in 1548. Thomas Silk, the prior, received the salary of £10 established by Bishop Carpenter, and the other two priests £8 and £7.4s. respectively. The lesser priests appear to have still been living in the guild house adjoining All Saints church, but the prior was not. He had a separate dwelling, which belonged to the guild, in the suburban parish of St Philip. His duties and those of his brethren remained the traditional ones: divine service each day and the celebration of regular obits, dirges and masses for the souls of the founders of the guild. Little remained of Carpenter's reforms. Of the four annual sermons which he had established, only three were now delivered and even these by a paid deputy. No mention is made of the library as a working institution, or of the prior's weekly lecture there, but as already stated there was still a chamber in the guild house 'vulgarly called the library'. The decline of the prior's evangelical work was fatal. If active, it might have commended itself to the authorities of the new Protestant Church of England; instead, the guild of Kalendars simply bore the appearance of a Catholic institution for intercessory prayers, and shared the fate of bodies of that kind.

7 Alexander Barclay, poet and educationist, presents a volume to one of his noble patrons. Not a realistic portrait, it shows the poet in the robes of a monk of Ely Cathedral, in one of the stages of his unusually varied career.

13

CHAUCER AND EDUCATION

Among the many matters which interested Chaucer and found expression in his writings, the education of young people occupied a place of moderate rather than major importance. Unlike religion, morality, love, or social satire, it is seldom a dominant theme of his work. In the romantic stories which form his main achievement, the heroes and heroines undergo sufferings, testings, and punishments, but they can rarely be said to experience education in the sense of acquiring knowledge. Only in two of his tales — those of the Wife of Bath and of the Squire — does Chaucer seem to lay a special emphasis on the training and instruction of the young.[1] His other important writings, the didactic works, are by definition concerned with teaching, but they are almost always directed to mankind as a whole, rather than to the young in particular. The *Treatise on the Astrolabe* stands out alone as a major project to instruct a young man, namely the author's own son. Even here the educational purpose was probably limited. The only other people envisaged by Chaucer in his preface as reading the *Astrolabe* were the "discret" or well-informed (*Astrolabe*, preface, 41-42).[2] Having served its initial purpose, the work appears to have been intended to circulate as an adult manual as much as an adolescent schoolbook.

Yet if the education of the young was seldom at the center of Chaucer's mind, it frequently entered the periphery. He was certainly aware of, and attracted by, young people who were involved in learning, or who had been so. Two of the Canterbury pilgrims — the Squire and the Clerk — belong to this category, and similar characters figure in several of the tales, particularly those told by the Miller, the Reeve, the Wife of Bath, the Squire, the Franklin, the Physician, and the Prioress. The width of Chaucer's interests and his keen awareness of the world around him meant that education, which was a feature of that world, was bound to attract his attention from time

1. These tales are discussed below.
2. All citations from Chaucer's work are taken from F. N. Robinson, ed., *The Works of Geoffrey Chaucer*, 2nd ed. (Boston: Houghton Mifflin, and London: Oxford Univ. Press, 1957).

to time. The references which he makes to the subject, when collected together, turn out to comprise a significant part of his work. The following study sets out to identify those of the greatest importance and to relate them to the educational system of Chaucer's day. A project of this kind has value for both the literary critic and the historian. The critic intent upon understanding Chaucer's mind, and the historian concerned to form as full a picture of his age as possible, both need to be informed of the extent and accuracy of his interest in education. The information should not be presented without a commentary. Since Chaucer's educational references grew out of an interest in life in general rather than education in particular, they are generally random and selective, illuminating certain aspects of the subject but neglecting others. Chaucer did not produce, even by accident, a *summa* of allusions to contemporary education, and so it is the duty of a modern commentator to remedy this deficiency.

Education can be defined for our purposes as that which children and adolescents, of both sexes, learn to fit them for adult life. It includes two aspects: first, the acquisition of knowledge about God, the world, society, and their laws; and second, the mastery of techniques such as manners, behavior, literacy, work, and play. Education in this general sense was provided by two kinds of institutions in the later Middle Ages: the family or household, and the school or university. Most medieval people lived in some kind of a household or family. Among the lower orders this consisted simply of a small group of kindred like that of the miller of Trumpington (A 3969-71), or the widow and her two daughters in the *Nun's Priest's Tale* (B² 4019). In the case of the wealthy it also included servants and retainers, ranging from the two employed by John the Oxford carpenter (A 3555-56) to the great households of the monarch and the aristocracy at which Chaucer hints in his treatments of Theseus (A 1414-41) and Cambuskan (F 91, 177, 189). Religious houses of monks, friars, and nuns can also be termed households, since they consisted of groups of clergy living together, with bodies of servants as well. Any kind of medieval household was likely to include young people: wards and pages in the households of the king and the aristocracy, choristers and clerks in those of the clergy, apprentices in those of merchants and craftsmen, and the head of the household's own sons and daughters. Since children who live with adults learn and are trained in many ways, albeit subconsciously and informally, the household can properly be termed an educational institution. It differed, of course, in basic respects from a school or university. It was only partially concerned with education, being also engaged in many other activities, whereas universities and schools concentrated upon the business of learning. On the other hand, the latter catered only for the small minority of male scholars who wished to be trained in literary studies, whereas the household provided some education for everyone. Even those who went to school or university also spent part of their childhood in a household, and most people spent all of it there. The family or household was thus the most basic and ubiquitous center of education in medieval England, and ought to be our starting point.

Chaucer's allusions to household education can be divided into two groups: those which relate to the ordinary population and those concerning the aristocracy. The very few references to education in religious houses can be treated along with the second category. Of the two groups, Chaucer has much less to say about the family or household education of the lower orders than about that of the aristocracy. This, no doubt, reflected the casual and unorganized nature of education in ordinary homes, which projected few features that would strike a contemporary observer. Chaucer is nevertheless aware of the need for and the existence of a system of education in the houses of the population as a whole. His remarks on the duties of parents in the *Physician's Tale* (C 93-104), though they occur in the context of a story about the aristocracy, are obviously addressed to Chaucer's readers in general and accord with the advice which contemporary moralists directed to society at large. Fathers and mothers, says the Physician, are responsible for the oversight of their children while the latter are under their government. They should set them a good example of life and rebuke them for doing evil, lest the children be lost (presumably to the Devil or to wicked human beings), like sheep to the wolf when the shepherd is careless. Chaucer also shares the contemporary opinion that parents should instruct by precept as well as by example. The medieval Church required parents and godparents to teach children basic religious prayers and observances, and this is depicted in the *Prioress's Tale*, where the widow instructs her seven-year-old son in one of those prayers, the Ave Mary, and in one basic observance: to kneel and repeat it in front of every image of the Virgin that he passes (B² 1695-1705).

Chaucer is also aware that a child at home will absorb precepts of a moral and cautionary nature. On three occasions in his works, his nonaristocratic characters recall pieces of advice which they learnt from their "dames" or mothers, apparently when they were young. One such maxim is quoted in the *Pardoner's Tale* by the boy who attends on the three "riotoures" (C 680-84), and seems to be based on a proverb or quotation warning that you should always be ready to meet your death.[3] In the *Manciple's Tale* the teller ex-

3. A Latin quotation meaning "Live as though you were to die tomorrow" is found in fourteenth-century Continental sources (Pierre Dubois, *The Recovery of the Holy Land*, trans. W. I. Brandt [New York: Columbia Univ. Press, 1956], p. 117). Or Chaucer may have had in mind Christ's call for readiness in Matthew 24-25, Mark 13, and Luke 12 and 21.

pounds forty-two lines of counsel which his mother gave him about
discretion in the use of speech (H 317-62). Here only the form, however, is based on oral teaching in the home, since the matter consists
of literary references to the *Distichs of Cato* and the *De Arte Lo-
quendi et Tacendi* by Albertano da Brescia, works unlikely to have
been known by any manciple's mother in real life. In the third example, the Wife of Bath attributes to her "dames loore" the subtle-
ties she uses to seduce her fifth husband, the clerk Jankin:

> I bar hym on honde he hadde enchanted me, —
> My dame taughte me that soutiltee.
> And eek I seyde I mette of hym al nyght,
> He wolde han slayn me as I lay upright. . . .
> And al was fals; I dremed of it right naught,
> But as I folwed ay my dames loore,
> As wel of this as of othere thynges moore.
> (D 575-84)

This passage indicates Chaucer's recognition that children may learn
less desirable matter from their parents than religion and morality —
here the female freemasonry of deception and seduction. In this respect he is a realist rather than an idealist about what happens at
home. He fails, however, to provide any description of home education in practice. Although a number of children appear in his works,
they are featured for their pathos or innocence, not as learners or
trainees.[4] He does not show them learning to understand the world
around them, to discipline themselves, to deal with other people, or
to master a trade or occupation. The widespread institution of apprenticeship, for example, finds mention only in the *Cook's Tale,*
and even here the poet's interest in the subject is a limited one (A
4365-422). Perkyn Revelour, the "hero," is an apprentice in one of the
victualling trades in London. He lives in his master's household in
order to learn the business, and serves or works in the shop beneath.
Chaucer does not evoke Perkyn's training, however, but rather his
riotous behavior out of hours, which leads to his master's dismissing
him at or before the end of his term. The *Cook's Tale* is unfinished,
but it lasts long enough to show Perkyn leaving his master to live with
a boon companion and his prostitute wife. It is obvious that Chaucer
used the apprenticeship as a point of departure, not as an object of
interest in its own right.

Compared with the household education of the lower orders, that

---

4. On Chaucer's treatment of children see D. S. Brewer, "Children in Chaucer," *A Review of English Literature*, 5 (1964), 52-60.

of the aristocracy receives much greater attention.[5] This accords with Chaucer's fuller treatment of noble life, and with the greater organization which aristocratic education had developed by the later Middle Ages, making its features more easily recognizable. Chaucer takes it for granted that the aristocracy make conscious and deliberate arrangements for their children to be educated. Queen Cenobia brings up her sons "in vertu and lettrure" (B² 3486), noble Cecilia is fostered from her cradle "in the feith / Of Crist" (G 122-23), and the marquess of Saluces orders his daughter to be reared "in alle gentillesse" (E 593). Aristocratic children in Chaucer's time usually began to be educated in their parents' own households, but when they grew older were often sent out to be trained as pages or damsels in other aristocratic households. Chaucer gives examples of both practices. Canacee in the *Squire's Tale* lives at the court of her father with her own governess (F 374-83), whereas the marquess of Saluces sends his children by Griselde to be brought up by his sister the countess of Panik at Bologna (E 589-93). The latter arrangement is part of the testing of Griselde, but only in its manner; the principle involved was a well-established one. In late medieval England, when aristocratic children had to be reared away from home, they often went for this purpose to nunneries or, in the case of older boys, to the households of bishops or abbots. Curiously, Chaucer makes very few references to the educational role of religious houses or clerical households in this respect. The most important one occurs in his portrait of the Prioress, where the emphasis on her behavior and accomplishments seems to betoken an awareness of the involvement of nuns with the education of noble girls (A 118-41). What are at first sight merely the Prioress's personal characteristics are also, in fact, a list of the major elements in the aristocratic female curriculum: religious devotion, French of the Anglo-Norman dialect, table manners, deportment, and good behavior. The only person whom Chaucer mentions as being educated in a nunnery, however, is not a noblewoman but the bastard daughter of the Cambridgeshire priest married to the Trumpington miller (A 3942-68). The fact is referred to with sarcasm: for all her "nortelrie" she was only "as digne as water in a dich," but it would probably be wrong to construe this as a general attack on education in nunneries, or even on its extension to girls who were not of noble birth. Several cases are known in which wealthy merchants and citizens sent their daughters to be fostered in this way, and there is no sign that Chaucer's contempo-

5. For a general survey of aristocratic education in medieval England see Nicholas Orme, "The Education of the Courtier," *English Court Culture in the Later Middle Ages*, ed. C. Ross and V. J. Scattergood (London: Duckworth, 1982); now above pp 153-75.

raries found the practice objectionable.[6]

Aristocratic children in late medieval England often had less contact with their parents than did their social inferiors. Kings, lords, and knights, and sometimes even their wives, were too busy or elevated to carry out fully the burden of rearing and teaching their offspring. Their newborn infants were immediately entrusted to a nurse, as was the son of Griselde (E 617-18). If the child were a boy, he usually remained under petticoat government from his mother, the nurse, or a governess until, at about the age of seven, he was thought able to be transferred to the rule of a male tutor. In the best-known cases, heirs to the throne, the tutor was an experienced knight who kept a general supervision over his charge, while professional instructors were brought in to teach the prince such specialized techniques as reading and grammar.[7] Among the rest of the aristocracy — peers and knights — the kind of tutor chosen probably varied, and could be either a knight or a cleric, depending on the family's status and the money available. If a cleric, he might well act both as a general supervisor and as a specialized teacher of religious knowledge and school learning. Chaucer's one portrait of a tutor is of the scholarly rather than the knightly kind, Nero's "maister" Seneca, who was the flower of "moralitee" in his time and taught his protégé "letterure and curteisye," meaning literary studies and good behavior (B[2] 3685-708). The portrait is an ideal one. While Seneca was able to dominate his pupil,

> He maked hym so konnyng and so sowple
> That longe tyme it was er tirannye
> Or any vice dorste on hym uncowple.
> (B[2] 3690-92)

Unfortunately, Nero's nature was so evil that, when he grew up and asserted himself, he shook off both the discipline and the teaching of his master, whom he forced to commit suicide. The lesson of the tragedy seems to be that a good tutor who exerts himself to bring up his pupil in the best way can achieve much. Nevertheless, education is not capable of reforming all those who by nature are strongly inclined to vice and wickedness.

Although Chaucer presents a tutor only once and in ideal form, he shows us three aristocratic pupils, one of them ideal and the other two quite the opposite. The ideal pupil is the Squire, the others are Nero and the son of the Franklin, whom his father deliberately contrasts with the Squire at the end of the latter's tale (F 682-94).

6. On education in nunneries see Eileen Power, *Medieval English Nunneries, c. 1275-1535* (Cambridge: Cambridge Univ. Press, 1922), pp. 261-84, 568-81.
7. Nicholas Orme, *English Schools in the Middle Ages* (London: Methuen, 1973), pp. 21-29.

Chaucer does not actually say that the Squire had been educated, as he says of the Clerk of Oxford, but the Squire's youth (he is twenty) and the close resemblance between his accomplishments and those taught in the aristocratic curriculum of the day, make it difficult to believe that Chaucer could have conceived the portrait without having in mind the curriculum as a frame of reference (A 79-100). Fourteenth-century aristocratic education covered several areas: religion and morality, war and athletics, and literary and cultural pursuits. The first two are missing from the Squire's portrait, but their omission is probably without significance. It arises from Chaucer's strategy of dividing the qualities of the ideal aristocrat among the Knight, the Squire, and the Franklin, the religious and moral material being given to the Knight (A 45-50, 67-72). With this exception, the list of the Squire's abilities accords so closely with what was taught in the curriculum that we can feel ourselves justified in calling the portrait "ideal."

First, the Squire is a well-trained warrior. This was expected of a good fourteenth-century nobleman or gentleman, whose duties included the protection of his tenants, the keeping of local law and order, and the defence of the realm, even if he followed a largely peaceful life at home. Next, the Squire has mastered the athletic and sporting pursuits of aristocratic leisure, which their participants held to be valuable for keeping themselves fit for military service and free from sloth and other vices. We are told he is skilled in two major elements of this part of the curriculum: horsemanship and the use of weapons. He has jousted, and medieval jousts, when they involved young men, can properly be regarded as educational exercises, providing an opportunity to learn and practice the techniques of fighting on horseback. Four other athletic pursuits engaged in by young medieval aristocrats, however, are not listed in relation to the Squire, though they are attributed to Chaucer's other young "hero," Sir Thopas: hunting, hawking, wrestling, and archery (B² 1926-31). It has been asserted that the two latter activities were not practiced by noblemen or gentlemen in Chaucer's day and are ascribed to Sir Thopas to give an effect of incongruity.[8] In fact, like hunting and hawking, they were both proper to a knight of the time, and can be traced in late medieval practice.[9] The satire upon them,

8. F. N. Robinson, *Works*, p. 738, notes to lines 738 and 740.

9. Aristocratic hunting and hawking, of course, were widespread. Archery was practiced by both noblemen and women (see, for example, Edward Duke of York, *The Master of Game*, ed. W. A. & F. Baillie-Grohman [London: Chatto & Windus, 1909], pp. 188-89, 194, 198). Wrestling was an accomplishment of Gamelyn, son of a knight, in the pseudo-Chaucerian "Tale of Gamelyn" (*The Complete Works of Geoffrey Chaucer*, ed. W. W. Skeat [Oxford: Clarendon Press, 1900], IV, 650-52), and also of King Henry VIII in 1510 (Edward Hall, *Chronicle containing the History of England* [London, 1809], p. 515).

if it is present, relates to the *manner* in which Sir Thopas pursued the activities, rather than to the activities themselves.[10]

The remainder of the Squire's accomplishments belong to the parts of the aristocratic curriculum which can broadly be called the literary and cultural. He has been trained for life indoors as well as out of doors. He is well mannered: "curteis," "lowely," and "servysable" and can do the symbolic service required of aristocratic youths in noble households, that of carving the meat for their lords and masters. He is skilled in music and can play the flute, the most popular instrument along with the harp among noblemen and gentlemen at the time. He can compose songs, though it is not absolutely clear whether this refers to the words, the music, or both, and can sing them. He can write, which implies (though Chaucer does not specify the fact) that he can read. On the basis of what his real contemporaries were taught, he would have learnt enough Latin to follow a missal or a breviary, but would have been most fluent in the reading and writing of French and English. He can also "purtreye": a word of equivocal meaning (A 96). Portrayal, in medieval usage, signifies the representation of something in writing, speech, or painting. The latter is Chaucer's commonest meaning, but it is inappropriate here since there are no indications that the English aristocracy could paint or draw, or were conceived of as doing so, until the sixteenth century.[11] More probably, the Squire is being praised as good at writing or speaking. It is worth noting that while he is not specifically mentioned as an orator in the *General Prologue*, the tendency of his tale is to imply that he was particularly ambitious in this respect. The *Tale*, as is well known, is told with an emphatic use of rhetorical devices. It goes out of its way to describe and to praise the king of Arabia's knight for his command of rhetorical rules and ability in speaking, and it concludes with praise from the Franklin for the Squire's eloquence (F 89-104, 675-77). In presenting him as a good speaker, Chaucer reproduces yet another element in the aristocratic training of his age.

The education of noble and gentle girls in Chaucer's day is also

10.   The main target of the satire may be only the piling up of the hero's attributes in medieval romances. If aimed at the attributes themselves, the significant points are the goshawk, usually associated with gentlemen below the rank of knight or with yeomen (Rachel Hands, *English Hunting and Hawking in* The Boke of St Albans [London: Oxford Univ. Press, 1975], pp. 55, 118); Thopas's use of archery in hawking rather than hunting, if that is the meaning of "therto" (B[2] 1929); and his entry into plebeian wrestling competitions in order to win the prize ram. Gamelyn also wrestles with commoners, but does so initially with the knightly motive of righting a wrong.

11.   The earliest example known to me is Sir Thomas Elyot, *The Governor* (London, 1531), Book I, Chapter 8.

well reflected in his writings.[12] Their upbringing during the later Middle Ages parallelled that of their brothers, for like them they were either brought up at home or boarded out in other aristocratic households or in religious houses. Their training was probably often supplied by their mothers or mistresses, since ladies had more leisure for this purpose than their husbands. In the case of the king's daughters, however, and at least a few of the great magnate families, the task was already deputed by the end of the fourteenth century to a governess, or "maistresse" as she was termed.[13] This lady, in the recorded instances, was usually the wife of a knight in the service of the girl's father, and was therefore herself of aristocratic rank and breeding. If Katherine Swynford, the "maistresse" of the daughters of John of Gaunt, was also Chaucer's sister-in-law, the poet himself must have been well aware of these ladies' existence and of the role they played.[14] There are two allusions to them in his work. The first relates to Canacee in the *Squire's Tale*, who is a king's daughter and (though her age is not recorded) probably in her 'teens. Her "maistresse" is mentioned only briefly, but enough is said about her to establish that she is old, wise, and possesses authority (F 374-83). She has to be asked for permission when Canacee wishes to rise early to walk in the palace grounds, and she is responsible for collecting an escort of ladies for the purpose. The second reference arises from the description of Virginia, the knight's daughter in the *Physician's Tale*. After praising her modest and retiring nature, Chaucer interrupts his story with an apology and admonition to all "maistresses . . . That lordes doghtres han in governaunce" (C 72-92). He characterizes them as being in their "olde lyf" or maturity, and suggests that they are chosen for their task either because they have kept their "honestee" or because, though they have fallen into "freletee" (evidently of an erotic kind), they have reformed, thus gaining (presumably) a reputation for experience. He ends by exhorting them not to slacken in keeping guard over their charges, in teaching them "vertu," and in discouraging them from vice.

It is Virginia who comes nearest among Chaucer's female charac-

12. For a general account of the medieval education of aristocratic women see Dorothy Gardiner, *English Girlhood at School* (London: Oxford Univ. Press, 1929), pp. 33-140.

13. On the mistresses of royal children in the age of Chaucer see Mary Anne Everett Green, *Lives of the Princesses of England* (London: Henry Colburn, 1840-55), especially III, 166, 230; and J. H. Wylie, *History of England under Henry the Fourth* (London: Longmans & Co., 1884-98), IV, 222, 241-42.

14. Katherine was the wife of Sir Hugh Swynford, one of the retinue of John of Gaunt. She occurs as "maistresse" to Gaunt's daughters Philippa and Elizabeth in 1376-80 (*John of Gaunt's Register, 1379-83*, ed. Eleanor C. Lodge and R. Somerville, Camden Society Series III, 57 [London: Royal Historical Society, 1937], pp. 302-03, 93).

ters to providing a model example of the well-educated aristocratic girl. The list of her virtues, which occupies twenty-seven lines, finds echoes in Chaucer's other noble heroines — Canacee, Dorigen, and Emilye — but whereas their qualities and accomplishments tend to emerge in passing, hers are set out in a conscious and studied way, proving that Chaucer had a well-developed concept of the ideal female education (C 43-71). Though a Roman pagan, Virginia embodies most of the fundamental virtues of the Christian tradition. She is chaste, not only in body but in mind, and humble, modest, and patient. Her dress and her bearing observe "mesure" or moderation, and her speech is accordant with her station, honest in manner, and admirable in content:

> No countrefeted termes hadde she
> To seme wys; but after hir degree
> She spak, and alle hire wordes, moore and lesse,
> Sownynge in vertu and in gentillesse.
>
> (C 51-54)

She is temperate in her way of life, a virtue shared by Canacee, who is also "mesurable" in this respect, going early to and from her bed (F 362-64). Virginia allows wine no mastery over her, and she is careful to spend all her time industriously, so as to keep away idleness. Finally, she avoids dangerous company,

> Where likly was to treten of folye,
> As is at feestes, revels, and at daunces,
> That been occasions of daliaunces.
>
> (C 64-66)

Her conduct is thoroughly approved by Chaucer, who observes that such occasions cause children to ripen and grow bold too soon. Boldness, he argues, is learnt quickly enough after marriage.

The portrait of Virginia as an ideal young female is something of a counterpart to that of the Squire. There is a difference between the two, however, in that hers is a moral portrait whereas his centers upon abilities and techniques. The treatment of Virginia gives a good insight into the behavior expected of well-educated aristocratic women, but the techniques which they were taught are not described by Chaucer at any one point and have to be gathered from various places in his writings. Most of the accomplishments learnt by medieval aristocratic women find a mention somewhere in the Chaucerian canon. A well-educated noblewoman or gentlewoman was brought up like Saint Cecilia in the Christian faith and taught how to pray and behave in church (G 120-26; compare C 118-20). She was encouraged to adopt modesty in behavior and speech, like Virginia, and schooled in good manners and table etiquette like the Prioress (A 127-41). She learned to sing, like Emilye (A 1055), and to dance, like Canacee and Dorigen (F 277, 900). She may also have practiced original musical composition, since Antigone in *Troilus and Criseyde* not only sings a song of love but identifies it as the work of an aristocratic lady: "the goodlieste mayde / Of gret estat in al the town of Troye" (*Troilus*, II, 824-26, 876-82). She was taught the arts of weaving and embroidery like Philomena, who

> lerned hadde in youthe
> So that she werken and enbroude couthe,
> And weven in hire stol the radevore   [tapestry]
> As it of wemen hath be woned yore.
> (*Legend of Good Women* 2350-53)

She was also introduced to forms of exercise: hawking (associated with Canacee) and hunting, in which Emilye and Ypolita take part in the *Knight's Tale*, like many of their real-life contemporaries (A 1685-87, F 631-51). Finally, Chaucer's frequent allusions to reading and writing by aristocratic ladies show that he took it for granted that they were literate in French or English. The total impression is that of a wide and varied curriculum, hardly inferior to the masculine one. If it was weak on the athletic side, it covered all the moral and cultural accomplishments and included, by means of the decorative arts, a dimension missing from the training of youths.

We shall now turn from the education of the household to that of the specialized institutions of the school and the university. This brings us back to the masculine world, since both were wholly confined to men in the later Middle Ages, except for a few elementary schools for young boys and girls in London and elsewhere.[15] By Chaucer's time there was a school open to the male public in most English towns of any importance, and several in London, one of which he may have attended himself.[16] Their primary purpose was to teach Latin, but they were probably also attended by persons who wished to acquire only enough facility in letters to read French or English. There were two grades of schools.[17] Some were elementary in character and taught "reading" (the Latin alphabet and the ability

15. Orme, *English Schools*, pp. 54-55.

16. There were three authorized public schools in fourteenth-century London: those of St Martin le Grand, St Mary Arches and St Paul, as well as some private and unauthorized ones (*English Schools*, pp. 169, 190, 210-14). It is impossible to say which one Chaucer attended.

17. On medieval schools in general see Orme, *English Schools*, especially pp. 59-86, and Orme, *Education in the West of England, 1066-1548* (Exeter: Univ. of Exeter, 1976), pp. 1-4.

to recognize Latin words) and "song" (the reading and singing of the ecclesiastical psalms, hymns, and antiphons). Others were grammar schools and taught, often alongside the elementary subjects, the ability to understand the Latin language, to speak and write it fluently in prose and in verse, and to read some of its easier authors. A well-taught youth who graduated from a medieval grammar school ought to have known enough Latin to embark on a career as a priest, lawyer, merchant, or secretarial clerk, or to undertake university studies, which were also carried on through the medium of Latin.

Chaucer's interest in schools was restricted. The only one he describes is that in the *Prioress's Tale*, nominally located in Asia but closely resembling an English elementary school or the elementary department of a grammar school (B² 1685-1740). In it he features two boy pupils at different stages of their education. The first is at the very beginning of the curriculum, learning the primer: a "litel book" or pamphlet containing the alphabet and the basic Latin prayers. The second has graduated one step to read the antiphoner: the church service book containing the words and music of the antiphons which, being written in large separate letters, were especially suitable for children to study.[18] The first boy hears the older pupils singing the antiphon to the Virgin, *Alma Redemptoris Mater*, and learns by ear the words and music of the first line or "vers." Later, the second boy teaches him the other five lines by word of mouth. At this stage neither of them knows the meanings of the Latin words they read and sing. The second boy has been told that the *Alma* is a salutation and a prayer to the Virgin, but he cannot translate it: "I lerne song, I kan but smal grammeere" (B² 1726). The grammar course, which imparted this knowledge, was the next stage of the curriculum. It is unfortunate for us that Chaucer fails to describe it. The very use of the word "grammar" in his writings is restricted to the single example just quoted. He was not ignorant of what was taught in grammar schools, since he alludes to several of the Latin authors boys were made to study.[19] In addition to the *Distichs of Cato*, which he mentions frequently,[20] he refers to Pseustis, one of the characters in the *Eclogues of Theodulus* (HF, 1228), to Ovid's *Remedia Amoris* (B² 2166, BD 568),[21] and to the *Facetus*,

18. Compare Orme, *English Schools*, pp. 60-63.

19. For the grammar curriculum see Orme, *English Schools*, pp. 87-115, and David Thomson, *A Descriptive Catalogue of Middle English Grammatical Texts* (New York and London: Garland, 1979), especially pp. 30-47.

20. See, for example, the references under "Cato" in J. S. P. Tatlock and A. G. Kennedy, *A Concordance to the Complete Works of Geoffrey Chaucer* (Gloucester, Mass.: P. Smith, 1963), p. 124.

21. The work is mentioned as a school text in *Hoccleve's Works: The Minor Poems*, ed. F. J. Furnivall and I. Gollancz, rev. Jerome Mitchell and A. I. Doyle, EETS, ES 61 (London: Oxford Univ. Press, 1970), p. 81.

a popular treatise in verse conveying advice on self-discipline and good behavior (A 3227-28).[22] But he nowhere describes a lesson in grammar or a schoolmaster, and his evocation of the schoolroom, its pupils and procedures, even in the *Prioress's Tale*, is of a minimal kind. In this respect Chaucer shared a shortsightedness general among his contemporaries. Medieval schools, though nominally under the jurisdiction of the Church, attracted little attention from the ecclesiastical authorities.[23] Their masters, few in number, modest in status, and often brief in their tenures of office, made equally little impact on the general public whose children they taught. As a result, references to schools and masters are scarce in medieval literature, in both the narrative and didactic genres, and Chaucer merely conforms to this pattern.[24]

There is one other matter related to schools, however, which finds a place in Chaucer's work, and that is corporal punishment. Brief as is his treatment of school life in the *Prioress's Tale*, he does not overlook its most notorious feature: beating, which could be expected, even by a seven-year-old who did not learn his book, "thries in an houre" (B[2] 1732; compare A 3759). Many medieval moralists were strong supporters of the "good sound thrashing" both by parents and masters, as an encouragement to virtue and a deterrent against vice. Langland, for example, puts Solomon's proverb, "who so spareth the sprynge spilleth his children," into the mouth of Reason itself, and goes on to encourage the use of the rod even by husbands on their errant wives.[25] Chaucer's attitude to corporal punishment, characteristically, is a milder one. Although he follows Langland in urging parents to "chastise" their offspring, the word in question is an equivocal one which can mean merely to rebuke, without recourse to physical action (C 98). His ideal tutor, Seneca, corrected his pupil Nero "discreetly, as by word and nat by dede," and there is no indication that Nero's adult vices are considered to have resulted from this mild regime (B[2] 3695-700). Nero's shortcomings arose from nature, not nurture. Most tellingly, in the *Parson's Tale*, Chaucer's principal reference to physical punishment is a hostile one:

> A philosophre upon a tyme, that wolde have beten his disciple
> for his grete trespas, for which he was greetly amoeved,
> broghte a yerde to scoure with the child; and whan this child
> saugh the yerde, he seyde to his maister, "What thenke ye do?"

22. Robinson, *Works*, p. 684, note to l. 3227.
23. Orme, *English Schools*, pp. 142-43.
24. On medieval lack of awareness of schoolmasters see Nicholas Orme, "Schoolmasters," in *Profession, Vocation and Culture in Medieval England*, ed. C. H. Clough (Liverpool: Liverpool Univ. Press, 1981); now above pp 59-62.
25. Langland, *Piers Plowman*, B Text, V. 32-47.

"I wol bete thee," quod the maister, "for thy correccioun."
"For sothe," quod the child, "ye oghten first correcte youreself,
that han lost al youre pacience for the gilt of a child." "For
sothe," quod the maister al wepynge, "thow seyst sooth. Have
thow the yerde, my deere sone, and correcte me for myn
inpacience."

(I 670-74; compare I 628)

It is surely significant that in this, his main treatment of the subject,
Chaucer extols the use of patience by a master, not the use of the
rod. A master ought to be patient, first because patience is one of
the cardinal virtues, and second because the "gilt" of a child is only
a petty matter. It may be unwise to assume that Chaucer ruled out
corporal punishment altogether, but he seems to have felt that verbal
reproof and charitable discipline were best. Nor was he alone in
this view. Vincent of Beauvais, the influential French Dominican
friar and educationist, had stated as long ago as the 1240s that in
discipline, gentleness leads but austerity repels.[26] More recently,
in the early fourteenth century, two eminent English friars of the
same order, John Bromyard and Robert Holcote, had urged the need
for kindness and lenience by masters, and had argued that beating
might sometimes be counterproductive.[27] William Wykeham conformed to their viewpoint in 1400 when he ordered the headmaster
of his new foundation, Winchester College, to punish the boys with
moderation.[28] Even in the Middle Ages there was a liberal tradition in English education, and it fits with Chaucer's general temper-
ance that he shared its opinions.

When he turns from schools to universities, a notable increase in
Chaucer's interest is immediately apparent.[29] The tradition that he
attended Oxford himself cannot be traced back earlier than the mid-

26. A. L. Gabriel, *The Educational Ideas of Vincent of Beauvais*, 2nd ed.
(Notre Dame: Univ. of Notre Dame Press, 1962), p. 28.
27. G. R. Owst, *Literature and Pulpit in Medieval England*, 2nd ed. (Oxford:
Blackwell, 1961), pp. 462-63; Beryl Smalley, *English Friars and Antiquity in
the Early Fourteenth Century* (Oxford: Blackwell, 1960), pp. 192, 332.
28. T. F. Kirby, *Annals of Winchester College* (London: H. Frowde, 1892),
p. 485.
29. On the two medieval English universities see J. H. Rashdall, *The Universities of Europe in the Middle Ages*, ed. F. M. Powicke and A. B. Emden (London: Oxford Univ. Press, 1936), vol. III; *The Victoria History of the County of
Oxford*, ed. H. E. Salter and M. D. Lobel (London: Oxford Univ. Press, 1954),
III, 1-19; [*The Victoria*] *History of the County of Cambridge and the Isle of Ely*,
ed. J. P. C. Roach (London: Oxford Univ. Press, 1959), III, 150-66; and
A. B. Cobban, *The Medieval Universities: their Development and Organization*
(London: Methuen, 1975), especially pp. 196-217. Chaucer's references to the
subject are surveyed in J. A. W. Bennett, *Chaucer at Oxford and at Cambridge*
(Oxford: Clarendon Press, 1974).

sixteenth century and is unproven,[30] but the *Treatise on the Astrolabe* shows that his son Lewis was sent to study there,[31] and the tales of the Miller and the Reeve indicate a familiarity with the topography of both Oxford and Cambridge. A third university, Orleans, appears in the *Franklin's Tale* (F 1118-1242). Academic locations, however, are less important to Chaucer than their inhabitants. Seven clerks appear in his works, in contrast with the single schoolboy: the Clerk of Oxford, Nicholas in the *Miller's Tale*, Aleyn and John in the *Reeve's Tale*, Jankyn in the *Wife of Bath's Prologue* (D 525-29), and Aurelius's brother and the magician in the tale of the Franklin.[32] As notable as Chaucer's interest in these characters is his approval of them. He treats them indulgently, and does not apply to them the criticisms which mark his handling of the Monk, the Prioress, the Pardoner, friars and summoners and even (at times) the parish clergy. His seven scholars share certain common features. Most appear to be secular clerks who have not yet committed themselves to the priesthood and are not members of religious orders. Those currently at university are mainly young, the studies of at least two of them (the Clerk and Nicholas) are related to the arts course (A 286, 3191), and four of them (the latter two and Aleyn and John) are characterized as "poor" (A 287-90, 3190, 4002). All can also be called extrovert or adventurous, since they become involved in escapades of love or of magic, and even the soberest of them, the Clerk, has journeyed to Padua (E 27). It is therefore apparent that Chaucer's image of a university scholar, in England at least, was of a young secular clerk of modest means, probably engaged in studying the arts course, and likely to have exploits of a non-academic kind. In forming this picture Chaucer responded to what was indeed the reality at Oxford and Cambridge, among whose scholars young men of this kind formed the largest group. The universities also contained bodies of monks and friars, however, who lived there in their own religious houses, and included four higher faculties (theology, canon law, civil law, and medicine) in which these regular clergy, along with the older secular clerks, were particularly active. These were areas of university life to which Chaucer did not do justice. His Monk and his friars are primarily members of their orders, rather than scholars who have had an academic education. Only once, in the *Summoner's Tale*, are we clearly told of its friar-villain that he had

---

30. A. B. Emden, *A Biographical Register of the University of Oxford to A.D. 1500* (Oxford: Clarendon Press, 1957-59), I, 396.

31. Ibid., pp. 396-97; *A Treatise on the Astrolabe*, 10.

32. There is a recent study of all these figures by J. Burke Severs, "Chaucer's Clerks," in *Chaucer and Middle English Studies in Honour of R. H. Robbins*, ed. Beryl Rowland (Kent, Ohio: Kent State Univ. Press, 1974), pp. 140-52.

gained the master's degree in "scole" or university, but it makes no difference to his characterization (D 2185-86).

Although Chaucer concentrated his attention on the secular clerks of the arts course, it would be unfair to say that he viewed them merely as stereotypes. On the contrary, he was aware that such scholars varied widely in their ways of life, and he reproduced several of the variations in his writings. He was not indeed interested in their social origins, though he sometimes indicates where they came from: Jankyn from Bath, Aleyn and John from "Strother" in the North, complete with Northern accents, and Aurelius's brother from Brittany (D 528-29, A 4014-15, F 1179). He is quite sensitive, on the other hand, to the economic differences which existed among them. He indicates most of the sources from which a scholar might draw his support. A man with no money of his own, like the Clerk, was maintained at university by his "friends," a term which could include his relatives or patrons as well as friends in the strict sense (A 299-302). Better off than the Clerk was Nicholas, who had some "rente" or income of his own besides what his friends provided, and seems to have lived in relative comfort (A 3220). A third situation, hinted at in the portrait of the Clerk, was that of a cleric who held a benefice and could support himself at university from its income (A 291-92). A fourth possibility, increasingly common as endowed colleges came to be founded at the universities after the mid-thirteenth century, was to secure a college scholarship with accommodation, board, and perhaps a stipend. Seven colleges existed for secular clerks at Oxford by 1400 and eight at Cambridge,[33] so it is not surprising that Chaucer observed and described such institutions. "Soler Halle," the Cambridge college to which Aleyn and John belong, is characterized as a large foundation, headed by a warden and employing a manciple (A 3989-4001). Of the contemporary colleges, King's Hall, Cambridge, seems to come nearest to this description, if the poet had in mind an actual place.[34]

Closely related to variations of income were differing life-styles. Chaucer's scholars, like their real counterparts, lived in a range of dwellings. Curiously, although the poet was aware of the colleges, he does not clearly evoke the most basic of all academic communities: the Oxford hall or Cambridge hostel, in which the majority of

33. Rashdall, III, 192-223, 295-312.

34. For recent discussions of the question, see A. B. Cobban, *The King's Hall within the University of Cambridge in the Later Middle Ages* (Cambridge: Cambridge Univ. Press, 1969), pp. 16-17; D. S. Brewer, "The *Reeve's Tale* and the King's Hall, Cambridge," *ChauR*, 5 (1971), 311-17; and J. A. W. Bennett, pp. 94-96.

students lived in groups.[35] No doubt these establishments interfered with his literary purpose of describing individual scholars having adventures on their own. Consequently he alludes only vaguely to Aurelius's brother sharing a study at Orleans with a bachelor of law (F 1123-28), and with Nicholas and the Orleans magician he indicates specifically that they lived on their own (A 3203-04, F 1183-88). Nicholas, who lodges in a private chamber in the house of John the Carpenter, belonged to a real-life genus of "chamber-deacons," who lived thus separately at Oxford until forbidden to do so by the university authorities in the early fifteenth century.[36] Though nominally "poure," Nicholas's enjoyment of privacy, together with his books, counters, astrolabe, and chest "ycovered with a faldyng reed," seems to indicate a scholar with resources well above the minimum (A 3187-220). Wealthier still is the magician of Orleans, who resembles the aristocratic students of Chaucer's day in occupying his own house, with a study full of books and a squire to wait upon him and to make him his supper (F 1183-88, 1207-16). Here too Chaucer reproduces variations of life-style and possessions which really existed.

We hear little more about university studies than we do about the school curriculum. Nicholas followed the arts course, and the Clerk had been long engaged with logic, which was one of its chief constituents (A 3191, 286). Chaucer alludes to some of the major works which figured in the arts course, including Boethius on music (B^2 4484), Euclid on geometry (D 2289), the *Almagesta* of Ptolemy (A 3208), and the works of Aristotle in general (A 294-95). Except for the Clerk, however, the scholars are all portrayed in their extracurricular moments, or when they have left the university. This, while it takes the attention away from their studies, enables Chaucer to express another truth about their contemporaries in the real world: their often secular way of life. As clerks in minor orders, they had not yet bound themselves fully to the rigors of ecclesiastical life, including celibacy and austere behavior, and they went on combining the secular with the ecclesiastical in an incongruous way. Thus Nicholas turns from study to melody upon his psaltery, and from singing the liturgical hymn *Angelus ad Virginem* to the erotic salutation of his landlord's wife (A 3213-16, 3271-75). So too Aleyn, saying farewell to the miller's daughter, identifies himself at once as lover and as clerk in the same few poignant lines:

35. On halls and hostels see *Victoria History of Oxford*, III, map between pp. 36-37; A. B. Emden, *An Oxford Hall in Medieval Times*, 2nd ed. (Oxford: Clarendon Press, 1968), pp. 1-59; *Victoria History of Cambridge*, III, 160-61.
36. Emden, pp. 30-31; W. A. Pantin, *Oxford Life in Oxford Archives* (Oxford: Clarendon Press, 1972), pp. 9-10.

> The day is come, I may no lenger byde;
> But everemo, wher so I go or ryde,
> I is thyn awen clerk, swa have I seel!
>
> (A 4237-39)

The sequel to this dual status was that scholars left the universities
both for ecclesiastical and for secular employment, and this too is
recognized by Chaucer. The Clerk may come in time to have a benefice or he may secure some office in the world, presumably in the
king's administration or that of a lay magnate (A 291-92). As for
Jankyn, he leaves the university early, returns to lodge at home in
Bath, and ends by marrying the Wife. Outwardly secularized, he
nevertheless retains enough of his identity as a scholar to spend the
evenings by his fireside reading a volume of antifeminist writings
in Latin (D 3327).

The literacy of Chaucer's scholars reminds us of a general rule
about the poet's characters: he has drawn a society whose higher
echelons are all literate The first estate of that society was the clergy.
Anticlerical writers in Chaucer's time, such as Langland and the
Lollards, often criticized its members for their alleged failure to
understand what they read or to improve their shortcomings by study.
Chaucer, significantly, does not level these charges. Rather, his rep-
resentatives of all the major kinds of male clergy include men of
education and learning: the Monk who has "an hundred" tragedies
in his cell, versified or in prose (B^2 3161-62); a friar, already mentioned, who has studied at university (D 2185-86); and the Parson,
who is able to preach a long analytical sermon on sin and penance
with citations from Ambrose, Augustine, and Isidore, as well as the
Bible and the Canon Law (I 75, 84, 89, 97, 931). Even a parish
clerk, in Oxford at least, can be reckoned to know enough Latin to
make "a chartre of lond or acquitaunce" (A 3327). Literate too, in
Chaucer's eyes, is the second estate of aristocracy, though its literacy
is based upon French and English rather than upon Latin as with
the clergy. Reading and writing are basic aristocratic accomplishments in Chaucer, for both sexes. Our first glimpse of the home life
of Criseyde, for example, is one in which

> two othere ladys sete, and she,
> Withinne a paved parlour, and they thre
> Herden a mayden reden hem the geste
> Of the siege of Thebes, while hem leste.
>
> (*Troilus*, II, 81-84)

It may be said against a reference like this that it portrays the aristocracy as listeners rather than readers, and consequently as people
written for rather than writers themselves. Yet their deputing of lit-

erary tasks to others was clearly a matter of convenience, not of necessity. Damian, the squire in the *Merchant's Tale*, when secrecy is required, is quite able to write a letter to his lord's wife May, just as she can compose a reply "right of hire hand" (E 1879-82, 1936-39, 1952, 1995-2004). Anelida can do the same to Arcite (*Anelida* 113-15, 208-10), and Philomena to Progne (*LGW* 2356-64), while Troilus and Criseyde correspond in holograph so often that

> The lettres ek that she of olde tyme
> Hadde hym ysent, he wolde allone rede
> An hondred sithe atwixen noon and prime. . . .
> (*Troilus*, V, 470-72)

Nor were these letters necessarily ungrammatical scrawls. When Pandarus urges Troilus to write to Criseyde in the first place, he is not worried about the prince's lack of ability for the purpose but worried lest he produce the wrong effect through overmuch care. Troilus should blot his words with his tears, rather than compose "dygneliche" or write "craftily," like a scrivener (*Troilus*, II, 1023-29).

Apart from the clergy and the aristocracy, the chief exponents of learning and literacy in Chaucer's writings, as also in his day, are the professional men and the great traders. The Sergeant of the Law is not only able to read the French and Latin of the statutes and judgments, but can himself "endite" or draw up what are presumably legal petitions and instruments, and has read in his leisure both Ovid's *Metamorphoses* and Chaucer's *Legend of Good Women* (A 323-27, B[1] 45-89). So too the Physician, though his study may be "litel on the Bible," is credited with the knowledge of fifteen Latin authors of medical treatises (A 429-38). The literacy of trade, based on the keeping of accounts, is well evoked by Chaucer in the *Shipman's Tale*, the merchant of which spends most of the morning in his counting house to reckon up his year's accounts:

> His bookes and his bagges many oon
> He leith biforn hym on his countyng-bord.
> Ful riche was his tresor and his hord,
> For which ful faste his countour-dore he shette;
> And eek he nolde that no man sholde hym lette
> Of his acountes, for the meene tyme;
> And thus he sit til it was passed pryme.
> (B[2] 1272-78)

It is only beneath the élite and among the population as a whole that Chaucer's references to literacy and learning dry up, as they probably did in reality. The Shipman boasts of "litel Latyn in my mawe" (B[1]

1190), and although the Summoner can speak a few words of that language,

> That he had lerned out of som decree —
> No wonder is, he herde it al the day;
> And eek ye knowen wel how that a jay
> Kan clepen "Watte" as wel as kan the pope.
> But whoso koude in oother thyng hym grope,
> Thanne hadde he spent al his philosophie.
>
> (A 640-45)

Chaucer's plebeian characters have plenty of first-hand experience and cunning, and second-hand knowledge of religious and secular literature, but the poet does not clearly attribute these to their own personal reading.

We have now surveyed the major kinds of educational references which occur in Chaucer's writings. To repeat what was said at the outset, they are scattered, unpredictable, and usually incidental to the works in which they occur, arising from the poet's general involvement in the world around him rather than from a specific concern with education itself. It remains to be asked whether Chaucer's interest in the subject was ever large enough to form a theme of his writings, as opposed to a mere ingredient. While the educational references are widely diffused, they come nearest to forming themes in two groups of the *Canterbury Tales*. The first consists of the three fabliaux of the Miller, the Reeve and the Cook. All take as their starting point young men who are engaged in education: three university scholars and an apprentice. In the first two tales, the scholars make use of their education to outwit the layfolk against whom they are pitted. Nicholas hoodwinks the carpenter by means of his knowledge of astrology, and it is Aleyn's acquaintance with the law that stimulates him to gain redress of his wrongs by sleeping with the miller's daughter (A 3299-300, 3513-21, 4177-87). The humorous tone of the fabliaux, however, precludes any deep or serious treatment of the educational theme. There is little to distinguish the confrontations they show between the educated and the uneducated from the clashes between other men of different occupations which characterize the Friar and the Summoner, for example, or the Cook and the Host.

It is by contrast in the "Marriage Group" that we find discussion of education both on a large scale and in a serious way. Of the five tales which the group contains, only that of the Merchant is without any educational connection. The *Wife of Bath's Prologue* features one of Chaucer's scholars, and her tale, as will be argued presently, has a major educational theme. The tales of the Clerk and the Squire are told by two of the pilgrims whose education Chaucer has stressed most, while that of the Franklin begins with educational observations and ends by featuring a scholar as "gentil" as an aristocrat. It would be difficult to argue that all these references relate to a single theme, or that education is here as important in Chaucer's mind as the problems of love and marriage. Nevertheless, this group of tales, if imperfect as a discussion of education, seems to contain Chaucer's most extended treatments of the subject. The *Wife of Bath's Tale* about the "bachelor" or young unmarried knight who had to learn what women most desire, is the clearest example of a Chaucerian story in which the education of the hero is the main theme. The tale, of course, is more than the mere solution of a riddle. It is the education of a young man, so insensitive to women that he rapes a virgin, into a husband schooled in "gentillesse" who concedes to his wife the "maistrie" of their marriage, which thereby achieves perfection. The story is not about education in the scholastic sense, but it certainly deals with training in human relations and, centering upon a young man, differs from the lifelong gathering of experience associated with the Wife herself.

The other tale in which education seems to be a major ingredient is that of the Squire. Here education is not the theme of the story, which is concerned with adventure and love, but relates to the manner in which the story is told. The very obvious and rather artificial devices of rhetoric which the Squire uses, and indeed stresses, have often puzzled commentators, who have sometimes been tempted to see them as a deliberate parody of the romance genre. This view by no means accords with the content of the story itself, the setting and incidents of which evidently interested Chaucer deeply and without parody. The disparity between manner and matter can be reconciled, however, if the telling of the tale is seen as an extension of the Squire's portrait in the *General Prologue*. Chaucer seems to be trying deliberately to convey how a tale would be told by an ardent young man of twenty, well-schooled in the techniques of rhetoric, but as yet lacking in the maturity to use them effectively. When the Franklin remarks with perception,

> As to my doom, ther is noon that is heere
> Of eloquence that shal be thy peere,
> If that thou lyve,
>
> (F 677-79)

he means that the Squire's perfection lies in the future, and has yet to be achieved. In this comment, and in the telling of the tale that preceded it, Chaucer seems to be associating education with immaturity. His feeling, apparently, is that while education is necessary and desirable in a young man, it takes him only part of the way along life's road, and requires to be improved by age and experience before it bears its best fruits. The Squire may indeed be Chaucer's model of the *young* well-educated aristocrat, but the poet's ideal of aristocratic perfection, surely, resides in that older man whom the Squire has yet to equal: the Knight himself.

14

LANGLAND AND EDUCATION

English literature, whether poetry, drama or prose, is a rewarding source for the historian of education in almost any era of the past. Single works and minor authors provide individual references of value, and the greatest writers—those who most fully describe and mirror the times in which they lived—reveal wide areas of the educational scene. Consciously or unconsciously they adopt (or reject) traditions of the past, they observe and allude to the ideas and systems of the day, and are moved to comment on and criticize them with an eye to future change. Two of the earliest writers in English whose works contain a wide and significant view of education in their times (the second half of the fourteenth century) are Chaucer and Langland. Both have an added attraction today, since their works are more accessible to a modern audience than many other sources of educational history in the middle ages, which are in Latin or French and often remain untranslated. The following article is intended to complement an earlier study of 'Chaucer and Education'[1] by drawing attention to the value of Langland's great poem, *Piers Plowman*, as a mirror of fourteenth-century childhood and education, and as an original (albeit an often idiosyncratic) commentary upon them. For those who are not familiar with Langland, it needs to be said that his poem was first written in the 1360s (the A text) and twice subsequently rewritten and enlarged in the 1370s (the B text) and the 1380s (the C text). References in this article are made to the earliest text in which the passage concerned occurs, but the serious student of the subject will do well to compare the changes which Langland sometimes made in his later additions and revisions. This can easily be done by using the two-volume edition of the poem by W. W. Skeat, which prints all three texts in parallel columns.[2]

Although Langland and Chaucer were writing at much the same period of time, their interest in education took somewhat different forms: a welcome trait since it widens the scope and value of their observations. Chaucer preferred to concentrate on the élites of society: the education of the aristocracy in great households and that of scholars at the universities. He has little to say of the more numerous (but less obtrusive) schools, of the training of apprentices or of the mere growing up of the great majority in their own homes. Langland, in contrast, says little about the élites and is more concerned with those aspects of upbringing and education which are common to everyone. Like other moralists and preachers, he singled out baptism as the chief event of childhood—an

---

1 Nicholas Orme, 'Chaucer and Education', *The Chaucer Review*, now above pp 221-42.
2 *The Vision of William concerning Piers Plowman*, edited by W. W. Skeat, (2 vols. Oxford, 1886). References in the following article are to this work, but with modernized punctuation. There is a good modern edition of the B text alone, with an introduction surveying Langland's life and work: William Langland, *The Vision of Piers Plowman: A Complete Edition of the B-Text*, edited by A. V. C. Schmidt (London, 1978).

occasion so important to him that it overshadowed birth itself, which he scarcely mentions. Whereas in our own society birth is considered the marvel and the beginning, and babies are objects of wonder irrespective of their baptism, Langland belonged to a religious tradition which saw a newly-born child as imperfect, unfreè and incapable, because it was not yet a Christian and might 'not so be saved':

> ...a child that is born of womb,
> Till it be christened in Christ's name and confirmed by the bishop,
> It is heathen as regards heaven and helpless as to the soul.
>
> (B XV 448–50)[3]

Baptism mattered in two respects. At a mere secular level it was the ceremony at which children received a name and acquired god-parents to assist their natural parents in caring for their needs (B IX 74–8). More important, as a religious sacrament, it released them from the bonds of Satan and admitted them into the freedom of Christianity. It gave them the chance of salvation but laid upon them the obligation to do God's will and observe the laws of His Church, which their godparents promised to do on their behalf as their sureties or 'borwes'. As Holy Church reminds the dreamer,

> I received thee first and taught thee thy faith.
> Thou broughtest me sureties to work my bidding
> And to love me loyally while thy life endured.
>
> (A I 74–6)[4]

It is therefore with baptism, not birth, that a child becomes, for Langland, a being to admire, because it has been granted salvation and has not yet forfeited the grant through sin. Nothing can be more chaste than 'a child that in church weepeth' (A I 154). 'Truth' sits in its heart 'in a chain of love' (B V 615–16), and over infants,

> ...the Fiend hath no power,
> For any act that they do, wicked or not.
>
> (A X 64–5)[5]

Children, then, are innocent, but they have no conscience (A X 58) and they do not yet know law (B IX 77). Left to themselves they may run astray in youth and render themselves unfit, through idleness, for proper adult life (B V 446–8); they must therefore be cared for, governed and educated. The most important agents of children's upbringing, to Langland, as to us, were their parents. Parents can be both good and bad, and children take after them by 'kind' or nature. Christ, he believes on the evidence of Matthew vii., 16–18, asserted

> That kind followeth kind, and never contradicts itself,
>
> (C XI 244)[6]

and he himself agrees:

> I find, if the father be false and a shrew,
> That the son in some measure shall have his sire's faults.

---

3 ...a barne that borne is of wombe,
   Til it be crystened in Crystes name and confermed of the bisshop,
   It is as hethene as to heueneward and helpelees to the soule.
4 Ich the vndurfong furst and thi feith the tauȝte.
   Thow brouȝtest me borwes my biddying to worche,
   And to loue me leelly while thi lyf durede.
5 ...the fend hath no miht,
   For no werk that thei worchen, wikked or elles.
6 That kynde folweth kynde and contrarieth neuere.

> Graft on an elder-tree, and if thy apple be sweet,
> Much marvel, methinks, and more of a shrew
> That bringeth forth any child unless it is the same.
>
> (B IX 145–9)[7]

Holy Church, in consequence, is good by virtue of being the daughter of God, and Lady Meed ('Illicit Reward') bad because she is the child of Falsehood and 'mannered like him, just as kind demands' (B II 27). So too in contemporary society, a maiden of good family is well-mannered (C XI 260), whereas beggars and their women beget bastards who will themselves become beggars by nature (C X 168).

The responsibilities of good parents, in Langland's view, include the maintenance, education, discipline and endowment of their children. He takes it for granted that parents will maintain their children with food, clothes and shelter, since he offers no advice to this effect or criticism that it was not done. He is very conscious, however, of the difficulties faced by the poor in bringing up their infants. When Piers confesses to Hunger what little food is available to him and his family during the shortage season of Midsummer, one of the most poignant items is the scanty fare that is all he can give to his offspring:

> a loaf of beans and bran, baked for my children,
>
> (A VII 270)[8]

food which elsewhere is associated with times of famine (B VI 184). Later, in the C text, Langland developed this theme into a heartfelt elegy on the lot of the poor and their children: particularly that of widows who toil by day for means to provide baby-food ('papelotes'), and are woken at night to rock the bed-side cradle:

> The most needy are our neighbours, if we take good heed,
> Such as prisoners in pits and poor folk in cottages,
> Charged with children and landlords' dues.
> What they may save with spinning they spend on house-rent,
> On milk and on meal to make milk-porridge
> To satisfy their children who cry out for food.
> Also they themselves suffer much hunger,
> And woe in winter-time with waking at night
> To rise to the bed-side to rock the cradle...
> This I know truly, as the world teacheth,
> What is the fate of one that hath many children,
> And hath no goods but his craft to clothe and to feed them.
>
> (C X 71–90)[9]

7 ...I fynde, if the fader be false and a shrewe,
  That somdel the sone shal haue the sires tacches.
  Impe on an ellerne, and if thine apple be swete,
  Mochel merueile me thynketh, and more of a schrewe
  That bryngeth forth any barne but if he be the same.
8 ...a lof of benes and bren i-bake for my children.
9 The most needy aren oure neighebores, and we nyme good hede,
  As prisones in puttes and poure folke in cotes,
  Charged with children and chef lordes rente.
  That thei with spynnynge may spare spenen hit in hous-hyre,
  Bothe in mylk and in mele to make with papelotes,
  To a-glotye with here gurles that greden after fode.
  Al-so hem-selue suffren muche hunger,
  And wo in winter-tyme with wakynge a nyghtes
  To ryse to the ruel to rocke the cradel...
  This ich wot witerly as the worlde techeth,
  What other by-houeth that hath meny children,
  And hath no catel bote hus crafte to clothy hem and to fede...

In his perception of these hardships and his pity for the poor, Langland accords with contemporary preachers such as John Bromyard, who also drew attention to the situation with forcefulness and compassion and called on the rich to amend it.[10] Like Bromyard, Langland seems to have seen the chief remedy in private charity. We should all give to our poor neighbours in need (C X 71). Wealthy merchants should dispose of their money to give poor children schooling, vocational training or marriage portions (A VIII 31–34), and religious communities should offer charity to children in their infirmaries (B XIII 109). The latter may mean either the maintenance of poor boys in monastic almonries or the casual feeding of children at abbey and hospital gates, both of which went on in practice during the fourteenth century.[11]

Next to the maintenance of children, we may consider their general education: the gaining of knowledge about the world around them and how to behave within it. Like most medieval writers, Langland gave little attention to education of this kind, either because he did not perceive it or took it for granted, and it receives only a few casual glances in his works. The religious upbringing of children—confirmation (usually administered soon after baptism, during infancy) and the teaching of basic prayers and devotions by parents, godparents or the clergy—is scarcely mentioned. Confirmation is simply referred to in passing (B XV 449), learning the paternoster emerges only in that slothful parishioners are accused of not learning it (B V 401), and religious devotions by children are absent completely. Fathers, however, are warned to guard their offspring from wantonness when they are young, and should be blamed if they fail to do so (A X 66–7). Langland, like Chaucer, also identifies parents as the transmitters of oral wisdom to their children, in the form of traditional proverbs:[12]

> I have learned how ordinary men have taught their children:
> That the stone that men tread on seldom groweth moss.
>
> (A X 100–1)[13]
>
> My father said so to me, and so did my mother,
> That the dearer the child, the more it needs teaching.
>
> (B V 37–8)[14]

and, metamorphosed into animal fable,

> I heard my father say, seven years ago,
> When the cat is a kitten the court is most miserable.
>
> (B Prol. 189–90)[15]

Elsewhere Langland makes a brief complimentary reference to well-mannered children (C XI 260), and he emphasizes the importance of obedience to one's parents, in accordance with the Fourth Commandment (A VI 57).

In order that children be steered from vice towards virtue, Langland followed Robert Mannyng, the English moralist of the early fourteenth century, in the advocacy of stern discipline. Mannyng had quoted the well-worn proverb of Solomon: 'he that spareth the rod hateth his son', adding only the *caveat actor* that the child's bones should not be broken in the process, and he had cited the fate of the high priest Eli and

---

10 G. R. Owst, *Literature and Pulpit in Medieval England* (2nd ed. Oxford, 1961), 299–303, 311, 327.
11 Nicholas Orme, *English Schools in the Middle Ages* (London, 1973), 179–80, 243–5.
12 *The Chaucer Review*, 16 (1981), 40–1.
13 I haue lerned how lewede men han lered heore children,
   That selden moseth the marbelston that men ofte treden.
14 My syre seyde so to me and so did my dame,
   That the leuere childe the more lore bihoueth.
15 ...I herde my sire seyn, is seuene ȝere ypassed,
   There the catte is a kitoun the courte is ful elyng.

his sons as the punishment of an indulgent father and his two spoilt children.[16] Langland too reproduces the Solomon proverb (B V 39–41) and the story of Eli (C I 109–10). He favoured corporal punishment throughout the family, advising husbands to cut staves to deal with idle or scolding wives (B V 28–33), and he has four clear references to the beating of children (A IV 103, A V 32–3, B V 174, A VII 72), notably in the B version of Reason's sermon to the English people:

> And then he charged chapmen to chasten their children:
> Let your profits not spoil them while they are young,
> Nor for any power of the pestilence please them out of reason.
> My father said so to me, and so did my mother,
> That the dearer the child, the more it needs teaching,
> And Solomon, who wrote the Book of Wisdom, said the same:
> *Qui parcit virge, odit filium*
> The English of this Latin is, whoever will know it,
> 'He who spares the switch spoils his children'.
>
> (B V 34–41)[17]

At first sight this appears to be the commonplace medieval view of a commonplace family practice. The reality was undoubtedly more complicated. First, the proponents of corporal punishment were complemented by other fourteenth-century writers— Bromyard, Robert Holcote and Chaucer himself—who approached the subject in a liberal spirit and recommended beating to be used either sparingly or not at all.[18] Second, the insistence of Langland on *discipline*, when he took so much else for granted about children's upbringing, must have arisen from a conviction that, in reality, parents were not correcting their offspring as they should. Society too may have been more liberal (or negligent) than we often believe. Mannyng had identified the rich as particularly indulgent to their children,[19] and Langland evidently had the wealthy in mind as well by his mention of 'chapmen' or merchants. His reference to the pestilence suggests another factor: that fear of the plague made parents more protective of their offspring and less willing to discipline them. Similar complaints were to be made in the early sixteenth century, when Edmund Dudley repeated the charge against merchants and Sir Thomas Elyot made parallel observations about the plague.[20] Clearly, child-beating was not universally practised; if it had been, some educationists would not have felt the need to insist upon it so emphatically.

The last dimension of education common to all medieval families was the preparation of children for adult careers: work for boys, housewifely duties for girls, and marriage in both cases. As with their training in knowledge and behaviour, this

---

16 *Robert of Brunne's 'Handlyng Synne'*, edited by F. J. Furnivall (London, Early English Text Society [hereafter EETS], original series, 119 (1901), 161–6 (lines 4849–5044)), based on Proverbs, xiii, 24, and I Samuel, ii–iv.
17 And thanne he charged chapmen to chasten her childeren:
Late no wynnynge hem forweny whil thei be ʒonge,
Ne for no pousté of pestilence plese hem nouʒte out of resoun.
My syre seyde so to me and so did my dame,
That the leuere childe the more lore bihoueth,
And Salamon seide the same that Sapience made:
Qui parcit virge, odit filium.
The Englich of this latyn is, who-so wil it knowe,
Who-so spareth the sprynge spilleth his children.
18 *The Chaucer Review*, 16 (1981), 49–50.
19 *Handlyng Synne*, 162 (lines 4904–4918).
20 Edmund Dudley, *The Tree of the Commonwealth*, edited by D. M, Brodie (Cambridge, 1948), 68; Sir Thomas Elyot, *The Governor* (London, 1531), book I chapter 13: 'theyr parentes wyll nat aduenture to send them farre out of theyr propre countrayes, partely for feare of dethe'.

process elicited as little attention from Langland as it did from Chaucer, and probably for the same reason: that it was not readily distinguishable from life in general. Langland seems to believe that the male children of bondmen and beggars should be put to labour, probably reflecting contemporary prejudices that they should continue in the work of their fathers and not be enabled to rise above their station by being ordained as clergy or apprenticed in towns (C VI 61–7). He specifically exhorts housewives to teach their daughters to spin and to make cloth, and approves the making of textiles and garments by women at all levels of society (B VI 9–16). He alludes once to the learning of duties as a servant in a household, in his image of the lordly monk who,

> ...unless his servant kneels, when bringing his cup,
> He scowls at him and asks him who taught him courtesy,

(B X 310–11)[21]

but he has most to say about apprenticeship, of which he has a rather jaundiced view. True, he approves of merchants who assist poor boys to be trained in a craft (A VIII 34) but all too often, he seems to feel, apprentices are trained in the wicked practices of their masters and not the good ones. Merchants make Guile their apprentice 'to serve the people' (A II 190), and the character Avarice receives his first lesson in dishonesty as apprentice to Simon atte Noke, with whom he learns to tell lies and weigh falsely. He studies the *Donet* or grammar of trade among the drapers, who teach him to stretch the cloth, and spends the rest of his youth among Lombards and Jews practising how to weigh coins and clip the heaviest (A V 115–128, B V 241–3). Langland's principal references to apprenticeship are therefore unfavourable, the blame attaching primarily to the master rather than (as in Chaucer's 'Cook's Tale') the apprentice himself.[22] Finally, Langland considers and criticizes the marriages which contemporary parents arrange for their children,

> For some, as I see now, truly to tell,
> For covetousness of wealth are wedded unnaturally ...
> It is an unseemly union by Christ, I think,
> To give a young wench to an old feeble man,
> Or to wed a widow for wealth of her goods
> Who shall never carry a child, except in her arms.

(B IX 154–5, 160–4)[23]

On the contrary, he asserts, young virgins of either sex should be matched together, the prohibited degrees of kinship should be respected, and weddings should not be arranged merely on economic grounds out of covetousness of the wealth to be won thereby (A X 172–95).

The home education of medieval children reached its greatest sophistication in the households of the aristocracy. By the fourteenth century there were treatises advising how noble children should be reared and educated, and specialized instructors (tutors

---

21　...but if his knaue knele that shal his cuppe brynge,
　　　He loureth on hym and axeth hym who tauȝte hym curteisye.
22　*The Works of Geoffrey Chaucer*, edited by F. N. Robinson (2nd ed. Boston and London, 1957), 61 (A 4403–13).
23　For some, as I se now, soth for to telle,
　　　For coueitise of catel vndkyndeliche ben wedded ...
　　　It is an oncomely couple bi Cryst, as me thinketh,
　　　To ȝyuen a ȝonge wenche to an olde feble,
　　　Or wedden any widwe for welth of hir goodis,
　　　That neuere shal barne bere but if it be in armes.

and mistresses) had developed to supplement the efforts of the parents.[24] Langland does not describe the educational system by which the aristocracy was trained, but he does allude to some of the values and accomplishments which the system was meant to instill. He has a clear concept of 'courtesy': the code of good behaviour learnt and practised by the aristocracy at court. It is divine in principle, since Christ Himself can be thought of as courteous (B XII 79, B XVII 241), and it is a standard to which the whole nobility should conform:

> It is becoming for a knight to be courteous and polite.
>
> (C IX 47)[25]

Langland portrays good kings and good knights as having the quality (e.g., A III 99, A VII 150), but he sees many noblemen in practice falling short in this respect. That all 'clerks and knights be courteous of their mouths' remains to be achieved (A IV 105). He does not mention the literary education of the aristocracy, but he draws the image of a lord who can write well, if there are pen and parchment to do so (B IX 38–40), and he says he has personally witnessed lords discussing theology over meals and voicing their disbelief in original sin:

> I have heard great men eating at table
> Talking of Christ and his powers, as if they were clerks,
> And ascribing faults to the Father that made us all...
> 'Why should we that live now, for Adam's deeds,
> Rot and be destroyed? reason won't have it'
>
> (B X 101–14)[26]

—speculations of which he strongly disapproves. This picture accords closely with documentary evidence that the contemporary aristocracy included many well-schooled men and women, experienced in religious devotions and used to reading religious books, including the Bible in French. When we consider that a few of them, the famous Lollard Knights, even absorbed the heresies of Wycliffe, there is no reason to doubt that episodes of debate and scepticism took place, along the lines that Langland describes.[27]

While the home of one's parents or the household of one's master was the scene of most people's educations in the middle ages, there were also the specialized institutions of schools and universities for the minority of boys and young men who required to be trained in the difficult art of letters. These institutions, being separate from everyday life, attracted notice from contemporaries in ways that the home did not, and to a disproportionate extent. This is the case in Langland's writings too. When in the C text he was moved to reveal some of his autobiography, he tells us nothing of his birth or

---

24 On this subject, see *The Chaucer Review*, 16 (1981), 41–7, and Nicholas Orme, 'The Education of the Courtier', *English Court Culture in the Later Middle Ages*, edited by J. Sherborne (London, 1982), now above pp 154–7, 226–9.

25 Hit by-cometh to a knyght to be curteys and hende.

26 I haue yherde hiegh men etyng atte table
   Carpen as thei clerkes were of Cryste and of his miȝtes,
   And leyden fautes vppon the fader that fourmed vs alle...
   'Whi shulde we that now ben, for the werkes of Adam,
   Roten and to-rende? resoun wolde it neuere.'

27 K. B. McFarlane, *Lancastrian Kings and Lollard Knights* (Oxford, 1972), especially 185, 199–204.

family but he singles out his schooling with pride as something which made him a clerk and introduced him to religious knowledge:

> When I was young, quoth I, many years ago,
> My father and my friends supported me at school
> Till I knew assuredly what holy writ meant.
>
> (C VI 35–7)[28]

It is worth emphasizing what an unusual record this is. One or two twelfth-century writers, such as Gerald of Wales, had previously recalled their childhoods and schooling, but the habit had not become widespread and reminiscences of past youth are rare in thirteenth- and fourteenth-century literature. Langland's account, brief though it is, stands out as an exception. Even such early fifteenth-century writers who exhibit tendencies twards autobiography start with student days, in the case of Adam or Usk, and marriage in that of Margery Kempe,[29] so that we have to wait until the 1480s for parallel reminiscences of schooling by William Caxton and Thomas Rotherham.[30] Langland moreover refers to several features of contemporary schools which establish their place in his consciousness. A reference to Guile as 'master' and 'a flatterer for his usher' (C XVIII 111–12) recalls the chief functionary of a medieval school and his deputy. Schoolmasters live by taking reward for their services (A III- 215), and this appears to be a lawful gain in Langland's eyes (compare A III 240–3). Children are maintained at school, as above, by their fathers or 'friends' (meaning patrons), and merchants are particularly encouraged to give their alms to scholars, as they are to others of the deserving poor (A VIII 34).

The schoolmaster rules through fear:

> ...Dread is such a master
> That he makes men meek and mild of their speech
> And all kinds of scholars to learn in schools.
>
> (A X 82–4)[31]

His instrument of power is the rod, a teaching aid as old as the curriculum itself. 'Grammar for children', says Dame Study,

> ...I began to write first,
> And beat them with a rod unless they would learn,
>
> (A XI 131–2)[32]

and Langland evidently approves of this method which harmonizes with the discipline he recommends for the home. Schooling is associated in his mind with the ecclesiastical sphere[33] and the study of letters confers clerical status, for which (says Langland

28 Whanne ich ȝong was, quath ich, meny ȝer hennes,
   My fader and my frendes founden me to scole,
   Tyl ich wiste wyterliche what holy wryt menede.
29 *Chronicon Adae de Usk, A.D. 1377–1421,* edited by E. M. Thomspson (2nd ed. London, 1904), 6, 22, 145, 168; *The Book of Margery Kempe,* edited by S. B. Meech and H. E. Allen, (EETS, original series, 212 (1940)), I, 6.
30 On Caxton, see *The Prologues and Epilogues of William Caxton,* edited by W. J. B. Crotch (EETS, original series, 176 (1928)), 96, and on Rotherham, see A. F. Leach, *Early Yorkshire Schools,* Yorkshire Archaeological Society, 32 (1903), II, 109–10, 150, or his *Educational Charters and Documents, 598–1909* (Cambridge, 1911), 422–5.
31 ...Drede is such a mayster
   That he maketh men meoke and mylde of heore speche,
   And alle kunne scolers in scoles forte lerne.
32 ...I gon furste to write,
   And beot hem with a baleys but ȝif they wolde lernen.
33 Discussed below.

sardonically) a boy may be grateful if he is ever threatened with the gallows. He may then claim 'benefit of clergy' and establish his claim by reading a verse from the psalter:

> Well may the child bless whoever set him to books,
> Since living by letters saved him, life and soul.
> *Dominus pars hereditatis mee* is a merry verse,
> That has taken from Tyburn twenty strong thieves.
>
> (Bb XII 187–91)[34]

The school curriculum is centred on Latin. It begins with learning to read the (Latin) abc (A VIII 119) and continues with Latin grammar, taught by means of an elementary textbook or *Donet* (A V 123) in question-and-answer form on the model of Donatus's *Ars Minor*. Emphasis is placed on the learning and understanding of grammatical rules and concepts (C IV 335–409). More advanced studies include *dictamen* (the writing of formal letters), Latin verse composition and the reading and translation of Latin poets (B XV 365–9). In practice several of the latter were read in schools, but Langland concentrates his attention on the most famous of them: *The Distichs of Cato*, which evidently much impressed him during his own school days. He makes some twelve allusions to *Cato*,[35] including several direct quotations from the poem, and regards it as the sin of sloth for a parish priest to be so unlearned that he 'cannot construe Cato, nor read like a clerk' (C VIII 34).

Besides these passing allusions, Langland made two deliberate observations on the school education of his day. The first is in the well-known passage, first found in the B text, in which he expressed his admiration for the worlds of the cloister and the school: the one for its peace and quiet, and the other for its learning and comradeship:

> For if heaven be on this earth and ease to any soul,
> It is in cloister or in school, I find on many grounds;
> For in cloister cometh no man to chide or to fight,
> But all is obedience there and books to read and to learn.
> In school there is scorn unless a clerk will learn,
> And great love and liking, for each of them loveth the others.
>
> (B X 300–5)[36]

'School' in the fourteenth century can signify either a school or a university. Langland more often uses it to mean the former, and his apparent lack of interest in universities as places, which we shall shortly encounter, makes school the likelier meaning in this passage. His love for the place was accompanied, however, as such love often is, by a conviction that the schoolboys of his maturity were not achieving the standards of his

---

34 Wel may the barne blisse that hym to boke sette,
   That lyuinge after letterure saued hym lyf and soule.
   Dominus pars hereditatis mee is a meri verset,
   That has take fro Tybourne twenti stronge theues.
35 E.g. A IV 17; C VIII 34; B VI 316; B VII 73; A VIII 135; A X 95; A XI 45; B X 189, 338; B XI 394; B XII 21; B XIX 291.
36 For if heuene be on this erthe and ese to any soule,
   It is in cloistere or in scole, be many skilles I fynde;
   For in cloistre cometh no man to chide ne to fiʒte,
   But alle is buxomnesse there and bokes to rede and to lerne.
   In scole there is scorne but if a clerke wil lerne,
   And grete loue and lykynge, for eche of hem loueth other.

youth. In a general lament on the decline of learning, also first made in the B text, he asserts that

> Grammar, the basis of all things, deceives children nowadays,
> For none of these new clerks, whoever will take heed,
> Can versify fairly or write formal letters;
> Not one in a hundred can construe an author,
> Or read a letter in any language but Latin or English.
>
>   (B XV 365–9)[37]

If Langland was born in the early 1330s (B XI 46, B XII 3), he would have had his schooling in the 1340s, just before the Black Death. At that time, according to Ranulf Higden writing in about 1340 and to John Trevisa in 1385, French, not English, was the second language of the grammar schools and was used by boys when they were required to translate anything into or out of Latin.[38] Trevisa adds that the Oxford schoolmaster, John Cornwall, began the use of English in his school instead of French at about the time of the Black Death, and that by the 1380s the practice was so general that schoolboys knew no more French than their left heels! This would explain Langland's scorn at grammarians who only knew Latin and English, if he himself came of a generation which had been expected to know French as well.

Paradoxically, however, Langland had become influenced by the rise of English in the schools by the time that he wrote the C text in the 1380s or 90s. This is the case in the long passage in Passus IV in which the author discusses 'mede' and 'mercede'—improper and proper reward—by means of a grammatical analogy involving the use of grammatical terms in English: 'react' and 'indirect', 'adiectif' and 'substantif' and so on.[39] The adoption of English as the second langauge of the grammar schools during the second half of the fourteenth century meant that schoolmasters had to develop a terminology of grammar in the new language and to coin and establish English words for the purpose. The first recorded usage of English in a post-Conquest grammatical textbook occurs, as Trevisa asserts, in a work of John Cornwall, the *Speculum Grammaticale* of 1346,[40] and Langland's Passus IV discussion is one of the next earliest examples. In it he uses about a dozen grammatical terms in English: 'gendre', 'numbre', 'case' and 'antecedent', besides the examples already mentioned, at a time when it was still so novel to do so that the king in the poem, to whom the terms are addressed, declares that 'English was it never' and has to have them explained to him. In using these words Langland reflected the change in schools which elsewhere he deplored. There is, perhaps, some evidence in support of his view that educational standards were declining. Since the Black Death it had become difficult to find graduate MAs to teach

---

37 Gramer, the grounde of al, bigyleth now children,
   For is none of this newe clerkes, who so nymeth hede,
   That can versifye faire ne formalich enditen,
   Ne nou3t on amonge an hundreth that an auctour can construe,
   Ne rede a lettre in any langage but in Latyn or in Englissh.

38 K. Sisam, *Fourteenth Century Verse and Prose* (Oxford, 1955), 148–9.

39 There are discussions of the passage by Margaret Amassian and J. Sadowsky, 'Mede and Mercede: a Study of the Grammatical Metaphor in "Piers Plowman" C:IV:335–409', *Neuphilogische Mitteilungen*, 72 (1971), 457–76, and by Janet Coleman, *Piers Plowman and the Moderni* (Rome, 1981), 90–6. For some other instances of grammatical metaphor in medieval literature, see J. A. Yunck, *The Lineage of Lady Meed* (University of Notre Dame Publications in Medieval Studies, 17 (Notre Dame, 1963)), 95, 120.

40 R. W. Hunt, 'Oxford Grammar Masters in the Middle Ages', *Oxford Studies Presented to Daniel Callus* (Oxford Historical Society, new series, 16, 1964), 168, 174—5. Cornwall's passage on the moods of the verb is printed by Brother Bonaventure, 'The Teaching of Latin in Later Medieval England', *Mediaeval Studies*, 23 (1961), 17.

even in leading English schools, and a more easily obtained degree of Master of Grammar was being developed for schoolmasters at Cambridge and at Oxford.[41] The teaching of grammar in the schools of Oxford in the late fourteenth century appears to have become more simple and basic,[42] and in the diocese of Exeter Bishop Grandisson castigated local schoolmasters in 1357 for the poor understanding of Latin achieved by their pupils.[43] Against all this it must be noted that John Trevisa considered the decline of French to have improved the work of the schools, since pupils were now learning grammar 'in less time than children were wont to do'.[44] The level of educational standards is always a difficult one to assess, and Langland's remarks may simply reflect the prejudices of a middle-aged man.

The trace of criticism in the poet's portrayal of schools becomes more pronounced when he turns to the higher studies of the universities. Unlike Chaucer, with his appreciative descriptions of university scholars and Oxford and Cambridge locations, Langland displays no interest in the universities as places or in their inhabitants. He does not mention Cambridge and Oxford by name, and says so little about their organization that it seems unlikely that he studied at either of them. This is not to deny that he was well acquainted with scholastic learning and techniques, acquired either through intercourse with university scholars or through private reading. As Dr Janet Coleman has demonstrated most recently, he was in touch with and influenced by the 'modern' theologians and philosophers of the fourteenth century, and reflects their ideas in his work.[45] He mentions most of the seven liberal arts on which the university arts course was based, and imagines himself disputing with the friars according to scholastic method—though the latter was not confined to universities but also learnt in schools (A IX 16–21). He certainly shared in the world of university learning, therefore, but whenever he stands back from it and tries to evaluate it, a strong vein of pessimism is apparent in his mind. Thus, though he concedes that few authors have bettered Aristotle as teachers, he observes that the Church considers Aristotle to be among the damned (like Solomon), and concludes,

> ...if I shall labour by their works to win myself heaven,
> And for their works and their learning go to hell,
> Then I would labour unwisely with all the knowledge that I learn.

(A XI 268–70)[46]

Similar contrasts of an unfavourable kind, between academic learning on the one hand and Christian faith and love on the other, are made on several occasions when Langland is moved to discuss the higher studies. 'Any science under the sun', he believes,

> ...the seven arts and all,
> Unless they are learnt for Our Lord's love, all the time is lost.

(B XI 166–7)[47]

---

41 Orme, *English Schools in the Middle Ages*, 151–3.
42 *Oxford Studies Presented to Daniel Callus*, 185–7.
43 *The Register of John de Grandisson, Bishop of Exeter*, edited by F. C. Hingeston-Randolph, (London and Exeter, 1897), II, 1192–3.
44 Sisam, *Fourteenth Century Verse and Prose*, 149.
45 Janet Coleman, *Piers Plowman and the Moderni*, 11–170, *passim*.
46 ...ʒif I shal werke be here werkis to wynne me heuene,
And for here werkis and for here wyt wende to pyne,
Thanne wrouʒte I vnwisly with alle the wyt that I lere.
47 ...the seuene artz and alle,
But if thei ben lerned for owre lordes loue, loste is alle the tyme.

Logic and law possess no virtue unless they accompanied by faith:

> Of logic or law in the lessons for saints' days,
> Little allowance is made unless faith helps them,
> For it is long before logic explains these lessons,
> And the law is loth to be loving unless it lacks money.
>
> (B XI 214–17)[48]

Astronomy, geometry and geomancy are vitiated by the use of them made for sorcery:

> ...astronomy is a hard thing and evil to know,
> Geometry and geomancy are guileful of speech.
> Whoever works with these three will be late in thriving,
> For sorcery is the chief book that belongs to those sciences.
>
> (A XI 152–5)[49]

Even theology is but 'a common thing' except in so far as it enshrines God's love and teaches men to that end:

> Theology hath vexed me ten score times,
> For the more I muse on it the mistier it seems,
> And the deeper I divine it the darker I think it.
> It is truly no science to argue subtly about;
> If it were not for the Love that lies in it, it would be an ordinary thing,
> But because it thinks most highly of Love, I believe in it the better.
>
> (A XI 136–41)[50]

His own knowledge of scholastic learning was thus accompanied by nagging doubts of its value by the highest Christian standards.

To a modern historian one of the most flourishing areas of higher education in the later middle ages was that of the friars, with their system of schools for training their members and their strong presence in the faculties of theology at Oxford and Cambridge. In the eyes of Langland, however, who waged a constant untiring vendetta against the four mendicant orders, their educational activity was simply of a piece with all their other detestable works. Making no recognition of their scholarly and pastoral achievements, he identified their motive in studying as envy of the 'possessioners'—the monastic and secular clergy—which led them

> ...to go to school
> And learn logic and law and also contemplation,
> And preach to men on Plato, and prove it by Seneca,
> That all things under heaven ought to be shared in common.
>
> (B XX 271–4, cf., 292–3)[51]

48 Of logyke ne of lawe in *Legenda Sanctorum*
  Is litel allowaunce made but if bileue hem helpe,
  For it is ouerlonge ar logyke any lessoun assoille,
  And lawe is loth to louye but if he lacche syluer.
49 ...astronomye is hard thing and vuel to knowe,
  Gemetrie and gemensye is gynful of speche;
  That worcheth with theose threo thriueth he late,
  For sorcerye is the souereyn bok that to that science longith.
50 Teologye hath teoned me ten score tymes,
  For the more I muse theron the mistloker hit semeth,
  And the deppore I diuinede the derkere me thouȝte.
  Hit is no science forsothe to sotilen ther-inne,
  Neore the loue that lyhth therinne a lewed thing hit weore.
  Bote for hit lat best bi Loue, I leeue hit the betere.
51 ...to go to scole
  And lerne logyk and lawe and eke contemplacioun,
  And preche men of Plato and preue it by Seneca
  That alle thinges vnder heuene ouȝte to ben in comune.

'Leave logic!', he exhorts them, on one of the rare occasions when he allows that they may still be reformed; let them remember the example of their founders, who gave up worldly and scholastic status in the pursuit of holiness:

> For love they left lordship, both of land and in school,
> Friar Francis and Dominic, for love to be holy.

(B XX 249–51)[52]

His sceptical view of academic learning was completed, also in the B text, by the same assertion of general decline that he made with respect to the learning of the grammar schools. Not only do astronomers, who were once able to predict the future, now find their art to fail them (B XV 352–3, 363–4), but even graduates of canon law and theology, who ought to be able to answer any questions, would be found to fail in their knowledge of philosophy if they were properly examined in academic disputation:

> Doctors of canon law and masters of divinity,
> That should study and know all kinds of learning
> And answer arguments on any subject—
> I dare not say it for shame: if such men were questioned,
> They would fail in their philosophy and in physic too.

(B XV 373–7)[53]

In all he sketches a melancholy picture, but one so individual and idiosyncratic that it is unnecessary to refute it here with all that emerges from the real records of university activity in his day.

There remains to be mentioned a final group of Langland's observations on contemporary education: those concerned with the uses of school and university learning and the careers into which their students went. Superficially, Langland reflected the tradition that the chief purpose of studying Latin was the reading of religious texts, and clerical life the destination of those who did so. When he mentions 'literature' ('lettrure') he generally implies religious writings not secular ones, much as we do when we talk about 'scripture' today. By 'the lettered' he usually means the clergy, and correspondingly his word for 'learning' or 'learned people' is often 'clergye'. Nominally religion and literature were still almost synonymous. At the same time he was perfectly aware of the development so well described and interpreted by Dr Michael Clanchy in his book *From Memory to Written Record*: the proliferation of secular documents and literate secular functionaries, which had begun in England during the twelfth and thirteenth centuries.[54] Indeed, impelled by the requirements of his alliterative form, he could hardly afford to ignore the large vocabulary of documentation which existed by his time: bille, breef, breuet, bulle, chartre, dede, feffement, lettre, parchemyn, pardoun, patente, registre, supersedeas, testament and writ—all of which he uses. He was familiar with the forms of some of these instruments,

52 For loue laft thei lordship, both londe and scole,
   Frere Fraunceys and Dominyk, for loue to ben holy.
53 Doctoures of decres and of diuinite maistres,
   That shulde konne and knowe alkynnes clergye,
   And answere to argumentz and also to a *quodlibet*,
   (I dar nou3t seggen it for shame), if suche weren apposed,
   Thei shulde faillen in her philosofye and in physyke bothe.
54 M. T. Clanchy, *From Memory to Written Record: England*, 1066–1307 (London, 1979), especially chapter 2.

as well as with the names. A badly written charter, he believes, deserves to be challenged at law and its maker to be scorned for his faults:

> A charter is challengeable before a chief justice;
> If false Latin is in it the law finds fault with it,
> Or if insertions are made or portions omitted;
> The man who writes such a charter is held to be a fool.
>
> (B XI 269–9)[55]

Indeed, he adopts documentary forms as his framework at certain points of his poem. The feoffment of property preceding the marriage of Meed and Falsehood (A II 60–82), the will dictated by Piers before he sets out on his pilgrimage (A VII 78–97), and the indulgence of Truth to Piers and his helpers (A VIII 3–95), each demonstrates a knowledge of the structure of its real equivalent.

He notices, too, the wide range of people, both lettered and unlettered, who are involved in drawing up these documents, conveying and receiving them. The clergy themselves, led by dignitaries and graduates who should know better in his view, are staffing the king's civil service and doing his secular business to the neglect of their duties as clerics:

> Bishops and bachelors, masters and doctors,
> That have charge under Christ and tonsures as tokens
> And signs that they should confess their parishioners,
> Preach and pray for them and feed the poor—
> They lie in London, in Lent and at other times.
> Some serve the king and count his money,
> Demand his debts in exchequer and chancery,
> Of wards and ward-meetings, waifs and strays.
>
> (B Prol. 87–94)[56]

Others are similarly employed and equally negligent in the administrations of the aristocracy:

> And some serve lords and ladies as servants,
> And sit and give judgements in the place of stewards.
> Their masses and their mattins and many of their hours
> Are said undevoutly; it is to be dreaded
> Lest Christ at his Judgement accurse many of them.
>
> (B Prol.95–9)[57]

He rightly sees great households as assemblies of literate people, what with the lord himself, already mentioned as able to write his own letters (B IX 38–40), the auditor of his reeves' accounts and the clerk who records the audit in the form of the reeve rolls

55 A chartre is chalengeable byfor a chief justice;
   If false Latyne be in the lettre the lawe it inpugneth,
   Or peynted parenterlinarie or parceles ouer-skipped;
   The gome that gloseth so chartres for a goky is holden.
56 Bischopes and bachelers, bothe maistres and doctours,
   That han cure vnder criste and crounyng in tokne
   And signe that thei sholden shryuen here paroschienes,
   Prechen and prey for hem and the pore fede—
   Liggen in London, in lenten an elles.
   Some seruen the kyng and his siluer tellen,
   In cheker and in chancerye chalengen his dettes
   Of wardes and wardmotes, weyues and streyues.
57 And some seruen as seruantz lordes and ladyes,
   And in stede of stuwardes sytten and demen.
   Here messe and here matynes and many of here oures
   Arn don vndevoutlych; drede is at the laste
   Lest crist in consistorie acorse ful manye.

(C XXII 461–6). A friar may obtain letters of recommendation from a lord to hold a parochial benefice, and the bishop (or rather his clerks) will give him a 'brief' or licence to do so (B XX 322–5). Pardoners, too, have bishops' letters with them as they ply their business with written pardons, bulls and patents (A Prol. 65–71, B V 648–9). The bishop and the archdeacon have their church courts, staffed by registrars (B II 173) and sending out letters of *supersedeas* in boxes to litigants by the hands of their summoners (C X 263). There are notaries attesting ecclesiastical documents (B XX 269–70), scriveners transcribing Bibles (C XII 97), and friars giving letters of confraternity to pious laymen (A VIII 178–9). There is the sheriff's clerk crying in Latin the words of a writ of *capias* (C V 164–5), the king's messenger riding swiftly with his letters even across the wheat (C XIV 33–64), and the merchant proceeding more slowly with his paper list of debts (*ibid.*). Regarding the lowest orders Langland confirms the evidence of Dr Clanchy concerning the thirteenth century: that even serfs encountered documents and used them, notwithstanding their illiteracy.[58] A churl may not make a charter without the assent of his lord (B XI 122), but a poor man can purchase an indulgence in the written form of a pardon (A VIII 90–3) and have his will drawn up (B VI 87)—perhaps even write it himself, in the wording adopted by some manuscripts of the poem (A VII 78).

What view did Langland take of all this literary activity? Like his opinion of academic learning, it was in part a sceptical one. In principle he respected both letters and literacy. Christ could write and the Holy Spirit inspires the writings of men (B XII 80, 103–4). 'Letterure' leads ordinary men to reason, and a literate clergy is necessary to guide the laity to Christianity and to salvation:

> Therefore, never find fault with logic, law or its customs,
> Or argue against clerks, I counsel thee for ever.

(B XII 99–100)[59]

In practice, however, he sees the literate frequently fall short of the illiterate in godliness. The priest who offers to read Piers's indulgence for him and who patronizes Piers for his knowledge of scripture—'thou art lettered, a little' (A VIII 90–1, B VII 130–1)—is castigated as a 'lewd lorel', an ignorant fellow, and contrasted with the humble ploughman who has been taught a superior knowledge by Abstinence and Conscience (B VII 132–7). Elsewhere, the clergy in the king's administration are abusing their status, the scriveners who copy the Bible may do so falsely, friars and pardoners use episcopal letters to cloak and justify their misdeeds, and the marriage feoffment is a contract between wicked people. This is a different emphasis from that of Chaucer, whose criticisms of the clergy avoid the topic of their literacy and learning.[60]

For those of us who trace the growth of schools, literacy and documentation in the middle ages it is natural to regard these things as good, because they lead towards the literate society which is considered to be civilized today. In the late fourteenth century not everybody viewed the situation in this way. The Peasants' Revolt of 1381 saw a widespread destruction of legal and financial records. The chronicler of St Albans alleges that the rebels forced schoolmasters to swear to give up teaching children, and at

---

58 Clanchy, *From Memory to Written Record*, 33–6, 182–97.
59 For-thi lakke thow neuere logyke, lawe ne his custumes,
   Ne countreplede clerkes, I conseille the for eure.
60 *The Chaucer Review*, 16 (1981), 53; now above p 238.

least one old woman at Cambridge thought and rejoiced, as she saw the bonfires of documents, that the learning of the clerks was also going up in smoke. Even the aristocracy in 1391 petitioned in parliament that villeins be prevented from sending their children to school to advance them by 'clergy' or learning.[61] Langland, too, stands out as a critic of education and literacy, albeit from higher and Christian motives.[62] It is salutary for us to remember his view that ordinary illiterate laymen, under clerical instruction, could achieve greater godliness and nobility by faith and good deeds than many of those who had the benefit of schooling and enjoyed the status of literacy.

---

61 For these references, see Orme, *English Schools in the Middle Ages*, 192–3.
62 In the tradition of I Corinthians, i.

15

ALEXANDER BARCLAY, TUDOR EDUCATIONIST

Few sixteenth-century Englishmen had such a varied career as Alexander Barclay. By origin a Scot, he spent most of his life in England but also travelled widely on the continent. By career, he was in turn a secular priest in a collegiate church, a monk, a friar, and finally (after the dissolution of the friaries), a secular priest again, this time a parish clergyman. He is best known today as a poet and translator, but he was also an educationist. He held at least two teaching posts, one in a song and one in a grammar school, and he wrote educational works. Yet much of his life remains obscure.[1] Even some of his contemporaries were doubtful whether he was born a Scot or an Englishman (the former is more likely), and the date of his birth is uncertain. It is usually given as 1475-6 on the grounds that he speaks in his *Eclogues* of being 38, parts of which were written as early as 1513-14. But we do not know when the statement of his age was written, and it may be better to postpone his birth nearer to 1484. This is the latest possible date, since Barclay had to be aged 24 in order to be ordained priest in 1508. He does not appear in records before his ordination, and all that we can gather of his previous life is that he journeyed in France and Italy. If he studied, he did not gain a university degree higher than that of BA. Only one reference before the 1530s calls him 'Master Barclay', and the rest describe him as if he were below the rank of MA.[2] The span of his life from 18 to 24 is enough to accommodate what we can infer of his early career, and to extend it by another eight years seems too long. On being ordained, as we shall see, Barclay took up a comparatively junior post, which also points towards a younger man.

The register of Hugh Oldham, bishop of Exeter, shows that Barclay was ordained subdeacon by Oldham at Exeter on 18 March 1508, deacon

---

[1] On Barclay's life, see principally his translation of *The Ship of Fools*, ed. T. Jamieson, 2 vols (Edinburgh and London, 1874), i, pp ix-xcii; *Dictionary of National Biography*, article by A.W. Ward; *The Eclogues of Alexander Barclay*, ed. Beatrice White, EETS, original series, clxxv (1926), pp i-liv, and Barclay, *The Life of St George*, ed. W. Nelson, EETS, original series, ccxxx (1955), pp ix-xxv.

[2] *Eclogues*, ed. White, p xli.

on 8 April and priest on 22 April.[3] He had not been previously living in
Exeter diocese but in that of Lincoln, and had 'letters dimissory' from the
bishop of Lincoln enabling him to be ordained elsewhere. His 'title' – the
means of support which ordinands had to show – was provided by the
collegiate church of Ottery St Mary, twelve miles east of Exeter,
evidently because the college was going to give him a job. Barclay
probably came to Ottery, therefore, in about March 1508. His stay at the
collegiate church is important because it was there that he translated his
first major work, *The Ship of Fools* by Sebastian Brant, but he did not stay
long. A note in the first printed edition of *The Ship of Fools* states that he
made the translation at Ottery in '1508' (which in terms of the early-
Tudor calendar means March 1508 to March 1509), being 'at that time
chaplain in the said college'.[4] The phrase 'at the time' indicates that
Barclay had left Ottery when the printing of the book was completed on
14 December 1509. His stay in Devon was therefore less than a year and
three quarters, and possibly only about a year. The most likely person to
have brought him to Ottery is Thomas Cornish, the warden or chief
officer of the collegiate church and a figure of some importance in the
south west of England. A graduate of Oxford, Cornish combined being
warden of Ottery, precentor of Wells Cathedral, titular bishop of Tine
and suffragan bishop in the dioceses of Exeter and Bath and Wells.[5] More
than anyone else at Ottery he had the wide connections capable of
bringing a young man from elsewhere to take up a job there. The
likelihood is strengthened when we find that Barclay dedicated *The Ship
of Fools* to Cornish, with an acknowledgement that Cornish had
'promoted' (presumably sponsored) him to holy orders and given him
many other benefits.[6] No other member of the college is mentioned in
the book with such respect.

On the basis of the word 'chaplain' applied to Barclay in the printed
book, he is usually thought to have held the post of chaplain (or clerk) of
the Lady chapel while he was at Ottery. The duties of this office were
twofold. He had to teach the choristers and adolescent clerks or
'secondaries' of the college to sing, and to organise the daily series of
services, accompanied by polyphonic music, which took place in the
Lady chapel in honour of the Virgin Mary.[7] These services were sung by

---

[3] Devon Record Office, Chanter XIII, ff 92^v, 95^v. The evidence was first brought to
light by W. Nelson, 'New Light on Alexander Barclay', *Review of English Studies*, xix
(1943), pp 59-61. The mentions of Barclay's 'admission by the schoolmaster' in the
bishop's register refer to John Calwoodleigh, master of Exeter high school, who acted as
one of the examiners of the ordinands (Orme, *West of England*, pp 50, 56).

[4] *The Ship of Fools*, ed. Jamieson, i, p cxvi.

[5] For Cornish's career, see Emden, *BRUO*, i, 491-2.

[6] *The Ship of Fools*, ed. Jamieson, i, pp cxvi-vii.

[7] J.N. Dalton, *The Collegiate Church of Ottery St Mary* (Cambridge, 1917), pp 93, 98,
100, 145, 262.

the choristers and secondaries, along with the adult vicars choral of the college. Barclay mentions the secondaries in *The Ship of Fools*, but he does not actually say that he was their teacher. We know, however, that he was not one of the dignitaries or canons of Ottery (whose names are recorded), nor (in view of his age) a secondary or chorister. It is unlikely that he would have come to the college to be a vicar choral, since many similar posts could be had elsewhere at more important places such as the cathedrals, and those at Ottery were probably filled by local men. There was only one office in the college apart from that of chaplain of the Lady chapel to which a man would be likely to have come from elsewhere: that of master of the grammar school. Barclay was well up in Latin grammar when he translated *The Ship of Fools*[8] and taught for a time in a grammar school, as we shall see, in the 1540s. But it was not necessary to be ordained to be schoolmaster of Ottery collegiate church, and if Barclay had held that office we would expect him to have been described in print as a schoolmaster, rather than as a chaplain. On the whole, the likelihood seems to favour Barclay having been chaplain of the Lady chapel, though the fact itself is never overtly stated.

The Ship of Fools by Sebastian Brant, published in Germany in 1494, is a long, rather diffuse poem, further extended by Barclay with his own additions. It satirises various groups in society: gentlemen, clergy and scholars, parents, women and children, and complains of their follies and faults. In the course of the work, opinions are stated about some aspects of education, notably parents and children, academic study, and the ignorance of gentlemen and clergy. On the first of these topics, Barclay is traditional and unexceptional. Parents should set a good example to their offspring, and correct them when they do wrong. In return, children should be obedient and care for their parents when they are old. To fathers who say that children are too tender to be chastised, Barclay replies like Langland,

> What hurtyth punysshement with moderacion
> Unto yonge children? Certaynely, no thynge;
> It voydeth vyce, gettynge vertue and cunnynge.

Like an Oxford writer of his own period, he asks is it not better for your son to be beaten than to grow up wicked and be hanged?[9] In the section on study, Barclay is more original because he takes sides with the humanists against the medieval grammarians. Many scholars who study logic and law, he says, do so without having mastered grammar properly, which is the basis of all the liberal arts. They read the old

---

[8] *The Ship of Fools*, ed. Jamieson, i, 144.
[9] Ibid., pp 45–52, 234–8; ii, 147–52. On hanging, compare *A Fifteenth Century School Book*, ed. W. Nelson (Oxford, 1956), p 14.

Doctrinale of Alexander of Ville-Dieu (a work then still in print in England), and disdain Priscian and Sulpizio, the classical and Renaissance authorities on grammar:

> If he have onys red the olde Dotrinall
> With his diffuse and unparfyte brevyte,
> He thynketh to have sene the poyntis of grammer all,
> And yet of one errour he maketh two or thre;
> Precyan or Sulpice disdayneth he to se.
> Thus many whiche say that they theyre grammer can,
> Ar als great folys as whan they firste began.[10]

When it comes to promotion to ranks and offices in the world, however, the studious do not get their just deserts:

> Eche is nat lettred that nowe is made a lorde,
> Nor eche a clerke that hath a benefyce.[11]

Criticism of clerical education was a well-worn theme among satirists, but Barclay shows the typical humanist tendency to extend it to the nobility and gentry. He was to repeat the charge a few years later in the preface to his translation of Sallust's *Jugurthine War* (published c. 1520). 'The understandyng of Latyn . . . at this tyme is almost contemned of gentylmen.'[12]

Some literary works tell us nothing about the places in which they were written. *The Ship of Fools* is not of that kind, since Barclay greatly enlarged the German text in his translation and took the opportunity to include several references, both complimentary and disparaging, to people whom he had met in Devon. Two of these people were dignitaries whose favour Barclay had or wished to have. The whole work, as has been said, was dedicated to Cornish, and in a section on foolish and wicked sheriffs and knights, Barclay explains that there is an exception to them: 'Kyrkham', who is not to be put into the ship along with the rest, because he is 'manly, righteous, wise, discreet and sad', a man of 'perfect meekness' and a supporter of men in poverty. Barclay asserts that he himself is Kyrkham's 'servitor, chaplain and bede-man'; he promises to remain so during his life, and prays to God to raise Kyrkham to honour and give him the favour of the king.[13] 'Kyrkham' was evidently Sir John Kirkham of Paignton, who had been sheriff of

[10] *The Ship of Fools*, ed. Jamieson, i, 142-7; compare *A Fifteenth Century School Book*, ed. Nelson, p 19.

[11] *The Ship of Fools*, ed. Jamieson, i, 21-2, 158.

[12] Sallust, *The Jugurthine War*, trans. Barclay (London, R. Pynson, c. 1520), f A5ᵛ. For similar contemporary references, see Richard Pace, *De Fructu* (Basel, 1517), p 15; John Skelton, *Poetical Works*, ed. A. Dyce, 2 vols (London, 1843), i, 334-5; Sir Thomas Elyot, *The Governor* (London, 1531), book i, chapter 12.

[13] *The Ship of Fools*, ed. Jamieson, ii, 81.

Devon two years previously, from December 1505 to December 1506, and was to hold the office a second time in 1523-4.[14] Barclay appears to have done some travelling while he was in Devon; he later mentions Exeter and Totnes as if he had visited them,[15] and it is possible that he met Kirkham either at Paignton or at Ottery. Sir John's third wife, Lucy, was the daughter of Sir Thomas Tremayle of Sand in Sidbury parish near Ottery, and the knight may well have passed by the collegiate church on visits there from time to time.[16]

As well as applauding his patrons, Barclay inserted six stanzas into *The Ship of Fools* in praise of 'his well-beloved friend Sir John Bysshop of Exeter' who, he said, was the first person to see his translation and encouraged him not to keep it in the dark but to publish it.[17] 'Bysshop', as Barclay makes clear, was a cleric, and there is no reason to dissent from the late Professor Nelson's suggestion that he was the John Bishop who was ordained deacon at Ottery on 4 December 1500 to the title of Ottery collegiate church.[18] The title implies that Bishop came from Ottery or nearby, and Barclay could easily have met him there on in Exeter. In 1508 Bishop may already have been rector of St Paul's church, Exeter,[19] the benefice he definitely held in 1522.[20] He seems to have been ambitious to rise in the Church and Barclay calls him 'covetous', though he also expresses a hope that Bishop's fortunes will grow and that he will one day be a bishop in fact as well as in name. This hope was not fulfilled. In 1522 the rectory of St Paul's was worth £10 a year and Bishop's own possessions were valued at £26.13s.4d., but he never got a better benefice, and his resignation of the parish in 1537 to become priest of the Grandisson chantry in Exeter Cathedral, worth a little over £6 a year, looks like a retirement by a man of failing powers.[21] It is the last that we

---

[14] *Lists of Sheriffs for England & Wales*, PRO, Lists and Indexes, ix (1898), p 36.

[15] *Eclogues*, ed. White, pp 19-20.

[16] On Kirkham, see John Prince, *Danmonii Orientales Illustres: or, The Worthies of Devon* (London, 1810), pp 554-6.

[17] *The Ship of Fools*, ed. Jamieson, ii, pp vii, 278-80.

[18] *Review of English Studies*, xix (1943), p 60; Devon Record Office, Chanter XII part ii, f 42.

[19] Devon Record Office, Deeds (Exeter, St Paul's), ED/BC/6-8. For another reference to Bishop, see PRO, C 1/287/78 (and possibly C 1/303/53 and C 1/317/53).

[20] *Tudor Exeter: Tax Assessments, 1489-1595*, ed. Margery M. Rowe, Devon and Cornwall Record Society, new series, xxii (1977), p 14.

[21] Devon Record Office, Chanter XIV, ff 88, 90; Nicholas Orme, *The Minor Clergy of Exeter Cathedral* (Exeter, 1980), p 83. The stipend of the Grandisson chantry was £5.6s.8d., but the priest could earn about another 19s.0d. by attending obit masses for the dead in the cathedral.

hear of him, and he probably died in the 1540s. Barclay, as the incumbent of two or three parishes in his last years, ended up better off than his former friend.

The rest of the local allusions in *The Ship of Fools* are unfavourable ones, suggesting that Barclay held a poor opinion of most Devonians, as did his fellow-poet Herrick a hundred and forty years later. It may be Ottery that he had in mind in his sketch of the disorders of contemporary church choirs: the musical director running hither and thither holding his staff of office, while the clergy gossip about the latest battle in France.[22] Barclay certainly mentions the eight secondaries of Ottery who, he says, are worthy to receive first place in the ship of fools because they know nothing and will learn nothing, even though they receive their tuition free of charge and live in a building next to the school itself.[23] He is scathing too about the local clergy, asserting as elsewhere that the least learned are promoted to the best benefices,

> For if one can flater, and bere a hawke on his fyst,
> He shalbe made person of Honyngton or of Clyst.[24]

Once in possession of these benefices, such people employ a hired chaplain to do their work – a 'Sir John of Garnesey' – and think themselves absolved of all responsibility.[25] No chaplain of this name can be discovered in early-Tudor Devon, so Barclay was either bestowing a nickname on some local priest who came from Guernsey, or using a stock name current at the time.[26] We should be careful, however, not to assume that the pre-Reformation clergy were as uniformly bad as he and other literary writers asserted. The secondaries of Ottery were probably a mixture of studious and ignorant, idle and conscientious youths, like their counterparts at Exeter Cathedral in the early sixteenth century.[27] And while we cannot now be sure which rector Barclay had in mind in the five parishes called Clyst, it is clear that his picture of the rector of Honiton was an inadequate one. Barclay may not indeed have had any personal knowledge of Henry Ferman, who held the parish from 1505 to 1527, since Ferman was studying at Oxford at about the time that Barclay was in Devon. But Ferman's ability to take a university degree in canon law, his promotion by the bishop to be precentor of Ottery in 1523 and his bequests to the fabric of Ottery and Honiton churches in 1526, shows that there was more to him than Barclay's canard suggests.[28]

Barclay reserved his rudest remarks for a group of people who seem to

[22] *The Ship of Fools*, ed. Jamieson, ii, 155.
[23] Ibid., i, 179. For the locations of the secondaries' house and the school, see Dalton, op. cit., p 75 and plan between pp 80–1.
[24] *The Ship of Fools*, ed. Jamieson, i, 22.
[25] Ibid., p 160.
[26] The term 'Sir John' for an ordinary priest was, of course, very common.
[27] Above, pp 194–5.
[28] For Ferman's career, see Emden, *BRUO*, iv, 202.

have been mainly lay inhabitants of Ottery. Foremost among them was a
certain Mansell, whom he portrays as a man with a huge belly who went
about seeking for prey and despoiling the poor, presumably as a steward,
rent collector, or summoner of the Church courts.[29] Barclay suggested
that if Mansell arrived too late to get into the fools' ship, he should be
made the captain of a separate barge of 'bawds' or scoundrels. Later, the
poet changed his mind and allocated Mansell a place in the filthiest part of
the ship – the stinking bilges – along with Jack Chard, Robin Hill, millers
and bakers who cheated with weights and measures, and 'all stealing
tailors' such as Soper.[30] The court rolls of Ottery manor mention a
Chard family in 1515-17,[31] but it is unfortunately impossible to identify
any of Barclay's enemies as such, due to a lack of contemporary local
records. Nevertheless, his criticisms of these people, along with the
absence of any compliments to the staff of the collegiate church
excepting Cornish, show plainly that Barclay was not very happy during
his stay in Ottery. In one respect *The Ship of Fools* was his revenge: a
squib to startle his enemies when he had left. It is amusing to picture their
indignation when Barclay's book exploded in Ottery, some time in
1510, when he himself was safely far away.

On leaving Devon, Barclay moved both geographically and
vocationally. By 1513 he had become a Benedictine monk of Ely
cathedral priory, and since in 1516 he is listed as sixteenth among the
thirty brethren, it is likely that he went there straight from Ottery. Was
the change due to economic or spiritual motives? He may have despaired
of getting patronage with which to leave Ottery and get a more
comfortable benefice, such as a parish church. Ely offered a better
standard of living, being a large and well endowed foundation, where a
monk would have his personal servant, a private room, and a good
library at hand. But Barclay had hardly been in Devon long enough to
feel a sense of failure in the search for patronage, and his later career
suggests a strong vocation to live in a religious order. His life at Ely must
have been relatively comfortable, and he was able to go on writing. Six
of his works were published wholly or partly during this period, up to
the mid 1520s, falling into two groups: literary and educational.[32] The
first were all translations of texts by classical or Renaissance authors: *The
Life of St George* by Battista Mantovano (published c. 1515), five *Eclogues*,
nos 4-5 by Mantovano (published 1518-21) and nos. 1-3 by Aeneas

---

[29] *The Ship of Fools*, ed. Jamieson, ii, 82.

[30] Ibid., ii, 307. In this reference Mansell is spelt 'Manshyll' in order to rhyme, and
perhaps in parallel with Prince Hal's gibe at Falstaff: 'a huge hill of flesh' (*1 Henry IV*,
II.iv.239).

[31] Devon Record Office, CR 1288, mm 105, 107ᵛ, etc.

[32] On these works, see A.W. Pollard and G.R. Redgrave, *A Short Title Catalogue of
Books Printed in England, 1475-1640*, 2nd ed., 2 vols (London, 1976-86), nos 1383.5-1386,
3545, 10752, 12379, 17242, 21626, 22992.1 and 23181.

Sylvius Piccolomini (published 1523–30), and Sallust's *Jugurthine War* (published c. 1520). The educational group began with a translation of *The Mirror of Good Manners* by the humanist scholar Domenico Mancini, a Renaissance work in the medieval genre of treatises on behaviour and etiquette aimed at young people. Next came a revision of John Stanbridge's popular *Vocabula* (published 1519), an early humanist vocabulary in Latin and English for use in schools, and successful enough in Barclay's edition to be reprinted in 1524 and 1526. Finally, an *Introductory to Wryte and to Pronounce Frenche* was published in 1522, the latest of a long line of such treatises in England, stretching back to the thirteenth century.[33] Barclay drew on these, admitting in his work that he had 'seen the draughtes of others' made before his time, and sometimes he perpetuated out-of-date spellings of French words. The book was treated scornfully by John Palsgrave, the author of a much longer work on French, *L'Esclarcissement de la langue francoyse*, published in 1530, who stated

> I have seen an old book written in parchment in manner in all things like to his said *Introductory* which by conjecture was not written this 100 years. I wot not if he happened to fortune upon such another.

But Palsgrave was self-consciously trying to write a new kind of treatise, in which French grammar was thoroughly reduced to rules. Barclay belonged to an older tradition which gave the learner practical advice, rather than aiming at grammatical completeness.[34]

The best known of Barclay's Ely works are the *Eclogues*, which were the first formal poems of their kind to be written in English. They belong to humanist literature since they are translations from two fifteenth-century Italian authors, but Barclay sympathised enough with pre-humanist Latin poetry to pay a compliment in his prologue to the *Eclogue of Theodulus*, the ninth-century poem which was widely read in English grammar schools up to the early sixteenth century:[35]

> What shall I speake of the father auncient,
> Which in briefe language both playne and eloquent,
> Between Alathea, Sewstis stoute and bolde,
> Hath made rehearsall of all thy storyes olde,
> By true historyes us teaching to obiect
> Against vayne fables of olde Gentiles sect.[36]

Barclay himself may have read Theodulus at school, and it is interesting that despite his acquaintance with humanist writing, he still valued its 'playne and eloquent' style and content (the debate of Pseustis and

[33] Above, p 11.
[34] Kathleen Lambley, *The Teaching and Cultivation of the French Language in England during Tudor and Stuart Times* (London and Manchester, 1920), pp 3–4, 77–80.
[35] Orme, *English Schools*, p 103.
[36] *Eclogues*, ed. White, p 2.

Alathea as to whether Greek mythology or Hebrew history was better). His opinion did not prevail, however, and Theodulus ceased to be printed in England after 1515.[37] Elsewhere in Barclay's *Eclogues* there are some brief but vivid references to childhood. The mother sits on the doorstep with her children on her lap, kissing and hugging them, delousing and combing them, and rubbing their necks with butter – perhaps to soothe sunburn. The street boys busy themselves with their tops in Lent, and sing and hop for joy in the fruit season. In winter, torn and ragged, they watch men killing pigs, in hope of a good dinner, and claim the bladder into which they put beans and peas to make it rattle, blow it up well, and play handball and football with it to drive away the cold.[38] There is also a more formal discussion about whether the royal court is a place of education for good or ill. Coridon, one of the shepherd characters, asserts that at court you find wise men, good music and the reading of chronicles which stir young princes to imitate the worthy deeds of their predecessors. But Cornix, who tends to represent Barclay, disagrees; most of the talk at court is of war, novelties and abominable deeds. The wise cloak their sayings with flattery to gain promotion. Some great men indeed send their sons to court to learn virtue and manners, but all that the youths absorb is malice, bad manners and vice. Courtiers boast of their sexual exploits, the murders they have done, the frauds they have committed, and you must not think to find any chaste or sober young men among them; instead 'all sueth vices, all sue enormitie'.[39] Once more the vein is the familiar humanist one of telling the aristocracy to reform their manners.

In the middle of the 1520s, somewhere between 1521 and 1528, Barclay's career experienced another change with his departure from Ely to become a Franciscan friar.[40] A move of this kind was most unusual – monks and friars had different traditions, objectives and ways of life – and it undoubtedly signified a major shift of outlook in the man himself. He ceased to write, either poetry or practical works, and his only important publication afterwards, the first three *Eclogues* of 1530, was probably written before he joined the friars. Instead, he acquired a reputation as a religious activist, even a nonconformist. In about 1528 the German informer Hermann Rinck wrote to Cardinal Wolsey that various dissidents, including 'William Roy, William Tyndale, Jerome Barlow, Alexander Barclay and their adherents, etc., formerly Observants of the Order of St Francis but now apostates, . . . ought to be arrested, punished and delivered up on account of Lutheran heresy'. As the others mentioned were all living in Germany, it looks as though

---

[37] Pollard and Redgrave, *Short Title Catalogue*, nos 23939.5–23943.
[38] *Eclogues*, ed. White, pp 184, 191-2.
[39] Ibid., pp 60-3, 128-9.
[40] For references to the rest of Barclay's career, unless otherwise given, see ibid., pp xli–liv.

Barclay was also settled there. The Observants were the reformed branch of the Franciscan Order, with six houses in England, and this is the chief evidence that Barclay joined them rather than the larger 'Conventual' section of the order. It seems to be supported by a letter to Wolsey of April 1529 by another Observant friar, John West, who was about to meet Barclay whom he accused of calling the cardinal a 'tyrant' and other 'opprobrious and blasphemous words'. The Observants were noted for their fervour, by contemporary religious standards, and if Barclay joined them, he did so as a religious challenge not merely for personal convenience. It is unlikely that he was a Lutheran. He may have been interested in some of Luther's writings (like other eventually conservative men of his day), but Rinck's letter is not wholly accurate (Tyndale was not a friar), and his linking of Barclay with the admittedly Lutheran Roy and Barlow may be a mistake. In the event Barclay remained a friar, returned to England and became known not for his Lutheranism but for his religious conservatism.[41]

We know little of Barclay's life as a friar, but friars were great students and it is likely that part of his time was spent studying theology at a university and taking a doctor's degree – a process of several years. He is described as 'Doctor Barclay' in 1538,[42] and if this is correct (as it certainly was by 1546), he must have taken his degree in the late 1520s or 1530s in a foreign university, since he does not appear in the degree registers of Oxford or Cambridge. Study in Germany would account for his mention there in 1528. In 1534 the Observant houses in England were closed because of their hostility to the king's supremacy over the Church, and the surviving members were transferred to the Conventual houses, themselves suppressed in 1538. Barclay thus experienced further changes of life, this time changes forced on him and unwelcome. The London chronicler Charles Wriothesley singled him out by name, under the year 1538, as one who was reluctant to give up wearing his friar's habit in public until he was compelled to do so, and John Foxe the martyrologist later recounted a story in which Thomas Cromwell personally threatened Barclay with a hanging unless he changed his clothes. In the summer and autumn of 1538 Barclay carried out a number of preaching engagements: at Barking (Suffolk) at Whitsuntide and in the diocese of Exeter in October. It is not recorded whether he revisited Ottery, but three reports of his demeanour subsequently reached

---

[41] On Roy and Barlow, see E.G. Rupp, *Studies in the Making of the English Protestant Tradition* (Cambridge, 1949); this contains no evidence of Barclay's involvement with them.

[42] Charles Wriothesley, *A Chronicle of England, 1485-1559*, ed. W.D. Hamilton, vol i, Camden Society, new series, xl (1875), p 82, assuming that the entry was written at the time.

Cromwell. At Barking he had not preached in favour of the king's supremacy or against the pope; at St Germans in Cornwall he had made his conservatism known, albeit in a circumspect way; and in Cornwall and Devonshire generally he was doing 'much hurt' with 'open preaching and private communication'.

What action Cromwell took, if any, is not clear, because Barclay drops out of records for the next eight years. When he reappears it is in the role of a beneficed clergyman, indeed a clerical pluralist – a different role by far from that of an Observant friar. This suggests that Barclay accepted that the friars were done for and decided to come to terms with the situation. In 1546 the subdean of Wells Cathedral presented him to be vicar of Wookey (Somerset), close to Wells and with an income of £12.15s.8d.; he probably lived in one or other of those places for the next couple of years.[43] Then, in the summer of 1547, the headmaster of Wells Cathedral School, Richard Edon, fell ill and Barclay was persuaded to take his place, probably on a temporary basis, with a further salary of £13.6s.8d.[44] He did the task until Michaelmas or Christmas 1548, when he moved abruptly from Somerset to the other side of England to become resident vicar of Great Baddow in Essex. It has always been said that Barclay was admitted as vicar of Great Baddow on 7 February 1547 (new style), but this is a mistake of the eighteenth-century historian Richard Newcourt. The true date is 1549, and we know from other evidence that Barclay went to live in Great Baddow in January of that year.[45] It was a more valuable benefice than Wookey, with an income of £18.6s.8d., and as Barclay obtained permission to go on holding Wookey as well,[46] his net income rose to a respectable £25 even if he paid a curate to serve his Somerset parish. In 1552 he was given a third, even wealthier benefice: the rectory of All Hallows Lombard Street, London, with an income of £22.6s.8d., which involved him giving up one of his other two parishes. In the event, before he could do so, he died at Croydon (Surrey), early in June 1552, and was buried there on the tenth of the month.

If we had to write his epitaph, it would be difficult to sum him up concisely. As a Latinist, he was a humanist, dismissive of Alexander of

---

[43] *The Registers of Thomas Wolsey, etc., Bishops of Bath and Wells, 1518-1559*, ed. Sir H.C. Maxwell-Lyte, Somerset Record Society, lv (1940), pp 113-14.

[44] Orme, *West of England*, pp 87-8, 90.

[45] Barclay was admitted as vicar of Great Baddow on 7 February 1549 (new style) (London, Guildhall Library, MS 9531/12 part i (The Register of Edmund Bonner), f 164^v). For the other evidence, see *Eclogues*, ed. White, pp xlviii-li.

[46] Barclay was licensed to hold an additional benefice with Wookey on 28 January

Ville-Dieu and steeped in classical and Renaissance literature. Yet he could write appreciatively of Theodulus, compile a treatise in French of a very traditional kind, and make customary observations about parents and children. He also became a monk and a friar, both of which we associate with the middle ages. Yet the humanist monk-poet of Ely is parallelled by Robert Joseph, the humanist monk-letter writer of Evesham,[47] and the old religious orders were perfectly capable of absorbing new ideas, not to mention heretical ones as we see with Roy and Barlow. Once upon a time, Barclay would have been called 'a transitional figure', with a foot in the medieval and the Renaissance worlds. The truth is that every generation is transitional, and that all innovators are conservative in some respects. We shall witness the same when we pass on to Shakespeare.

1549 (D.S. Chambers, *Faculty Office Registers, 1534-1549* (Oxford, 1966), p 316).
    [47] Above, pp 39-40.

16

SHAKESPEARE AND EDUCATION

The historian of education needs to interest himself in many things. There are the institutions which provide it, the studies it entails, and the people it depends on: benefactors, teachers, parents and pupils. There is also a fourth dimension: its reputation in society. How was it perceived and valued by those not directly involved with it? The history of public attitudes to education in the middle ages and the Renaissance is not easy to write, but something can be learnt about it from the great literary authors of the time. Chaucer and Langland suggest to us what was noticed about education in the fourteenth century, and Shakespeare does the same between about 1590 and 1612. Comparing him with them also helps us to estimate whether people's perceptions of education changed during the intervening two hundred years. There are dangers, of course, in expecting literary authors to provide information about a technical matter like education. They were not experts; their information is restricted by their literary genres, their own interests, and the kind of audience they wrote for. Yet reading them is also a rewarding experience. Great authors, being detached, may give us a truer account of the status of education than is given by professional educationists. Literary writers notice certain things, often unconsciously, and ignore others; approve of this and disapprove of that. They point to the impact which education was making at the time, and the extent to which people took it seriously. Such information is hard to acquire elsewhere, in the centuries concerned.

Shakespeare's writings are a good source for the historian of education because they say so much about the subject.[1] They show an awareness of childhood and adolescence by both the author and the audience whom he expected to understand what he wrote. The subject is not uniformly treated, however, throughout the canon of Shakespeare's works. It is most apparent in the plays of his early and middle periods, from about 1590 to about 1600: the early comedies, the English histories, and the early tragedies (*Titus Andronicus*, *Romeo and Juliet*, and *Hamlet*). These were written when Shakespeare was young himself (he was born in 1564), and feature many young people whose education is still going on

---

[1] All references to the plays are to the Arden edition, 2nd edition, ed. Una Ellis-Fermor, H.F. Brooks and H. Jenkins (London, Methuen).

or has only just finished. Later, he transferred his attention to older men and women in the great tragedies, and not until his last five plays from about 1608 to 1612 (the romances and *Henry VIII*) did he again return to the growing up of the young. We shall therefore concentrate on the plays before about 1600 and after 1608. Most of these contain significant educational material, touching on birth, childhood and adolescence; schools, teaching and schoolmasters; and educational policy. Like Chaucer, Shakespeare noticed many things in the contemporary world, and education as a part of that world attracted his notice from time to time. More rarely, it seized his attention fully, leading him to write two plays in particular which are 'about education', though they are also about other things. *The Taming of the Shrew* (c. 1590) centres on the making of Katherina the shrew into a good wife, a process arguably educational, and compares this with the formal tuition of her sister Bianca by schoolmasters. *Love's Labour's Lost* (c. 1593-7) belongs to the same category. Its main plot concerns the vow of the king of Navarre and his courtiers to study for three years in seclusion from the world, and it has a sub-plot dominated by a schoolmaster discussing school topics. These plays embody a greater primary concern with education than we find in the fourteenth-century writers, and justify us saying that Shakespeare was interested in the subject, as opposed simply to mentioning it.

He is still like Chaucer, however, in another important respect. His fullest attention is given to the aristocracy, which for convenience we apply collectively to royalty, nobility, gentry, and wealthy merchants with a similar life-style. Only they are fully explored in childhood and adulthood, comedy and tragedy, whereas the commonalty are treated less fully, chiefly comically and in adulthood. The births and christenings that we hear about are even more restricted, for they are entirely of royal children. Several queens give birth in the plays, and as in contemporary practice this is done in the presence of women alone. Men are excluded, and the king waits to be told the news of the birth by an aristocratic lady.[2] In the unusual circumstances of Tamora's illegitimate childbirth in *Titus Andronicus* and Thaisa's delivery at sea in *Pericles*, there is only a nurse at hand and she brings the tidings.[3] Real fathers often rewarded the bearers of the news, and this is shown in *Henry VIII* when the king promises the Old Lady a hundred marks (£66.13s.4d.), which she correctly thinks to be inadequate. Henry VIII had expected a son. He was disappointed on hearing that his new child was a daughter (Elizabeth), and his gift did not compare well with those of earlier kings.[4] Later, having visited the

[2] *The Winter's Tale*, II, ii, 25; iii, 64, 6; *Henry VIII*, V, i, 158-69.
[3] *Titus Andronicus*, IV, ii, 61; *Pericles*, III, i, 15-22.
[4] *Henry VIII*, V, i, 170-6.

queen, Henry changes his mind and a magnificent christening takes place, as usual on the very day of birth. The return of the christening party from church was shown on the stage, in one of the splendours of production for which *Henry VIII* became famous:

> Enter Trumpets sounding: then two Aldermen, Lord Mayor, Garter, Cranmer [the godfather], Duke of Norfolk with his marshal's staff, Duke of Suffolk, two noblemen bearing great standing bowls for the christening gifts: then four noblemen bearing a canopy, under which the Duchess of Norfolk, godmother, bearing the child richly habited in a mantle, &c.; train borne by a lady: then follows the Marchioness Dorset, the other godmother, and ladies.

Henry comes behind separately. He has chosen the godparents but not apparently attended the christening or given the baby's name, since he asks what it is. He also praises the costliness of the christening presents. The queen is also absent, and the christening party pays a courtesy call on her afterwards.[5]

Aristocratic mothers, like Hermione in *The Winter's Tale*, usually refrained from suckling their children personally,[6] and procured other women to do so when the birth was expected. Shakespeare portrays four such nurses in his plays, notably the Nurse in *Romeo and Juliet* who is not just a functionary but a fully realised character, one of the earliest of her profession in English literature.[7] Of lowly rank, she is a married woman with a baby of her own, and feeds her new charge too until the third year. The child, Juliet, is then discouraged from further breast feeding by putting wormwood on the breast to give it a bad taste. The Nurse retells all this at length, and goes on to recall when Juliet was first able to walk,

> For then she could stand high-lone, nay, by th'rood,
> She could have run and waddled all about;
> For even the day before she broke her brow,
> And then my husband – God be with his soul,
> A was a merry man – took up the child,
> 'Yea', quoth he, 'dost thou fall upon thy face?
> Thou wilt fall backward when thou hast more wit,
> Wilt thou not Jule?' And by my holidame,
> The pretty wretch left crying and said 'Ay'.[8]

The genre of the drama made it difficult to include young child-actors, but Mamillius in *The Winter's Tale* is evidently young. He must be under seven, since he is still in the hands of his mother and her ladies, not yet under male tutelage. His smudged nose, his wish to fight and not be spoken to like a baby, and his tale 'of sprites and goblins' – 'there was a

---

[5] Ibid., V, iv; compare V, iii, 196–203.
[6] *The Winter's Tale*, II, i, 56.
[7] *Romeo and Juliet*, I, iii; *3 Henry VI*, V, vii; *Titus Andronicus*, IV, ii; *Pericles* III, chorus and i.
[8] *Romeo and Juliet*, I, iii, 16–48.

man . . . dwelt by a churchyard', are delightful touches of childhood,
but he is also a vulnerable figure. Even as his father Leontes is talking and
playing with him, Leontes is conceiving jealousy against the child's
mother, Hermione, and in the end Mamillius's life is short. When she is
imprisoned, he falls ill and dies 'with mere conceit and fear' of her
misfortunes.[9]

This introduces us to two essential qualities of childhood in
Shakespeare: it is a time of pleasure, but also of vulnerability. Neither
perception was new. Medieval and Renaissance writers both saw play as
a natural inclination of children,[10] and social observers since at least the
twelfth century had noticed children's games and described them.
Shakespeare does the same in metaphor. His characters compare life and
its happenings with boys pursuing summer butterflies, killing flies for
sport and scrambling in a 'muss' or melée. Boyish games are mentioned
like push-pin, span-counter and tops, riding the wild mare and learning
to swim with bladders.[11] But children are also at the mercy of adults.
Chaucer depicted the murder of a schoolboy by the Jews, and the
starvation of the count of Pisa's children in prison. In Shakespeare we
have the birth of Marina in a storm at sea, the setting adrift of Miranda as
a child alone with her father, and the frightening of Lucius Andronicus
by his maimed aunt as he learns his lessons.[12] There is the ominous entry
of Edward V and his brother into the Tower of London and the grasp of
Richard III, the coming of the executioners to blind Prince Arthur, the
murders of Macduff's young son and of the twelve-year-old earl of
Rutland.[13] As much as possible is made of these events for dramatic
purposes. Rutland pleads at length for his life to be spared and Macduff's
son shouts defiance, but to no avail, and although Arthur's eloquence
averts his fate, he dies soon afterwards escaping from prison. Children
are not safe from the horrors of the times they live in.

In normal circumstances, however, the young are protected by their
parents. Aristocratic fathers in particular are shown taking a close
interest in their children's welfare. Edward IV, Henry VIII and Pericles
appear with their wives' newly-born babies, taking delight in them and
planning their futures.[14] Leontes, as we noticed, watches over
Mamillius, and the Pages in *The Merry Wives of Windsor* voice their

---

[9] *The Winter's Tale*, II, iii, 9–17; III, ii, 144–5.

[10] E.g. J.A. Burrow, *The Ages of Man* (Oxford, 1986), pp 44, 49, 150; *The English Works of Sir Thomas More*, ed. W.E. Campbell, 2 vols (London and New York, 1931), i, 332–3.

[11] *Coriolanus*, IV, vi, 95; *King Lear*, IV, i, 36–7; *Antony and Cleopatra*, III, xiii, 91; *Love's Labour's Lost*, IV, iii, 167; *2 Henry VI*, IV, ii, 150–1; *The Winter's Tale*, II, ii, 103; *2 Henry IV*, II, iv, 243–4; *Henry VIII*, III, ii, 358–9.

[12] *Pericles*, III, i, 15–31; *The Tempest*, I, ii, 132–58; *Titus Andronicus*, IV, i, 1–4.

[13] *Richard III*, III, i; *King John*, IV, i; iii, 1–10; *Macbeth*, IV, ii; *3 Henry VI*, I, iii.

[14] Ibid., V, vii; *Henry VIII*, V, iv; *Pericles*, III, i; iii.

concern that William their son should profit from his schooling.[15] Parental cares are heaviest in adolescence. Then, fathers and mothers worry themselves about their offspring's behaviour like Polonius about Laertes in *Hamlet*, or their careers like Antonio about Proteus in *The Two Gentlemen of Verona*, or their marriages like the Capulet parents about Juliet.[16] Shakespeare believed, with the moralists of the middle ages and the Renaissance, that parents and children each had duties: maintenance, discipline and teaching on the one hand, and obedience on the other. Parents support their children, at much expense in the case of older boys as Silence wrily remarks in *Henry IV Part Two*.[17] They exercise discipline, including corporal punishment if necessary, for as with Langland it is only 'fond' or indulgent parents who spare the rod, with bad results:

> as fond fathers
> Having bound up the threat'ning twigs of birch
> Only to stick it in their children's sight
> For terror, not to use, in time the rod
> Becomes more mock'd than fear'd.[18]

At the same time, punishment should be distinguished from tyranny, 'to hang clogs on them', as Desdemona's father is tempted to do in *Othello*.[19] Parental authority lasts through adolescence and includes the right to arrange a child's marriage, even against its will, to a suitable partner. Bertram is married to Helena in this way by his substitute-father, the king of France, in *All's Well That Ends Well*.[20] It may be significant that children who marry secretly without their parents' consent, as Juliet and Desdemona do, often come to tragic ends.[21]

Parents are also involved in teaching, both in a moral and in a technical sense. Biblical, classical and medieval literature all featured parents giving wise advice to their offspring, from simple proverbs to large treatises,[22] and this continues in the world of Shakespeare's plays. Oddly enough, one earlier example which he handled, he did not develop. This was the death-bed counsel of Henry IV to Prince Hal, which is mentioned both by contemporary writers and later chroniclers. Shortly before Shakespeare wrote about it, John Stow in his *Annals of England*

---

[15] *Merry Wives of Windsor*, IV, i, 5-13.

[16] *Hamlet*, I, ii, 57-61; iii, 55-81; II, i; *Two Gentlemen of Verona*, I, iii, 1-43; *Romeo and Juliet*, I, ii-iii; III, iv-v.

[17] *2 Henry IV*, III, ii, 8-11; *Taming of the Shrew*, V, i, 60-2; *Hamlet*, II, i, 1.

[18] *Measure for Measure*, I, iii, 23-7.

[19] *Othello*, I, iii, 195-8.

[20] *All's Well That Ends Well*, II, iii, 105-83.

[21] An exception is that of Anne Page and Fenton in a more lighthearted play (*Merry Wives of Windsor*, V, v, 217-37).

[22] Orme, *From Childhood to Chivalry*, pp 103-6.

(1592) made it into a discourse of a couple of pages long on how to rule, but the dramatist seems to have followed Holinshed's shorter account.[23] In his own play Henry IV's oration takes the form of an apology for past life with only one piece of advice:

> Be it thy course to busy giddy minds
> With foreign quarrels, that action hence borne out
> May waste the memory of the former days.[24]

The point is interesting: Shakespeare did not develop educational topics instinctively on every occasion. Instead, his chief example of a father's advice to his son is that of Polonius when Laertes leaves for France. This by contrast is extended into a speech of 23 lines containing ten precepts of good behaviour and wise policy.[25] The writing down of such advice is frequently found in the late sixteenth century by, for example, William Cecil, Sir Walter Raleigh and Sir Henry Sidney to their sons,[26] but there is nothing new about it in principle; it had been going on for centuries.

Technical teaching by noble parents, particularly of letters, is also hinted at. In *Titus Andronicus*, Titus's daughter Lavinia reads literary works to his grandson Lucius in the manner that the historical Cornelia did to her sons the Gracchi:

> Ah, boy, Cornelia never with more care
> Read to her sons than she hath read to thee
> Sweet poetry and Tully's Orator.

Later, we see Titus teaching the boy to shoot well with his bow.[27] In *The Tempest*, Prospero himself is schoolmaster to his daughter Miranda, but this is due to the unusual fact of them being alone on a desert island.[28] It is more frequent to hear of the employment of specialised instructors. Sometimes the teaching is provided privately, within the family's own household. In classical and medieval times, kings and noblemen had maintained various kinds of tutors for their sons: knights, chaplains and professional schoolmasters. Shakespeare refers to two of these: the chaplain, who appears as tutor to the earl of Rutland in *Henry VI Part Three*, and the professional schoolmaster, represented by the master in *Antony and Cleopatra* whose historical original was the instructor of Mark Antony's children by Cleopatra.[29] A king's or nobleman's sons were often joined by other boys in their upbringing: their father's wards, or

[23] *2 Henry IV*, ed. A.R. Humphreys (London and Cambridge, Mass., 1966), pp 201, 215-18.

[24] Ibid., IV, v, 213-15.

[25] *Hamlet*, I, iii, 58-80.

[26] Ibid., ed. H. Jenkins (London and New York, 1982), pp 440-3.

[27] *Titus Andronicus*, IV, i, 12-14; iii, 2-3.

[28] *The Tempest*, I, ii, 171-4.

[29] *3 Henry VI*, I, iii; *Antony and Cleopatra*, III, xi, 71-2; xii, 2-25.

the children of his friends and dependents sent to his household to cement alliances or acquire patronage. Hamlet, we are told, was brought up with Rosencrantz and Guildenstern who were presumably the sons of Danish noblemen, and the same is said (less credibly) of Leontes and Polixenes in *The Winter's Tale*.[30] Relationships thus formed are close, but they are not proof against the animosities of later life. Those who could not afford a private schoolmaster (the majority in practice, though not in the plays), sent their boys to a public grammar school. Here William Page is Shakespeare's chief example.[31]

Not all of Shakespeare's children go to school, however, since for common people childhood is a time of work and service. The plays include many boy servants, partly because the actors' companies themselves employed such boys and gave them minor stage-roles, and partly because boys were familiar and necessary figures in real contemporary households, where they were cheap to hire. Most of these boys were plebeian, but some were aristocratic pages, as Falstaff is said to have been in the household of the duke of Norfolk,[32] and real pages often combined their duties with attending school. Boys who did not become servants were set to learn a trade or formally apprenticed to a master. Othello tells us that he entered military life at the age of seven,[33] and there is a gunner's boy on active service at the siege of Orleans in *Henry VI Part One*.[34] But Shakespeare, like Chaucer, took little interest in the learning of trade or apprenticeship. Christopher Sly remembers in *The Taming of the Shrew* that he was 'by birth a pedlar, by education a cardmaker' (in the cloth industry),[35] and *Henry VI Part Two* includes an armourer's apprentice, Peter Thump, who denounces his master for treason. The master claims that this was a revenge for being disciplined, they fight, and Peter wins because his master is drunk.[36] Apprentices also appear in *Sir Thomas More* (c. 1595-8), to which Shakespeare is thought to have contributed the scene where they riot and are quelled by More's wise oratory.[37] Yet even these brief mentions are unusual, and only Moth the page in *Love's Labour's Lost* and Falstaff's page are given more than casual

---

[30] *Hamlet*, II, ii, 11-12; *The Winter's Tale*, I, i, 21-4.

[31] *Merry Wives of Windsor*, IV, i.

[32] *2 Henry IV*, III, ii, 24-5.

[33] *Othello*, I, iii, 83-5.

[34] *1 Henry VI*, I, iv.

[35] *Taming of the Shrew*, induction, ii, 17-21.

[36] *2 Henry VI*, I, iii, 190-202; II, iii.

[37] 'Sir Thomas More', ed. H. Jenkins, in William Shakespeare, *The Complete Works*, ed. C.J. Sisson (London, 1953), pp 1,245-7.

mention.[38] The latter reappears in *Henry V*, dies at Agincourt and was obviously close to Shakespeare's heart, but as a vulnerable child as much as a trainee man.[39]

When boys reached adolescence, it was more feasible to introduce them on stage and to make them main characters in a story. In consequence, the plays up to about 1600 portray numerous young noblemen on the verge of adulthood who are being brought up away from home in order to give them wider experience of life. The question of how to educate such youths is treated at some length in *The Two Gentlemen of Verona*. The wealthy Antonio has been keeping his son Proteus at home, a policy questioned by the boy's uncle:

> He wonder'd that your lordship
> Would suffer him to spend his youth at home,
> While other men, of slender reputation,
> Put forth their sons, to seek preferment out:
> Some to the wars, to try their fortune there;
> Some, to discover islands far away;
> Some, to the studious universities.
> For any, or for all these exercises,
> He said that Proteus, your son, was meet,
> And did request me to importune you
> To let him spend his time no more at home,
> Which would be great impeachment to his age,
> In having known no travel in his youth.

Antonio agrees:

> I have consider'd well his loss of time,
> And how he cannot be a perfect man,
> Not being tried and tutor'd in the world:
> Experience is by industry achiev'd,
> And perfected by the swift course of time.
> Then tell me, whither were I best to send him?

He is advised:

> I think your lordship is not ignorant
> How his companion, youthful Valentine,
> Attends the Emperor in his royal court . . .
> 'Twere good, I think, your lordship sent him thither:
> There shall he practise tilts and tournaments,
> Hear sweet discourse, converse with noblemen,
> And be in eye of every exercise
> Worthy his youth and nobleness of birth.[40]

---

[38] *Love's Labour's Lost*, I, ii &c.; *2 Henry IV*, I, ii &c.
[39] E.g. *Henry V*, III, ii.
[40] *Two Gentlemen of Verona*, I, iii, 1-43.

These speeches affirm a belief and a policy. Experience in the world is needed to perfect a man, particularly a nobleman who ought to have it in proportion to the highness of his birth. And it is best acquired in an organised noble or semi–noble environment: a royal court, a university, an army or an expedition overseas.

The first three of these organisations all appear in Shakespeare's work, though their educational function is not described to any great extent. We do not see the emperor's court, and the exploits of Proteus and Valentine take place outside it. We learn no more of the training of other young men at courts, such as Bertram in *All's Well* and Hamlet, Horatio, Laertes and 'young Osric' at the court of Claudius in *Hamlet*.[41] The plays feature plenty of military campaigns, and in *Henry VI Part One* John Talbot earl of Shrewsbury brings along his son

> To tutor thee in stratagems of war,
> That Talbot's name might be in thee reviv'd.[42]

It could be argued that the young men in some other wars are educated or miseducated. Bertram, perhaps, becomes better fitted through his Italian campaign to be a good husband to Helena, and Richard III is the worse because of the Wars of the Roses. But Shakespeare does not labour the point, not even when he features young men at university, a place of overt education. We learn from *Hamlet* that Polonius was at university a long time ago, and that Hamlet and Horatio were recently at 'school' (which means the same) at Wittenberg, but little is made of the fact.[43] Laertes in Paris may be at university, but we are never told so, and when Polonius sends him letters, money and a spy to report on his doings, it is the extra–curricular ones that Polonius wants to know about. Does he gamble, drink, quarrel or go to brothels; not, does he apply himself to his books?[44] Lucentio is sent by his father to study at Padua in *The Taming of the Shrew*, but all we see him study is his heart.[45] Oxford is only mentioned twice by Shakespeare as a place of learning: once when Silence sends his son there, and once in a complimentary reference to Wolsey's foundation of Cardinal College (now Christ Church).[46] Another great centre of Tudor education, the inns of court and chancery in London, figures a little in Shallow's reminiscences about them in *Henry IV Part Two*.[47] Cambridge does not appear at all.

The agencies of noble education, then, from school to court, war and university, are shadowy, but there is no doubt about the value attached

---

[41] *All's Well That Ends Well*, I, ii; II, i; *Hamlet*, passim.
[42] *1 Henry VI*, IV, v, 1–3.
[43] *Hamlet*, I, ii, 112–13, 164, 177; III, ii, 97–8.
[44] Ibid., II, i, 58–61.
[45] *Taming of the Shrew*, I, i, 1–9; V, i, 60–2.
[46] *2 Henry IV*, III, ii, 8–10; *Henry VIII*, IV, ii, 57–63.
[47] *2 Henry IV*, III, ii, 12–23, 189–205, 274–5, 302–4.

to education in principle. Princes and noblemen should be trained in a formal way and in literary studies, and those deficient in such training are satirised. Medieval writers had mocked shortcomings of politeness and military skill in noblemen, but satire on literary failings was a more recent development of the Renaissance period, traceable in England to 1500-10.[48] 'What say you then to Falconbridge, the young baron of England?' asks Nerissa of Portia in *The Merchant of Venice*, Falconbridge being one of Portia's suitors and presumably a tourist in Italy. She replies,

> You know I say nothing to him, for he understands not me, nor I him: he hath neither Latin, French, nor Italian, and you will come into the court and swear that I have a poor pennyworth in the English: he is a proper man's picture, but alas! who can converse with a dumb-show?[49]

He has not profited from his Latin lessons at school, nor has he learnt a modern language. His counterpart in *Twelfth Night* is Sir Andrew Aguecheek, 'a foolish knight' whom Sir Toby Belch brings in to woo his niece on the grounds that Andrew can play the viol-de-gamba and speak three or four languages word for word without book. In truth, the knight is little more than a physical specimen, like Falconbridge: 'as tall a man as any's in Illyria'. He likes music and can dance, but he cannot recognise a well known quotation from the school Latin grammar, and he does not know much French:

> What is *pourquoi*? Do, or not do? I would I had bestowed that time in the tongues that I have in fencing, dancing and bear-baiting. O, had I but followed the arts!

By the end of the play, even his crony Toby dismisses him as 'an ass-head, and a cox-comb, and a knave'.[50]

Negligence in acquiring education is bad; so equally is failure to provide it, in a gentleman's case. Here the example is that of Orlando in *As You Like It*, a story based on the fourteenth-century *Tale of Gamelyn*, in which an eldest son deprives his youngest brother of his rightful inheritance and keeps him in a style of life beneath his rank. Thomas Lodge rewrote the story as a prose romance in 1590 with a brief mention of education, and Shakespeare expanded the latter to become a major issue, hitherto unusual in such stories. In the play, we are told that the knightly father charged the eldest son in his will that Orlando should be well-educated, which has not been done. He is maintained below his station with 'keeping for a gentleman of my birth, that differs not from the stalling of an ox', and he is ill-educated. His brother's 'horses are bred better; for . . . they are taught their manage . . . but I . . . gain nothing

48 Orme, *From Childhood to Chivalry*, p 215; see also above, p 262.
49 *The Merchant of Venice*, I, ii, 63–70.
50 *Twelfth Night*, I, iii, 14–37, 89–93, 118–21; V, i, 204–5.

under him but growth', like Falconbridge and Agucheek. Orlando's gentle birth is being undermined by his education, and he is 'not taught to make anything'.[51] The grievance is stressed when the play begins, in order to explain the hero's behaviour towards his brother, but it is then discarded. As we shall see in due course, Shakespeare also subscribed to the idea that true noblemen possessed an inner 'virtue' which compensated for lack of education. As Oliver the brother remarks of Orlando, 'yet he's gentle, never school'd, and yet learned, full of noble device'.[52] Despite his poor upbringing, he possesses good manners, generosity, eloquence and martial prowess. Moreover, though Shakespeare approves of literary study, it is not enough by itself as we see from the careers of Henry VI and the young Prospero. His ideal seems to be a man of varied talent and experience: 'a scholar and a soldier', like Portia's eventual husband Bassanio, or Hamlet's 'courtier's, soldier's, scholar's, eye, tongue, sword'.[53] Sixteenth-century writers inherited from the middle ages the ideas that the hero's *curriculum vitae* should be wide: inclusive of literary, artistic, moral and physical attainments. They emphasised the literary element more than before, but it remained a part of a larger scheme.

Most of Shakespeare's references to aristocratic education, as an organised process, relate to men. This accords with another medieval tradition of showing men being taught by instructors and acquiring skill, while women were praised for developing good characters. Only a few exceptional women in medieval history or romance were credited with literary studies to a high standard, a motif inherited from classical literature in which such women were portrayed. The coming of humanism to England in about 1500 modified these views. Beginning with the daughters of Henry VII, aristocratic women began to be given formal schooling in Latin like their brothers, but by masters at home not at a public school. Shakespeare's plays reflect this previous history. His reference in *Pericles* to Marina

> At Tharsus and by Cleon train'd
> In music, letters; who hath gained;
> Of education all the grace,
> Which makes her both the heart and place
> Of general wonder

could well be taken (as it professes to be) from medieval literature, depicting an exceptional woman.[54] There is also much of the past in *The Taming of the Shrew* in that the education of Katherina by Petruchio

---

[51] *As You Like It*, I, i, 1-25, 30, 66-74.
[52] Ibid., 164-9.
[53] *The Merchant of Venice*, I, ii, 108-10; *Hamlet*, III, i, 153-6.
[54] *Pericles*, IV, chorus, 5-11.

centres on the acquisition of a good nature as a wife, not on the development of skills. The *Shrew* reflects the Renaissance, however, in depicting Katherina's sister Bianca gaining an education in various intellectual pursuits. Her father Baptista belongs to the new age by importing professional teachers for her benefit:

> And, for I know she taketh most delight
> In music, instruments, and poetry,
> Schoolmasters will I keep within my house
> Fit to instruct her youth.

Two 'schoolmasters' duly appear (Hortensio and Lucentio in disguise), the former 'cunning in music and the mathematics' and the latter 'long studying at Rheims . . . cunning in Greek, Latin and other languages'.[55] The learning of English by Katherine of France in *Henry V* is also worth noticing, for though it is informally acquired from a lady in waiting, it is still the depiction of a woman learning a skill, unusual in earlier literature.[56] At a plebeian level, too, the mentions of school-maids in *Measure for Measure* and the teaching of parish girls in *Love's Labour's Lost* remind us of the increasing admission of girls to elementary schools, which was taking place in the sixteenth century.[57]

Not a great deal more than this divides Shakespeare's and Chaucer's perceptions of aristocratic education. The dramatist probably made more educational references than the poet, but then he wrote more. He placed more emphasis on literary education for men and women, but in other respects both writers depict the aristocracy in a similar way. Difference is more apparent when we turn to the second main body of educational topics in Shakespeare's work: schools, school studies and schoolmasters. Chaucer introduces a school only once, in the Prioress's tale, where he describes two pupils and a little of their study, but no master. In Shakespeare, school references are numerous. Holofernes, the schoolmaster in *Love's Labour's Lost*, teaches at an envisaged place at the top of the hill.[58] Mistress Page escorts her son to a school entrance near Windsor, and though we are not shown a school at work as we are in Chaucer, the Windsor schoolmaster gives a good demonstration of examining a boy in the classroom manner.[59] Shakespeare knew of the foundation of endowed schools, which had taken place since Chaucer's time. In *Henry VI Part Two* one of Jack Cade's ridiculous charges against Lord Say is that he had 'most traitorously corrupted the youth of the realm in erecting a grammar school', along with encouraging printing and paper-making.[60] Since the historical Say did not endow a school,

[55] *Taming of the Shrew*, I, i, 92–9; II, i, 55–60, 98–101.
[56] *Henry V*, III, iv.
[57] *Measure for Measure*, I, iv, 47–8; *Love's Labour's Lost*, IV, ii, 75–6.
[58] Ibid., V, i, 77–81.
[59] *Merry Wives of Windsor*, IV, i, 5–6.
[60] *2 Henry VI*, IV, vii, 30–2.

Shakespeare was simply taking a familiar kind of charity, common in his own day, and ascribing it retrospectively. He was aware that such schools had been founded in previous times since he mentions the refoundation of Ipswich school by Wolsey, in *Henry VIII*:

> in bestowing, madam,
> He was most princely: ever witness for him
> Those twins of learning that he rais'd in you,
> Ipswich and Oxford; one of which fell with him,
> Unwilling to outlive the good that did it,
> The other (though unfinish'd) yet so famous,
> So excellent in art, and still so rising,
> That Christendom shall ever speak his virtue.[61]

Nor was the dramatist's view of education confined to grammar schools and noble tutors. He brings on stage the clerk of Chartham in Kent, who teaches boys to write, and uses the metaphor of the 'pedant that keeps a school i' th' church' – humble sources of teaching which really existed.[62]

School is perceived as an organised place which keeps to hours and appointed times.[63] Pupils approach it reluctantly and leave it with alacrity:

> Love goes toward love as schoolboys from their books,
> But love from love, toward school with heavy looks.[64]

The image reappears in *As You Like It*:

> Then, the whining schoolboy, with his satchel
> And shining morning face, creeping like snail
> Unwilling to school,[65]

and in the disbandment of the rebel army in *Henry IV Part Two*

> like a school broke up,
> Each hurries toward his home and sporting-place.[66]

Teaching begins with the alphabet and prayers written on a board protected with horn, or in a little 'absey' book. Holofernes 'teaches boys the horn book', and they no doubt reply with 'answer like an absey book', glibly and predictably.[67] One can 'sigh, like a schoolboy that hath lost his abc'.[68] Learning to read is followed by writing lessons. The clerk of Chartham was arrested 'setting of boys' copies', meaning while giving

---

[61] *Henry VIII*, IV, ii, 56–63.
[62] *2 Henry VI*, IV, ii, 84; *Twelfth Night*, III, ii, 72–3.
[63] *Taming of the Shrew*, III, i, 19. Compare the emphasis of Ulysses on 'degrees in school' in *Troilus and Cressida*, I, iii, 104, which could refer to schools or universities.
[64] *Romeo and Juliet*, II, ii, 156–7.
[65] *As You Like It*, II, vii, 145–7.
[66] *2 Henry IV*, IV, ii, 104–5.
[67] *Love's Labour's Lost*, V, i, 46; *King John*, I, i, 196.
[68] *Two Gentlemen of Verona*, II, i, 21–2.

out exemplars to be copied, and Hamlet was drilled in writing 'fair'
which he abandoned when he grew up in favour of the individual
illegible hand of a statesman.[69] Progress is encouraged by corporal
punishment. William Page is threatened with 'breeches', a whipping on
his breeches or buttocks, and Bianca reminds her masters that she is no
'breeching scholar in the schools', but a lady who determines the course
of her own lessons.[70] There are also holidays, some of them
unpredictable (called 'remedies') when the master decided or was
persuaded to close school for the day, as Sir Hugh Evans does in *The
Merry Wives of Windsor*. The homely Mistress Quickly approves of this
('Bless his heart'), but certain Tudor educationists did not, and criticism
of the practice may be mirrored in the reaction of Mistress Page to the
news. 'My husband says my son profits nothing in the world at his
book.'[71]

Shakespeare also makes several references to the grammar
curriculum.[72] This marks an advance on Chaucer and Langland, who
seem to have regarded *Cato* as about the only school book which their
readers would readily recognise. Langland uses grammatical terms in
English on one occasion, but with much explanation and almost
apologetically.[73] By the sixteenth century, matters were different. More
lay readers and listeners knew more Latin, and in 1540-2 uniform
elementary and advanced Latin grammars were officially prescribed for
use in every school. Act IV Scene 1 of *The Merry Wives* is almost wholly
based on the elementary one, *The Shorte Introduction of Grammar*, Sir
Hugh Evans questioning William Page on the definition of nouns and the
declension of the definite article. Interestingly, although *The Short
Introduction* departed from earlier elementary grammars which took a
question-and-answer form, in favour of simple statements, Sir Hugh
reverts to the older technique, turning the statements into questions to be
answered. There are several direct quotations from the two grammars as
well, including an example in *Twelfth Night*, when Sir Toby remarks to
Sir Andrew, '*diluculo surgere*'.[74] The audience (originally a learned one, at

[69] *2 Henry VI*, IV, ii, 84; *Hamlet*, V, ii, 31-6.

[70] *Merry Wives of Windsor*, IV, i, 68-9; *Taming of the Shrew*, III, i, 18-20.

[71] *Merry Wives of Windsor*, IV, i, 7-13.

[72] The grammar-school references are exhaustively examined in T.W. Baldwin,
Shakspere's Small Latine and Lesse Greeke, 2 vols (Urbana, 1944).

[73] Above, p 252.

[74] *Twelfth Night*, II, iii, 1-5.

the inns of court) was expected to know the rest of the phrase, '*saluberrimum est*', but as usual, Sir Andew does not. Another occurs in *Titus Andronicus*, when Titus sends a message to the villainous Goths Demetrius and Chiron:

> *Integer vitae, scelerisque purus,*
> *Non eget Mauri iaculis, nec arcu.*

Chiron recognises this,

> O, 'tis a verse in Horace; I know it well:
> I read it in the grammar long ago,

but he does not understand its meaning for him, and Demetrius knows no better. Here the point is laboured, however, and explained by other characters, the play being a more popular one and its audience less well schooled.[75]

Once grammar was learnt, pupils practised translation from Latin to English and vice versa. The first of these tasks is shown in Bianca's lesson,[76] and it is mentioned in *The Merry Wives* when Falstaff compares the wooing of Mistress Ford with the translation of Latin into English:

> I can construe the action of her familiar style, and the hardest voice of her behaviour, to be Englished rightly, is, 'I am Sir John Falstaff's.'

Pistol observes,

> He hath studied her will, and translated her will, out of honesty into English.[77]

The Latin authors read in contemporary schools were chiefly classical and Renaissance poets, and they are also reflected in Shakespeare. In *Love's Labour's Lost*, another play for a relatively learned audience (probably the court), the schoolmaster recites

> *Facile, precor gelida quando pecus omne sub umbra*
> *Ruminat,*

the opening line of Battista Mantovano's *Eclogues*, very popular in Tudor schools, though he goes on to identify its author:

> Ah! good old Mantuan. I may speak of thee as the traveller doth of Venice . . .
> Who understandeth thee not, loves thee not.[78]

Another school-text, Ovid's *Heroides*, is quoted in Bianca's lesson and in the dying utterance of the young earl of Rutland, in a scene also featuring his tutor.[79] Two more, Ovid's *Metamorphoses* and Cicero's *Orator*, are

---

[75] *Titus Andronicus*, IV, ii, 20-8.
[76] *Taming of the Shrew*, III, i, 26-43.
[77] *Merry Wives of Windsor*, I, iii, 42-6.
[78] *Love's Labour's Lost*, IV, ii, 92-8.
[79] *Taming of the Shrew*, III, i, 28-43; *3 Henry VI*, I, iii, 47.

mentioned being studied by Lucius in *Titus Andronicus*.[80] There are, of course, a great many other allusions to classical literature read in the classroom which show the contribution of the schools to the culture of Shakespeare's day. But these need not detain us now, because they are not presented in the context of the classroom.

There is a greater attention to schoolmasters, as well. Chaucer featured only one, and that was an historical figure, Seneca tutor to Nero; contemporary masters do not appear in his work. Shakespeare by contrast has up to nine characters wholly or partly in this role. Two or three are presented seriously, and the rest humorously. One is heroic: the earl of Rutland's tutor, whose brief lines include a wish to die with his pupil.[81] Another is stoic: Mark Antony's schoolmaster, who is sent to Octavian Caesar as an ambassador. This signifies the collapse of Antony's cause; he has nobody better to send, and the master admits it:

> Such as I am, I come from Antony:
> I was of late as petty to his ends,
> As is the morn-dew on the myrtle leaf
> To his grand sea.

He is a downcast, modest figure, though he speaks adequately.[82] The clerk of Chartham stands on the borderline between tragedy and comedy. His name is Emmanuel (a common word to inscribe on deeds and letters), but when he admits he can write he is ordered to be hanged with his pen and ink-horn round his neck.[83] Of the altogether comic masters, two need little comment. Pinch, described as one in a stage direction in *The Comedy of Errors*, is based on the doctor in Plautus's play *Menaechmi*, and seems intended as a doctor in Shakespeare's version.[84] His pedagogic attribution must be a mistake, or an idea not developed. There is also a Pedant in *The Taming of the Shrew* who is brought into the plot to provide a counterfeit father for Lucentio. He is shown to be innocent and gullible, and is easily tricked into playing his part.[85]

That leaves four characters more fully portrayed as schoolmasters. Hortensio and Lucentio only assume the role in the *Shrew*, so we must beware of supposing them to be realistically depicted, but they have a whole scene to themselves. It is noteworthy that Lucentio as grammar-master wears 'the habit of a mean man', and is called by the music master 'pedant' and 'pedascule'.[86] Sir Hugh Evans in *The Merry Wives of Windsor* is more fully realised, though he combines the roles of schoolmaster and

[80] *Titus Andronicus*, IV, i, 42-3.
[81] *3 Henry VI*, I, iii, 6, 8-9.
[82] *Antony and Cleopatra*, III, xii, 7-25; xiii, 14-16.
[83] *3 Henry VI*, IV, ii, 81-104.
[84] *The Comedy of Errors*, stage direction after IV, iv, 37; compare 45-50.
[85] *Taming of the Shrew*, IV, ii, 72-121.
[86] Ibid., stage direction after II, i. 38; III, i, 46-8.

clergyman in a way often found at the time. He is competent in a basic way when he questions William Page on elementary Latin, and he has some status as the associate of Shallow the JP and others of the gentry. In other respects, however, he is an object of ridicule with his Welsh pronunciation, his curious use of nouns instead of verbs, his pedantic objections to people's language, and his quarrel with the equally comic Frenchman, Dr Caius. Much the same is true of Shakespeare's chief creation of the genre, Holofernes, who dominates two scenes in *Love's Labour's Lost* and is present in a third. Holofernes is the most absolute schoolmaster, doing nothing but teach and teaching everything from the abc to Mantuan. He has an equal status with the parish curate, and he is sometimes styled 'Master Holofernes' or 'Master Schoolmaster'. Academically he seems better than Evans: learned, able to converse wittily, a skilled poet who devises the pageant of the Nine Worthies and writes the songs with which the drama ends. He is also generous in sharing hospitality extended to himself. But he is garrulous like Evans, pedantic, critical of others' speech, and full of curious information: one who has been 'at a great feast of languages and stolen the scraps'. In the end, the courtiers of Navarre mock him cruelly. They call him a pedant, a cittern head, the head of a bodkin, a death's face in a ring, the face of an old Roman coin (scarce seen), an ass, Jud-as. He replies with justice, 'this is not generous, not gentle, not humble', but retires humiliated.[87] It is sad, but not surprising. Schoolmasters are indeed given greater attention by Shakespeare than by most previous writers, but their status in his world is still modest. They are more often laughed at than regarded seriously, and though they sometimes come into contact with great and important people, they count for little in such company.

After about 1600 Shakespeare's interest moved away from education for a time. *Hamlet* (c. 1600-1) and *All's Well* (c. 1603-4) are the last plays of his middle period to centre on young men who have recently been, are being, or ought to be educated. Instead, for the next few years, the dramatist wrote tragedies involving older men and women whose upbringing was over and whose character and experience mattered more. Later, he returned again to the portrayal of children and adolescents in his last, romantic plays, but his approach in these was somewhat different from most of his work in the 1590s. The four romances, *Pericles*, *Cymbeline*, *The Winter's Tale* and *The Tempest*, were all written between about 1608 and 1611, and to them we may add *Henry VIII* (1612-13) which has much in common. Each of the plays depicts a crisis among mature men and women, which is subsequently healed by the birth or growing up of their children: Pericles's daughter Marina, Cymbeline's sons Arviragus and Guiderius, Perdita in *The Winter's Tale*, Miranda in *The Tempest*, and Elizabeth I in *Henry VIII*. All the children

---

[87] *Love's Labour's Lost*, especially IV, ii, 75-9; V, i, 37-8; ii, 589-623.

are royal, and all are lost in some way, for an interval, before returning to help inaugurate a new era.[88] As we have already seen, Shakespeare provided for the education of two of these children, Marina and Miranda,[89] but the treatment of Cymbeline's sons and Perdita is different. Their stories involved them growing up in remote places, the boys in a cave with an ex-courtier and a nurse, and the girl in the countryside with a shepherd and his wife. This raised the question whether they were fitted to return to court life as princes and a princess.

Shakespeare answers the question in a way that he had done once before. We saw how he portrayed Orlando as unjustly deprived of education, yet recompensed with an innate virtue which made him naturally behave like a gentleman. In *Cymbeline* and *The Winter's Tale*, Shakespeare likewise asserts that noble virtue makes up for lack of education. Arviragus and Guiderius instinctively act like kings' sons: they are brave, intelligent and polite. In the words of Belarius their guardian,

> O thou goddess,
> Thou divine Nature; thou thyself thou blazon'st
> In these two princely boys: they are as gentle
> As zephyrs blowing below the violet,
> Not wagging his sweet head; and yet as rough
> (Their royal blood enchaf'd) as the rud'st wind
> That by the top doth take the mountain pine,
> And make him stoop to th'vale. 'Tis wonder
> That an invisible instinct should frame them
> To royalty unlearn'd, honour untaught,
> Civility not seen from other, valour
> That widely grows in them, but yields a crop
> As if it had been sow'd.[90]

Likewise of Perdita, apparently merely a shepherdess, it is said that

> nothing she does or seems
> But smacks of something greater than herself,
> Too noble for this place.[91]

---

[88] In Elizabeth's case the 'loss' is very brief and exists only in Henry VIII's disappointment that she is not a boy, but there is subsequently a joyful sense of rediscovery as in the other plays (*Henry VIII*, V, i, 161-76; ii, 194-5; iv, 63-8).

[89] *Pericles*, IV, chorus, 5-11; *The Tempest*, I, ii, 172-4.

[90] *Cymbeline*, IV, ii, 169-81.

[91] *The Winter's Tale*, IV, iv, 157-9.

Far from being uninstructed, she seems to be educated above the average:

> I cannot say 'tis pity
> She lacks instructions, for she seems a mistress
> To most that teach.[92]

It follows that if virtue transcends education, so too does natural vice. In *Titus Andronicus* Shakespeare had already featured one man, Chiron, whose grammar-school education had not counteracted his innate wickedness.[93] Likewise in *The Tempest* Caliban is Perdita's opposite: educated but unimproved. Miranda tried to elevate him by teaching:

> I pitied thee,
> Took pains to make thee speak, taught thee each hour
> One thing or other: when thou didst not, savage,
> Know thine own meaning, but wouldst gabble like
> A thing most brutish, I endow'd thy purposes
> With words that made them known. But thy vile race,
> Though thou didst learn, had that in't which good natures
> Could not abide to be with,

only to earn Caliban's reply,

> You taught me language; and my profit on't
> Is, I know how to curse. The red plague rid you
> For learning me your language.[94]

It would, no doubt, be wrong to regard the romances as questioning the value of education, so much insisted on in the earlier plays. The survival of the lost children, in a repeated word, is a 'miracle', and their experiences are not meant as models to be followed. We are merely reminded, more so than in the earlier plays, of the importance of human nature which, if good, supplies defects in education, but if bad, can scarcely be improved by any training.

In this as in much else Shakespeare subscribed to tradition. Chaucer too had distinguished nature from education. Innate gentility overcame low birth, poverty and lack of formal education in Griselde in the Clerk's tale, just as education only briefly tamed the vices of Nero in the Monk's. Other survivals from Chaucer in Shakespeare, as we have now seen, are the attention given to aristocratic education, and within that to the learning of skills by boys and the development of character by girls, though the latter is a little modified in Shakespeare. Several of the main elements of childhood are similarly portrayed: parental responsibilities, children's vulnerability, the role of nurses, households, schools, courts, war and even university, and the diversion of ordinary children to service

---

[92] Ibid., 582–4.
[93] *Titus Andronicus*, IV, ii, 20–8.
[94] *The Tempest*, I, ii, 355–67.

and work. At the same time, there are differences between the two writers due to the cultural changes of the intervening years. The foundation of endowed schools and the enhanced identity of schoolmasters leads to more mention of schools and teachers in Shakespeare. The greater emphasis of humanist scholars on the teaching of Latin, both to boys and girls, results in a greater attention to that subject and its learning by a girl. The Reformation is responsible for the smaller role of the clergy and clerical institutions in Shakespeare's education, and for the uniform grammar enabling more references to be made to the school curriculum. In short, there is both continuity and change between the two writers, as is usually the case in English history. They belong to one evolving tradition, in which there were indeed phases and eras, but not independent 'medieval' and 'Renaissance' worlds divided by a chasm in between.

INDEX